Israel in History

The comparative dimension is, all too often, missing from writing on Israeli history. Zionist ideology restricts comparisons between Zionism and other forms of nationalism. At the same time, Zionist claims to have initiated a rupture with the Jewish past mask continuities between Israel and the experiences of modern diaspora Jewry. Some scholars have presented Israel as a variant of settler-colonialist societies such as the United States and South Africa. This framework of continuity across space commands attention, but it lacks nuance and is often built upon politicized foundations. Besides, it neglects areas of continuity across time, between Israel and the Jewish past.

Israel in History: The Jewish State in Comparative Perspective seeks to address these issues. The essays in this book combine a variety of comparative schemes, both internal to Jewish civilization and extending throughout the world. These frameworks include:

- modern Jewish society, politics and culture
- historical consciousness in the 20th century
- colonialism, anti-colonialism and post-colonial state-building.

The benefit of comparison is not limited to a richer understanding of the circumstances under which Israel was born and has developed. Rather, an open-ended, comparative approach offers a useful means of correcting the biases found in so much scholarship on Israel, be it sympathetic or hostile.

Israel in History: The Jewish State in Comparative Perspective will appeal to scholars and students with research interests in many fields, including Israeli Studies, Middle East Studies, and Jewish Studies.

Derek J. Penslar is the Samuel Zacks Professor of Jewish History and Director of the Jewish Studies Program at the University of Toronto. His books include *Zionism and Technocracy: The Engineering of Jewish Settlement in Palestine, 1870–1918*, *Shylock's Children: Economics and Jewish Identity in Modern Europe*, and *Orientalism and the Jews* (co-edited with Ivan Kalmar).

Israel in History

The Jewish State in Comparative Perspective

Derek J. Penslar

LONDON AND NEW YORK

First published 2007
by Routledge
2 Park Square, Milton Park, Abingdon, Oxon OX14 4RN

Simultaneously published in the USA and Canada
by Routledge
270 Madison Avenue, New York, NY 10016

Routledge is an imprint of the Taylor & Francis Group, an informa business

Typeset in Times New Roman by Taylor & Francis Books
Printed and bound in Great Britain by Antony Rowe Ltd, Chippenham, Wiltshire

British Library Cataloguing in Publication Data
A catalogue record for this book is available from the British Library

Library of Congress Cataloging in Publication Data
A catalog record for this book has been requested

ISBN 0-415-40037-6 ISBN13 978-0-415-40037-4 (pbk)
ISBN 0-415-40036-8 ISBN13 978-0-415-40036-7 (hbk)

Contents

Acknowledgments vii
Introduction 1

PART I
Writing Israeli history 11

1 Israel's "new history": from innovation to revisionism 13

2 Beyond Revisionism: current directions in Israeli historiography 25

3 Historians, Herzl, and the Palestinian Arabs: myth and counter-myth 52

PART II
Continuity and rupture 63

4 Is Israel a Jewish state? 65

5 Is Zionism a colonial movement? 90

6 Antisemites on Zionism: from indifference to obsession 112

PART III
Zionism as a technology 131

7 Zionism as a form of Jewish social policy 133

8 Technical expertise and the construction of the rural Yishuv 150

PART IV
From Jewish to Israeli culture 167

9 The continuity of subversion: Hebrew satire in Mandate Palestine 169

10 Transmitting Jewish culture: radio in Israel 187

Notes 207
Select bibliography 244
Index 262

Acknowledgments

The material in this book has taken form over many years, on three continents and in more than a half-dozen countries. I owe thanks first and foremost to my home institution, the University of Toronto, which has provided a stimulating academic and a warmly collegial environment. My colleagues Tim Brook, Sean Hawkins, Eric Jennings, Ivan Kalmar, Michael Marrus, Paul Rutherford, and Janice Stein have read or commented on early versions of one or more of the chapters. The number of colleagues at other universities who have done the same is vast; I can only hope to have remembered them all here: Guli Neeman Arad, Israel Bartal, Michael Berkowitz, Menachem Blondheim, Michael Brenner, Tobias Brinkmann, David Biale, Dan Diner, Alan Dowty, Todd Endelman, Sidra Ezrahi, Gabriel Finder, Yoav Gelber, Sander Gilman, Zvi Gitelman, Nachum Gross, Mitch Hart, Paula Hyman, Elihu Katz, Eran Kaplan, Jonathan Karp, Hillel Kieval, Lital Levy, Tamar Liebes, Benjamin Nathans, Emanuel Ottolenghi, David Rechter, Aron Rodrigue, Anita Shapira, Michael Silber, Sarah Abrevaya Stein, David Sorkin, Michael Stanislawski, Kenneth Stow, Yfatt Weiss, Ruth Wisse, Steven Zipperstein, Yael Zerubavel, and Ronald Zweig.

Research support was provided by the Social Sciences and Humanities Research Council of Canada, a University of Toronto Connaught Fellowship, the Yitzhak Rabin Institute in Tel Aviv, and the Hebrew University's Institute for Advanced Study. The staffs of the Central Zionist Archives, the Archive of the Israel Defense Force, the Israel State Archives, YIVO, the Leo Baeck Institute, Harvard University's Widener Library, the New York Public Library, and the Jewish National and University Library extended me every courtesy. Benjamin Fisher, Daniel Heller, Merav Katz, Tatjana Lichtenstein, and Sagit Yakobovic provided invaluable research assistance.

The chapters in this book are drawn from previously published material; some have been revised and expanded, while others appear in English for the first time. I am grateful to the following publishers for allowing me to make use of material that first saw the light of day under their purview: Indiana University Press: "Innovation and Revisionism in Israeli Historiography," *History & Memory* VII, 1 (1995), 125–46; and "Transmitting

Jewish Culture: Radio in Israel," *Jewish Social Studies* X, 1 (2004), 1–29; Editions de l'Ecole des Hautes Etudes en Sciences Sociales: "Nouvelles orientations de l'historiographie israélienne: au-delà du révisionnisme," *Annales* 59, 1 (2004), 171–93; Taylor and Francis: "Theodor Herzl and the Palestinian Arabs: Myth and Counter-Myth," *Journal of Israeli History* 24, 1 (2005), 65–78; "Zionism, Colonialism, and Post-Colonialism," *Journal of Israeli History* 20, nos. 2–3 (2001), 84–98; and "Antisemites on Zionism: From Indifference to Obsession," *Journal of Israeli History* 25, 1 (2006), 11–29; Praeger Publishers: "Normalization and its Discontents: Israel as a Diaspora Jewish Community," in *Critical Issues in Israeli Society*, ed. Alan Dowty (2004), 223–49; Merkaz Zalman Shazar: "Ha-tsiyonut ke-tadmit shel ha-mediniyut ha-yehudit ha-hevratit," in *Idan Ha-tsiyonut,* eds. Jay Harris, Jehuda Reinharz, and Anita Shapira (2000), 65–89; Springer Science and Business Media: "Technical Expertise and the Construction of the Rural Yishuv, 1882–1948," *Jewish History* XIV, 2 (2000), 1–25; and "The Continuity of Subversion: Hebrew Satire in Mandatory Palestine," *Jewish History* 20, 1 (2006), 19–40.

Last on the page, but always first in my heart and on my mind, is my wife Robin. This book is dedicated to her.

Toronto
January 2006

Introduction

Most of the chapters in this book were written over the past five years, but I have been engaged with Israel for over half of my life. While in graduate school during the 1980s, I began to probe the points of connection between three overlapping yet distinct targets of historical study: modern Europe, modern Jewry, and the state of Israel. My exposure to the first and second had come when I was an undergraduate, especially while studying for a year in Berlin. Not long thereafter I spent several months in Israel, learning Hebrew and working at Ma'agan Michael, one of the most beautiful and prosperous kibbutzim in the country. A rite of passage for Jewish adolescents of a previous generation, the kibbutz was, for me, a transformative experience.

Situated on the Mediterranean coast just north of Caesarea, and sandwiched between a lovely sand beach and the foothills of the Carmel range, Ma'agan Michael appeared to me to be a proletarian paradise. Its fishponds reflected the blue of the clear winter sky, and in its citrus groves the leaves of grapefruit trees sparkled after a night of rain. The groves of banana trees, a riot of tropical colors and luridly shaped flowers, evoked an Aubrey Beardsley Orientalist fantasy. The cowshed and various work areas were a bit untidy and run down, as I believed a farm should be, but the plastics factory was impressively sophisticated, and the residential areas were anything but rustic. Neat, trim low-rise housing blocs surrounded well-manicured lawns, and the dining hall featured an enormous picture window overlooking the sea. I remember sitting in that dining hall, or strolling through the kibbutz grounds, thinking that here, in this small corner of the world, a just society had finally been established on earth: one that demanded labor and sacrifice but in return provided a comfortable life, care for the ill and elderly, and, despite the kibbutzniks' impressive physiques, a commitment to education and culture.

I idolized the kibbutzniks, especially my adoptive kibbutz parents: he an engineer, she a teacher, both of them bronzed by the sun and grayed by toil, combat, and loss. As youths, they fell in love in the tomato fields at Kibbutz Deganiah Bet and fought for Israel's independence; in middle age they buried their son's fiancée, the victim of a terrorist attack. When I departed the kibbutz, their farewell gift to me was a children's biography of the legendary Alexander Zaid, a founder of the first Zionist militia, *Ha-Shomer*. It was the first book I ever read in Hebrew.

My story is that of scores of thousands of North American and European youths who, throughout the twentieth century, found in a secular Zionism a meaningful collective identity, often more satisfying than whatever their parents' home offered (in the case of my milieu, an amorphous suburban Judaism, flecked with a residue of ethnic Yiddishkeit). For some Jews this ideology propelled them to attempt new lives in Palestine or, later, Israel; for others it became the base of an associational identity that linked them with other like-minded Jews throughout the diaspora, with whom they collaborated in fundraising or political activism on behalf of the Jewish state; for still others it was merely a phase, outgrown and forgotten, or a way station en route to a deepened religiosity.

For me it was something different. Although I returned from Israel with a deep sense of attachment to the country, from the start my feelings were nuanced by academic curiosity. While in Israel, romantically learning Hebrew by flashlight in my ramshackle quarters or striving valiantly to argue about politics with my comrades in the chick hatchery, I continually asked myself how Israel had come to be. When I returned to the United States and the Ph.D. program at UC Berkeley, I thought that some new answers might come from my previous academic training as a European historian. I became a comparativist, writing a dissertation, and then a book, on the influences of German social thought and colonial practice on early Zionist settlement.[1] Over the course of the past twenty years, I have continued to write on Israel in addition to various topics in European Jewish history, and the constant movement back and forth keeps me thinking about Israel in terms of other spaces and times, although the frameworks have broadened and multiplied, and the original *Leitfrage* – "How did this state come to be?" – is now supplemented by the rather gloomier "Did it have to turn out this way?"

This choice of field turned out to be somewhat eccentric. To be sure, systematic inquiry into the history of Zionist ideology had been undertaken in North America since the late 1950s, and in the 1970s the role of Zionism as a mobilizing force for diaspora Jews figured in the emerging field of modern Jewish social history.[2] But via a tacit division of labor the study of Zionist diplomacy, and even more so the development of Palestine's pre-1948 Jewish community (the Yishuv) and the young state of Israel – that is, Zionist state-building, whether in the centers of power in Europe's capitals or the boardrooms of the Histadrut headquarters in Tel Aviv – was until the late 1980s overwhelmingly the province of scholars in Israel. The strictures of Zionist ideology as well as the parochialism of Israeli academic life kept foreign scholars away from close inquiry into the gritty details of the transformation of Palestine from an Arab land into a Jewish state. On many occasions during the 1980s, I was told by older Israeli scholars that no one who has not made his life in Israel could understand the Yishuv well enough to write about it, and that in addition someone who cared enough about Israel to write its history should move there.

Throughout much of Israel's history, this sort of ideological passion inhibited critical comparisons between Zionism and other forms of nationalism. Comparison was employed instrumentally, in order to justify Zionism's legitimacy as a *bona fide* European nationalist movement, while highlighting its allegedly exceptional qualities, in keeping with Marc Bloch's famous dictum that comparative analysis should establish "the perception of differences" along with similarities.[3] The bedrock of Zionist discourse was not comparison, but rather the assertion of continuity and rupture. The former imagined a constant yet evolving connection over the millennia between the Jewish diaspora and the Land of Israel (*Eretz Yisrael*). The latter claimed that Zionism diverged radically from patterns of diaspora Jewish life and sensibility, but the purpose of this rupture was the preservation (or revival) of whatever Jewish civilization's most essential or valuable characteristics were believed to be. Both forms of discourse were ideological constructions, manufacturing a usable, mythologized past. The one concealed vast fissures, gaps, and contradictions in Jewish relationships with the Land of Israel across space and time, just as the latter masked the extent to which modern Israel has replicated various aspects of diaspora Jewish societies.

Over the past twenty years, Israeli historiography has gradually shed its ideological armor, and social scientists, both in Israel and outside of it, have striven to portray Israel in a wide variety of comparative contexts. A talented political scientist has produced a fascinating comparative analysis of Israel and "Asian Tiger" states such as South Korea,[4] but, by and large, the comparative work done thus far has generated models of Israel as a variant of ethnic democracies (like Slovakia and Northern Ireland) or settler-colonialist societies (such as the United States, Australia, and South Africa).[5] Frameworks of synchronic continuity between Israel and colonial states command attention, but often they lack nuance and are built upon politicized foundations. Moreover, the new schools of critical Israeli historiography and social science have neglected areas of diachronic continuity between Israel and the Jewish past.[6]

As a methodology, comparative history usually involves the study of two or more states, although in recent years this nationally centered approach has been challenged in the name of comparative local and regional studies and transnational categories, including diasporas.[7] In the case of Jewish history, spatial comparison is virtually unavoidable since throughout most of their history Jews have lived in a global diaspora, and although Jewish historiography often focuses on developments in one land, there is nonetheless ready acknowledgment of the transnational qualities of Jewish religious, economic, and communal life. For the study of Jewish modernity, processes of emancipation, acculturation, and social integration are understood to be global, although their specific contours vary greatly from one land to another. Few Jewish historians include Palestine/Israel in their global comparative network, yet such inclusion is essential, since throughout most of the twentieth century the Jewish population of Palestine, then Israel, consisted largely of recent immigrants, bearing cultural imprints of their place of origin. The study of Zionism can benefit in particular from the comparative historian's interest in cultural transfer – that is, the movement of ideas and sensibilities across borders – especially because, in the case of the cosmopolitan Jewish culture that took form in twentieth-century Palestine, borders between "here" and "there," between lands of birth and the land of immigration, between "Jewish" and "gentile" forms of knowledge and discourse were porous to the point of dissolution.

This book's underlying theme is the need to study Israeli history within multiple and overlapping comparative frameworks. The benefit of comparison is not limited to a richer or more illuminating understanding of the circumstances under which Israel was born and has developed. Rather, an open-ended, comparative approach offers a useful means of correcting the biases found in so much scholarship on Israel, be it sympathetic or hostile. Advocates for Israel are almost always exceptionalists, arguing that the eccentric aspects of Jewish nation-building, i.e. colonizing an inhabited land in the name of return to an ancient home, were fully justified given the historic abnormality of Jewish existence; that is, the durability of its civilization despite millennia of dispersion and persecution. Anti-Zionist literature is no less exceptionalist, although it waves the banner of comparison by presenting Israel as an exemplar of western colonialism. This is comparison in bad faith, for its underlying goal is the depiction of Israel as embodying colonialism in such a concentrated and lethal form as to comprise a category unto itself.

To be sure, as Chris Lorenz has cautioned, comparison in and of itself provides no "guarantee against empirically false judgments, because just like politicians, historians may try to prove anything by comparison."[8] Historical comparison can easily hide a political agenda in its choice of what Lorenz calls the "contrast class" or "comparison situation"; that is, the analytical framework against which one's subject is set determines the subject's appearance. If applied judiciously, however, comparative approaches towards the study of Zionism can steer a safe course between the Scylla of Zionist myth and the Charybdis of anti-Zionist counter-myth. In order to do so, the historian must apply multiple frameworks simultaneously; for example, an approach that examines Israel solely through the lens of modern Jewish society might promote an ethnic parochialism, whereas global comparative approaches run the risk of diluting Israel into insignificance, although the much more common outcome is the assertion of exceptionalism under a different name. The chapters in this book offer and combine a variety of comparative schemes, both internal to Jewish civilization and extending throughout the world, all the while acknowledging that the internal and external are not clearly separated but constantly shape each other and themselves through dynamic interaction.[9] The frameworks constructed here include modern Jewish society, politics, and culture; nationalist ideology and movements in modern Europe; the relationship between technology and state-building in the twentieth century; and the matrix of western colonialism, Third World anti-colonialism and post-colonial state-building.

The book is divided into four parts, one on historiography and three on specific themes within Zionist and Israeli history. Part I begins with a chapter on the origins of Israeli historical writing and the place of the new Israeli historiography and sociology within the framework of twentieth-century historical revisionism in the western world. Written in 1995, the chapter pays particular attention to the most salient aspects of the new Israeli historiography at that time: its emphasis on the origins of the Arab–Israeli conflict, overtly adversarial stance *vis-à-vis* the Israeli academic establishment, and often dubious claims to scholarly objectivity. Chapter 2, written a decade later, continues the comparison into the twenty-first century, when the decline of overarching national narratives has led to a weakening of revisionism's adversarial ethos and has encouraged a proliferation of historiographical approaches. The impact of this development upon Israeli historiography may be seen in the rapid growth of a sophisticated and variegated literature and an acceptance, in Israeli universities if not in the educational system as whole, of many of the new historiography's arguments that had been so hotly debated just a few years before. Israeli historiography has reached new heights of analytical depth and methodological sophistication, yet its future is clouded by the paucity of scholars outside of Israel who work in the field and by constant politicization due to the Arab–Israeli conflict.

The relationship between politics and historiography is central to Chapter 3, a focused study of pro-Zionist and pro-Arab scholarly depictions of Theodor Herzl's attitudes towards the Palestinian Arabs. This chapter's historiographical focus expands beyond the Israeli academic world to include Middle Eastern historians, thus demonstrating the lines of intellectual affinity linking some practitioners of the new history with the familiarly hostile view of Zionism and Israel prevalent in the field of Middle East studies. Herzl's relations with Arabs are interpreted by scholars sympathetic or hostile to Zionism in profoundly different ways, reflecting the existence of two distinct historical narratives, situated within separate points of departure and arrival. The former begins with persecution, reaches a nadir in the Nazi genocide, and then leads towards the glory of statehood before veering off into a dizzying mixture of hubris and panic. The latter begins with colonialism and ends with exile; it is a tale of humiliation redeemed by an as yet inconclusive armed struggle. The two narratives constitute different literary genres: the Palestinian story is a tragedy, whereas that of Zionism is a romance, an endless quest that contains aspects of both the tragic and the triumphant.

Part II of the book seeks to expose the myriad areas of continuity and rupture between the Zionist project, modern Jewish society and western colonialism. Chapter 4 asks an apparently obvious question about Israel's Jewish character, but its answers downplay the political character of the state in favor of its social, economic, and cultural structures. Analysis of these structures reveals that Israel has replicated or paralleled developments in the diaspora far more closely than conventional wisdom would have it. Israeli religious life is no less variegated than that found in North America and Europe; its economic values and structure have been steadily converging with those of the Jewish diaspora in the West as well. In its political culture, Israel preserves many characteristics of Jewish governmentality as practiced throughout the globe in the nineteenth and twentieth centuries. Even post-Zionism, which strives to normalize Israel as a state of all its citizens, is fueled by the same idealization of the liberal state that drove the maskilim, the nineteenth-century "enlightened" Jews whose struggle for radical collective change was, like that of post-Zionists today, carried out in the Hebrew language and within a Jewish public sphere.

Chapter 5 engages the debate about Zionism's relationship with European colonialism. I contend that Zionism rooted itself simultaneously in European colonialism and Afro-Asian anti-colonialism. Seeking the protection of the Great Powers, early Zionist leaders became embroiled in imperialist intrigue, and they espoused the typical European view of the Orient as desiccated and degenerate. Lacking a mother country, however, the Zionists had little in common with the practices of colonialist ventures that exploited native labor and resources for the benefit of the metropole. A better case may be made for Zionism as a form of settlement colonialism practiced by Europeans in the New World or the Boers in South Africa, although the Zionist project featured many eccentric, even unique, features as well. Moreover, there are lines of continuity between Zionism and anti-colonial political movements, just as the culture of modernizing Jewish intellectuals closely resembled that of colonial intelligentsias in twentieth-century Asia and Africa.

Chapter 6, the last in Part II, is a comparative study of antisemitism in Europe and the Middle East from the late 1800s to the mid-twentieth century. It argues for a clear distinction between European antisemitism, which was directed against the Jew as religious and social pariah, and its Middle Eastern counterpart, which, although not lacking in religious and social components, was overwhelmingly political, a response to the growth of Zionism and, after 1948, the plight of the Palestinians. My key sources here are the texts produced by Europe's most notorious antisemites, who all but ignored Zionism because it was superfluous to their pre-established worldview, and by early Arab nationalists who treated Zionism in a far more realistic, albeit often hostile, fashion.

All of the chapters in the book's first two parts deal, in one form or another, with the Arab–Israeli conflict. Even the chapter on Israel's Jewish characteristics dwells on the dynamic interaction between the conflict and collective memory of the Holocaust in the formation of Israeli historical consciousness. I have no desire, however, to fall into the mold, replicated throughout the academic world, of presenting Israel's history solely in terms of the conflict. (There are many broad, synthetic works and textbooks about the Arab–Israeli conflict but very few on the history of Zionism or Israel.)[10] Thus Part III of the book seeks to account for the Israeli state's formation beyond the parameters of its political or military history. Instead, the two chapters here look to the Zionist project's debt to the developmental ethos of the modern state; that is, they present Zionism as a technology, one that requires situation in both a Jewish and global context.

Chapter 7, taking as its starting point Jürgen Habermas's classic depiction of the structural transformation of the public sphere, argues that, beginning in the late nineteenth century, the philanthropic activities of European Jewish communities melded into a vast new Jewish public sphere, an agent of an international social politics whose chief beneficiary was the Jewish community of Palestine. This chapter blurs the distinctions between Zionism and other forms of Jewish politics in the modern world and between Zionist schemes for Jewish settlement and other forms of Jewish social engineering throughout the twentieth-century world, from Argentina to the Soviet Union. Chapter 8 presents the Yishuv as a case study of technology transfer, as technical expertise and technological innovation were exported from the West to Palestine, undergoing fundamental transformations to accommodate the peculiar political structure and sensibilities of the Zionist labor movement that was advancing towards hegemony. The hierarchical administrative structures found in both the capitalist West and its colonial dependencies foundered in the contentious, egalitarian environment of the Yishuv's labor movement. The result was a uniquely informal environment and high level of independence accorded to the creators of Israeli scientific knowledge, ranging from the citriculture of the 1930s to the computer-processing and software technology of our own generation.

The book's final section, Part IV, returns to Israel's relationship with the Jewish past by focusing on the lines of continuity and rupture between Israeli and diaspora Jewish culture. The key transitional period under analysis is that of the Yishuv and the first two decades of Israel's existence. Much has been written on the high Hebrew literary culture of this period, but we know far less about popular, ephemeral forms of cultural expression. The production and reception of Israeli popular culture are essential objects of study if we wish to understand which aspects of Israeli culture were native to the new Zionist Yishuv and which emerged from and were porous to influences from abroad. Chapter 9 traces the transformation of Jewish parody from its origins in eighteenth-century Eastern Europe through

Israeli statehood. I argue that the Jewish Enlightenment's heritage of learned Hebrew parody flourished only briefly in Palestine before it took on the forms of a highly politicized satire, with the Talmud replaced by the straightforward Passover Haggadah as the parodied text of choice. During the interwar period, Haggadah parodies enjoyed considerable popularity, but in recent decades, even this basic text has lost its literary valence among secular Israelis. The loss of the genre of sacred parody testifies to the powerful changes in the Jews' lettered tradition wrought by the conditions of statehood and the multiple traumas endured by Israelis in the second half of the twentieth century.

The book's last chapter moves from popular literature to even more widely disseminated forms of cultural communication, the mass media. I have chosen to focus not on the press, whose literary and cultural reportage was accessible to a limited audience, or cinema, which was available only in discrete units of limited duration. Instead, the chapter traces the history of radio in Israel from the 1930s, when the Palestine Broadcast Service was founded under British auspices, until the early 1970s, by which time television had replaced radio as Israelis' primary source of electronic entertainment consumed within the home. Despite radio's novelty as an electronic mass medium, Zionist elites in the Yishuv and young state of Israel were determined to employ it as a tool for the creation and dissemination of a Zionist culture laced with traditional Jewish motifs. Beginning on the micro level of broadcasting policy, content analysis of specific programs, and reception history (made possible due to exhaustive listeners' surveys), the chapter broadens out to explore the relationship between the oral and written sign in Jewish religious culture and the revolutionary transformation of Jewish aurality in the era of electronic communication.

Throughout the book, but particularly in the chapters touching upon the Arab–Israeli conflict, I attempt to present historical truth as falling in between what have become staked-out ideological positions. This stance may strike some readers as a manifestation of weakness, a refusal to take a stand, an epistemological equivalent of the legendary diffidence of Israeli prime minister Levi Eshkol, of whom it is said that when asked if he wanted coffee or tea, he replied "both." However healthy and satisfying the golden mean may be when applied to the conditions of daily life, there is something quintessentially academic and irritating about what appears to be its application to the realm of historical understanding. Yet nuanced historical explanation is not relativist; nor is it a form of deductive judgment. The arguments made in this book clearly establish a claim to historical truth, set forth a coherent conceptual framework, and draw upon a large evidentiary base.

More important, the attribution of a single underlying cause to a multifaceted historical event defies rational understanding of the complexity of social relationships. The attribution of responsibility in an ethnic conflict, such as that between Israelis and Palestinians, entirely to one of the antagonists is a product of volition and filtered cognition, an assertion by the will more than an exercise of judgment. Operating in unintended symmetry, champions and revilers of Israel have constructed historical narratives that free their constituencies of accountability for their actions.

The normalization of Israeli historiography demands removing it from the framework of competitive victimhood. The comparative approach, as applied throughout this book, attempts to seal off access to this polarizing and ultimately destructive conceptual universe. Appreciating commonalities as well as differences between Israeli Jews and Palestinian Arabs, Jews in Israel and in other lands, between Israel and other lands, we move not towards relativism but rather its opposite – towards truths that are sufficiently broad and subtle to encompass the untidy vastness of historical experience. The comparative framework, if applied in good faith, constantly forces the scholar to confront his own tendencies to think in exceptionalist terms. Of course, scholarship is often engaged – it would not be produced at all without the writer's sense of mission that propels her into a life of labor with often uncertain rewards, a high level of drudgery, and, at times, at least in the field of Middle Eastern studies, no small level of professional or even personal risk. My own personal confession, with which this Introduction began, is that of a man who as a youth came under the spell of an ideology. Over the past quarter-century it has both faded and matured, no longer a guide to perception or action, but still a source of inspiration about the power of humanity to reshape the world and of admiration, albeit mixed with sorrow and anger, for the creation of a polity where Jews enjoy the privileges, but also bear the responsibilities, of sovereignty.

No writer should pretend to transcend engagement. The *bona fide* scholar's distinguishing trait is not disinterest but rather a wholehearted acceptance of the rules of presentation and documentation that allow for a rational critique of any individual work by other scholars competent in and possessed of access to the relevant sources. The best scholarship on Israel and the Arab–Israeli conflict is such that one does not know, before opening the book and beginning to read, what it is going to say. This acid test is not often passed.[11] Part of the problem lies in the predetermination of answers, but scholars must also strive to be open-minded and imaginative in their framing of questions. There are myriad unanswered questions regarding Israel's origins and development, about causation and consequence, intention and happenstance, consensus and contestation. This book raises a few such new questions and tries to address them in a fresh and accessible manner. It is critical yet highly respectful of existing historiography. It accepts that even scholars who strive to avoid the pitfalls of myth and counter-myth will inevitably present differing, even clashing, narratives, not simply because of political engagement or bias, but because of differing points of departure and arrival. Yet, to offer an analogy to a Cartesian grid, the competing narratives do not exist only in separate quadrants, with no

point of intersection. Quite the contrary; the narratives are more like waves of varying amplitudes, which intersect, diverge, and conjoin yet again. As in the past, so in the present and the future, the points of convergence provide a moment of authentic encounter, a possibility for agreement, and the beginning of a new narrative. I hope that the chapters in this volume will make a contribution in that direction.

Part I

Writing Israeli history

1 Israel's "new history"

From innovation to revisionism

In an essay of 1988, the Israeli historian Benny Morris made a distinction between the terms "revisionism" and "new history," rejecting the first and adopting the second for the historiography of the 1948 Arab–Israeli War which he and several other scholars were producing. Morris claimed that the term "Revisionist" only applied when there was a "solid, credible – if wrongheaded – body of historiography" about a particular subject which "latest fashion is bent on overthrowing."[1] Previous Israeli treatments of the 1948 War, Morris contended, were not serious scholarship, but rather tendentious and apologetic works of official history, written by career officers, bureaucrats, and public figures. Thus, Morris claimed, he was part of the first generation of *bona fide* historians of the 1948 War and, by extension, of the birth and establishment of the state of Israel.

Unlike most of the criticism that has been published about the "new historians," it is not my primary intent here to impugn their claims about Israeli behavior during the 1948 War. Rather, I wish to call into question their historiographical understanding, self-image, and theoretical frameworks. The new historians do Israeli historiography a disservice by depicting their relationship with previous scholarship solely in terms of an opposition to an official military history which they are the first to challenge. Morris poses a neat dichotomy between "a generation of nationbuilders" who lived through 1948 as "committed adult participants" and a new generation, born around 1948 and raised in a "more open, doubting, and selfcritical Israel than the pre-1967, pre-1973, and pre-Lebanon War Israel of the old historians."[2] This statement flattens the entire period from the mid-1960s to the early 1980s into a single point, thus conjuring away an entire generation of scholars who founded the study of Zionism and the Yishuv as a serious academic discipline. Israeli historiography is admittedly a young creature, but it was not born with the emergence of the new history in the mid-1980s. Rather, as this chapter will explain, the "new history" represents a continuation of and response to the generation of Yishuv scholars who came of age during the early 1970s. The new history is part of an ongoing process of innovation – innovation which began before the advent of this new cohort and which goes on outside of it.

The debates about the new history which have saturated the Israeli press tend to be "Israelicentric," underplaying the parallels between the Israeli literature and contemporary historiographical controversies in other lands. In the new history, innovation assumes shapes which, Morris's protests aside, resemble various forms of historical revisionism currently being produced in Europe and the United States. This chapter seeks, therefore, to contextualize the new history both vertically, within the framework of Israeli historical selfunderstanding, and horizontally, within contemporary historical discourse in the western world.

This chapter speaks of two generations of Israeli historians, one crystallizing in the first half of the 1970s and the other in the second half of the 1980s. By "generation" I mean a cohort of scholars not only of more or less the same chronological age, but also sharing similar concerns and values. To be sure, many historians of Israel do not fit neatly into one of these generations. Moreover, scholars whom I would place within a particular generation may and do differ over myriad issues, personal as well as professional. My quest here is for neither inclusiveness nor uniformity, but rather for identification of select groups of individuals who, through personal dynamism and scholarly accomplishment, have most strongly influenced the production of historical writing about Israel over the past twenty-five years.

In 1976, the Israeli historian Israel Kolatt contributed a thoughtful programmatic essay to the first issue of *Cathedra*, a journal devoted to the Jews in Palestine from antiquity to the recent past. In the mid-1960s, the article contends, academic study of the Yishuv was made possible by two factors: the general growth of the Israeli universities and a sense that the generation of the founders of the state was passing and that the current crop of graduate students, who had experienced the foundation of the state as children or at most adolescents, would be able to write the Yishuv's history unburdened by private memory. Kolatt added that a deepening of the gap between older and current scholarship on Zionism and the Yishuv had occurred after the 1973 Arab–Israeli War, which had occasioned historical rumination about the long-term political and social causes of Israel's military failures. Kolatt appeared to place Israeli historiography somewhere between two paradigms: "western," which was adversarial and devoted to the shattering of myths, and "Third World," which served the interests of nation-building.[3]

All of the factors mentioned by Kolatt, working together over the period from the mid-1960s to the mid-1970s, made possible the formation of the first generation of academic Yishuv historians. Kolatt himself was the founder of this cohort, completing his dissertation in 1964. Other scholars of this generation include Dan Giladi, Elkana Margalit, Yosef Gorny, and Anita Shapira.[4] Equally significant are the historically oriented social scientists of this generation: Yonathan Shapiro, Dan Horowitz, and Moshe Lissak.[5] Most often, the Yishuv historians wrote their dissertations under the direction of the older generation of historians of European Jewry. (Kolatt's dissertation was supervised by Jacob Katz and Jacob Talmon; Shapira's by Daniel Carpi, a historian of Italian Jewry.) The production of Zionist and Yishuv historiography was aided by institutions such as Tel Aviv University's Weizmann Institute (founded in 1963), which provided financial support for scholars such as Gorni and Shapira. Along with publishing monographs, research institutes founded journals emphasizing Yishuv history, such as the Weizmann Institute's *Ha-Tsiyonut* (1970) and the Ben Zvi Institute's *Cathedra* (1976).[6]

More than anything else, the political history of the Zionist Labor movement was the object of the first generation's historiographical gaze. The historians had, for the most part, been raised in the Labor movement and were steeped in its ideology.[7] As a gesture of emancipation from their past and recognition of Labor's decline during the 1970s, the historians tended to be sympathetic critics of Labor Zionism, its institutions, and its heroes. For example, although Carpi, the first editor of *HaTsiyonut*, saw the journal as operating within the framework of such classic Zionist principles as *kibbutz galuyot* ("ingathering of the exiles") and *shinui arakhim* ("transformation of values"), he also recognized a growing tendency to question beliefs held sacred by the founding generation of the state.[8] As the historian Israel Bartal has noted, today's established Israeli historians considered themselves rebels during the 1970s, criticizing and rejecting what they thought were the Bolshevik aspects of the heritage of Mapai, Israel's long-hegemonic Labor–Zionist political party.[9] For Yonathan Shapiro, the term "Bolshevik" must be taken literally, for he traced the influence of Bolshevik political thinking and organizational tactics on the Ahdut ha-'Avodah apparatchiks of the Third Aliyah. Equally unflattering was Anita Shapira's presentation, in her first monograph *The Futile Struggle*, of the Labor parties' capacity for political violence during the 1930s.

To be sure, the members of this generation conflicted with each other over major interpretive and methodological issues. (Josef Heller has nicely laid out these differences in a review essay.)[10] But it is nonetheless possible to construct an ideal-type of the first-generation academic Israeli historian: a political historian and specialist in the Labor movement, of which he was an in-house critic. This ideal-type to some extent replicated itself among a younger cohort of scholars. One encounters this type among the likes of Dina Porat and Yehiam Weitz, who have written important books on the response of the Yishuv leadership to the Holocaust.[11] But the decline of the Labor movement through the 1970s did more than encourage introspective histories of the Zionist Left; it also stimulated, from the mid-1970s onward, the production of history not written from a Labor perspective. This includes work on the Orthodox Yishuv,[12] the Zionist Right,[13] Yishuv economic history,[14] and historical geography.[15] The latter two put the kibbutz, Histadrut (General Federation of Labor), and other creations of the Labor movement into perspective by demonstrating the centrality of private capital, capitalist initiative, and British expenditures in the construction of the Yishuv in Ottoman and Mandatory Palestine.

The historiography referred to above redressed some of the imbalance in the work produced by the first generation of Yishuv scholarship, but until the turn of the twentieth century the literature continued to suffer from certain limitations. The historiography remained overwhelmingly political, diplomatic and institutional. Although economic history made some inroads, social history did not, and the study of gender relationships in the Yishuv was relegated mostly to sociologists.[16] Even within the sphere of political history, the amount of material on some crucial subjects, such as the Zionist Right, remained scandalously small. Although there were sparkling exceptions, Yishuv historiography was often positivist and conceptually narrow.[17] The best work in political history often took the form of biography, a worthy medium to be sure, but which does nothing to nudge the historiography into a more analytical paradigm.

Yishuv historiography bears the signs of being produced and consumed entirely within the Israeli cultural sphere. Much of this literature, including work deserving of an international audience, remains untranslated; and even those works which are rendered into English are often composed in so internalistic a style that the reader needs to know Hebrew and have a good knowledge of the subject matter in order to follow the narrative. On this point there is a notable distinction between Yishuv historiography and that of Zionism, that is, Jewish nationalist ideology, the international Zionist movement and Zionist diplomacy. These subjects have tended to attract a more cosmopolitan and polyglottal pool of authors than Yishuv studies. So, for example, at the time when the first generation of Israeli academic historians was producing Hebrew volumes on one aspect of the Labor movement or the other, the political scientist David Vital published *The Origins of Zionism* (1975), a work from which uninformed English readers derive great benefit.[18]

Whereas scholarship in the history of Zionism is written by individuals from many lands, virtually every work of Yishuv historiography written since 1970 has been the work of a permanent resident of the state of Israel or an Israeli expatriate. When I ask Israeli scholars why this is so, they reply that non-Israelis rarely know Hebrew well enough to work with the sources. But this is not the case. In the United States, within the field of Jewish studies there are hundreds of academics who can read Hebrew sources far more esoteric than the minutes of the meetings of the Mapai Central Committee. Moreover, there is an intriguing juxtaposition between the scarcity of foreign historians studying the history of the formation of the state of Israel and the number of non-Israeli political scientists who write on Israeli foreign affairs and the Arab–Israeli conflict. The issue is not one of linguistic competence, but one of individual motivation. Since most non-Israeli scholars of Jewish history are themselves Jewish, the study of the Jewish past is, for them, a highly personal affair; they prefer to think about issues meaningful to a diaspora Jew (e.g. antisemitism, acculturation, Jewish identity) rather than the political quarrels of the Yishuv or its socio-economic construction. The Arab–Israeli conflict is another matter altogether. A variety of motivations, including heartfelt idealism, an appreciation of the global significance of the conflict, and fears for Israel's future should the conflict remain unresolved, propel foreign scholars into a field of inquiry which is certainly no less complex or demanding than the domestic history of the Yishuv.

As a result of these factors, Yishuv and Israeli historiography tends to be a cottage industry. Given the small size of the country and the tight interconnections between academia, government, and the military, members of the Israeli educated elite are far more likely to know each other and share common experiences than would be the case in a more spacious environment. In Israel, as in other young countries, the writing of national history often takes a polemical form, but, as is the case in other small countries, it has the quality of family history as well. In family history every individual is sacred and no detail can be left out. Synthesis is thus not a strong suit of Israeli historiography. Comprehensive histories of the Yishuv tend to be popular or pedagogic rather than works of analytical scholarship.

The cottage-industry quality of Yishuv historiography, combined with its methodological peculiarities, makes for interesting parallels with the historiography of small countries in general. Historically overshadowed and often dominated by larger nations, small countries feature a defensive, introspective historiography which asserts national distinctiveness and integrity. Small-country historians remain engaged in the mental process of nation-building long after historians of Great Powers slide into post-nationalist skepticism. Physical isolation and nationalist ideology reinforce each other, discouraging methodological innovation. A recent survey of Czech historiography has noted that, although the literature can be imaginative and far-reaching, there continues a general preference for political and macrostructural history.[19] Bulgarian historiography, according to the Balkan historian Maria Todorova, tends to be dull; the Bulgarian scholars are so busy chronicling history "wie es eigentlich gewesen ist (as it really happened)" that they fail to note "was es eigentlich bedeutet (what it really means)."[20] Finally, the history of small countries, like that of Israel, is written primarily by and for people from those lands. I have heard Israeli scholars express doubts whether foreigners, Jewish and gentile alike, can really understand Israeli history; many Estonian and Finnish historians harbor similar suspicions about foreigners, even if of Baltic background, who probe the Baltic past.[21]

I am not suggesting that Israeli historiography lies immobile in a Ruritanian stupor. Far from it; the "new historians," a cohort of Israeli historians which began to form in the mid-1980s, have in many ways overcome the limitations of their predecessors. First, the new historians are likely to be outsiders within the Israeli academic establishment and they have a cosmopolitan orientation which differentiates them from the earlier generation. One of the most widely read new historians, Tom Segev, holds a doctorate in history but has made his career is a journalist.[22] Morris has spent much of his life abroad (although he now holds a tenured position in Beersheba) and the historian Avi Shlaim has made his career at St. Antony's College, Oxford.[23] Morris and Shlaim write fluent English; more important, they conceptualize their work and present it in a fashion that makes it immediately accessible to the English-reader. (Unlike most books by Yishuv historians, these authors' publications do not assume prior knowledge of Israeli history.) One encounters a similar style as well in another new historian, Ilan Pappé, who was educated at Oxford and holds a tenured position at the University of Haifa.[24]

To be sure, the books of Morris, Shlaim, and Pappé find western publishers and readers in good measure because of their subject matter, which is of greater general interest than, say, the internal quarrels within the Yishuv's Labor parties during the 1940s. Their generally critical evaluation of Israeli behavior also strikes a sympathetic chord in the hearts of many readers abroad. But these reasons alone are not sufficient to account for the authors' popularity. The military historian Uri Milstein has written highly innovative and critical analyses of Israeli actions during the 1948 War, but because of his work's bulk, overwhelming detail, and internalistic presentation, Milstein remains virtually unknown outside the Hebrew-reading public, this despite the fact that much of his work has been translated into English.[25] Unlike Milstein, the new historians under analysis here enjoy a wide international audience, and they do so because they intentionally write for one.

So much for style, but what about substance? Unlike the earlier literature, the newer history actively seeks to come to grips with Israel's most traumatic past experiences. It offers a painstaking (and often painful) examination of Jewish–Arab conflict in Palestine, the 1948 War, and the institutionalization of the Arab–Israeli conflict by 1956. Although each historian has his particular interpretation, there is a general agreement that Israeli behavior toward the Arabs was more aggressive and less justified, from either a strategic or moral perspective, than most Israelis have previously thought. The new historians are indeed correct in claiming that they are the first to engage in sustained archival study of this conflict. Prior Israeli scholarship on the subject had palpable biases and employed inadequate documentation, whereas the first generation of academic Yishuv historians avoided the subject.

Coming to terms with the traumatic events of the 1940s is something that many nations have attempted only in the past decade or so. Moreover, outsiders to the national academic establishment are frequently the first to produce critical studies of a country's tarnished past. We have seen these developments in both France and Germany, whose wartime misdeeds were, until recently, chronicled by foreign, mostly North American, scholars or homegrown investigative journalists. To be sure, there are good reasons to resist comparisons between Israel's behavior, no matter how unsavory, during the 1948 War and the responsibility of the Germans and those who collaborated with them in the commission of acts of unparalleled evil during World War II. But although we do not fully understand them, the mechanisms of collective memory and collective denial appear to operate in similar fashions in disparate environments and are of greater importance to us than the radically opposed historical realities of Israel in 1948 and Europe in World War II.

Moreover, Israel shares an important structural similarity with both France and Germany: all are, to use the terminology of the political scientist Pierre Birnbaum, "strong states," with a powerful public sector and close connections between academia and government.[26] Until thirty or so years ago, academic historians in all three of these "strong states" saw themselves as engaged in a state-supporting enterprise. On the other hand, "weak states" like the United States, with its decentralized educational structure, have a stronger tradition of critical, anti-statist scholarship.

It was an American scholar, Robert Paxton, who in 1972 offered the first thorough critique of Vichy France as a manifestation of an indigenous Gallic fascism and not, as French "official memory" claimed, a Germanic implant. In 1981 Paxton and the Canadian historian Michael Marrus went far beyond French scholarship in their book *Vichy and the Jews*, a powerful indictment of French complicity in the Holocaust. Only thereafter did French historians begin to confront the Vichy period, and Henry Rousso's 1987 study of French representations of Vichy aroused a storm of controversy.[27]

During the 1960s and 1970s American and British scholars of Nazism produced a steady stream of critical accounts of the behavior of the German populace toward the Jews and other persecuted groups. German scholars did not ignore the Nazi period, but their focus was the diplomatic and military history of the Third Reich as well as the institutional and social structure of the Nazi state. During the 1980s it became more routine for German scholars to work on antisemitism and the Holocaust, but, as we learned from the *Historikerstreit* (a much-publicized academic controversy about the relationship between Nazism and the German past), many German historians displayed significant resistance to this line of inquiry and the political judgments that came with it.[28]

In the *Historikerstreit* and comparable controversies in other lands the term "Revisionist" frequently appears in analyses of the historiographical approaches of one or the other side. "Revisionism" is a protean word which, when employed as an abstract noun, has been used in the past century to describe the evolutionary socialism of Eduard Bernstein, the territorial irredentism of the European powers after World War I, or maximalist political Zionism. But when used in a historiographical context, the term, although at times descriptive of the routine process of scholarly innovation, often refers to controversies surrounding the origin of wars, public scandals, and other traumatic events in the life of a nation. (It is precisely the association of the term "revisionism" with calamitous events that has led Holocaust deniers to take shelter under this term.)

Let us recall that the essay by Benny Morris cited at the beginning of this chapter denied the applicability of the term "Revisionist" to the new historians because there was no substantive body of literature for them to revise. Morris also argued in that essay that the close association of the term "revisionism" with an American diplomatic historiographical school of the 1960s rendered it inapplicable to the Israeli context. But parallels between Israeli new history and American revisionism, and indeed with Revisionist historiography as such, are substantial and illuminating. It does not matter that the Israeli new historians have rarely used the term "Revisionist" to describe their own work, or that the epithet was most probably assigned by their opponents. Such is often the case with abstract, classificatory nouns such as "Imperialism," which in Victorian England was employed by Liberal opponents of Tory foreign adventurism, or "Canaanism," a derisive term coined by the socialist-Zionist poet Abraham Shlonsky to describe the literary movement that asserted the existence of an autochthonous Hebrew-Palestinian culture and rejected Zionism's sense of mission to diaspora Jewry.[29]

In the countries that were defeated in World War II, the term "revisionism" is associated with rightist historians combating the incriminatory national historiography that became normative during the 1970s. One encounters this usage not only in Germany but also in Italy, where "Revisionists" are those who refuse to accept a structural link between Italian fascism and Nazism. Contrarily, among the victors in World War II the term is associated with left-oriented scholars attacking a triumphalist historiography that depicted the war as a Manichean struggle between western civilization and totalitarian barbarism.

Israel, the victor of 1948, falls into the latter camp, and its new historians subject Israel to the same sort of criticism employed in the 1960s by the self-styled Revisionist school of American diplomatic historiography. The Revisionist literature on the origins of the Cold War accused the Truman and Eisenhower administrations of unwarranted aggressiveness toward and hysterical fear of the Soviet Union.[30] These lines of argumentation are certainly familiar to any student of the new Israeli historiography. Like the Israeli new historians, the American Revisionists unleashed a stormy national debate about the morality of the country's foreign policy and the justice of its use of force. As the historian Peter Novick has written, "Given the centrality of the cold war in American society since the 1940s, it is only a slight exaggeration to say that cold war revisionism threatened the myth which defined and justified the postwar American polity. . . . "[31] Substitute the term "Arab–Israeli conflict" for "cold war," and "Israeli" for "American," and you have a good summary of the public ramifications of the Israeli new historians' contentions.

It was the very sensitivity of the subject matter, its ability to provoke a public furore, that linked the American and Israeli situations. The 1990s brought a fresh crop of American scholarship critical of American policy during World War II, the dropping of the atomic bombs on Japan and, as before, the origins of the Cold War. The intersection between this literature and the production of works of public history, such as the mid-1990s star-crossed Enola Gay exhibition at the Smithsonian Institution, turned an academic debate into a *cause célèbre*. The matter percolated into the mass media, which were, in general, hostile to the exhibition's "Revisionist" qualities. The call by some American historians not just to remember the Alamo, but rather to reconstruct it, evoked a similar visceral reaction. The impassioned polemics of Shabtai Teveth and Aharon Megged against the new historians in Israel thus had numerous parallels in American political culture.[32]

Morris, Shlaim, and others brought to Israeli historiography the adversarial ethos which had been typical of American historiography since the 1960s. Let me take a moment to clarify what I mean by "adversarial," first in the American and then in the Israeli context. By the end of the 1970s the vigor of radical historiography in American academe had been spent; today's neo-conservative criticisms of universities as hotbeds of anachronistic radicalism are themselves anachronistic.[33] But if today's academic historiography is by and large uninformed by a radical agenda, neither is it an exercise in defense of the status quo. The basic mood of academic historians at major research universities in the United States is not revolutionary, but it is resentful: sympathetic with the downtrodden and hostile to Whiggishness of all sorts. In the contemporary narrative of oppression, history is portrayed as a tale of perpetrators and victims, not an account of the progressive activity of enlightened elites or revolutionary masses. And this is precisely the spirit of the Israeli new historiography. It is adversarial in its harsh critique of the Yishuv leadership and its resentment against Zionist triumphalism in any form. Whereas the first generation of Yishuv historians were sympathetic critics of Labor, the new historians save their sympathy for those whom they perceive as Labor's victims: Arabs, Oriental Jews, even (for Segev) German Jews, dominated in Palestine by their Polish brethren and reduced to stammering in broken Hebrew.[34] The first-generation scholars present the Yishuv leaders as flawed and troubled heroes, but heroes nonetheless; for the new historians there are no heroes, only victims.

Like American Revisionists of the 1960s and 1970s, the new Israeli historians have marshaled vast amounts of recently declassified archival material in the service of the construction of a counter-narrative of considerable validity. No rational person can dispute, after reading Morris, Shlaim, and Pappé, that in 1948 many of the Palestinian Arabs were driven from their homes by Israeli force, or that the leaders of the Arab states were torn by doubts about the desirability or feasibility of a war of annihilation against Israel. But the adversarial ethos which informs the new Israeli historiography can affect its arguments in negative ways as well. American Cold War Revisionists have been criticized for offering too schematic a presentation, which conceals the uncertainty and improvisation of policy formulated under extreme conditions. Although Morris's careful scholarship avoids this pitfall, Shlaim's does not; his book's greatest weakness is its persistent exaggeration of the amorphous accords between the Yishuv leadership and King Abdullah.[35]

Moreover, the new historians' desire to compensate for the errors of official Israeli military historiography can skew their presentation. Morris's books make only a modest effort to convey the traumatic effects of the 1948 War on the Israelis, and the books of Shlaim and Pappé elide this subject almost completely.[36] Pappé's *The Making of the Arab–Israeli Conflict* offers an apparently impartial (if questionable) distinction between the 1948 War's military history, which he describes as "microhistorical" and hence unimportant, and its political-diplomatic history, which is "macrohistorical" and thus the center of the author's attention. True to form, Pappé's book overlooks Jewish military defeats and massacres of Jewish civilians, but the mass murder of Arabs at Deir Yasin counts as "macrohistorical" and thus receives close attention. Moreover, Pappé and other new historians are more likely to employ moralistic and uncomplimentary language when describing Israeli behavior than when describing that of the Arabs. For example, although Shlaim argues explicitly that Palestinian militancy and rejectionism left the Yishuv no choice but to thwart the creation of a Palestinian state, he describes Israeli military action in the Arab areas of the UN partition resolution as "Jewish aggressiveness." In Pappé's work, Arab aggression, such as the renewal of fighting in July 1948, is termed an "Arab initiative." Since it was during the subsequent days of fighting that Israel conquered much of the territory beyond the partition resolution boundaries, Israel is portrayed as the aggressor in the July fighting which, he acknowledges, the Arabs started.[37]

The new historians, like any scholar with a sense of mission, stretch their arguments further than their own evidence warrants. To be sure, the Arab states were not certain of their military goals in 1948, but Pappé strains credulity by presenting the drift into war as a result of a fit of absentmindedness.[38] Morris and Pappé are right to show that the Zionists' military forces were approximately equal to those of the Arabs, but, according to Pappé and Shlaim, the Zionists themselves did not know this, nor did they know that Ernest Bevin, the much-despised British foreign secretary, was resigned to the establishment of a Jewish state.[39] Finally, the new historians' documentation, although massive, is no less questionable than that of their official predecessors. For example, for their understanding of Arab intentions and policies the new historians rely heavily on Arabic published sources such as correspondence, diaries, and memoirs, although they have stressed the inadequacy of relying on Hebrew sources of this type and the necessity of employing contemporary archival documentation.

It is the adversarial ethos, rather than any methodological or analytical innovation, which makes the new historians a distinct and cohesive force in contemporary Israeli historiography. For Morris, scholars who worked with recently declassified archival materials on the Arab–Israeli conflict but did not share his conclusions were not serious historians. He therefore described Itamar Rabinovich and Michael Oren, whose scholarship blames the Arab states more than the Israelis for the failure of the post-1948 peace negotiations, as members of "a new school of 'official' Israeli historians perhaps 'new old historians.'"[40] As I have remarked above, there is nothing at all unusual in contemporary western historical scholarship about the new historians' adversarial ethos. More striking is Morris's odd refusal to admit to having a particular political perspective (though admittedly one that has changed over time; his apparent move from Left to Right is analyzed in Chapter 2). In response to his various critics, Morris has steadfastly claimed the high ground of objectivity, a search for truth without preconceptions. "I collected evidence, tried to reconstruct what happened and why things happened as they did, and then drew conclusions." "My objective in writing about 1948 was to ascertain and explain what happened. I did not judge or apportion blame." "I am not sure that writing history serves any purpose or should serve any purpose that strays beyond the covers of each book."[41] And so on. Shlaim makes similar claims to objectivity:

> I did not set out with the intention of writing a Revisionist history. It was the official documents I came across in the various archives that led me to explore the historical roots of the Palestine Question, drew my attention to the role of Transjordan, and led me to reexamine some of my own assumptions as well as the claims of previous historians.[42]

These claims might well be made in good faith. Let us return to our comparison between the Israeli new history and American Cold War revisionism. American New Left historiography of the 1960s featured a combination of political radicalism, on the one hand, and a staunch epistemological objectivism and hostility to relativism, on the other.[43] Relativism, after all, would weaken the moral certainty of one's cause; the clearer one's concept of how things should be, the more certain is the depiction of the past "as it really was." Like the precipitate that remains in a container whose liquid has evaporated, the compound of subversion and positivism remains long after its catalyst, Marxist ideology, has melted into air.

The new history's methodology is as traditional as its conclusions are revolutionary. It operates within the confines of diplomatic and high political history, combating older narratives of the 1948 War on their own terms. (Such is usually the case with revisionism; who can imagine a book more stodgy in its methodology than Fritz Fischer's masterful exposé of German war aims in World War I?)[44] Greater methodological innovation has come from Israeli historical sociologists who, in the spirit of Shapiro, Lissak, and Horowitz, propose unifying analytical frameworks that transcend the who-wrote-what-to-whom model of diplomatic historiography. For example, the work of the sociologist Baruch Kimmerling refreshingly focuses not on the debate over 1948 but instead on broader conceptual issues facing scholars of Yishuv society. In his classic book *Zionism and Territory* and other works, Kimmerling claims that Lissak and other scholars have isolated nation-building institutions such as the Jewish National Fund from the Arab sphere in which they operated and upon which they had a traumatic impact. According to Kimmerling, the Zionist economy, and especially its collectivist aspects, owes its structure to the presence of Arabs, which necessitated the creation of a dual-market economy.[45]

Kimmerling has attempted to construct a comprehensive paradigm which unites Yishuv history from its origin into the period of statehood. He seeks a conflation of domestic and foreign affairs, as well as diplomatic, political, social, and cultural history. Unfortunately, the search for a new paradigm, admirable in itself, can lead to a determinist monism. Gershon Shafir's application of this sort of framework on a monographic level in his highly influential 1989 book on land and labor markets in Ottoman Palestine was not completely successful. Although stimulating and wide-ranging, Shafir's book is marred by factual errors, and the author repeatedly forces evidence into a Procrustean theoretical frame.[46]

Problematic though it may be, this line of sociological thinking is promising and welcome, as it has pushed the new history beyond controversies surrounding the birth of the state of Israel. Most students of the new history see its purview moving inexorably forward; thanks to the ongoing declassification of Israeli documents, particularly after thirty years, we have a growing Revisionist literature of the 1956 and 1967 Wars. At the same time, scholars are shifting their glance backward and rethinking the history of Zionism and the project of Jewish nation-building as a whole.[47] No doubt, these studies, like the first generation of Yishuv scholarship and the newer Israeli historiography, will operate within distinct ideological frameworks. Nevertheless, one hopes that these works, and others that will follow, will be able to overcome the analytical and methodological limitations of the earlier scholarship and, at the same time, avoid the reflexive adversarialism that characterizes so much of the new Israeli historiography.

2 Beyond Revisionism

Current directions in Israeli historiography

Some twenty years ago, the Israeli academic establishment was shaken by the publications of a small group of historians who claimed to shatter conventional Zionist myths regarding the birth of the Israeli state, the Palestinian refugee problem, and the Arab–Israeli conflict.[1] This body of scholarship, interchangeably called "new" or "Revisionist" Israeli historiography, was, by and large, critical of Israeli policy, seeing Israel as militarily aggressive and in good measure responsible for its conflict with its Arab neighbors. For over a decade, furious debates between practitioners of the "new history" and defenders of traditional historical views filled the halls of Israeli universities and the columns of the Israeli press.[2] The Revisionists claimed to be objective scholars, their vision unclouded by Zionist ideology and the resulting impulse to apologize for Israel's actions and exculpate its leaders. Benny Morris, the most prominent of the Revisionists, went so far as to argue, in a manifesto of 1988, that the new history was, in fact, Israel's first serious professional historiography. The literature produced to date, he claimed, had been official history, produced by governmental or quasi-governmental bodies, or the representation of private memory presented in memoirs. In both cases previous historiography had been produced without access to Israeli archives, which normally grant access to documents only after the passage of thirty years.[3]

Critics of the new history thought differently. Staunch defenders of David Ben-Gurion and the Labor Zionist elite that established Israel argued that the new history was the work of guilt-ridden leftists hostile to the existence of Israel as a Jewish state. The Revisionists' oeuvre was accused of being little different in approach and intent from the inveterate anti-Zionist scholarship produced in the Arab world or by its sympathizers in the West. There was widespread concern that the new history would undermine Israelis' confidence in the justice of the Zionist dream, thereby weakening their will to continue the ongoing struggle for Israel's survival in a continuously hostile environment. The distinguished Israeli writer Aharon Megged went so far as to describe the new history as a manifestation of "Israel's suicidal impulse."[4]

Over the past few years, a paradoxical development has taken place. While the number of scholars championing a critical approach to the Israeli past has grown markedly, the rhetorical storm has died down. The new historical revolution continues, but it has passed from its Jacobin period into its Thermidor and has taken on a more subdued form. To some degree, the arguments of Revisionist historians have been incorporated into the mainstream historiographic consensus and even into popular historical consciousness in Israel. The more extreme arguments have been marginalized, called into doubt by the preponderance of evidence or delegitmized by the open political biases of some of their champions. The Revisionist writings of the late 1980s and early 1990s were suffused with an adversarial ethos, a missionary zeal to shatter Zionist myths of Israeli rectitude, catalyzed by a generational struggle between young scholars against mandarin professors who controlled access to teaching positions at Israeli universities. By the end of the 1990s the first generation of new historians were, for the most part, professionally secure. Ironically, Morris, whose writings have depicted Ben-Gurion in highly unflattering terms, is now a tenured professor at Ben-Gurion University of the Negev.

One important reason for the waning of the Israeli historians' controversy is the rapid attenuation of traditional Zionist ideology in Israeli academia and, to an only slightly lesser extent, among the members of Israel's secular and professional elite who dominate the mass media. The New history's counter-narrative was coherent and powerful because it challenged a well-established master narrative. Traditional Zionist proclamations about the Jews' historic and moral right to a homeland in the ancient Land of Israel, the obligation to undergo a physical and psychic transformation from a people of peddlers into a nation of warriors and laborers, and a mission to "ingather the exiles" from throughout the diaspora have lost relevance as Israel has matured into a highly industrialized, urbanized, materialistic society with an economy based in high-technology manufacturing and services. After fifty-five years, the ideological scaffolding that supported the state through its youth has come down, leaving an unobstructed view of a political edifice which, albeit in many ways unattractive, stands on its own.

The Oslo peace process is widely viewed as responsible for the weakening of traditional Zionism, as substantial numbers of Israelis began to imagine a future in which they would dwell in a normal state at peace with its neighbors and thus no longer making constant demands upon its citizenry for heroic sacrifice and struggle. In fact, such a striving for normalization was very much in keeping with classic Zionist ideology, according to which antisemitism was omnipresent but not eternal, and the establishment of a Jewish state would stabilize the position of Jews in the world. By transforming Jews from a "ghost people," as the Zionist founding father Leo Pinsker called them, into an empowered, territorialized nation, they would be accepted into the community of nations. It was the *failure* of the Oslo peace process in the wake of the renewed Intifada in 2000 that promoted the collapse of Zionist political consciousness and its replacement with the beliefs that anti-Jewish sentiment is indelibly ingrained into human sensibility and that Israel is doomed to fight for its very survival into the distant future. In such an atmosphere, Israelis are far less likely than in the past to be offended by historians' accusations that Israel's wartime behavior has been less than exemplary. To be sure, Israelis can still be outraged by the findings of military historians, for example Motti Golani's recent discovery that during the 1956 Sinai campaign Israeli soldiers murdered Egyptian prisoners of war in the Mitla Pass.[5] But such cases are now the exception, not the rule, as the world-view of Israelis becomes increasingly pragmatic and jaundiced.

Moreover, with the decline of the Ben-Gurionist vision of a unified, secular Israeli culture, Israeli society has taken on the form of a jigsaw puzzle of competing interest groups divided along ethnic and religious lines – the veteran European-Jewish (Ashkenazi) elite, immigrants from the Middle East and North Africa and their descendants (Mizrahi, or "Oriental" Jews), new immigrants from the former Soviet Union, ultra-Orthodox Jews, and a large Arab minority. In such an atmosphere, the public's historical interest has turned inward, to the mass immigration of the state's early years, the impact of the Holocaust and of Holocaust survivors on the young state, the suppression of the immigrants' languages and cultures, the historic domination of Ashkenazim over Mizrahim, and transformation within the Orthodox community and its relations with the secular majority.

Although developments within Israeli academia cannot be separated from the broader social developments described above, there are also important internal factors within Israeli university culture that account for the moderation of the historians' controversy. First off, the new history of the 1980s and 1990s was not as revolutionary as its practitioners claimed. Professional, archive-based history of the Zionist movement and Yishuv dates back to the 1960s. This literature featured a critical, although fundamentally sympathetic, approach to Zionist ideology and the Yishuv's political leadership. When archives for the years surrounding 1948 became available, Revisionist historians approached them with the same traditional, diplomatic- and military-historical approach that had been taken by previous generations, and, although their findings were controversial, they were not rejected out of hand in Israeli academia. (By means of example, Morris's first scholarly article on the subject of the Palestinian refugees was published in the staid Tel Aviv University journal *Studies in Zionism*.)[6] Israeli universities are riven with conflict, both political and personal, but the historical discipline as practiced there is highly professionalized, and so given to the process of self-correction that is integral to scholarly endeavor in the modern western world. It was only a question of time before the new history would cease to be new, its arguments tested, rejected or confirmed by other scholars and incorporated, at least in part, into the historiographic mainstream.

Second, historians at Israeli universities are acutely aware of developments within the historical discipline in the West. They have kept abreast of, and sometimes pioneered, historiographical innovation in the fields of social, gender, and especially cultural history. (The journal *History & Memory*, housed at Tel Aviv University, has been a focal point for scholarship on collective memory.) In recent years, as the writing of Israeli history has shed its conservative and state-supporting agenda, historians of the Yishuv and state of Israel have begun to catch up with their colleagues in other fields, and, although the bulk of historical writing about Israel is still political, diplomatic, and military, there is a new wave of literature on the intersection of class, gender, ethnicity, and race in the construction of the Israeli state.

Third, recent Israeli historiography has been powerfully influenced by Israeli sociologists, who have tended to be politically more radical and methodologically more innovative than their historian colleagues. Much of the most important work on the mass immigration, relations between immigrant and veteran Israelis, and the suppression and invention of ethnic identities in Israel has been the work of historically informed sociologists. Sociologists preceded historians in positing linkages between foreign and domestic policy, locating the militarization of Israeli society in the cultural milieu of the first Palestinian-born generation of Zionist youth and in the vast social and ideological cleavages that fissured the young Israeli state's fragile society.

The critical discourse on recent Israeli historiography often, and mistakenly, conflates historical Revisionism with post-Zionism. These terms need to be carefully defined and their relationship delineated. Revisionism in the sense of a coherent critique of an entrenched historical paradigm originated in debates during the 1920s about the origins of World War I. Since then, the term has been applied to controversies about the origins of other conflicts, including World War II and the Cold War, and it has been associated with a wide variety of political orientations, from Left to Right. In Israel, the unpopular 1982 Lebanon War and the first Palestinian Intifada (1987–93) fostered the development of Revisionist historiography on the Arab–Israeli conflict, and to this day the terms "Revisionist" or "New" historiography continue to be applied largely to literature on Israeli military policy and statecraft.

Revisionist Israeli historiography is on occasion, but not regularly, informed by a post-Zionist conceptual framework. Revisionist historical literature has devoted itself to deconstructing historical perceptions cemented in Zionist ideology but does not by definition impugn the legitimacy of the Zionist project itself or of Israel as a Jewish state. The term "Revisionist" or "New" historian has been linked with such disparate scholars as the arch-positivist and increasingly hawkish Benny Morris, the positivist and dovish Avi Shlaim, and the relentlessly post-colonial and anti-Zionist Ilan Pappé. Clearly, then, self-proclaimed Revisionist historiography of Israel, not to mention the field of Israeli historiography as a whole, cannot be tied to any particular political ideology or orientation. Israeli historiography is in a state of both fragmentation and evolution, of what could be called constructive deconstruction. This is a global process in which self-conscious Revisionism is ultimately less significant than incremental innovation as a force for the creation of knowledge. Yet the production and nature of Israeli historiography display persistently parochial characteristics, the product of a complex interaction between the fading, yet still present, influences of Zionist ideology and the all-consuming conflict that dominates the field of Israeli historical vision.

Historiographical revolution and its aftermath

Israeli Revisionist writings on the 1948 War paralleled the wave of reassessments of fascism and World War II that rolled through European academia from the 1960s through the 1980s. The topics under review varied widely – for example the roots of Nazi expansionism in Germany's territorial aims in the First World War I, French popular support for the Vichy regime and complicity in the Holocaust, similarities between Italian fascism and Nazism, or between Stalin's gulags and the Nazi death camps – as did the political perspective of their authors. While these debates raged in Europe, historians in the United States challenged conventional views about the origins of the Cold War, claiming that they lay not so much in a *bona fide* Stalinist threat as in American neo-colonial expansionism and anti-communist paranoia. Throughout the western world, as in Israel, the critical re-evaluation of the causes of war and conflict was made possible by the passage of time, the opening of archives, high levels of freedom of expression (as did not exist behind the Iron Curtain or in the Arab world), and, most important, the 1960s' cultural revolution, which replaced the state-supporting ethos of traditional academic historiography with an adversarial one.[7] A good example of the new adversarial ethos was the Bielefeld School of German historiography, which claimed that Nazism was not an aberration from German historic norms but rather a natural outgrowth of the allegedly dysfunctional and authoritarian Wilhelmine Empire.

Over the past decade these controversies have died down. Revisionist counter-narratives, which were as coherent and all-encompassing as the master narratives they attacked, have been replaced by more nuanced, less politicized approaches. To return to the German example, over the past twenty years the Bielefeld School has been supplanted by a more sympathetic view of Imperial Germany as an integral component of Western Europe, with a mature bourgeois society and an evolving political system. Culture and the region have replaced politics and the nation-state as the privileged loci of attention. There is a flourishing of writing on gender relations, social networks, locality (*Heimatsgeschichte*), and daily life (*Alltagsgeschichte*).[8] We shall see below that Israeli historiography is beginning to be influenced by this diffusion and de-politicization of historiographical focus.

The Revisionist strain in Israeli historiography may also be compared with a somewhat different type of historical inquiry, not of dominating states but rather of the peoples they have historically dominated. The Israeli Revisionist controversy of the late 1980s and 1990s was similar in many ways to developments in the field of Irish historiography some twenty years earlier. In both cases, the passage of about two generations after statehood and the transformation from an impoverished into a First World national economy moderated feelings of historic victimization. Irish Revisionist historians claimed that Ireland's historic relationship with Britain, long seen as one of unrelieved oppression, was often economically beneficial to the Emerald Isle.[9] Similarly, over the past two decades the image of Mandatory British rule in Israeli historiography has improved considerably. Britain, previously seen as reneging on the Balfour Declaration, throttling Jewish immigration, and conspiring with the Arabs to thwart the establishment of the Jewish state, is now appreciated for having played an invaluable role in developing Palestine's infrastructure and promoting the growth of the Yishuv's political and military institutions.[10] (A nostalgic image of British rule has been presented in two recent bestselling books in Israel, Tom Segev's popular history *One Palestine, Complete* and Amos Oz's fictionalized memoir *A Tale of Love and Darkness*.)[11]

The Irish Revisionist controversy has been debated almost entirely within Ireland, yet modern Irish history is written by scholars throughout the globe. In Israel the opposite is the case: for many years the Israeli new history was represented, often in a charged and polemical form, in the North American and European Jewish press, and the new historians attained considerable notoriety. Yet despite the size and educational attainments of the Jewish diaspora, the production of Israeli Revisionist historiography, indeed of Israeli historiography as such, has been almost entirely the work of scholars in Israel. This phenomenon deserves further scrutiny.

Israeli historians and historians of Israel

Since the late 1950s, scholars in North America and Europe have produced outstanding overviews of the history of Zionism and Israel, but original, monographic research on the subject has been produced almost entirely in Israel.[12] There is nothing unusual about the historiography of small countries, especially those whose official languages are difficult and obscure, being dominated by natives of and universities in those lands. But Israel is unique among small nations for its centrality in global politics and religious consciousness. Modern Hebrew is not as difficult as Slavic languages or Arabic, and a knowledge of the latter eases the acquisition of Hebrew considerably. What is more, at least among Jewish academics, there are substantial numbers who learned Hebrew as part of their basic or professional education. Finally, and most important, there is a thriving field of Israel studies in North America (less so in Europe), but it is dominated by scholars in the social sciences, mainly political science and sociology. Although some of this literature is historically informed, its emphasis is presentist, concerned with the contemporary Arab–Israeli conflict or sites of social tension within the Israeli state.[13]

Clearly, then, the neglect of Israeli history by North American or European academics has little to do with a lack of supply of competent scholars. One must look instead to "demand" factors; that is, the configurations of academic faculties and research frameworks, on the one hand, and the socio-psychological factors behind a scholar's choice of field, on the other. Israel does not fit neatly into any of the geographic fields upon which history departments in the western world are structured. It is in, but not of, the Middle East. I do not refer here merely to political considerations, the antipathy towards Israel that reigns throughout the region and is certainly to be found in North American and European universities. I also mean that in a technical sense a historian of Israel is unlikely to fit into a department of history that seeks a Middle Eastern specialist with expertise in Arabic (which many Israeli historians have not mastered), Islam, and other factors common to the modern Middle East – the heritage of colonialism and anti-colonialism, pan-Arabism, state socialism, and, more recently, Islamic radicalism. Given the state of Israel's European origins, courses on Israeli history are often, incongruously, considered part of the "European" field, but a young scholar with expertise in Israeli history is not likely to find a position in a faculty of European historians unless (s)he has mastered European languages and has research expertise in topics of direct interest to European historians. Thus, in order to become part of a history department in the western world a scholar of Israeli history must in fact pursue this subject as a second field in addition to one that fits into the department's structure and will be of use to its program for graduate training. (There is an exception to the above generalizations in the form of a handful of Middle East historians currently employed in American universities who know Hebrew and have serious interests in Palestine/Israel. Yet because of the demands and expectations of their fields most of their publications treat the Arab world, and what they do publish on Palestine often features a pronounced anti-Israel political bias.)[14]

In contemporary North America, Israel studies flourishes far more readily in the social sciences than in history departments. Sociologists and political scientists can claim to locate in Israeli statecraft or society models that are relevant to their disciplines as a whole. Often, these models are explanatory tools for ethnic strife, discrimination, or international conflict, with Israel presented as exemplifying one form or another of social pathology. Scholars who adopt these approaches free themselves of suspicion of an apologetic or sympathetic stance towards Israel, which, as opposed to a bias in favor of Arab causes, is rarely considered academically respectable. Even still, only a handful of the elite research universities in North America have on staff social scientists with specific research interests in Israel. Most of the social scientists who dominate the Association for Israel Studies teach at good, but not elite, public universities or at second-tier institutions.

The limitation of the study of Israeli history to Israel itself is also the product of the collective psychology of Jewish studies scholars and the programs in which they teach. In the field of Jewish studies, as it has flourished in North America over the past three decades, historical study has focused primarily on issues of immediate concern to Jews in their lands of residence: antisemitism and the Holocaust, assimilation and ethnicity, religiosity and cultural expression. Although Zionism can be of considerable interest to historians as a mobilizing force and a source of Jewish identity in a particular time and place (for example interwar Poland, the United States during the 1970s), Jewish historians outside of Israel tend to look upon international Zionist politics, the development of the Yishuv, and the history of the Israeli state as something distant, even foreign. Given history's venerable role as the handmaid of nationalism, Jewish studies scholars outside of Israel have implicitly accepted the claim, commonly made in Israeli academia, that only those who have made Israel their home and have come to know it intimately are qualified to write its history. One may also conjecture that the sort of Jewish scholar willing to commit his or her life to the field of Jewish studies often has profound Zionist convictions that could be undermined by getting to know Israel's history too well. If Israel is studied with the same historiographical tools and conceptual frameworks that are applied to any other country, it loses much of its exceptionalism, upon which Zionist fervor so often depends.

Like the dissipating wake of a ship that has long passed, the patterns of production of Israeli historiography testify to the ongoing influence of Zionist ideology, even as it recedes into the distance. For the foreseeable future the subject and object of Israeli history will remain identical, and the country's past will be probed mostly by its own citizens. The result has been, and will continue to be, the ever-present threat of blinkered historiographical vision, of parochialism born of the fact that the literature is produced by at most a hundred tenure-stream faculty in a minuscule country with only five research universities. Israeli historians are, by and large, remarkably well traveled and well read, but, precisely because they live their lives in the small land about which they write, national history risks being reduced to local history. The broad comparative sweep, the novelty of approach, and the dispassionate gaze that historians bring to countries that are their summer-and-sabbatical, adopted homes – for example American historians of Germany, Japanese historians of Egypt – do not come easily to Israeli historians of their own country. Yet, despite these challenges, Israeli historiography has, in recent years, not only advanced our factual knowledge of the country's past but also adopted analytical frameworks universally employed by historians regardless of provenance or field.

Major trends in the history of Israeli society

The bulk of recent Israeli historiography is political, diplomatic, and military, followed by traditional intellectual history, particularly the history of Zionist thought. Social history is gaining ground, either in the form of labor history (including comparative studies of Jewish and Palestinian workers) or, more often, immigration history, which blends into political history because of its frequent focus on the state's elites and on policy as opposed to the lives and experiences of the immigrants themselves. Israeli economic history, which until the 1980s focused almost exclusively on the labor sector, is now giving proper due to the private sector, from citrus plantations and rural marketing co-operatives to light industry. Younger scholars are beginning to write the gender and cultural history of the Yishuv and early state. An environmental history of Israel has recently been published, although it is essentially a history of state policy rather than of landscape.[15] Most of the work in these fields is neither self-consciously Revisionist nor apologetic. Save for the book review section of Israel's respected daily newspaper *Ha-Aretz*, this literature attracts little public attention, partly because there is no polemical edge to the scholarship and partly because the authors do not push themselves into the limelight of the mass media. This literature, however, contributes fundamentally to our understanding of the state of Israel's origins and subsequent development. (On a similar note, George Boyce and Alan O'Day have noted that the most innovative, exciting Irish historiography of recent years has been only indirectly touched, if at all, by the Revisionist controversy.)[16] Moreover, whereas ten years ago only the most controversial or general works of Israeli historiography were translated into English, much of the more specialized literature is now becoming available in translation. The *Journal of Israeli History*, produced at Tel Aviv University, and Ben-Gurion University's journal *Israel Studies* publish both original work and translations or adaptations of articles originally published in Hebrew.

An important trend in Israeli political history is the identification of the nexus between politics and culture, locating the intellectual field in which Israel's leaders operated and exposing the ideological tensions that were never resolved, nor even suppressed, but only temporarily displaced by the founding of the state. Joseph Heller, the author of a pioneering study of the Israeli far right, has recently published an important monograph on David Ben-Gurion's arduous struggle to establish functional political unity among the Yishuv's warring factions during the five years leading up to the establishment of the state. As Heller points out, the emphasis in the Revisionist historiography on war and Arab–Jewish conflict obscures the fact that most of the energy of the Yishuv's governing elite was directed towards machine politics, coalition-building, and the construction of a viable national economy.[17] Political and ideological rivalries within the Yishuv were all-consuming. Ben-Gurion faced constant revolt from the left wing within his own Labor

Zionist Mapai party, and during the 1948 War he went to the brink to force the Yishuv's most powerful militia and elite strike force, which were dominated by parties to the left of his own, into a regular state army. (Strife with the right-wing militias Etzel and Lechi was even more divisive; as I have found in my own research, in the spring of 1948 the Israeli public feared all-out civil war between the government and the radical right.)[18] Given high levels of domestic instability, Heller argues, a peaceful partition of Palestine (although not necessarily the creation of a Palestinian state) was vastly preferred over armed conflict, and the expulsion of the Arab population of the future Jewish state was a far less significant policy issue than the mass immigration of Jews from Europe.

Tensions between religion and state, between Judaism and Zionism, were a constant threat to the elusive yet essential consensus without which the state of Israel could not be founded or long survive. Ehud Luz's monograph *Parallels Meet* (1988) and a book of essays by Yosef Salmon (1990) concentrated on Zionism's early decades and on the formation of an Orthodox centrist core that accommodated Zionism on pragmatic grounds (as a means of saving endangered Jews) or pietist ones (as a vehicle of collective religious revival, promoting Torah study in the sacred Land of Israel, and tilling its soil, which was associated with a variety of sanctifying commandments).[19] In a major work of 1994, Aviezer Ravitzky offered a detailed analysis of Orthodoxy's more extreme responses to Zionism, ranging from a fervent embrace to an uncompromising rejection. Both extremes sprang from messianic yearnings. The former was activist, calling on Jews to initiate messianic redemption through settlement of the Land of Israel, while the latter embraced traditional Jewish passivity. Taken to its extreme, ultra-Orthodox anti-Zionism claimed that not only the establishment of a Jewish commonwealth, but even the agricultural settlement of the land, was a sacrilege; the former because it preceded the advent of the messiah, and the latter because it transformed a wild, sacred ruin into a mere object of human will.[20]

Ravitzky's book threw considerable new light on the origins of activist-messianic Orthodoxy in the thought of Isaac Abraham Kook, the first Ashkenazic chief rabbi in Mandatory Palestine. In 1999, Arye Naor, cabinet secretary under Prime Minister Menachem Begin, published *Eretz Yisrael ha-sheleimah: emunah u-mediniyut* (The entire Land of Israel: theology and policy), which traces Kook's influence upon future generations through Kook's son, Zvi Yehuda, and the Merkaz Ha-Rav Yeshiva, which became the spiritual center of the religious settler movement that exercised considerable influence over Israel's post-1967 policies in the Occupied Territories. In his search for the intellectual roots of the post-1967 settler movement's territorial maximalism, Naor ranges beyond religious Zionism *per se* to the entire gamut of Zionist ideology, dating back to the grandiose territorial vision of the early twentieth-century Zionist leader Menachem Ussishkin. Ussishkin and, after him, the Revisionist Zionist leader Vladimir

Jabotinsky, conjured up a hash of historic and strategic justifications for a Jewish state that would extend over the East Bank of the Jordan and up into today's Lebanon. Their rhetoric employed religious language – Jabotinsky referred to the Jordan as a "sacred river" – although these expressions were for the most part metaphorical, expressive of political convictions about the territorial needs of the Jews as a nation rather than beliefs in the inalienable spiritual patrimony of Jews as a faith community.[21] Yet a sufficient coalescence of sensibility and blurring of rhetoric took place within Zionist ideology to foster widespread support, by Labor as well as Likud governments, for the settlement movement after 1967.

Historians of Zionism have long argued that Labor Zionism harnessed considerably greater religious energy than Revisionism, as it sublimated traditional Jewish messianism into striving to settle or, tellingly, to "redeem" the land, to sanctify the Jews through productive labor, and to create a Jewish state that would be a model of social justice, a veritable Light unto the Nations.[22] In a controversial book of 1995, Zeev Sternhell, a historian with expertise in the history of right-wing and fascist thought in Europe, turned his attention to Labor Zionism, and he took a far more critical tack than previous historians of the subject. Sternhell argued that although early twentieth-century Labor Zionism professed an allegiance to social democracy, its spiritual energy and uncompromising nationalism quickly overpowered its socialist tendencies. The result was an anti-democratic, pseudo-socialist, and quasi-totalitarian Labor Zionist hegemonic regime, suffused with an aggressive territorial maximalism and a militaristic ethos that were curbed only by the needs of the moment.[23] Sternhell's book was brilliant in its analysis of Labor Zionism's intellectual debt to the radical neo-romanticism of the extreme ends of the *fin-de-siècle* European political spectrum (integral nationalism on the Right and anarcho-syndicalism on the Left). The result was a celebration of experience and distaste for theoretical system-building which, paradoxically, presented itself in the form of pragmatic empiricism and positivism. The book was also significant in that it represented an avowedly Revisionist approach to the domestic, as opposed to the military-diplomatic, history of Zionism and Israel. But the book's numerous and glaring factual errors, its distortion of evidence, and its unfavorable comparison of Labor Zionism to an idealized European social democracy that never existed rendered the book all but useless as a piece of serious scholarship and endeared it only to readers with a visceral predisposition against its subject.[24]

Sternhell was right that Labor Zionist political culture was imbued with militarism, but one can encounter this argument in a wide variety of scholarship written from varying disciplinary and political perspectives. The 1980s witnessed the formation of a school of Israeli sociology known as critical sociology, which can be seen as adumbrating and then running parallel with the "new history" that came to the fore at the end of the decade. Thanks largely to the influence of the late Yonathan Shapiro, who pioneered the field of Israeli historical sociology and trained many students, a number of important studies in the field began to appear from the mid-1980s onward. The University of Haifa has been a stronghold of critical sociology and in 1995 Haifa's Uri Ben-Eliezer published a finely crafted monograph, *Derekh ha-kavenet: hivatruto shel ha-militarizm ha-yisre'eli 1936–56*, which appeared in English three years later under the title *The Origins of Israeli Militarism*.[25] The book argued that during the 1930s and 1940s philosophical differences between Labor and Revisionist Zionism regarding the use of force were minimal. Palestinian-born Jewish youth scorned what they believed was the impractical humanism of their European-born parents and believed that they alone possessed the will and ability to fight. European-born leaders of the Labor Zionist movement viewed the raw militarism of the native youth with distaste, but they eventually co-opted it and transformed it into the reigning ethos of the new Israeli state. Thus if Israel managed to avoid the plague of military coups affecting most post-colonial democracies, the reason was not because the army stayed in its barracks, but because the body politic and the barracks were coterminous.

Ben-Eliezer's book, however critical its presentation of the foundations of the Israeli state, was not as novel as it may seem. Many of its arguments had already been made, albeit in a form somewhat more sympathetic with its subjects, by the most prominent representative of what might be considered the Israeli historiographical establishment, Anita Shapira, in her 1992 book *Herev ha-yonah: Ha-tsiyonut ve-ha-koah* (English version: *Land and Power: The Zionist Resort to Force*).[26] Similarly, the nostalgic glow that suffuses sociologist Oz Almog's typological study of the native-born Israeli, *Ha-Tsabar* (1997; English version: *The Sabra*, 2000), does not obscure the sabra's preference for direct action, his belief that conflict with Arabs can only be resolved through grim determination and the use of force. The military historians Martin Van Creveld and Motti Golani, who identify with neither the Revisionist nor critical sociological schools, have recently published powerful critiques of the Israeli militarist ethos' negative effects on Israeli statecraft (for example the lack of an effective counterweight to the Israeli military in the formation of national security policy during the crises and subsequent wars of 1956, 1967, and 1973).[27] Golani's work makes the particularly astute, albeit counterintuitive, argument that since the 1973 War Israeli society has increasingly questioned the capacity of force to solve the Palestinian problem, even as exponentially greater quanta of force have been applied, as was the case during the massive Israeli air assault against Lebanon in 1982.

The most recent historical monograph on Israeli militarism is the journalist Yonah Hadari-Ramage's *Mashiah rakhuv 'al tank* (Messiah rides a tank).[28] Hadari-Ramage explores the connection between war and the pervasive sense in Israeli society, throughout most of the state's history, of a failed utopia or lost paradise. Hadari-Ramage shows that on the eve of the

1956, 1967 and 1973 Wars Israeli youth were decried in the media as degenerate, materialistic, and hedonistic (for example, dancing the tango and listening to jazz). In all three cases, wars redeemed the youth of the nation by transforming them into heroes and martyrs. The soldier–messiah figure so well known from the 1967 war was adumbrated by the conquerors of the Sinai in 1956. In 1956, as eleven years later, popular songs produced in the wake of the war were replete with biblical imagery, and images of rabbis, Torah scrolls, and young soldiers at the foot of Mt. Sinai foreshadowed David Rubinger's famous photograph of Shmuel Goren, the Israel Defense Force's chief rabbi, sounding the shofar at the Western Wall on June 7, 1967. Although it would not be justified to argue that domestic malaise alone pushed Israel into three major wars with the Arab world, Hadari-Ramage has exposed the vulnerability of the Zionist project in the face of its own fulfillment: the dialectic between the achievement of "normalization" of the Jews and the psychic deflation that inevitably resulted, and the excessive burdens placed upon youth in Israel's revolutionary, puritanical, and highly mobilized society.

The recent wave of literature on Israeli militarism has been respectfully reviewed in the Israeli press and has aroused little controversy. Similarly, although back in the 1980s there was considerable resistance in Israel, among scholars and the public alike, to the first critiques of Israeli immigration policy during the 1950s, it is now conventional wisdom that the Ashkenazic governing elite looked upon the two main reservoirs of immigrants, European Holocaust survivors and North African/Middle Eastern Jews, with not only compassion but also condescension, mistrust, and even contempt. The kibbutzim, hallmarks of the Hebrew national revival, were reluctant to accept new immigrants, and the Labor movement as a whole was slow to divest itself of the prevalent belief during much of the Mandate period that immigration must be highly selective, limited to the young and able-bodied.[29]

The most sensational critiques have attracted, as one might expect, the most attention in the West, for example Tom Segev's *1949*: *Ha-yisre'elim ha-rishonim* (1984; English edition: *1949: The First Israelis*, 1986) and Idith Zertal's *Zehavam shel ha-yehdim: Ha-hagerah ha-yehudit ha-mahtertit le-erets yisra'el 1945–48* (1996; English edition: *From Catastrophe to Power: Holocaust Survivors and the Emergence of Israel*, 1998).[30] Segev, a talented journalist with a fluent style, presented colorful, if rather selective, evidence of the instrumentality with which Israel's leaders treated what was called the "human material" before them and the horrific conditions under which the new immigrants from Middle Eastern and North African lands were forced to live, sometimes for years after their arrival in Israel. Zertal's book focused specifically on the clandestine immigration of Holocaust survivors to Palestine, an issue that has been mythologized in Israeli collective memory as a source of salvation to vast numbers of individuals and an important factor behind the creation of the state. Zertal argues that between

1945 and 1948 scarcely any shiploads of illegal immigrants managed to dodge the British blockade, that officials of the Yishuv's Agency for Clandestine Immigration were well aware of this, and that the transports of survivors on unseaworthy ships were essentially public relations stunts. Holocaust survivors were, in the words of one immigration official, "wonderful propaganda for the entire human world."[31] Zertal presents the Yishuv leadership as far less interested in bringing Holocaust survivors to safety in their putative homeland than in using them to win public opinion over to the Zionist cause.

Many of Zertal's arguments were made before her by the Tel Aviv University historian Dina Porat.[32] The difference between Zertal and Porat is not really a dispute over facts so much as one of historical judgment. Both authors agree that the leaders of the Yishuv were incapable of distinguishing between the fate of Holocaust survivors as individuals and the transformation of the fledgling Yishuv into a viable state. Zertal, applying contemporary post-Zionist moral standards to her subjects, charges them with insensitivity and even criminal disregard for the tragic consequences of their actions (for example the sinking of a refugee ship or the incarceration by the British of its cargo of human skeletons in internment camps). Porat, however, adopts a more empathetic and less judgmental stance. Porat's approach is shared by Esther Meir-Glitzenstein in a recent monograph on the tragic fate of Iraqi Jewry in the mid-twentieth century. Meir-Glitzenstein shows that after World War II Zionist and Israeli officials sincerely believed that an independent Jewish state was immediately needed to provide a safe haven for Middle Eastern Jews, even though the creation of the state would be a primary cause of the persecution from which they would need to be rescued.[33]

It took several years after Segev's *1949* for academic historians to begin paying serious attention to the experience of immigrants from the Islamic world.[34] Sociologists, however, had been working on the subject since the 1960s. The first studies of the immigrants attributed the social dysfunction of Oriental Jews to backwardness, which would be remedied over time through integration into a uniform, Ashkenazic-dominated Israeli political culture. In the early 1980s, Shlomo Swirski switched the focus from alleged Oriental backwardness to the discriminatory mentalities and practices of the Ashkenazic elite, which resulted in social closure, impeding access to the educational institutions and employment opportunities, without which economic mobility was impossible.[35] (At this time academic discourse on the immigrants and their descendants became increasingly politicized, as the Oriental vote was a key issue in Israel election campaigns and eventually expressed itself in the founding of the political party Shas in 1984.) In the 1990s, under the influence of theoretical innovations in gender and cultural studies, some Israeli sociologists moved beyond empirical analyses of ethnic discrimination to the discursive field in which Israel's governing elite fabricated a coherent "Oriental" Jewry out of a mosaic of variegated immigrant communities (Iraqi, Yemenite, Moroccan, etc.) with little in common save their origins in the Islamic world.[36]

By arguing that the Mizrahi Jew was not only oppressed but also invented by the Ashkenazic elite, scholars such as Ella Shohat, Gil Eyal, Aziza Khazzoom, and Yehouda Shenhav foster the post-Zionist proliferation of ethnic, sub-national Israeli identities, and in particular champion the reintegration of Middle Eastern and North African Jews into Arab cultures, against which mainstream Zionism has set itself in a stark dichotomous fashion. The notion of Mizrahi Jews as, at heart, Jewish Arabs or Arab Jews is fueled by a political agenda to reconfigure the relationship between Arab and Israeli Jewish culture, to break down the barriers between Israelis and Palestinians just as those barriers are taking material form in the shape of the separation barrier between Israel and the Palestinian Territories. This political agenda may be a noble one, but it is untrue to the historical experience of Oriental Jewry, which, despite its infusion into Middle Eastern cultures, spoke distinct Jewish dialects and retained considerable cultural and socio-economic particularity. Nor is the new wave of critical sociology accurate in presenting Mizrahi Jews as bearers of an alternative Zionism, inclusive and communitarian, as opposed to the allegedly domineering and aggressive Zionist ideology of the Ashkenazic founding elite.[37]

Historians of immigration to Israel and, before it, the Yishuv, are approaching their subject without an overt political agenda, and the direction in which their research is going suggests that with the passage of time the story of Jewish immigration to Palestine/Israel will cease to be a political issue, a site for justifying or undermining the tenets of Zionist ideology, and will become, as the current research of Hagit Lavsky and Gur Alroey proposes, one chapter in the general history of Jewish population movement in the twentieth century.[38] This is a fruitful line of inquiry particularly for the Mandate period, when the vast majority of Jewish immigrants to Palestine were neither ideologically Zionist nor assisted by Zionist institutions. The motivations behind immigration, the social and family structure of the immigrants, the construction of economic and social networks upon arrival, and acculturation into the new environment are issues common to the history of immigration in general, and in the case of modern Jewish history comparisons may be made across different points of arrival in Western Europe and the New World. (See, for example, the work of Anat Helman, a young scholar at the Hebrew University of Jerusalem, who has produced a number of publications on the urban history of Tel Aviv, including an intriguing comparative study of Jewish immigrant associations in Tel Aviv and New York.)[39] Israeli social history shifts the focus from the state and political elites to the experiences of individuals as members of groups defined by familial affiliation, community of residence, class, and gender. This approach does not deny the ongoing influences of politics and ideology on society and sensibility but presents those influences more in dialectical than unidirectional forms. The diminution of the state and of state-controlled

institutions also makes possible the development of new approaches to the history of the Israeli economy, which, as demonstrated by the veteran scholars Nachum Gross and Jacob Metzer, and more recently by Nahum Karlinsky, has from the start been heavily dependent upon private capital, in the form of both transfers from abroad and investments by local entrepreneurs.[40]

The history of gender relations and of women in Israel is still in its infancy. To be sure, there is a tradition of scholarship on the gendered inflection of Zionist ideology, which incorporated *fin-de-siècle* western notions of honor and masculinity in its idealization of what the Zionist leader Max Nordau called "muscular Judaism." It is well known that the Zionist celebration of physical fitness, productive agricultural and industrial labor, and self-defense represented an attempt by Jewish males to combat the feminization of the Jew that was essential to European antisemitic discourse. Studies of actual gender relations among Jews in the Yishuv and Israel, as opposed to ideological constructs, have been far fewer. *Pioneers and Homemakers: Jewish Women in Pre-State Israel*, an edited volume published in 1992, treated a number of important topics in the history of Ottoman and Mandatory Palestine: the role of middle-class women activists in pushing for universal suffrage in elections for the Yishuv's representative institutions under the British Mandate; the rise and fall of an independent women's voice in the umbrella trade union the Histadrut; and the exclusion of women from the ostensibly egalitarian kibbutz labor community and their relegation to child-rearing responsibilities, albeit in a collective rather than familial environment.[41]

In 2001, a volume of essays titled *Ha-'ivriyot ha-hadashot* (perhaps best translated as The New Shebrews) pushed the study of Jewish women back into the "Old," or pre-Zionist Yishuv of the nineteenth century and forward into the period of statehood. As in other works of Israeli social history, the emphasis in this volume is on immigration, although entirely new perspectives are gained through the focus on women's experience. For example, Mikhal Ben Ya'akov's essay, on North African female immigrants in the nineteenth century, demonstrates that women were often the dominant force pushing their families to emigrate to Palestine and that single women, mostly widows, comprised a surprisingly large percentage of North African immigrants during the late Ottoman period.[42] Ben Ya'akov's argument for North Africa is expanded to the Yishuv's new arrivals as a whole in Margalit Shilo's important recent monograph *Nesikhah o-shevuyah?* (Princess or prisoner?), a history of women in the Old Yishuv. Shilo notes that in the nineteenth century the immigrant pool, which was almost entirely Orthodox, consisted for the most part of families, but with a surplus of single women. (There were twice as many single female immigrants as bachelors.) The single women were of various types: widows suffused with pietist devotion, freed by the deaths of their husbands and maturation of their families to make the pilgrimage to the Holy Land; *agunot* (women whose husbands had abandoned them or gone missing, leaving their marital status in limbo and preventing them from remarrying), and impoverished women from Yemen and North Africa. Taken together, these women formed the bottom of the Old Yishuv's social ladder.[43]

In the New Yishuv, we learn from Yossi Ben-Artsi's essay in *Ha-'ivriyot ha-hadashot*, single Jewish women continued to immigrate to Palestine, although their motives were now markedly different: a desire for independence, an escape from the bourgeois social conventions that restricted them to the spheres of the family and caring professions, and a search for fulfillment. Just as women played an important but heretofore unappreciated role in the history of Jewish immigration to the Old Yishuv, either as solo actors or as the guiding forces behind their families, so too did women help mold the face of the New Yishuv's society during the Mandatory period. The historical development of the Yishuv's agricultural settlements, which often began as temporary labor brigades and land-clearing collectives but then, over time, evolved into permanent collective and co-operative arrangements, is usually attributed to the dialectic between socialist-Zionist ideology and the physical and economic conditions of life in rural Palestine. Ben-Artsi presents a third force behind the evolution of Zionist settlement: pressure from the collectives' female members. Communes devoted to labor-intensive tasks such as building roads, clearing land, and draining swamps were perceived as less likely to accord to women equal responsibilities and rights than permanent settlements based on a variety of agricultural and manufacturing activities, many of which women could easily perform.[44]

All of the literature discussed thus far tells stories about Jews, not the Arabs who comprised as much as 90 percent of Palestine's population in 1900 and two-thirds on the eve of the 1948 War. It is here, in the history of the Palestinian Arabs, that one encounters perhaps the most striking contrast between stridently Revisionist and quietly innovative historical scholarship within the field of Israeli history today. The history of modern Palestine is a vast field, studied by scholars throughout the world, but, intriguingly, few of the scholars who associate themselves with Israel's new history or critical sociology write about the Palestinians, and when they do Arabs are likely to be treated summarily and abstractly as objects or historical victims, rather than as subjects and historical agents.

The sociologist Gershon Shafir's 1989 book *Land, Labour and the Origins of the Israeli–Palestinian Conflict, 1882–1914* has attained considerable influence for its argument that, from the start, Zionist settlement patterns and policies were dictated by the need to obviate the native Arab labor market and create an artificially distinct Jewish national economy. Shafir's argument has much merit, although it is overstated, as the presence of a large indigenous labor market was but one of several factors influencing the planning of early Zionist settlement. More important, in Shafir's analytical framework "Arab labor" is no less abstract than in the world-view that Shafir attributes to the Zionists. On-the-ground interactions between Jews and Arabs, the sites of contact, contestation, and possible concord, are neglected. Zachary Lockman, a Middle East historian at New York University, made a serious effort to fill this gap in his 1996 book *Comrades and Enemies: Arab and Jewish Workers in Palestine, 1906–1948*.[45] Lockman centers the book around what he calls the "relational paradigm" of Jewish–Arab interaction in modern Palestinian history. According to this paradigm, which is laid out with great fanfare and sharp criticism for conventional approaches to Israeli history, the development of the Yishuv as a body politic and national economy cannot be separated from that of the Palestinian Arab nation in the making, as the Palestinian Zionist labor movement devoted considerable effort to countering and co-opting organizations of Palestinian laborers, and Palestinian laborers were deeply affected by their interactions with Jewish workers in those fields where they worked side by side, as in the state railways and the foreign-owned oil refining industry. Lockman's narrative of the making of a Palestinian Arab working class is fascinating yet fragmentary; the bulk of the book is about Zionist politics, particularly infighting within the Zionist Left about the Arab labor issue, and the centrality of that issue is not convincingly demonstrated. The relational paradigm, therefore, promises a bit more than it delivers.[46]

Similar problems plague Ilan Pappé's *A History of Modern Palestine* (2004).[47] The book's introduction promises a revolutionary approach to the subject, first in presenting the story of Jewish and Palestinian nationalism within a single narrative, but, more important, in refusing to reduce the history of the two peoples to that of their national movements. In the mid-twentieth century, argues Pappé, the Yishuv, and even more so Palestinian Arab society, often functioned within pre-, sub-, or extra-nationalist frameworks, some of which promised alternate paths to the course of endless conflict which, Pappé believes, was taken by the Zionists during the years leading up to and immediately following the establishment of the Israeli state. Pappé hopes to rescue from oblivion the life stories of the masses of individuals who were neither leaders nor the faithful cadres of nationalism. Pappé's critics have tended to focus on the book's overt pro-Palestinian political bias (to which the author readily admits right from the start), but a far more serious shortcoming is the book's inability to fulfill its methodological promises. For the period up to 1948, Jewish and Arab society are for the most part depicted separately. There is some important material on arenas of Jewish–Arab economic co-operation during the Mandate period, although Pappé does not attempt to assay the political or economic significance of occasional joint Jewish–Arab strikes, as opposed to their moral value as an indicator of bi-nationalist brotherhood. Pappé's depiction of the Zionist Yishuv's dependence upon the British colonizing state is entirely conventional. For the period after 1948, the book takes the form of a standard history of the Palestinian–Israeli conflict and (for the years after 1967) Palestinian society in the Occupied Territories. There is some treatment of Mizrahi ("Arab") Jews, but otherwise developments within Israel are sorely neglected. Finally, despite the Introduction's claim to deconstruct hegemonic narratives of nationalism and modernization, nowhere does the book seriously engage any alternative theoretical models, such as those generated by the Indian scholars who have pioneered the field of subaltern studies, which could do so much to account for the dynamics of Palestinian society. (For example, there is useful factual material on Palestinian women's activity during the first Intifada, but no analysis of their perceived and constructed roles in the Palestinian national liberation movement or its ideology.)

Although lacking Lockman's or Pappé's elaborate theoretical framework, a sophisticated social history of the Palestinians is now being written by scholars throughout the globe, including in Israel. Both Palestinian and Jewish Israelis have contributed to this literature. Avoiding traditional political-historical approaches to the Arab Revolt of 1936–9, Mahmoud Yazbek has analyzed how social dislocation suffered by recent migrants from the countryside to cities helped spawn violence, and Mustafa Kabha has examined the role of the media in mobilizing support for the mass strike with which the revolt began. Another recent article by Yazbek examines the complex social stratification of Haifa's Arabs during the Mandatory period; this analysis does much to promote understanding of the response of Haifa's Arabs to the crisis of 1948.[48] This literature adds depth and nuance to the important, yet introductory, general history of the Palestinians written by the Israeli sociologist Baruch Kimmerling and his American colleague Joel Migdal.[49]

Kimmerling is also the author of an important synthetic work on the development of Israeli society, *The Invention and Decline of Israeliness* (2001). This book and Gershon Shafir's and Yoav Peled's *Being Israeli: The Dynamics of Multiple Citizenship* (2002)[50] represent the state of the art of Israeli historical sociology, and their illuminating analytical perspectives provide a fitting conclusion for this section of the chapter.

Kimmerling's focus is the construction and deconstruction of a hegemonic, secular-Zionist Israeli national identity from the early years of the Zionist movement to the present. Kimmerling offers a sophisticated analysis of the historic alliance and tensions between the Israeli state and other sources of central power, such as the political and economic arms of the Israeli labor movement. He demonstrates that the decline of Israeli "stateness" – that is, self-conscious aggrandizement of the state and conflation of Israeli identity with devotion to it – has been the result not of the weakening of the Israeli state, but rather of the collapse of its historic rivals. "Stateness" has thus been replaced by silent hegemony. In turn, the failure by the Israeli state to annex the Territories captured in 1967 is an expression not of weakness but of strength, for annexation would challenge Jewish ethnic domination of the state, whereas the status quo allows for all the benefits of annexation with none of the liabilities.

Kimmerling believes that the rise in the 1980s of Mizrahi Jews via the political party Shas may be traced to power and cultural shifts within the Ashkenazic political elite since the creation of the state in 1948. The geographic displacement of post-1948 Israel from the heart of the ancient biblical homeland to the historically gentile coastal plain fostered the creation of a secular Zionist culture, which was disseminated by governmental and party apparatchiks in the camps for new immigrants from Middle Eastern lands and by the state-centered educational system, whose National Religious stream was dominated by Ashkenazim. With the conquest of the Territories in 1967, the National Religious Party rose from a junior partner to the leading sector in the Israeli polity, thus weakening Israeli statism by elevating religious and ethnocentric forms of Israeli identification. The triumph of Ashkenazic religious Zionism thus made possible the rise of Mizrahi ethnic Zionism.

Shafir and Peled, too, are concerned about the rise in Israel of an ethnonationalist identity, one which conflates membership in the Israeli polity with Jewish ethnicity. They believe that this form of political identity is now struggling for dominance with an individualist and materialist post-Zionist ethos. Both of these forms reject the old republican ethos of Labor Zionism, which sought to create a model community by fostering civil virtue. (Shafir and Peled are not at all nostalgic about the republican form of Israeli citizenship, which they present as collectivist, quasi-authoritarian, and militaristic.) The book's analysis of the development of an Israeli liberal-individualist ethos is highly illuminating. Shafir and Peled trace the transformation of the Israeli economy from the 1950s, when access to capital markets were tightly regulated and pensions funds were forcibly invested in state enterprises, to the 1980s, when Israel entered the neo-liberal world economic order by releasing foreign currency restrictions, privatizing state-owned enterprises, and fostering the growth of the Tel Aviv stock exchange.[51] Shafir and Peled note the parallels between these developments and the liberalization of Israeli political culture through the growing power of the Supreme Court, which prior to the 1980s had rarely asserted the right to review parliamentary legislation, but which in recent decades has become an advocate for individual civil freedoms and a neo-liberal economic order.[52]

The main flaw of these two books is their neglect of the religious life of Israeli Jews and the lines of continuity between post-1948 Israeli society and its diaspora Jewish predecessors and counterparts. This problem is typical in the work of secular Israeli sociologists who are removed from Jewish culture and whose historical focus does not extend beyond Palestine and the twentieth century. Nonetheless, the books' major arguments are eminently reasonable, and it is safe to say that they represent a certain consensus on the major trends in Israeli society since the creation of the state. As we shall now see, there are signs that similar lines of agreement are beginning to coalesce around a far more controversial topic, the Arab–Israeli conflict.

The Arab–Israeli conflict: the new consensus

Twnety years after the appearance of the first fruits of the new history, many of its arguments have been accepted into the Israeli historiographical mainstream. It is now conventional wisdom that, as Benny Morris argued back in 1987, substantial numbers of Palestinians were expelled from their homes in 1948, and the Arab states' military capabilities were far less, and those of the Zionists far greater, than raw numbers would suggest. Similarly, a number of Israeli scholars agree with Avi Shlaim that during the years leading up to the war there were extensive contacts between the Zionist leadership and the emir of Transjordan, King Abdullah, regarding their common interest in thwarting the establishment of a Palestinian state and having the West Bank incorporated into the Hashemite Kingdom. (There remain serious disagreements, however, whether these contacts actually led to a secret, unwritten agreement that Jordan would not attack lands designated by the United Nations for the Jewish state.) Finally, there has been no serious challenge to Ilan Pappé's arguments that in 1948 Arab leaders went to war reluctantly, pushed ahead by public opinion, and that Britain considered Israel's victory in 1948 to be inevitable and was resigned to the creation of a Jewish state.

When the new history, and the controversy surrounding it, first appeared there was an obvious link between the various parties' historical and political viewpoints. Those who offered unflattering portrayals of Israeli actions in 1948 tended to be critical of government policy at the time of the first Palestinian Intifada (1987–93). With the passage of time, however, visceral political sentiment and historical judgment have begun to separate from each other. Morris's own political views have, over the past two years, turned sharply to the Right, and in a number of public opinion pieces he has denounced the Palestinian leadership as utterly opposed to reconciliation with Israel and responsible for the failure of the Oslo peace process. Yet Morris's historical research is, if anything, more likely than before to portray Israel as the aggressor in its War of Independence.[53] In his most recent monograph *The Road to Jerusalem: Glubb Pasha, Palestine and the Jews* (2002), Morris analyzes the 1948 War from the perspective of John Glubb, the British commander of the Jordanian Arab Legion, as well as of Emir Abdullah himself. Glubb, Morris argues, favored the partition of Palestine into Jewish and Transjordanian realms, and he states that "Jordan invaded Palestine not in order to attack Israel but in order to 'save' its Arab-populated eastern parts from Jewish conquest and ultimately to annex them."[54] The Arab Legion's fierce, and successful, defense of the Latrun salient must be seen as a defensive act, for it was in an area earmarked by the Partition Resolution for the Arab state, and Latrun's strategic location made it the gateway to Jerusalem and the West Bank. Morris writes:

> At virtually no point did Jordanian forces attack and occupy the Jewish state area. . . . If Israel and Jordan entered the 1948 War with a secret, unwritten understanding of mutual non-belligerence, it was primarily Israel that violated it in May and June and then again in July and October 1948, not Jordan.[55]

Morris is particularly interested in the war's Jerusalem theater, where the bloodiest battles of the conflict were fought and which would appear to belie claims of a non-aggression pact between Israel and Transjordan. In Morris's view, Abdullah's motivations for attacking Jerusalem, all of which was to be placed under international supervision by the United Nations' Partition Resolution, were twofold: a desire to proclaim Hashemite rule over the sacred Muslim sites in the Old City and fear lest the Zionists attempt to take the city by force. These fears were intensified at the end of April by the Haganah's assault on the Arab neighborhood of Katamon in mostly Jewish West Jerusalem. After the British officially left Palestine and Israel declared statehood in mid-May, for several days Abdullah deliberately chose to keep his troops out of Jerusalem out of deference to the UN's mandate and to his British patrons. But Abdullah succumbed to fears of an Israeli conquest of the city and ordered his Arab Legion into its eastern part.

Morris's book aroused little controversy, most likely because its main arguments do not differ in the main from the general picture of Zionist–Jordanian relations painted by historians with such diverse political perspectives as Avi Shlaim on the left and Yoav Gelber on the right. Besides, with the passage of time and the opening of archives from later periods, the 1948 War has lost its centrality among Israeli political and military historians and yielded to the ongoing crises of the 1950s and 1960s. In contrast with the vociferous debate that first greeted the Revisionist historical literature on 1948, reaction to recent studies of the Suez Crisis has been markedly muted. Whereas the 1948 War constituted Israel's foundational myth, and impugning Israel's behavior during that war implicitly undermined the legitimacy of the state, the 1956 War is more easily understood within the framework of unresolved tensions between Israel and Egypt over the Palestinian refugees, misunderstandings regarding Nasser's intentions towards Israel, and the confluence of Israeli interests with those of the fading colonial powers, England and France.

A nuanced, yet critical, approach to the war has been offered by Motti Golani, a historian at the University of Haifa and an employee of the Israel Defense Force's historical branch.[56] (Golani encountered heavy-handed military censorship in the preparation of the book and his findings outraged veteran commanders of the war.) Golani's main argument is that in the spring of 1955 Chief of Staff Moshe Dayan and Prime Minister David Ben-Gurion decided that an assault against the Gaza Strip and the Sinai Peninsula was required in order to redress Israel's vulnerability to border skirmishes and an inability to defend the country from the existing armistice lines. Although Ben-Gurion himself was sometimes hesitant about launching an all-out invasion, he was pushed ahead by Dayan and the young director-general of the Defense Ministry, Shimon Peres. This view of the 1956 Sinai campaign as an "initiated war" (*milhamah yezumah*) contrasts with that of Mordechai Bar-On, author of the standard history of the Suez Crisis, who has argued for a more prolonged and later decision-making process, beginning at the end of 1955, after the signing of the Egyptian–Czech arms deal, and taking final form only with the tripartite agreement between Israel, England, and France in the wake of the nationalization of the Suez Canal in July of 1956.[57] More important, Golani, like Morris, author of an earlier work on the origins of the 1956 War, claims that Israel entered the conflict with far-reaching war aims, including the overthrow of Nasser and conquest of the West Bank (should Jordan intervene) and even of southern Lebanon. Morris and Golani have their points of difference: Morris places the origins of the war even further back, in the creation of the state, its militaristic culture, and an assumption that a "second round" with Egypt was inevitable. But the differences that divide Golani, Bar-On, and Morris are more of interpretation than of fact, scholarly rather than political, and, as demonstrated by a recent exchange between the three, amenable to civilized discussion.[58]

Given the trajectory of the new history thus far, one would expect the first major archive-based works on the 1967 war to come from scholars identified in one form or another with the Revisionist camp. Yet this is not the case. Michael Oren, author of the phenomenally successful *Six Days of War: June 1967 and the Making of the Modern Middle East*,[59] is a former Israeli military officer and Israeli government official, and is currently affiliated with the neo-conservative Shalem Institute in Jerusalem. Oren's book is notable in many ways. It makes extensive use of Arabic and Russian as well as Hebrew sources, thus providing a much deeper analysis of Arab decision-making processes than what most of the earlier Revisionist historians attempted in their studies of 1948. It presents the Egyptian move towards war as gradual and conflicted, characterized by tension between an often hesitant Nasser and his consistently aggressive minister of war, Abd al-Hakim ʻAmr. Jordan's King Hussein, who in his later years was wont to present himself as an unwilling ally of Egypt, dragged into battle against his better judgment, entered the war willingly and entertained far-reaching war aims.[60] Although sympathetic to Israel, Oren deconstructs myths about the war that have long dominated Israeli collective memory. For example, Syrian barrages from the Golan Heights against Israeli villages in the Upper Galilee are regularly invoked to justify Israel's conquest of the plateau during the last days of the war. Yet Oren argues that most Syrian attacks were limited to the demilitarized zones established by the United Nations as part of the 1949 armistice. (Such arguments have long been made by members of the Israeli extreme left but have been rejected summarily by mainstream public opinion.) Moreover, the decision to open a Syrian front in the war was made abruptly by Defense Minister Dayan, who ordered the assault without cabinet approval.[61]

It is intriguing to compare Oren's work with the treatment of the 1967 war in Avi Shlaim's highly critical account of Israeli foreign and military policy in his recent overview *The Iron Wall: Israel and the Arab World* (2000).

As one might expect, the two differ markedly on key issues; for example, Shlaim believes that the most important factor behind the 1967 war was "Israel's strategy of escalation on the Syrian front,"[62] whereas Oren looks more to Egypt's posturing *vis-à-vis* the Arab world. Yet even Shlaim argues, like Oren, that Israel's attack on the West Bank was piecemeal and unplanned – "the one thing it [the Eshkol government] did not have was a master plan for territorial aggrandizement"[63] – and that King Hussein would not have lost the West Bank or eastern Jerusalem had he not attacked. Moreover, the two agree that there was more to the Khartoum Arab Summit of August/September 1967 than just the infamous "three nos" to negotiations, reconciliation, and peace with Israel. Shlaim contends that underneath the hostile rhetoric lay subtle clues indicating an openness to indirect negotiations leading to a de facto peace. Oren acknowledges the presence of that way of thinking at the time but is rather less sanguine, noting that Nasser clearly called for a military solution to the conflict.[64] Clearly, Shlaim and Oren approach the history of the conflict from radically differing perspectives, the former from the Olympian heights of St. Antony's College, Oxford, and the latter from the heart of Fortress Israel. Yet the scholarly integrity of Oren's book rises above political differences and accounts for the highly respectful reception that Shlaim has accorded to it.[65]

In his splenetic attack against Revisionist Israeli historiography, Efraim Karsh argues that many of the new historians' contentions regarding Israeli–Jordanian collusion during the 1948 War were adumbrated by earlier scholars with impeccable Zionist credentials, and that in general the new history was not at all new – at least on those points where it had any measure of credibility.[66] There is a critical difference, however, between what is merely on the record and acknowledged on the periphery of consciousness, on the one hand, and what is central to collective memory, on the other. Admissions in passing or elliptical statements in memoir literature and obscure scholarship reveal embarrassing historical truths only to conceal them through strategies of marginalization and deflection. In this sense the new history performed an essential service to Israeli political culture in that it brought to center stage painful questions regarding the circumstances of Israel's birth and its behavior throughout its struggle with the Arabs. Something similar, one could argue, applies to critical sociological studies of the ethnic inequities in Israeli society and the complex simultaneous processes of the invention and suppression of Mizrahi Israeli Jewish identities.

The new history and critical sociology adumbrated Israel's transition to a post-Zionist epoch, and the fading of the academic controversies accord with the general disengagement from history that characterizes a post-nationalist *Zeitgeist*. Twenty years ago, Anita Shapira's biography of the Labor Zionist leader Berl Katznelson was a national bestseller, but it is doubtful if any work of biography or history would have this kind of impact today.[67] At that time, the Israeli labor movement was in decline, but its sensibilities, including the typical nationalist yearnings for justification through history and self-commemoration, were still widespread among the Israeli populace. In Hegel's famous saying, the owl of Minerva, the goddess of wisdom, flies at dusk; the same may be said of Mnemosyne, the goddess of memory.

Whereas Labor Zionism was nourished by mythologized history, its successor, the militantly populist Likud, preferred historicized myth. The Likud did not cultivate research institutions devoted to its Revisionist roots; even today, the archives and libraries dedicated to the labor movement are far superior to its rightist counterparts. The Likud's fervent attachment to the borders of the ancient Israelite kingdoms fostered glorification of biblical heroes and the ancient warrior-cum-messiah Shimon Bar-Kokhba. The alliance between the Likud and the post-1967 religious settlement movement was made possible not only by common interests but also by a common aversion to historicism and an embrace of myth. Labor Zionism, too, cultivated myths about Jewish antiquity, but this manipulation of the distant past was secondary to a detailed, positivist scrutiny of the Jews' situation in modernity, which, although refracted through thick ideological lenses, encouraged constant re-view and re-vision. In this sense, the new history represented a natural outgrowth of as well as reaction against Labor Zionist-dominated historiography. Along the same lines, there are significant areas of continuity as well as rupture between the rightist neo-Zionism of the 1970s through 1990s and politically leftist or quiescent post-Zionism, which suspects coherent historical narrative of masking discourses of oppression, hierarchy, and exclusion. Tellingly, the most influential sources of historical information in contemporary Israeli culture are novels, which filter and manipulate historical situations in an overt, self-conscious manner.[68]

The decline of the Israeli historiographical controversies of the 1980s and 1990s reflects Israel's place in the post-modern western world, where the constant flow of information and rapid technological change have flooded the human mind and occluded historical consciousness, leaving in its place an uneasy sense of eternal present. Within Israeli universities, however, the historiographical enterprise continues, seeking not so much to legitimize or exculpate the state of Israel as to account for it. Writing in an entirely different context, that of ancient Jewish civilization, the historian Amos Funkenstein once noted that the Hebrews were imbued by a sense of their own novelty and frailty, of wonder at their very existence.[69] The Israeli historian, in turn, is bemused not only by the specific research question (s)he poses but also by the presence of the object being studied. Israel is an improbable country, whose founders faced the daunting task of creating the preconditions for its own existence: a population *in situ*, a national economy, a civil society, and autonomous political and military institutions. The state's existence has simultaneously fulfilled, stoked, and thwarted traditional Jewish yearnings for a return to the Land of Israel in messianic time.

Engaged in constant conflict against Palestinians and other Arabs, Israel is, simultaneously and paradoxically, among the world's frailest and most powerful nations. It is thus the historian's challenging, yet deeply rewarding, task to map the vectors of possibility that account for the state of Israel's creation and subsequent development. The ongoing Arab–Israeli conflict, which, as I write, is sinking to ever-greater levels of brutality, extremism, and despair, will surely influence a scholar's framing of her subject but must not predetermine the inquiry's outcome. History, including that of Israel, has many futures.

3 Historians, Herzl, and the Palestinian Arabs

Myth and counter-myth

However bitterly historians of the Arab–Israeli conflict may dispute among themselves, there is a tacit agreement among them about the centrality of certain matters behind the creation of the Jewish state and of Palestinian statelessness. In a historiography that mirrors the Arab–Israeli conflict, there have developed rules of scholarly engagement dictating where, and upon what points, battle shall be joined. Pro-Zionist and pro-Palestinian scholars offer radically different interpretations of issues such as the Balfour Declaration or the Peel Commission's partition proposal or Zionist military strategy in the spring of 1948, but all agree to their importance. Regarding Theodor Herzl, however, there is a fascinating and unusual disjuncture between the pro- and anti-Zionist historiographical camps.

To be sure, all historians of Zionism, regardless of perspective, agree to Herzl's significance as a political leader within the Jewish world and as a representative of Zionist interests to the European colonial Great Powers. Yet Herzl's musings on the Palestinian Arabs – their current situation and future position in a Jewish state – are the subject not merely of different interpretations by pro- and anti-Zionist scholars but also of a totally dissimilar form of evaluation. Herzl's views on the Arabs are a peripheral topic in Zionist historiography yet central in its anti-Zionist counterpart.

According to conventional Zionist historiography, Herzl thought little about Arabs, but what he did have to say about them reflected benign and progressive, albeit paternalistic, liberal sentiment. Herzl, like most Zionists before World War I, believed that Ottoman imperial assent was the key to the success of the Zionist enterprise. The local Arabs constituted little more than an extension of the Palestinian landscape, and their hostility to the Zionists, like malaria, swampy soil, and stony fields, would all be cleared away in due course through the appropriate combination of technology and humanitarian zeal. On the other hand, Palestinian scholars, and those who sympathize with the Arab cause, take umbrage at Herzl's obliviousness to Palestine's Arabs and are offended by the disparaging tone of the few comments he did make upon them. More important, for critics of Zionism, underlying the paucity of Herzl's comments on Arabs was a conspiracy of silence, for already in 1895, at the time when Herzl was just sketching out his vision of the future Jewish state, he was allegedly planning the expulsion of the Palestinians, although he only confided this dark scheme to his diary, which was not published until after Herzl's death.

This chapter intends to throw new light upon Herzl's attitudes towards Arabs, and Palestinians in particular. I also wish to explore a variety of historiographical questions raised by the gulf that separates the camps of scholars who have written on this subject. I would like to trace the origins of politicized historical arguments to their source – not the historical subject itself, but rather scholars whose writings assume a canonical status among like-minded readers. Moreover, as this chapter will focus on Herzl's diary, I will critique the historian's tendency to privilege early sources over later ones (origins of ideas over their development or extension) and the unmediated over the mediated source, the diary over the novel, the archival document over the published report. Specifically, I will ask, were Herzl's diary entries, particularly those written during his celebrated manic fit of June 1895, truly more reflective of Herzl's Zionist sensibilities and program than his later public statements and published writings?

I begin with an overview of what the standard Zionist historiography has to say on our subject. The overwhelming consensus is that during the "Herzl era" (1897–1904) and its immediate aftermath discussions within the international Zionist movement about Palestine's Arabs were few and far between and were usually considered of little relevance. This is not to say that the Zionists were ignorant of the native population. Eliezer Be'eri, among other scholars, has refuted the myth that Herzl saw Palestine as a "land without a nation for a nation without a land" (Be'eri attributes that notorious phrase to Israel Zangwill).[1] Moreover, there were a few cases of Zionist leaders directly addressing the Arab question, such as Leo Motzkin's address at the Second Zionist Congress of 1898, at which he spoke of a Palestinian population of some 650,000 occupying Palestine's most fertile lands, or Max Nordau's speech at the 1905 Congress, when he proposed a Zionist alliance with the Ottoman Empire against what he saw as a destabilizing Arab nationalism. By and large, however, most Zionists denied the Arab presence or refused to consider it seriously, while a small minority nervously kept track of Jewish–Arab clashes and predicted future, and more serious, confrontations.[2]

Herzl himself paid but little heed to Arabs during his 1898 visit to Palestine, but he was made aware of the spectre of Arab as well as Ottoman opposition to Zionism from a brief exchange of letters in 1899 with Youssuf Zia al-Khalidi, a former mayor of Jerusalem and veteran senior Ottoman bureaucrat. Al-Khalidi believed the Zionist cause to be just but warned that the mass settlement of Jews in Palestine would provoke violent and unceasing resistance by the native population. In his reply Herzl assured al-Khalidi that the Zionists would bring only benefit to the native population and that opposition would melt away once the Zionists' benevolent intentions were fully perceived. A similarly irenic perspective suffuses Herzl's utopian novel *Altneuland*, in which a sole Arab character, the German-educated Reschid Bey, speaks glowingly of the vast material and technological progress that the Jews have brought to the land. The consensus among pro-Zionist historians is that Herzl, speaking through Bey, intended there to be a substantial Arab presence in the future Jewish state, which would both include Arabs as equals in civil society and respect their religious culture.[3]

Intriguingly, very few scholars writing from a Zionist perspective have engaged the controversial text in Herzl's diary entry of June 12, 1895, in which he writes:

> We must expropriate gently the private property on the estates assigned to us. We shall try to spirit the penniless population across the border by procuring employment for it in the transit countries, while denying it employment in our own country. The property owners will come over to our side. Both the process of expropriation and the removal of the poor must be carried out discreetly and circumspectly. The property owners may believe that they are cheating us, selling to us at more than [the land is] worth. But nothing will be sold back to them.[4]

This text, we shall see, is central to anti-Zionist propaganda and even to respectable recent scholarship that examines Zionism from a critical perspective. But it is not addressed in any of the standard biographies of Herzl[5] and in most literature by Israeli scholars on early Zionism's approach to the Arabs. Shabtai Teveth does not mention it in his 1989 pamphlet on the idea of transfer of Palestinians outside of a Jewish state. (He does, however, pay attention to other pre-1914 figures, including Israel Zangwill, Nachman Syrkin, Leo Motzkin, and Aaron Aaronsohn.)[6] Among reputable Zionist historians, Anita Shapira stands out for engaging Herzl's diary entry in her book *Land and Power*, although she is perhaps too lenient in interpreting the passage as meaning that "needy segments of the native population would be persuaded to leave" by finding them work elsewhere.[7]

The only works of Zionist historiography that take Herzl's diary entry seriously are those written from a pro-transfer or Revisionist viewpoint. Such works wish to derive legitimacy for their own maximalist programs from Herzl, the father of political Zionism. Most of this literature is eccentric and propagandistic, as, for example, the monograph of Chaim Simons, a resident of Kiryat Arba, which suggests that from Herzl's time through the 1940s support for transfer within the Zionist movement was widespread yet the subject was deliberately kept away from public forums.[8] A more reputable study came from the pen of the Revisionist activist Joseph Nedava, who in 1972 published a brief article on "Herzl and the Arab Problem." Departing from mainstream Zionist historiography, Nedava claimed that Herzl was well aware of Palestine's native population and its resistance to a substantial Jewish presence. Thus Nedava accounts for Herzl's opposition to piecemeal infiltration of settlers, which only stimulates native anger, and his insistence upon a charter, issued by the Ottoman sultan or one of the European Great Powers, that will usher in unstoppable mass immigration.

One intriguing source for Nedava's argument is Abraham Shalom Ezekiel Yahuda (1877–1951), an Egyptologist who, as a youth, met Herzl in London in 1896 and warned him that the consent of the native population would be necessary for the success of the Zionist venture. Yahuda claims to have met Herzl again on the eve of the first Zionist Congress, at which time he informed the Zionist leader that the Muslim Arab majority in Palestine could be won over to Zionism but that Christian Arabs presented a formidable threat as they were influenced by the antisemitic Church. (This was a common Zionist fear at the time: Christian Arabs were seen as carriers of European antisemitism and as forming a commercial bourgeoisie that feared Jewish competition.) Herzl allegedly replied to Yahuda that the Arabs in Palestine were of no import, and that the fate of Palestine was entirely in the hands of the sultan.[9]

Nedava deals squarely with Herzl's diary entry, claiming that the evacuation of the landless Palestinian population would be a necessary tactic to avoid economic catastrophe in the Jewish state aborning. Nedava lauds Herzl's "compassionate" approach, which, as Herzl lays out in his diary, would prohibit forced expropriation of landholders who, whether through old age, infirmity, or tenacious disposition, refused to part with their property. The apologetic and tendentious nature of Nedava's treatment of this issue is obvious, yet one wonders why serious questions on Herzl's views and policies regarding Arabs have been so marginalized in the mainstream literature and left for admitted dilettantes and activists like Nedava to explore.

Perhaps a sign of change in this regard is Benny Morris's addition of a chapter on "The Idea of 'Transfer' in Zionist Thinking" in the recently published revised edition of his classic monograph on the origins of the Palestinian refugee problem. In that chapter, Morris refers to Herzl's diary entry and to the published musings on the desirability of transfer by the likes of Motzkin and Zangwill. Unlike Teveth, who presents these expressions as idiosyncratic and without long-lasting importance, Morris claims that a subtle and subterranean discourse of transfer was already forming within the Zionist movement before World War I but that it was kept under wraps lest it poison relations between the fragile Yishuv, on the one hand, and Palestine's native population and Ottoman suzerain, on the other.[10] Morris's inclusion of this material represents a response to the work of Nur Masalha and other writers who claim that plans to expel Palestinian Arabs were central to Zionist thinking from the movement's inception. He deals with Herzl briefly and superficially, however, unlike the anti-Zionist authors to whom we shall now turn.

Zionism's sympathizers and critics agree that Herzl wrote little about Arabs and barely noticed them when he traveled, but the latter interpret this neglect in a far more ominous light than the former. For example, in an article on Herzl's colonialist programs, Walid Khalidi, the doyen of Palestinian historians, takes offense at Herzl's stray references to Palestine's Arabs as a mixed multitude of beggars or as potential drainers of swamps for Jewish settlers. Moreover, the contrast between Herzl's public flattery of the Ottoman sultan Abdul Hamid and the vicious caricature of the sultan in Herzl's private diary furnishes Khalidi with proof of Herzl's duplicitous nature, for, Khalidi maintains, the sultan had treated Herzl with the utmost courtesy and graciousness.[11] Zachary Lockman, author of a major study of Jewish–Arab labor relations in late Ottoman and Mandate Palestine, begins his book with the accusation that Herzl willfully shut Palestine's Arabs out of his consciousness. Lockman brings as proof the fact that when Herzl visited Egypt in 1902 he wrote in his diary about meeting educated young Egyptians and reflected upon their eventual resistance to British rule. Lockman faults Herzl for not making the same observation about Palestinians, although he does not discuss whether there was an equivalent Palestinian intelligentsia at the time.[12]

Unlike pro-Zionist readings of *Altneuland*, a recent article by Muhammad Ali Khalidi dwells on Herzl's contempt for Palestine's population in 1901, when the novel begins, and his vision, also mentioned in his diary, of expelling the population of the Old City of Jerusalem. (Khalidi does not acknowledge that the majority of the Old City's population at the time was Jewish, and that Herzl's schemes for social engineering demanded the radical reconfiguration of Jewish no less than Arab society.) Turning to the futuristic vision of the Jewish homeland, *Altneuland*, in 1923, Khalidi infers from the description of *Altneuland*'s pristine landscape that "the Arab villages have been removed from the landscape" and that "the indigenous inhabitants have been largely expelled."[13] Pro-Zionist scholars emphasize Reschid Bey's prominence in the novel, his references to Arab gratitude for the Zionists' technological bounty, and his allusions to the maintenance of traditional Arab family life and gender roles within *Altneuland*'s progressive society. Khalidi, on the other hand, notes that Bey is the only Arab character in a novel peopled virtually entirely by Jews, that the novel's descriptions of Arab villages are altogether indirect, limited to Bey's own testimony, and that at an interfaith Passover seder bringing together Jews and Christians of various denominations no Arab cleric, Muslim or Christian, is present. Khalidi agrees with pro-Zionist authors that Herzl's novel envisioned an ethnically diverse society which would embody the best of the multinational heritage of Herzl's native Hapsburg Empire while overcoming the ethnic hatreds that were tearing at its seams and making life particularly perilous for its Jews. Thus the highly negative portrayal of the character Geyer, a demagogic politician who aspires to deny voting rights to *Altneuland*'s non-Jews. Khalidi astutely observes, however, that a multicultural society is an entirely different thing from a bi-national one; Herzl depicts Arabs as one of many tolerated minorities in a Jewish commonwealth as opposed to an indigenous people with national rights of its own.

For critics of Zionism, Herzl's disregard or scorn for the inhabitants of the Middle East pales in comparison with Herzl's alleged paternity for the concept of expelling the Palestinians from their native land. The Internet lists hundreds of sites with references to the June 12, 1895, diary entry, identifying the citation as marking the beginning of an organized plot to expropriate the Palestinians. These sites are, for the most part, fonts of antisemitic and pro-Arab propaganda, but the diary entry is also central to the somewhat more learned polemics of the Israeli anti-Zionist writer Uri Davis and, more important, the late Edward Said, for whom Herzl's vision of an *araberrein* Palestine figures prominently in his seminal 1979 essay "Zionism From the Standpoint of Its Victims."[14] The association between Herzl and transfer is not limited to polemics but has recently crept into the work of serious historians such as Lockman, who claims that Herzl's diary entry specifically envisioned "dispossessing and displacing Palestine's Arab peasantry," although in fact at that time Herzl had not determined the location of the Jewish state.[15]

Said's reference is not Herzl's diary but rather Desmond Stewart's highly critical 1974 biography of Herzl. It makes sense that Stewart's book would have held much meaning for Said, for, whereas conventional biographies of Herzl, whether hagiographic like Bein's or ironic like Elon's, treated the Arab issue as a peripheral matter, Stewart makes it central to his caustic and hostile deconstruction of the Zionist leader. (Stewart claims that twenty pages of the June 12 diary entry dealt with the expropriation of the native population, although in fact the entire entry takes up about twenty printed pages, of which only three are devoted to the land issue.) Stewart admits that at the time of the writing of these passages Herzl was unsure where the Jewish state would be established and believes Herzl was leaning towards Latin America, far away from what Herzl called "militarized and seedy Europe." Rather than emphasize the utopian aspect of this scenario, in which a Jewish state would develop without European interference and corrupting influences, Stewart focuses on Herzl's diary entries that call for the establishment of a vast Jewish army, which must grow in strength until it is more than a match for all the other Latin American republics put together. Only then would its security be assured. In the meantime, those natives who had not yet been expelled would be put to work exterminating wild animals, such as big snakes, and would be well paid for their skins. Even if Herzl's eyes were gazing across the Atlantic, writes Stewart, Herzl's heart was in South Africa. Stewart attaches the utmost importance to Herzl's letter to the German emperor explaining that his idea for a Jewish Chartered Company was patterned after the British Chartered Company for South Africa. Confusing form with substance, Stewart assumes that all the brutal empire-building tactics employed by Cecil Rhodes were emulated by Herzl and that "Herzl's stencil for obtaining a territory and then clearing it for settlement was cut after the Rhodesian model."[16] Unlike Rhodes, Herzl did not have diamonds to fuel the Zionist colonial project, but he believed that the Rothschilds' and Hirsch's fortunes would serve the same purpose.

Stewart sets Herzl's alleged colonialist fantasies into a framework of a dictatorial and opaque political regime. The Jewish state as imagined in Herzl's diary entries will feature secret administrative police, and political agitation against the state will be punished by banishment or even death. The state will be an aristocratic republic, led by a Doge, who will employ the guidelines bequeathed to him by Herzl yet keep them shrouded in secrecy: "When this book is published, the prescriptions for the organization of the government will be omitted. The people must be guided to the good according to principles unknown to them."[17] Similarly, according to Stewart, Herzl's musings on the expropriation and transfer of the natives were never intended for publication. Thus the secretive practices of the Jewish state will replicate the private, hidden reflections in Herzl's diary, where one can locate the essence of Herzl's psyche and program.

Stewart's crudely Straussian approach to Herzl's thought cries out for a more nuanced reading of Herzl's writings, both private and public. The underlying operating assumption by Herzl's critics is that the diary entries were coherent, lucid, programmatic, and far more significant than Herzl's later conciliatory statements about Arabs in public speeches or his rosy vision of Jewish–Arab relations in *Altneuland*. But is an unpublished source always to be accorded primacy in indicating an author's state of mind or intent over a published one? Does mediation always imply adulteration or concealment?

Let us consider the *mise en scène* for the infamous June 12, 1895, diary entry. Between June 5 and 15, Herzl experienced a manic fit, during which time he wrote constantly, producing eighty-three pages of printed text as per the 1922 German edition of the diaries. A portion of this text comprised the "Address to the Rothschilds," the seedbed of the pamphlet *The Jewish State*. The rest contained random jottings, scribbled on individual sheets of paper, about a welter of topics, most but not all connected with Herzl's inchoate Zionist vision. During this storm of inspiration Herzl feared that he was losing his mind; and, indeed, the entries feature the proverbial lucidity of the mad. He produced detailed prescriptions for every aspect of the Jewish state: the accoutrements of the Jewish high priests and military officers; state monopolies on liquor and tobacco; regulation of the insurance business and stock exchange; the public shaming of suicides; the necessity for dueling to maintain honor and refinement. In this great outburst of logorrhea, Herzl indulged in an orgy of narcissistic fantasies about power, control, and domination. Early on in the June 12 entries Herzl expresses a yearning to fight a duel with the antisemitic agitators Georg von Schoenerer or Karl Lueger. If he was shot he would die a martyr to the cause of fighting antisemitism; but if he killed his opponent he would captivate the court with so thrilling a speech on the Jewish Question that he would be released. In his musings on the Jewish state, Herzl saw himself personally leading spot inspections of businesses to ferret out corruption, determining when workers shall labor and rest, and intervening in their disputes.

In the midst of scores of pages of wish-fulfillment fantasy and unleashed anger from the bowels of his psyche, Herzl scribbled the notorious paragraph about the expropriation of the natives. The paragraph is immediately followed by one guaranteeing the freedom and property rights of people of other faiths. This apparent contradiction is resolved in the next paragraph, however, where it becomes clear that the freedoms Herzl has in mind are to be guaranteed to visitors to, not natives of, the Jewish state:

> At first people will avoid us. We are in bad odor. By the time the reshaping of world opinion in our favor has been completed, we shall be firmly established in our country, no longer fearing the influx of foreigners, and receiving our visitors with aristocratic benevolence and proud amiability.[18]

Herzl goes on to outline how land purchase must take place – quickly and uniformly lest land prices climb sky-high. After finishing his musings on these topics – which take up, all told, less than three pages in print – Herzl moves on restlessly to other unrelated matters, such as details about the Jewish state's flag and ideas for a new novel about Jewish honor.

Herzl's diaries are certainly revealing, and they provide grist for the mill of Herzl's critics, most recently Daniel Boyarin, who finds in Herzl's pathetic fantasies about male honor the source of his colonial ambitions (what Boyarin portrays as prancing in "colonial drag"), favoring a Jewish state in South America or Africa because these were "the privileged sites for colonialist performance of male gendering."[19] But such *ad hominem* comments do little to assist us in reconciling Herzl's diary entries with the humanitarian (albeit Eurocentric, condescending, and paternalistic) references to Arabs in the future Jewish state that dot his Zionist speeches and essays, the letter to al-Khalidi, and *Altneuland*.

One could argue that feverish thoughts confided to a private diary express innermost yearnings and augur future actions; yet, more likely, the encounter with realistic power politics would force any would-be political leader to modify all sorts of views, especially ones that were marginal to begin with. This was certainly the case for Herzl, who, after 1896, entered Zionist politics, founded the World Zionist Organization (WZO), committed himself to Palestine as the site of the Jewish homeland, initiated negotiations with the Ottoman government and European Great Powers, and was compelled to formulate a pragmatic and long-range strategy for the Jewish presence in Palestine. Consider Herzl's rationale for opposing in May 1903 the proposal, made by the Zionist opposition, which favored immediate settlement activity, to purchase lands in the Jezreel Valley made available for sale by the Sursuk family. Herzl displayed not only principled opposition to "infiltration" but also the conviction that, according to his first biographer, Adolf Friedmann, "Poor Arab farmers must not be driven off their land."[20] Two months previously, after visiting the pyramids near Cairo, Herzl had jotted in his diary that "the misery of the *fellahin* by the road is indescribable. I resolve to think of the *fellahin* too, once I have the power."[21] This statement could be easily dismissed as yet another puerile fantasy of power and control, but if one is going to approach the diaries in a fundamentally skeptical fashion, consistency should be maintained regardless of the orientation of the entry in question.

How much of what was scribbled in the diary was an outpouring of the id or the libido, released verbally only to be sublimated into constructive political action? Herzl did not, after all, run the WZO in the dictatorial and secretive fashion envisioned in his diary. (Herzl's critics within the WZO often made such accusations, but the fact that they came from within the WZO's own democratically elected bodies, and that Herzl had no choice but to acknowledge alternate and competing approaches to his own, demonstrated the inaccuracy of the accusations.) Although Herzl choreographed the Zionist Congresses with great care, the delegates wore evening dress, not operatic costumes, and although there was a WZO Court of Honor, saber duels were not fought in the corridors of the Basel Casino. Psychobiographical observations, even if based in fact, do not elucidate questions about the formation and implementation of policy. And, of course, the vast majority of the items in Herzl's June 1895 diary entries were never acted upon.

Was the plan to expropriate the natives of the future Jewish state nothing more than a flicker in Herzl's feverish vision of 1895? Before answering this question definitively we must take into account a final piece of evidence: a draft charter, drawn up in 1901 by Herzl and the Hungarian-Jewish Orientalist Arminius Vámbéry. The charter calls for the formation of a Jewish–Ottoman Land Company, empowered by the Ottoman sultan to purchase and develop lands in Palestine and Syria. Unlike Herzl's call in the 1895 diary entries for total separation between the Jewish polity and neighboring states, in this document the Jews are required to become Ottoman subjects and provide military service to the Empire in a Syrian-Palestinian army division. Yet in language echoing the June 12, 1895, diary entry, albeit in far more measured tones, Article III confers the following right upon the JOLC:

> the right to exchange economic enclaves of its territory, with the exception of the holy places or places already designated for worship. The owners shall receive plots of equal size and quality procured by it [the JOLC] in other provinces and territories of the Ottoman Empire. It will not only compensate those owners for the costs of resettlement from its own funds, but it will also grant modest loans for the building of necessary housing and the acquisition of the necessary equipment. These loans are to be repaid in equal installments over several years, and the new plots can be used as collateral [for the loan].[22]

In a draft charter drawn up six years later by Herzl's ally and successor David Wolffsohn, although much of Herzl's original wording remains intact this paragraph does not appear, thus suggesting that Herzl displayed a particular receptivity to the idea of transfer, albeit on a highly limited scale and under the most humane of conditions.[23]

Herzl's hopes to establish an Ottoman–Jewish colonization company are laid out in diary entries for June 1901 and February 1902, and his negotiations to obtain this concession have been well chronicled. Yet the draft charter itself has been neglected in Zionist historiography. It has long been accessible in the form of an appendix to the first volume of Adolf Boehm's massive history of Zionism, *Die zionistische Bewegung*. It is mentioned in a handful of other works, including Ben Halpern's classic *The Idea of the Jewish State*.[24] Halpern summarizes the main points of the draft charter, lumping together the contents of several of its articles, including the one on expropriation. Otherwise it is ignored. Nor did the charter receive much attention in pro-Palestinian literature until it was published in English translation by Walid Khalidi in 1993.[25] Not only has the document been far less visible than Herzl's diaries; it also lacks their dramatic flair and sweep. One may also question the document's historical significance, as it was never acted upon or even debated in any public Zionist forum, but, then again, neither were most of Herzl's diary entries, which are perused with voyeuristic zeal.

I would compare the relationship between the draft charter and Herzl's June 12, 1895, diary entry with that between the evening dress required of delegates at the first Zionist Congress's inaugural session and the silver breastplates that Herzl dreamed in his diary of girding on to the officers of the Jewish state. The former was the product of political calculation and a realistic frame of mind; the latter was pure fantasy. By 1901 Herzl had come to believe that in the interests of state-building some native landowners might need to be coaxed to cede their property and move elsewhere. But this charter, drawn up after years of negotiation and politicking both within the Zionist movement and among the crowned heads of Europe, is a far cry from the program for total expropriation jotted down in the late spring of 1895, before Herzl had even effectively formulated a Zionist program. The draft charter reflected Herzl's characteristic audacity, yet it was also the product of political maturity.

Muhammad Ali Khalidi sees in the 1901 charter's colonial-capitalist framework proof that Herzl had no serious intentions of erecting the social utopia envisioned in *Altneuland*, published a year later.[26] Herzl was indeed more solidly wedded to a colonialist economic scheme than some of his apologists would like to believe, but there is no necessary contradiction between the perception that the Zionist project must begin as a colonialist venture and the aspiration that it mature into a model of European social progressivism. The blueprint for a social utopia laid out in *Altneuland* may be dismissed as yet another hare-brained scheme like those that dot the diaries, a further embarrassing example of Herzlian self-aggrandizement. But this one was public, not secret; it was carefully, soberly, and painstakingly crafted for public appeal, and thus of far greater importance for our understanding of what Herzl thought would resonate with the Jewish public and international community than murky fantasies confided to and confined within a private diary. Thus the ongoing need for a serious confrontation with the image of Arabs in *Altneuland*, an image riddled with ambiguities and absences, depicted with benevolence yet condescension, Eurocentric to the core yet scathingly critical of Old World corruption and decadence.

The case of Herzl's views on the Arabs reminds us of the responsibility of all responsible historians of Zionism and Israel to unhesitatingly confront highly sensitive issues lest the field be abandoned to propagandists on either side of the conflict. Moreover, historians favorably disposed to Zionism have allowed their sympathies to distort their moral judgment by presenting Herzl's dismissive attitude towards Arabs or his other prejudices as merely products of his age, the sort of sentiment one would inevitably expect from a bourgeois European gazing from what he believed was the pinnacle of civilization upon the benighted Orient. *Fin-de-siècle* Europe featured many activists and intellectuals who were not merely products of their era but who sought to transcend the constraints of time and cultural convention. Imperialism had its many champions in Europe but also its opponents. Antisemitism at the *fin de siècle* was not justified simply because it was pervasive; the same is true for racial or ethnic prejudices of the era. To that end, Herzl's views on the Arabs deserve serious attention, even if they did not have the prognosticative powers accorded to them by Zionism's zealous opponents.

Part II

Continuity and rupture

4 Is Israel a Jewish state?

The subject of this chapter is Israel, but its predicate is the Jewish diaspora. The Zionist project was, on its surface, revolutionary, as it vowed to overthrow the *ancien régime* of diaspora Jewish political and religious culture. Yet many of the Zionist movement's goals, and the ways in which they have been achieved, reflect deeply preservationist impulses. Much of contemporary Israel's political, economic, and social structure, as well as many of its cultural norms, is largely consonant with those of diaspora Jewish communities at various points in time from the nineteenth century to our own day. Looking back from the perspective of the early twenty-first century, one can argue that the Zionist project was in many ways counter-revolutionary, a defensive measure against assimilatory forces that threatened to transform Jewish society beyond recognition. Zionism, like all modern nationalist movements, was, like the Roman god Janus, a two-faced creature, with one side pointed towards the unknown future and the other gazing into the immemorial past.

Many of the persistent continuities linking Israel and the diaspora have been neither consciously willed nor ideologically justified. They are the products of social forces over which Jews in the past century have had little awareness or control and that have been obscured from view by a Zionist ideological filter. Zionism, like any nationalist movement, rarely presented itself as a vehicle of gradual historical development, one in an ongoing series of manifestations of collective life, which is periodically directed along a different path. Instead, Zionism proclaimed its mission to be one of restoring long lost glory (for example the Hebrew language, a flourishing Jewish life in the Land of Israel) and abandoning shameful behaviors, such as political and physical passivity, that were associated with the diaspora experience. Revival and rupture are, therefore, two sides of the same discursive coin, as opposed to relatively smooth continuities, which, I claim, lie at the heart of the historical and contemporary relationship between Israel and the Jewish diaspora.

This chapter represents a plea for a greater integration of the study of the Zionist project and its realization, on the one hand, with the study of the history and culture of world Jewry in modern times. In both Israel and the diaspora, the academic study of Zionism and Israel has been deeply affected by notions of Israeli exceptionality. The idea that Zionism was qualitatively distinct from other Jewish political movements in modern times and that Israel wrought a sea-change upon its immigrants has promoted an unfortunate separation between the fields of Israel and Jewish studies. Israel studies is far more often seen as a province of social scientists, with a highly presentist orientation, than as overlapping with the history of the people who, after all, settled in, founded, and developed the world's only Jewish state. To be sure, social-scientific work on Israel has often made use of historical argumentation. Pioneers of Israeli social science employed a schematic historical narrative, incorporating the entire Jewish experience from Genesis to the kibbutz into overarching theories of Jewish social or political behavior, and reading sources, including sacred texts, uncritically.[1] A more theoretically sophisticated historical approach informs the work of some members of Israeli sociology's second generation, which came of age in the 1970s, and of the following generation, practitioners of what has become known as "critical sociology." The primary sources employed by such scholars, however, are limited to the Yishuv and state of Israel. Although Israeli critical sociology sets great store by comparative analysis, the reference group is either Palestinian Arab society or European colonial regimes, not Jews outside of Palestine.[2] The most important recent sociological studies of Israel, *Being Israeli: The Dynamics of Multiple Citizenship*, by Gershon Shafir and Yoav Peled, and Baruch Kimmerling's *The Invention and Decline of Israeliness*,[3] are decidedly ahistoric and "ajudaic"; the latter summarizes the entirety of Jewish history up to Herzl in six pages before jumping to twentieth-century Palestine, and it treats Israel without any reference to diaspora Jewry save as a source of immigration. Thus the most innovative sociological work on Israel emphasizes a selective synchronic comparison: between the "Jewish state" and other states, Jews and Arabs, but not between Jews "here" and "there," or past and present.[4]

Many historians of modern Jewry write about Zionism, but they do so within the framework of the states or geographic regions that are the objects of attention. Scholars of European, Middle Eastern, and North American Jewry incorporate material on the Zionist movement in these lands into their writings, but few historians of world Jewry engage in comparative studies including the Yishuv or Israel. One exception to this rule is a group of historians of nineteenth-century Eastern European Jewry who have studied the religious currents that bore thousands of Orthodox Jewish immigrants to Palestine, where they lived lives of, to employ the title of one book on the subject, "exile within the Holy Land."[5] There is also a small body of work, written by specialists in European Jewish history, which analyzes Zionism within the comparative framework of modern Jewish politics.[6] Israeli history is written, for the most part, by specialists who, to their credit, are masters of the archival sources and possess an intimate knowledge of the Israeli landscape, and who have some familiarity with the European intellectual traditions imbibed by the state's founding fathers, but, with the passage of time and the passing of the older immigrant generations, increasingly lack foreign languages other than English and are disconnected from the European or Middle Eastern terrain, including its Jewish communities.

My remarks in this chapter are both historical and historiographic. In pointing out areas of continuity, or at least contact and correspondence, between the Zionist project and the modern diaspora, I will note the work that has already been done along these lines and suggest what more could be accomplished by mapping the Zionist project on to the modern Jewish experience as a whole. I am aware of the dangers of essentializing the "diaspora," of assembling Jews who have lived in diverse environments into a coherent whole and asserting the existence of common characteristics that span time and space. After all, the uprooting of Jews from their particular historical and cultural contexts lies at the heart of Zionist ideology, wherein Jews, regardless of specific circumstance, are claimed to be members of a national body. My approach is, I hope, somewhat more sophisticated. Modern Jewish identity is indeed flexible, even liquid. Jewish religious, political, and cultural behavior varies widely across time and space, and even within one particular environment Jews adopt multiple, often contradictory, forms of collective identity. Individuals of Jewish origin may make some form of Jewish identity central to their sense of self, while for others Jewishness is compartmentalized, marginalized, or extruded altogether from the field of vision. Thus when I speak of "the Jews" I do not have in mind what Benedict Anderson calls a "bound seriality," an entity like a state, whose members can be confidently tallied up and located in a particular space. Rather, "the Jews" constitutes, to use another of Anderson's terms, an "unbound seriality," borderless and of indeterminate, yet finite, quantity.[7] Jews, like all ethnic or religious communities, are unbound serialities, as their numbers shift depending upon how one defines them, and the very act of observing and measuring them (for example through opinion polling) can affect their self-definition.

The approach presented here rejects classic Zionism's "negation of the diaspora," but it also critiques those aspects of post-Zionism that, striving for universalism and escape from the shackles of Zionist ideology, generate a willful ignorance of Israel's Jewish heritage. At the same time, the mantra of multiculturalism that is invoked by some post-Zionist thinkers opens the way to an embracing of Judaism and Jewishness. Thus post-Zionism is a fitting object of attention for this chapter, both for its linkages with previous intellectual currents within modern Jewish history and for its value as the source of a new method for probing the Jewish past.

Language

In the contemporary Jewish world Hebrew and Yiddish have switched their historic positions. Hebrew, traditionally the sacred tongue of prayer, has taken the conventional place of Yiddish as *mameloshen*, the mother tongue of millions of Jews, both in Israel and in a growing Israeli diaspora. As a rapidly evolving vernacular whose speakers come from all corners of the globe, contemporary Hebrew, like Yiddish prior to the Holocaust, contains a vast quantity of loanwords, and, like the Yiddish spoken on the pre-Holocaust Eastern European street, is often inelegantly presented, with little attention paid to the niceties of grammar. In Israel, Hebrew is spoken increasingly by ultra-Orthodox Jews, not only in their conversations with outsiders but among themselves as well, though it is often blended with Yiddish into a creole popularly termed *yeshivish*. At the same time, in the western world Yiddish has assumed some of the trappings of *lashon ha-kodesh*, the traditional appellation for Hebrew. As most of the world's Yiddish speakers pass away, the language is being kept alive by scholars of Yiddish literature, university classes, and journalism. Cherished as the fragile legacy of a lost civilization, Yiddish is cultivated in the classroom or library like a prize orchid in a hothouse. Yiddish studies is carried out primarily in the diaspora, yet Yiddish language and literature are taught on a modest scale at Israeli universities.

The simultaneous inversions of Yiddish and Hebrew point to the diversity of linguistic development and the inadequacy of a dichotomous distinction between dead and living languages. The vernacularization of a language transforms its nature but does not necessarily ensure its viability. Languages limited to the spheres of religion, government, and higher learning – what Benedict Anderson calls "truth languages" – can survive for millennia, whereas peasant vernaculars can be wiped out in short order if the community of speakers is uprooted or conquered by speakers of a different tongue. Truth languages have been widely spoken, with Latin being the official language of instruction at Polish and Hungarian universities into the eighteenth century. The relevance of these issues to the study of modern Hebrew are obvious. As Ron Kuzar has observed in an intriguing new book, Hebrew linguistic scholarship today is divided between champions of "revivalist" and "non-revivalist" schools. The former see Hebrew as a dead language whose revival in the early twentieth century was a unique and heroic accomplishment, whereas the latter attempt to fit modern Hebrew into a global pattern of pidgins and creoles. Clearly, modern Palestinian Hebrew does not fit into the narrow definition of a pidgin as a language of slaves of diverse provenance which then matures into a more stable creole as it passes to the slaves' children. But if a pidgin is conceived as the common language of any group of individuals of varied origins, and creolization as the nativization of that pidgin, then these terms can be fruitfully applied to modern Hebrew.[8]

Kuzar claims that the members of the Old Yishuv in nineteenth-century Palestine spoke a simplified, stilted Hebrew, a language of commerce, and for some a highly bookish tongue used for administration and jurisprudence. Many residents of the Yishuv were also conversant with the

Hebrew writings of the Eastern European Haskalah, which were disseminated via a substantial journalistic and belletristic literature. An additional source of Old Yishuv Hebrew was what Eliezer Glinert calls the "unsupervised" language of correspondence and popular pietistic literature. Thus the second wave of Zionist settlement that began in 1904 did not revive Hebrew so much as set into play a process of standardization of an already spoken language. Even before the second wave there was a generation of Palestinian Jewish children raised speaking Hebrew, children who were taught, ironically, in the schools of a non-Zionist German-Jewish philanthropic organization, the Hilfsverein der deutschen Juden, which advocated Hebrew as the Yishuv's most viable lingua franca given its population of such diverse origins.[9] The lexicon was highly limited, and new words were invented in droves by a number of authorities, the most famous of whom was Eliezer Ben-Yehuda. Because the Yishuv was predominantly of Eastern European stock, spoken Palestinian Hebrew was strongly influenced by Yiddish syntax, though its morphology was Biblical Hebraic. The phonology was influenced by European Jewish factors as well, not so much how the Ashkenazic Palestinian Jews pronounced Hebrew as how they spoke Yiddish. On the eve of World War I, the Hebrew Language Committee proclaimed that spoken Hebrew would henceforth employ Sephardic pronunciation, not out of deference to the land's long-resident Sephardic minority, but because Sephardic pronunciation was believed to conform more closely to ancient biblical speech.[10] Yiddish continued, however, to exert powerful lexical and syntactic influences on spoken Hebrew (for example in word order within sentences).

Kuzar's study has important implications for our understanding of contemporary Hebrew and, by extension, the relationship between the Zionist project and the Jewish past. Israeli Hebrew may be filled with slang and Americanisms, but I disagree with Benjamin Harshav's claim that it is essentially a western language in Hebrew characters with biblical grammar.[11] After all, Hebrew has always incorporated sizeable numbers of loan words, and rabbinic Hebrew owes as much to Greek as modern Hebrew draws on English. Today's Hebrew vernacular is a natural product of generations of speaking and writing by Jews, and there is as much continuity as rupture between the diaspora and Palestinian environments in which modern Hebrew developed. Israeli Hebrew grew out of many European languages, but primarily out of Yiddish, in combination with selected components of biblical and rabbinic Hebrew.

Now that Ashkenazi hegemony has all but disintegrated and a solid majority of Israel's Jews are of Middle Eastern and North African (Mizrahi) origin, Hebrew's future development will take a different tack. The language is not likely, however, to be Arabized as it was molded by Yiddish, given the suppression of Arabic and of Judeo-Arabic culture among Israel's Mizrahi Jews through decades of government policy and assimilationist striving.[12]

In the interpretation presented here, modern Hebrew is even more "Jewish" than the revivalist approach would suggest, for in the latter view modern Hebrew's glory depends upon its links with the biblical and Mishnaic forms of the language, and the more it secularizes and borrows from other cultures, the more it becomes a bastard tongue. The non-revivalist approach, on the other hand, is populist without romanticizing popular linguistic usage. It demonstrates that jettisoning ideologically inspired historical myths does not necessarily weaken attachment to a nation or its culture. Quite the opposite: in this case, a non-revivalist approach to Hebrew roots the language deeply into Jewish history and can enhance Israeli pride in greatly expanding the cultural fabric of modern Jewish life.

Religion

In 1991 and 1999, the Guttman Center of the Israel Democracy Institute carried out comprehensive surveys of Israeli Jewish religious behavior. The surveys indicated that, contrary to popular belief, Israeli Jews were not divided between a small, zealously Orthodox minority and a secular, anti-clerical majority. Rather, Israeli Jews fit into an only slightly lopsided bell curve, with (according to the 1999 figures) 16 percent claiming to be strictly observant, 20 percent observant to a great extent, 43 percent somewhat observant, and 21 percent totally non-observant. What is more, many of the totally non-observant preserved shards of Jewish ritual: two-thirds always participate in some kind of Passover seder, and one-third thought it important to fast on Yom Kippur. Although a majority of Israeli Jews favor reducing the power of the state to enforce religious law in areas such as public transportation or civil marriage, Israeli Jews do not, by and large, desire a total disengagement of the state from the promotion of Jewish tradition and culture.[13]

During the decade after the 1991 report was issued, support for disestablishment of the Israeli church grew considerably, as witnessed by the phenomenal electoral success in the 2003 elections of the anti-clerical party Shinui, which at this time commands almost 15 percent of the Israeli parliament. The leftist secular party Meretz received another 5 per cent of the vote. Thus approximately one-fifth of Israeli voters, or, setting aside Israel's Arab minority, one-quarter of Jewish voters, voted for parties with an avowedly secularist platform. On the other hand, most Israeli Jews preferred parties with a pragmatic and instrumental approach to religion (for example the Likud, Labor), and a substantial minority chose parties with an explicit religious agenda, often linked with a hyper-nationalism.

A second important change between the 1991 and 1999 surveys is the effects of the immigration over the past fifteen years of over one million Jews (and 250,000 accompanying non-Jews) from the former Soviet Union. This immigration wave does much to account for the fall in overall levels of religious observance among the Israeli Jewish population; between 1991 and

1999, the percentage of Jews calling themselves "non-religious" increased from 38 to 43, while the percentage of "traditional" Jews fell from 42 to 35. The Jews among the immigrants were often highly assimilated in their lands of origin and have been likely to be fiercely secular once in Israel. Secularism, however, is not necessarily consonant with anticlericalism. The political parties established by and representing Jews from the former Soviet Union have been zealous in protecting the Jewish character of the state, and they have not made significant efforts to separate church and state, reduce funding for Orthodox institutions, or diminish the political power of Orthodox parties. Moreover, between 1991 and 1999 there was a sizeable *increase* in the percentage of Israelis holding traditional Jewish beliefs, with half to two-thirds now professing faith in the existence of God, divine providence, reward and punishment, the divine origins of the Torah and mitzvot, the chosenness of the Jewish people, and the afterlife.

The first Guttman report elicited a storm of controversy. Many commentators observed that the differences dividing the somewhat or largely observant from the strictly Orthodox core were vast, and that, for all but the truly Orthodox, observance was primarily a manifestation of national, ethnic, and cultural identity as opposed to pietist sentiment. Critics of the report claimed that the religious practices of most Israeli Jews were syncretistic, illogical, and spotty, and that without strict religious observance a recognizably Jewish identity would not be transmitted across generations. Orthodox Israelis impugned the legitimacy of partial Jewish observance and bemoaned the transformation of the halakhah from an all-embracing way of life to a freely chosen and fluid lifestyle. But there is no gainsaying the fact that most Israeli Jews (including, we learn from the 2000 survey, immigrants from the former Soviet Union) engage in some forms of Jewish ritual behavior and that an overwhelming majority feel part of the Jewish people, as opposed to merely the Israeli nation.

In terms of normative ritual observance, Israelis are, as an aggregate, somewhat more "Jewish" than their counterparts in the diaspora. Drawing on various surveys carried out during the 1990s, Sergio DellaPergola reports that, whereas approximately 76 percent of Israeli Jews fast on Yom Kippur, the figure is 65 percent in France and 49 percent in the United States. About 14 percent of American Jews keep separate dairy and meat dishes, but in Israel the figure approaches 50 percent. In the United States, 22 percent of men go to synagogue once per month or more, while in Israel 32 percent of men attend prayers every Sabbath evening and morning. Moreover, Della Pergola's data, like the Guttman reports, point to important differences between true Orthodoxy and high levels of observance in Israel. Just over half of Israelis do not listen to the radio on the Sabbath and 39 percent do not watch television, yet under 30 percent abstain from travel and only 14 percent of men attend synagogue daily – the same percentage as those Israeli Jews who call themselves "strictly observant."[14] (Thus daily participation in a minyan can be seen, at least for men, as a benchmark of

Orthodoxy, although there are some exceptional cases, such as Reform or Conservative rabbis or rabbinical students who do attend daily prayers.)

The comparison offered here may be questioned on the grounds that Jewish practice does not necessarily correlate with Jewish literacy. It is often asserted that most non-Orthodox Israeli Jews know far less about the Jewish textual canon than diaspora Jews with some day-school education. So far as I know, however, this claim has not been empirically demonstrated, and a serious comparative study of Israeli versus diaspora Jewish literacy is a major desideratum.

The significance of the data summarized here extends beyond Israel's own borders, as it illuminates both changes and continuities in Jewish religious life throughout the globe. Comparisons between the report's findings and those of surveys of diaspora Jewish life indicate that Israeli religious behavior, like that of contemporary Jews in the West, can be plotted along a smoothly flowing curve, and although the bulges are somewhat different, there are numerous correspondences between the two shapes. In order to determine if this has always been the case, we must move from spatial to historical comparison and measure changes in patterns of observance over time in both the Yishuv/state of Israel and various diaspora communities.

It is a truism that the Labor Zionist movement contained within it deep religious impulses, which took on a secularized form in the guise of redemption of the land, the creation of a utopian society, and the veneration of the Hebrew bible as national epic. These impulses were manifested as well in the observance of certain traditional rituals, the most enduring of which during the period of the Yishuv, as in our own time, was the Passover seder. As Anita Shapira has observed, even in the highly secular kibbutzim of the Mandate period Passover was too powerful a force to be ignored, so it was subverted through the production of alternative haggadot: at first satiric renditions of the traditional text, then more serious texts incorporating newly invented traditions, and culminating in the 1940s with the production of authorized haggadot by the kibbutz movements.[15]

To take another example, statistical studies of radio and television use suggest that as early as the 1960s there was a considerable gap between the percentage of Israeli Jews who considered themselves "traditional" and those who were Orthodox. According to a Kol Yisrael listeners' survey of 1965, 30 percent of Israeli Jews refrained from listening to the radio on the Sabbath, although less than half that number voted for religious political parties.[16] This figure is lower than the almost 40 to 50 percent who now avoid the electronic media on the Sabbath, but the percentage of Orthodox Jews in the Israeli population has increased, as has, more importantly, the percentage of Israeli Jews of Middle Eastern and North African origin or descent. In the twentieth century, Muslim lands underwent a less explicit and widespread secularization than the West, and neither a radical Haskalah nor a reactionary Orthodoxy developed, thus sparing Oriental Jewry the sharp polarization that characterized modern Ashkenazic Jewish society.

Jews of Middle Eastern origin are overrepresented in the Guttman Report's "observant to a great extent" and "somewhat observant" categories, and they are likely to observe the commandments more selectively and flexibly than Ashkenazim.[17] Thus a substantial number of non-Orthodox Israeli Jews attempt to create a *shabbesdik* atmosphere in their homes by shutting off the electronic media's assault on the senses and endless flow of depressing news.

Contemporary Israeli religious life can be better understood by looking across the sea as well as back in time. Israel Bartal has wisely observed that today's Israel has a national church, the chief rabbinate, which is the incarnation of the old Russian Empire's State Rabbinate, designed to provide for the religious needs of a population for whom religion does not play a major role in daily life. The state of Israel, argues Bartal, has thus normalized Judaism along the lines of the Haskalah and the tutelary modern state.[18] Indeed, Israel is the child of the European Enlightenment project, which, by and large, sought not to eliminate religion so much as compartmentalize it. Non-Orthodox Israelis of earlier generations often possessed Jewish learning and visceral *yidishkayt*, and today one finds at least some secular Israelis groping towards a similar synthesis through involvement in what is known as "the Jewish Bookshelf" (*aron ha-sefarim ha-yehudi*). The term, said to have been coined by the Israeli writer Chaim Be'er, describes a yearning for Judaic knowledge that is increasingly disseminated through private learning groups, pluralistic *batei midrash* and *yeshivot*, radio talk shows on rabbinic texts, and, increasingly, journalism.[19] In January of 2002, Bambi Sheleg, a woman from a national-religious background, founded a new journal, *Eretz aheret: ketav et al yisre'eliyut ve-yahadut*, which seeks to bridge the chasm between secular and religious forms of Israeli identity. The journalists Adam Baruch and Amiel Kosman, writing in the Israeli daily newspapers *Maariv* and *Ha-Aretz*, respectively, interpret religious issues and texts for the secular public.

Because secular perusers of the Jewish Bookshelf often have close ties with the West, and because some of the institutions that purvey Jewish knowledge in a liberal environment are financed and run by North Americans, it is tempting to locate this phenomenon's origins in the contemporary United States. I would suggest, however, that the Jewish Bookshelf's highly intellectualized approach to Judaic identity has more in common with Weimar Germany's *Lehrhaus* movement than with contemporary American Judaism, imbued as it is with heartfelt religiosity and communitarian zeal.[20] Israel's Ashkenazic intellectual elite may be dying out, but it is still widely overrepresented in the media and universities, and this elite bears traces of European erudition and, at least when dealing with religious matters, emotional reserve. The Jewish Bookshelf does not enjoy wide popularity, but neither did the *Lehrhaus*. They are both important examples of a particular type of Jewish religious awakening, distinct from the emotionally fraught *hazarah bi-teshuvah* that is so common in contemporary Israel and North America and that has virtually no parallel in past forms of Jewish life. (There is the famous exception of Nathan Birnbaum, a *fin-de-siècle* secular Zionist ideologue who went on to become a founder of the ultra-Orthodox Agudat Yisrael.) Before the Holocaust, acculturating and secularizing Jews had little reason to resist the blandishments of the ambient society. Although some German Jews, from the turn of the century through the 1920s, underwent consciousness-raising as the result of contacts with their Eastern European brethren, the new sense of Jewish identity in Weimar Germany was ethnic, cultural, and esthetic rather than spiritual. This appropriation of Jewish texts for the enhancement of a worldly sense of self- and collective consciousness is occurring as well among some secular Israeli Jews today.

Ironically, the most spectacular displays of Jewish religiosity among secular Jews in contemporary Israel are the least bound with previous forms of Jewish life. The "conversion" of some Israeli popular entertainers or public figures to Jewish observance, and their appearance in recent months in confessional talk-show formats, such as the program hosted by the former Shas leader and convicted criminal Arieh Deri, is a profoundly anti-traditional phenomenon. So is the syncretistic toying with Jewish ritual, often mystical in nature, which stimulates the jaded palates of some high-flying Israelis, similar to the embrace of Lubavitch Hasidism in the United States by celebrities such as Steven Spielberg. This phenomenon is novel not so much in its selective approach to Jewish observance, which has been part of the warp and woof of Jewish life worldwide for almost two centuries, as in its blurring of distinctions between Judaism and other faiths, its liberal blending of Jewish concepts and practices with those from other religions, including Eastern non-monotheistic faiths, and its transformation of the kabbalah from something esoteric, with highly restricted access, to a universally available set of teachings, part of entry-level Judaism. All of these qualities have, as is well known, characterized the contemporary culture of Jews in North America. The Jewish Renewal movement employs meditation and chanting techniques borrowed from the Far as well as Middle East, and popularizations of the kabbalah fill the bookshelves of Judaica sections in major bookstores. Thus today's Israel features, in addition to a zealous, fundamentalist *hazarah bi-teshuvah*, two other forms of religious return, with parallels in the diaspora: the cerebral Jewish Bookshelf, and a sentimental and sensual New Age Judaism.

Politics

Ironically, one of the most important rabbinic justifications for Israel's existence as a sovereign state is based on talmudic discussion about Jewish life after the loss of sovereignty. In 1958, Rabbi Ovadyah Haddayah wrote on whether the rabbinic concept of *dina de malkuta dina* (the law of the land is law), which sets out the parameters within which Jews may obey laws proscribed by their host societies, applies to the state of Israel. The talmudic text refers to a "king" whom Jews must obey so long as his decrees do not contravene the halakhah. Drawing upon the medieval and early modern codes, Haddayah ruled that this royal figure could be Jewish as well as gentile. Just as David's and Solomon's kingdoms produced a body of royal decrees and regulatory laws that did not derive from the Torah, so can the state of Israel create a political and legal framework outside of the Torah. Moreover, according to Haddayah the "king" was a metonym for any authority figure, including a prime minister. The Israeli republic was thus no less, but also no more, legitimate than any polity in the diaspora.[21]

Haddayah's need to hearken back to the short-lived Biblical Hebrew commonwealth reflects the Jewish political tradition's lack of experience with dealing with conditions of sovereignty (as opposed to Islam, which dominated much of Eurasia for more than a millennium, and which has always had to grapple with the problem of reconciling divine law with secular power).[22] Sovereignty is, however, only one particular form of political life. Government by Jews over others (normally Jews, but in certain situations non-Jews as well) has taken place within the framework of the biblical kingdoms, the satrapies of pagan antiquity, and a host of autonomous institutions over the ages. Thus, unless carefully defined and delimited, the concept of "Jewish politics" can be so broad as to be meaningless. The political scientist Daniel Elazar attempted to sketch out a comprehensive theory of Jewish political thought and behavior centered around the concept of covenant, a form of contract in which one party is the entire Jewish people, or some part thereof acting on its behalf and representing it metonymically, and in which God figures as either a second party or guarantor.[23] There are a number of problems with this approach. The historicity of much of the biblical narrative is uncertain, and during the more than two millennia of post-biblical history Jewish life has assumed vastly differing forms. The divinely-inspired or sanctioned covenant is so widespread in both Islamic and Christian political traditions that it is difficult to speak of particularly Jewish qualities, save for those that can be attributed to the Jews' status from late antiquity through the beginnings of modernity as a tolerated but vulnerable minority.

One may argue that Rabbinic Judaism inspired a particular approach to politics by according to human beings creative freedom in the interpretation of sacred texts and imposing upon the Jews a matrix of ritual activity that sanctified the everyday world. The centrality of the concept of salvific knowledge – gleaned from texts that were, in principle, obtainable by all – encouraged widespread male literacy, a flourishing of cultural production, and a fluidity of social relationships. This fluidity did not foster democracy so much as permeable oligarchy and meritocracy. Throughout the Middle Ages and early modern period the Jews were a people of burghers, lacking the peasantry and landed aristocracy that were the pillars of every host society in which Jews lived. Their politics, in turn, were those of an ethnic bourgeoisie, like German or Armenian merchants in the Polish-Lithuanian kingdom or Greek Orthodox in the Ottoman Empire. Jews zealously preserved communal autonomy (akin to the Magdeburg Law followed by German communities in Eastern Europe), developed networks of mutual solidarity such as poor-care and the ransoming of captives, and strove to separate themselves from others culturally while engaging in unfettered economic interaction with the outside world.

In modern times, Jewish political activity entered a new phase. In mid-nineteenth-century North America and Western Europe, where European Jews benefited from emancipation and economic mobility, Jews founded defense organizations and agencies that lobbied on behalf of their oppressed brethren in Rumania, Russia, and the Middle East. In the Pale of Settlement, the 1880s and 1890s witnessed the birth of radical Jewish politics, which mooted a wide variety of solutions to the "Jewish Problem," ranging from territorial nationalism to communist internationalism. Zionism's revolutionary rhetoric and call for the use of force in self-defense were part of the warp and woof of Jewish politics in Eastern Europe. Many other aspects associated with the Zionist movement – political factions, mass memberships, using the press and the pamphlet to marshal public opinion – were developed prior to and alongside of international Zionism.

The conditions of sovereignty in Israel transformed the means by which Jews exercise power, but the psychological underpinnings of centuries of Jewish political behavior were still in place. In his book *The Jewish State: A Century Later*, Alan Dowty notes that Israeli politics is informed by the Jews' traditional fear of gentiles, sense of perpetual vulnerability and imminent catastrophe, and unwillingness or inability to conceive of gentiles (here, Arabs) as a collectivity with equal status to the Jews. This sense of isolation strengthened greatly after 1977, with the accession to power of the Likud party and its leader Menachem Begin, who, as we will discuss in the section on historical consciousness below, made the Holocaust central to Israeli political discourse. Moreover, following a number of Israeli social scientists, Dowty presents Israeli politics, like Jewish politics in the modern diaspora, as consociational rather than majoritarian, meaning that decisions are reached through consensus between interest groups rather than negotiations between representatives who are directly responsible to a grassroots constituency. Dowty claims as well that Israelis preserve the collective memory of life in the Russian and Ottoman Empires, where corruption was rampant and state authority rarely benign. Therefore Israelis distrust the state, distance themselves from it, and display at best limited and conditional respect for the law.[24]

I would disagree with Dowty on this last point and favor Baruch Kimmerling's view that in recent years the high levels of militarization in Israeli society and the dependence of many of its citizens upon transfer payments have cemented the individual to the state more strongly than ever, even though classic Zionist ideology has faded.[25] The Israeli polity is no longer responsive to the sort of message proclaimed by David Ben-Gurion in his 1954 essay "The Eternity of Israel":

> Without an extended and continuous effort . . . supported by the entire people, the ingathering of the exiles will be impossible, the cultivation of the desert will not be accomplished, and security will not be established. This effort requires consolidating the people's powers and activating its general will.[26]

Ben-Gurion offered a Rousseauian vision of a tutelary state and mobilized population as necessary for the accomplishment of Herculean tasks of social and material transformation. The Israeli state now has no national tasks save the defense of its population or the economic support of interest groups such as organized labor, ultra-Orthodox Jews, and settlers in the Occupied Territories.

In this militarized, yet de-ideologized, atmosphere, ultra-Orthodox Jews breathe more easily and are willing to grant the state of Israel at least de facto recognition. There is growing willingness among them to perform some sort of national service, and now there is little distinction between the views of the ultra-nationalist Orthodox and the formerly anti-nationalist ultra-Orthodox over the necessity to retain and continue settling the Occupied Territories. True, the ultra-Orthodox reject the authority of the Israeli Supreme Court, whose legal decisions are based on a complex blend of *mishpat ivri* ("halakhah without its theological references or its ritual codes"),[27] Jewish historical practice, British common law, and contemporary western jurisprudence. The dictum *dina de malkuta dina*, discussed at the beginning of this section, does not apply if the laws of the state force the Torah-true Jew to violate the halakhah, and it is the opinion of many ultra-Orthodox Jews that under the tenure of the secular and highly activist Chief Justice Aharon Barak the court has moved deep into this forbidden terrain. Since the outbreak of the second Intifada, however, the alliance between ultra-Orthodoxy and the de-ideologized Israeli state has muted the former's threats of civil disobedience.

The continued militarization of Israeli society and the engagement in a protracted low-intensity war against the Palestinians will strengthen the bonds between virtually all Orthodox Israeli Jews and the state. As the Israeli state sheds its former devotion to the creation of a new Jewish politics based in a unifying, secular civic culture, a sense of participation in the community of nations, and a pragmatic approach to the use of force, and as its vision is delimited by the domain of self-preservation, the more easily will it be able to negotiate between the conflicting interests that beset it, and the more will its politics conform to those of diaspora Jewish communities in centuries past, despite Israel's possession of sovereignty and one of the world's most potent armed forces.

Economics

Israeli politics and economics are symbiotically linked. Labor Zionism's concept of Jewish territorial sovereignty included the transformation of the

Jews from a people of peddlers, beggars, yeshiva *bokhers*, and starveling craftsmen into a robust laboring nation, an *'am oved*. This view was widely, although not universally, shared in the early Zionist movement. The first European Zionist organization, the Lovers of Zion, was cold to Labor Zionism's Marxist rhetoric, as were the overwhelming majority of Jewish immigrants to Palestine at the turn of the century, but that did not keep thousands from attempting to wrest a living from the harsh Palestinian soil. Theodor Herzl, the founder of modern political Zionism, decried the Lovers of Zion's yearnings to create a Jewish peasantry as romantic, if not reactionary, but in his own writings he envisioned a society of skilled, technologically savvy agriculturalists organized along co-operative lines and employing sophisticated machinery. The association between the Jewish return to the Land of Israel and economic transformation was well-nigh universal in Zionist ideology, resisted only by Revisionism, which glorified the individual entrepreneur and admired the Jew as a pioneer of modern capitalism. Vladimir Jabotinsky yearned to reshape the Jews politically and militarily, but he intended to leave their occupational structure intact, protected by a populist, yet capitalist, economic policy.

As things have turned out, the mainstream Zionist program of economic transformation was realized far less successfully than Revisionism's call to transplant diaspora economic life to Palestine. To be sure, all but the most puritan forms of Zionist ideology called for Israel to become a prosperous, technologically advanced society, as has indeed been the case. Israel's per capita gross domestic product is greater than that of southern European states and approaches that of the United Kingdom.[28] Regardless of the bucolic dreams of many of the country's founders, however, Israel has been, from the start, one of the world's most urbanized countries. Moreover, since 1967, manual labor has been performed increasingly by Arabs and foreign workers. (At its peak in the early 1990s, the Palestinian labor force accounted for one-quarter of all agricultural employment and 45 percent of all construction work in Israel. Over the 1990s, the number of Palestinian laborers dropped precipitously, but imports of foreign labor grew apace, and in 2003 there were as many as 300,000 foreign laborers in Israel, half of them there illegally.)[29] Meanwhile, the Israeli managerial and entrepreneurial elite displays classic diaspora Jewish talents for risk-taking and innovation in new fields, such as computer technology. Finally, despite Zionist ideology's attempts to root Jews into the soil, Israelis are among the most mobile people in the world. Israeli diasporas flourish in every major North American city, and, in recent years, the deteriorating security situation in Israel has prompted wealthy Israelis to purchase property or multiple properties abroad. According to stories in the Israeli press, Israeli businessmen considering new careers abroad pride themselves on their acumen, linguistic dexterity, and adaptability. As I have written elsewhere, such a positive self-image characterized Jewish men of affairs in Europe and North America throughout much of the century preceding the Holocaust and constituted an important counterweight to gentile, and later Zionist, criticism that Jews were economic parasites.[30]

Although the young state of Israel was stamped by a culture of material modesty, even austerity, over the past thirty years Israeli material wealth has grown exponentially, albeit unevenly. Israel now features one of the greatest income gaps in the western world between the top and bottom deciles, and 40 percent of income earners in Israel do not reach the minimum threshold for paying income tax.[31] (Transfer payments reduce these inequalities; for example, in 1999 transfers reduced the percentage of Israeli families living in poverty from 34 to 16.)[32] In these developments, Israel is merely following patterns of economic change throughout the developed world, wherein wealth is steadily increasing yet for the most part concentrated in the hands of a small minority.

Studies of the contemporary Israeli economy use the West, or, less often, "Asian tiger" states like Taiwan and South Korea as a frame of reference. The most important anomalous factor affecting the Israeli economy, according to such studies, is high government expenditure, especially for defense, but also for subsidies and transfer payments of various kinds.[33] The nature of these transfer payments, however, is inextricably linked with broader religious and social issues in that many of Israel's poorest citizens are Arab, Ashkenazic-Orthodox, or Mizrahi (of Middle Eastern and North African origin). Mizrahim identify with the political party Shas, whose leadership is solidly Orthodox even if barely one-quarter of its electorate is strictly observant. The two poorest cities in Israel today are Bnai Brak and Jerusalem – one a stronghold of ultra-Orthodoxy, the other a blend of Orthodox Jews of sundry origins, secular or semi-secular Mizrahi Jews, Arabs, and a diminishing secular minority. The system of government handouts to Orthodox institutions and families, like the controversial exemptions from military service for yeshiva students, was rooted in the fabric of the newly established state of Israel, and it has been augmented by a vast network of private transfer payments from Orthodox charities throughout the world. Contemporary Israel's political economy cannot be properly understood, therefore, without a synchronic and diachronic understanding of Orthodox economic life in both its generative (the production of goods and services) and distributive (spending patterns and philanthropic activity) aspects.

Indeed, given Israel's long history of reliance on capital transfers from a variety of global Jewish philanthropies, the most important of which is the United Jewish Communities–United Jewish Appeal, and the heightened role expected of these philanthropies since the collapse of the peace process and the intensification of the Palestinian–Israeli conflict, Israel's economy cannot be separated from that of global Jewry. In my own work, I have argued for the necessity of studying the history of Jewish political economy, philanthropy, and social politics in order to appreciate what is truly unique about Israeli economic life and what has been imported from the diaspora.

But there have been few serious attempts to compare the economic behavior, for example investment and risk-taking strategies, of Jewish entrepreneurs in the modern diaspora, Yishuv, and state of Israel. This is an important topic, as throughout the history of Zionism and Israel private capital transfers, in the form of capital imported with immigrants or invested by Jews living abroad, have far exceeded the public capital raised by Zionist fundraising instruments.

In an excellent recent book, Nahum Karlinsky has produced a collective study of the Yishuv's key capitalist entrepreneurs, the citrus growers of the coastal plain, over the years 1890–1939. The citrus growers, overwhelmingly of bourgeois Russian and Polish origin, saw themselves as true pioneers – self-sacrificing, noble-minded, and socially responsible, unlike the youthful laborers who, as the growers saw things, spouted romantic or Marxist rhetoric and strove to stifle individual initiative through hegemonic unions and political parties.[34] Eli Shaltiel's biography of Pinchas Rutenberg, who brought hydroelectric power to Palestine under the British Mandate, adds to this picture.[35] (Rutenberg, who in his youth was a Russian revolutionary, became a highly successful entrepreneur with political ambitions, a type all too well known in contemporary Europe and North America.) Such books demonstrate the important links between early twentieth-century Eastern European Jewish economic life and the material factors that made possible the creation of the state of Israel. They also suggest that contemporary Israel's strongly capitalist economic fabric began to be woven more than a century ago, and that even before the decline of the kibbutz and the Labor Economy in the 1980s their cultural hegemony did not necessarily match their material contributions.

Historical Consciousness

If Jewishness is defined in terms of a sense of historic victimhood and vulnerability, and if the diaspora experience is associated with feeling alone in a hostile world in which antisemitism is pervasive and ineradicable, then over the past thirty years Israel has undoubtedly developed a diaspora Jewish mentality. Classic secular Zionism expressed sympathy with diaspora Jewry's many centuries of suffering but maintained that once restored to their ancient patrimony Jews would no longer live in fear. The state of Israel was born in the shadow of the Holocaust, the greatest catastrophe ever to strike the Jewish people, and it loomed large in public consciousness during the state's first decades. But public memory was directed into selected, state-sanctioned channels. In Israeli Holocaust commemorations and history textbooks produced during the 1950s, emphasis was placed on the ghetto rebellions and other forms of heroism, such as the doomed mission of Hannah Senesh. In Israeli schools, the Holocaust was studied within the framework of World War II and all the suffering it wrought, thus minimizing Israeli shame for the ignominious destruction of European Jewry and the passivity with which most Jews allegedly accepted their fate.

The 1961 trial of Nazi war criminal Adolf Eichmann encouraged the adoption of a more inclusive and empathetic approach to the Holocaust. This transformation of Israeli self-consciousness accelerated between 1967 and the mid-1970s, as the result of frequent wars, terrorism, international isolation, and the passing of the generation of founders of the state. The Holocaust came to be seen increasingly as a collective tragedy, in which all Jewish victims could be viewed with equal compassion, and although the burden of guilt remained with the Nazis, the burden of shame was shifted from the Jewish victims to the world as a whole, which was divided into realms of perpetrators, who collaborated with the Nazis, and bystanders, who were too cowardly or opportunistic to intervene on the Jews' behalf.[36]

The growing centrality of the Holocaust to Israeli collective memory became apparent after 1977 when Menachem Begin was elected prime minister. Under the tenure of Begin's education minister, Zevulun Hammer of the National Religious Party, the Holocaust became a mandatory, separate topic within the high-school curriculum, and in 1981 the Holocaust became a separate category for the high school matriculation examinations. The subject was taught by means of a textbook authored by two survivors, who presented the tragedy as unique in the history of humanity and claimed that any attempt to approach the subject in terms of comparative genocide amounted to Holocaust denial.[37] Begin himself practiced and legitimized the use of the Holocaust as a cognitive filter for understanding the Arab–Israeli conflict. To be sure, Israeli society had always associated Arabs with Nazis, as in the widespread fear in the 1950s that former Nazi rocket scientists were working for Nasser, or the image in the popular film *Hill 24 Doesn't Answer* (1955) of an Arab taken prisoner in the 1948 War who turns out to be a former SS officer. But in the 1980s these occasional flights of fancy became embedded in Israeli political discourse at the highest level. On the eve of the invasion of Lebanon in 1982, Begin proclaimed that the only alternative to invasion was Treblinka, and the editor of the Israeli daily *Yediot Aharonot* claimed that compared to Yasir Arafat, Hitler was a "pussycat."[38] Moshe Zuckerman has observed how in 1988 the confluence of the first Palestinian Intifada and the trial of accused Nazi war criminal Ivan Demjanjuk deepened even further the associations between present and past, although memory of the Holocaust became increasingly abstract and mythologized, a signifier torn from its historical context and now ritually invoked to justify the occupation of the Territories.

During the Persian Gulf War, Zuckerman argues, not only did the Arab enemy (Arafat, Saddam Hussein) become an avatar of Hitler, but Israelis felt themselves re-experiencing the Holocaust as they huddled in sealed rooms and fearfully awaited attacks by missiles loaded with poison gas. In this atmosphere, Zionist confidence in the Israeli military gave way to a desperate religiosity. A massive prayer rally was held at the office of the chief rabbi, and ultra-Orthodox Jews recited a special prayer for the American president George Bush, while Lubavitcher hasidim saw in the low casualty count a sign of the imminent coming of the messianic era. Even secular Israelis felt the hand of divine providence at work, and journalists for the mainstream dailies employed religious language of salvation and deliverance. The hard-boiled prime minister, Yithzak Shamir, donned a *kippah* and recited psalms on national television. This act, claims Zuckerman, was not merely one of unifying the people or engaging in public relations, but rather

> a symbolic, striking, focussed expression of a very real component of the Israeli political reality, that potentially catastrophic grafting between the secular Zionist ideology in general (and that of Shamir's "national camp" in particular) and a relatively new type of religiosity – a religiosity that transformed gradually, in the wake of the conquests of 1967, the principle of "the sanctity of the land" to the prominent slogan of a conquering and enslaving chauvinism, a trampling and destructive religiosity.[39]

In such an environment, Arabs became an eternal, implacable enemy, ripped out of context in space or time. The Arab became Amalek.

The return of the diaspora in Israeli historical consciousness need not be a negative phenomenon. There is nothing inherently wrong about the increasing popularity of sending Israeli youth to Poland; the problem is that, rather than explore the gamut of Jewish life in the Ashkenazi heartland, the tours, precisely like the March of the Living trips for North American Jewish youth, focus on to visits to death camps, where teenagers forge a neo-Zionist identity based on an unhealthy combination of victimhood and empowerment. (As Motti Golani has written, "There is nothing more dangerous than a victim bearing arms: He has no inhibitions.")[40] Thus the historical distortion, but also present danger, inherent in then Chief of Staff Ehud Barak's 1992 comment, when visiting Auschwitz, that "we arrived here ... perhaps fifty years too late,"[41] or the recent statement by Jewish Agency chief Sallai Meridor that, given forecasts that the population of world Jewry might increase in the next century from 12 to 18 million, "[o]nce again, the fate of 6 million Jews hangs in the balance, only this time, their fate is in our hands."[42] Israel's re-occupation of the West Bank in April 2002 was justified by Prime Minister Ariel Sharon as being part of a war for the very survival of the Jewish people – a statement that not only absolves Israel of any responsibility for the catastrophic security situation but also conflates Israel with the diaspora. There was little difference between Israeli and diaspora Jewish interpretations of the contemporaneous outburst attacks against Jews and synagogues in Europe and North America. Both the Israeli government and diaspora Jewish organizations drew a direct line between 2002 and the 1930s, between the torching of a synagogue in Paris and *Kristallnacht*. It is ironic and deeply disturbing that such an interpretation neglects the vast differences between the two situations. Then, the Jews were defenseless, and now they possess a militarily powerful state.

Antisemitism is always irrational and indefensible, but surely it matters that its current awakening comes in the wake of a political struggle following thirty-five years of Israeli military occupation of the Palestinians, whereas the antisemitic image of the Jew in interwar Europe was nothing but a reflection and reification of European society itself.

In Israeli society, historical consciousness is molded primarily by political discourse and the media rather than formal education. Over the decades, history curricula in the middle and high schools have reflected more than adumbrated patterns of Israeli historical self-understanding. In the Israeli history curricula of the 1950s, when Israeli society was mobilized in the service of Zionist ideology and dominated by Ashkenazim, Jewish and "general" history were entirely separate units, and the history of Jews outside of Europe was all but ignored. The 1970 curriculum, a sign of the relaxation of Israeli society in the post-Ben-Gurion era, increased the amount of attention paid to world history, but the field was still taught separately from Jewish history, the result being that teachers in the public secular schools could (and did) neglect Jewish in favor of general history. The 1995 curriculum was the product of a further distancing from classic Zionist ideology, and it was criticized as embodying the post-Zionist spirit of the Israeli leftist intelligentsia. The neo-conservative ideologue Yoram Hazony, for example, decried the curriculum's integration of Jewish and world history, which allegedly presented Judaism and the Jews as epiphenomenal within the context of the march of the world's great civilizations. Ironically, however, the new curriculum could actually increase student awareness of Jewish history precisely because of its holistic approach. Moreover, the presentation of Middle Eastern Jewish history and culture is much enhanced (although still problematic) and, unlike the older textbooks, the new ones are engagingly written and visually stimulating.[43] Critics of the curriculum claim, drawing on a few isolated sentences from the textbooks' treatment of the Arab–Israeli wars, that the textbooks undermine Israeli patriotism. For the most part, however, these books seek merely to inculcate the sort of critical thinking skills that are expected from educated youth in any developed country. A holistic and pluralistic approach to the teaching of history in Israel indeed opens the way to discussions about sensitive topics such as Palestine's Arabs and the extent of Israeli responsibility for its conflict with the Arab world. It also makes possible a heightened and deepened evaluation of the diaspora communities, be they in Europe, the Middle East, or North Africa, from which Israeli Jews or their immediate ancestors came.[44]

Post-Zionism

The revision of history curricula for Israeli schools is part of a far larger set of possibilities and problems raised by the revision, over the past twenty years, of Israeli academic historiography from a state-supporting enterprise to an adversarial one. This subject, which has attracted a great deal of attention (and about which I have written elsewhere),[45] is not of immediate concern to us here, as the Revisionist historical oeuvre has devoted itself to deconstructing historical perceptions cemented in Zionist ideology rather than constructing a new Israeli identity based on an unblocked historical vista. That is, the "new history," as this body of scholarship is called, is not necessarily informed by post-Zionism, which is a project of abandoning collectivist ideologies and crafting an inclusive, truly democratic state that allows untrammeled personal freedoms.[46]

Post-Zionism appears to be at best indifferent and at worst downright hostile to any form of Jewish religious or cultural expression and to advocate cutting all ties with the Jewish diaspora. When the term was first employed by the leftist journalist Uri Avneri in 1968, it was meant to describe a new era, in which Israel could shake off its historic obligations to the diaspora and adopt an entirely pragmatic approach to life in the Middle East that stressed accommodation and cultural bonding with Israel's Arab neighbors. Avneri's vision was a variety of Canaanism, a 1950s ideology that conceived of Israel as utterly distinct from the diaspora, as a Hebrew rather than Jewish polity. (According to the Canaanite world-view, an ancient Hebraic spirit dominated the entire Near East and would do so again, this time in the form of a pan-Semitic federation, with the Hebrew state in the forefront.) In a somewhat gentler fashion, Amos Elon and Menachem Brinker spoke of post-Zionism, in 1971 and 1986, respectively, to refer to the successful completion of Zionism's mission of the ingathering of exiles. Avneri, Elon, and Brinker all used the word "post-Zionism" in a chronological-spatial sense – that is, to describe an epoch in history – as opposed to the conceptual and methodological meaning of the term in the 1990s, when it became shorthand for a manifesto against Zionist narratives of truth and knowledge.[47]

Whereas in its first phase post-Zionism respectfully acknowledged the diaspora, in its second phase the diaspora is usually not even within the field of vision. Much of contemporary Israeli literature and cultural criticism aspire to universalism in their embrace of western literary and philosophical models but they also feature an unnoticed parochialism and historical amnesia, an Israeli-centeredness, manifested in ignorance of the social, economic, and cultural fabric out of which the state of Israel was cut. Post-Zionism does not, as many of its critics mistakenly claim, harbor a leftist agenda to undermine the foundations of Zionist ideology. Rather, as exemplified by the stories of the writer Gafi Amir, post-Zionist thought is frequently apolitical and pro-capitalist in its glorification of individual autonomy. The free market and consumerism are linked with the cult of free choice; thus the privatization of political identity is tied up with the globalization of economic life.[48] For example, Amir's story "By the Time You're Twenty One You'll Reach the Moon" features two Tel Avivans, a man and his former girlfriend, seeking solace for their aimless lives in consumerism and removed from Judaism to the point of skipping attendance at the family's

Passover seder. The Jewish Bookshelf has been utterly abandoned by these lost souls.[49]

Post-Zionism, as presented thus far, would appear to be distant from any form of modern Jewish sensibility save radical assimilation. Yet post-Zionism contains within it unmistakable signs of its Jewish ancestry. First off, there is a variety of post-Zionism, originating in the Right end of the Israeli political spectrum, which combines militant religiosity and territorial maximalism with an unfettered allegiance to economic neoliberalism – the same celebration of personal freedom that one encounters in the post-Zionist Left. This approach, associated with Jerusalem's Shalem Center, rejects the concept of socioeconomic revolution and "normalization" that, as argued above, were central to mainstream Zionism. Moreover, although the settlers in the Occupied Territories usually claim to be the only true successors of the Labor Zionist pioneers, the settlers' journal *Nekudah* recently featured a fascinating article by one Yair Shapira, claiming that even in the Land of Israel Jews would and must remain particular, distinct, and *unheimlich* – that is, strangers in their own land.[50]

More important, even secular post-Zionism opens the door to Jewishness – however that may be defined – through its championing of multiculturalism and pluralism. A recent article in the flagship journal of post-Zionist thought, *Teoryah u-Vikoret*, featured a detailed critique of recent government-funded position papers on multiculturalism, with which the papers claimed to be sympathetic, but which, according to authors Yossi Yonah and Yehouda Shenhav, they sought to repress. The papers are said to endorse only a highly constrained form of multiculturalism within a Jewish-national framework, without room for Arabs or immigrant workers, and where the state remains a powerful force of social molding, unlike a truly multicultural model wherein the state is separated from society. Yonah and Shenhav believe the state should reflect social movements from below rather than mold them from above. Most of the arguments in this article concern the incorporation of Arabs, immigrant laborers, and homosexuals into Israeli society, but there is also criticism of discrimination against ultra-Orthodox and especially Mizrahi Jews. In true postmodern form, Yonah and Shenhav are attacking the society's dominant discursive structure, which is Ashkenazic and secular, and so they end up championing the interests of Mizrahi Jews, for most of whom religious and ethnic identity are inseparable, and even ultra-Orthodox Jews, as legitimate components of a multicultural society.[51]

This line of thinking has been taken several steps further by the historian Amnon Raz-Krakotzkin, who claims that hypocrisy lies behind many post-Zionists' conciliatory stands towards the Palestinian Arabs and multiculturalism within Israel. Raz-Krakotzkin believes that post-Zionism was the creation of secular Ashkenazic intellectuals who, in the wake of the Oslo Accords, hoped that the creation of a separate Palestinian state would allow Israel to live in western-style comfort and avoid a meaningful engagement with the ubiquitous Arab culture – neither western nor secular – surrounding the Jewish state. Many post-Zionists, writes Raz-Krakotzkin, do not really wish to engage authentically with ethnic difference or authentic religiosity. By idealizing western universalism, they are incapable of valorizing Arab culture and Islam, on the one hand, or Judaism and Jewishness, on the other. Raz-Krakotzkin's particular concern is Mizrahi Jews, who represent the worst of both worlds, being of Middle Eastern origin and often bound to Jewish tradition.[52]

Indeed, multiculturalism can serve as not merely a slogan or an abstraction, but rather a framework for the cultivation of a Jewish sensibility with deep and broad roots And in an unexpected, engaging fashion, one encounters just such an approach in an essay written some ten years ago by Adi Ophir, the founder of *Teoryah u-Vikoret*, on the liturgy for Yom Kippur. The essay is a series of reflections on the transcendent power of the liturgy and its structure of emotionally compelling references, which mask a vague and perhaps non-existent referent (that is, God). Most of the essay could easily have been written by a contemporary American or, more likely, French Jewish philosopher. If one substitutes the words "secular diaspora Jew" for "Israeli" in the narrative, the story would be told of the diaspora. For, as Ophir argues, there is no room in the Yom Kippur liturgy for a Zionist narrative, religious as well as secular. Ophir's discussion of the Day of Atonement's assembling the Nation of Israel refers to a collective, not necessarily a territorialized one.[53] When Ophir writes of secular Jews sitting side by side with the Orthodox in synagogue, the description may sound uniquely Israeli, as in most of North America non-Orthodox Jews can attend the synagogues of sundry denominations, but the coming together of Jews of all stripes, from the most assimilated to the most pious, into a single space for the holiest day of the Jewish year was typical of an earlier era, in the North America and Europe of a century ago, and is still commonplace throughout much of the world today.

Despite its self-proclaimed attempts to escape history, post-Zionism itself can and must be historicized and contextualized. Although many post-Zionists are not postmodernists, in Israel postmodernism is mediated through post-Zionism, just as for Jews in nineteenth-century Germany historicism was mediated through the scholarly study of the Jewish heritage, the *Wissenschaft des Judentums.* Jewish civilization filters new systems of thought through the prism of the Jews' particularistic concerns with their own existence and future. Jewish culture concretizes and personalizes epistemological innovation. Like a rebellious child who bears an unmistakable resemblance to his parents, post-Zionism is inextricably bound to the Jewish past. Its trenchant self-criticism, declamatory style, and self-righteousness; its sense of mission; its fervid faith in the power of the intellectual to reshape Jewish society; and, finally, its oxymoronic blend of parochialism and universalism – in all these ways, post-Zionism is the legatee of its predecessors, the major intellectual movements in modern diaspora Jewish life, from the Haskalah to Zionism.

Conclusion

Powerful counter-arguments could be raised against the claims I have raised in this chapter. In Israel, unlike anywhere in the modern diaspora, an empowered Jewish polity is the sole locus of coercive force. Under conditions of sovereignty, the rhythms of political, economic, religious, and cultural life are often incomparable with their diaspora counterparts. Like the basic elements of Israeli sovereignty, Israel's longstanding conflict with the Arab world in general and the Palestinians in particular confounds neat linkages between Israeli and diaspora Jewish life. The rupture may be discerned not only in the status of Jews as the dominant population in Israel, but also, paradoxically, from the presence of substantial non-Jewish minorities within the Jewish state.

To provide but one example, the presentation at the beginning of the chapter of modern spoken and literary Hebrew as a common Jewish cultural possession is challenged by the fact that almost one-quarter of the population of the state of Israel is not Jewish. It is expected, indeed necessary, for Israel's one million Palestinian citizens to speak fluent Hebrew. For these Arabs, Hebrew is a language of state, an instrument of power, imposed from without. A very different, yet still problematic, case is provided by the more than 250,000 non-Jewish immigrants who have entered Israel from the former Soviet Union, and whose children born in Israel speak native Hebrew. Although these children are not halakhically Jewish, mastery of Hebrew, coupled with attendance at state schools and service in the army, can and will lead to their complete absorption into secular Israeli society – or at least up to the point when they will confront Orthodox religious authority over matters of personal status (for example marriage, divorce, burial). In this contemporary scenario, therefore, Hebrew becomes a vehicle for the manufacturing of Jewishness rather than a manifestation of it.

These and other counter-arguments notwithstanding, it is undeniable that contemporary Israel has inherited the cultural legacy and psychological traumas of the modern Jewish diaspora. At times, the chain of transmission is easily visible, as in the case of religious behavior or collective memory, whereas at times it is opaque, unnoticed, or denied. This chapter has dealt largely with structural processes, social and cultural transformations that must not be confused with self-conscious manifestations of Jewish collective solidarity. With the passage of time, the collective psychology and social ethos of Israeli and diaspora Jews are converging, yet Jews perceive a growing divergence between the two. According to the Guttman surveys discussed in the body of the essay, between 1991 and 1999 the percentage of Israeli Jews believing that diaspora Jews constitute a distinct people rose from 57 percent to 69 percent, while the percentage of Israeli Jews who feel a sense of shared fate with diaspora Jews fell from 76 to 70. Survey data from the United States demonstrates a steady decline in Jewish bonds to Israel, with more than half of Jews in their seventies but only one-third of

younger Jews claiming that "caring about Israel" is a major aspect of their Jewish identity.[54]

These two apparently paradoxical phenomena may be causally linked. As the state of Israel has shaken off its Zionist ideological scaffolding, its complex relationship with the diaspora, characterized by a sense of deep-seated difference yet firm obligation, has changed. Few Israelis today wish to play the role cast for them by the Zionist labor movement and Ben-Gurionist state of the doughty sabra, the laborer cum warrior whose valor, dignity, simplicity, and straightforwardness represented the antithesis of the stereotypical diaspora Jew.[55] In fact, the sabra always contained within its ideal-type many quintessentially diaspora Jewish qualities, such as perseverance, resourcefulness, and a powerful sense of solidarity. It was precisely the fact that the sabra was recognizable by as well as alien to diaspora Jews, that underneath the tanned and muscular body beat a warm Jewish heart, that so endeared Israel to diaspora Jews during the state's first decades. The more Israeli Jewish society has normalized along the lines of the modern Jewish experience, the more it resembles a diaspora community, the less it can serve Jews living outside of Israel as a source of romantic inspiration or psychic revival. There are of course exceptions, such as those Orthodox Jews who have absorbed national-religious ideologies that cement them to Israel and render it central to their religious identity. There is also the small but vocal community of rabbis, educators, and activists in Jewish organizations who, whether out of choice, the demands of their careers, or both, sojourn extensively in Israel. For most diaspora Jews, however, the lowest, indeed only, common denominator linking them with Israel is concern about the state's security. Israeli and diaspora Jews alike have cast aside the optimistic, forward-looking qualities of classic Zionism in favor of an ethos of survivalism.

Israel is more than a Jewish state; it encases a Jewish society. The current debate about the future of Israel as a Jewish state elides this crucial fact. In years to come, Israel may continue its current course and become an apartheid state, with a Jewish minority ruling over a disfranchised Arab minority. If it divests itself of the Territories, it may attempt to remain an ethnic democracy featuring Jewish hegemony, or it may alter its character and become a state of all its citizens, in which equal rights to all citizens are constitutionally guaranteed, and church and state are separated. There is even a chance, albeit minuscule, that Israel and the Territories will, some day, form a unitary democratic state. No matter what path it chooses, however, Israel will be home to the world's largest Jewish community (it is already close to surpassing that of the United States, and demographic trends are definitely in Israel's favor), with a deeply rooted Hebrew culture, a flourishing system of religious education (even without massive state subsidies), and an interlocking network of social institutions that constitute a Jewish civil society. The Israeli polity will continue to nurture that Jewish civil society even it no longer does so exclusively or at the expense of other nationalities.

Along with the positive aspects of continuity between today's and the future's Israeli Jewish society will come negative ones as well. Even with a separation of church and state, tensions between religious and secular Jews will remain. The challenge of assimilation, whether into an Americanized, globalized habitus or into the Arab culture that surrounds and suffuses Israel, will confront Israeli Jewish society no matter what political direction the state follows. No less than diaspora Jewry, Israel will need to address these questions about religious practice and collective identity, questions that constitute the unfinished business of Jewish modernity, which has been accumulating for two centuries and shows no sign of going away on its own.

5 Is Zionism a colonial movement?

The relationship between Zionism and colonialism, long a highly controversial subject among scholars throughout the world, has in recent years become a primary source of friction between champions and opponents of revisionism within Israeli historiography and sociology. Until the 1980s, most scholars of Israel studies teaching in Israeli universities denied or qualified linkages between Zionism and late nineteenth-century imperialism. This approach is still taken by a number of younger scholars in Israel, but in the past fifteen years there has risen a cohort of Israeli academics who, following the lead of Arab and western scholarship on the modern Middle East, have made linkages between Zionism and colonialism central to their scholarly endeavors.

Regardless of their political stance, historians of Israel have sought to reconstruct the sensibilities and mental universe of their subjects, just as scholars of Israeli sociology have focused on broad sociocultural and economic structures. Traditional Zionist historiography emphasized that the founders of the state of Israel did not think of their enterprise as colonial in nature and, in fact, abhorred contemporary European colonialism for its parasitical profiting from the expropriation of native land and the exploitation of native labor. Classic Israeli social science, in turn, has contended that the Zionist movement and Yishuv did not conform to any conventional model of a colonizing state and that the structural barriers between Jewish and Arab society before 1948 were so great as to render impossible any consideration of the Jewish–Arab relationship as one between colonizers and colonized.

Some of the more recent Israeli historiography, on the other hand, claims that Zionist thinking, like that of *fin-de-siècle* Europeans as a whole, operated on multiple levels and that feelings of benevolence, humanitarianism, and sympathy could easily blend with condescending, Orientalist, and racist views of the Palestinian Arabs. Israel's current crop of critical sociologists, claiming that Jews and Arabs in pre-1948 Palestine constituted a common socioeconomic and political matrix, argue that Zionism conformed closely with typical European settlement-colonialism, in which, as Ronen Shamir has put it, "employers and employees belong to the same ethnic group ...

and in which that ethnic group has effective control over the land in ways that enable it to extract and utilize its resources."[1]

One serious problem with the discussion on the relationship between Zionism and colonialism is the attempt to establish complete congruence or total separation between the two phenomena. Another, related, problem is the failure to include additional categories of analysis such as anti-colonialism (Zionism as an act of resistance by a colonized people) and post-colonial state-building (understanding Israel within the political and economic framework of twentieth-century Asia and Africa). This chapter will contend that the Zionist project was historically and conceptually situated between colonial, anti-colonial, and post-colonial discourse and practice. Colonial and anti-colonial elements co-existed in the Zionist project from its inception until the creation of the state in 1948. From the time of Herzl onward, the Zionist political elite was eager to appeal to the interests of the Great Powers, and the Zionist movement as a whole was shot through with Orientalist conceptions of Arab degeneracy and primitiveness. At the same time, pre-state Zionism possessed anti-colonial elements present in sundry national liberation movements in the modern world. Moreover, underlying Zionist thought, preceding and running alongside of it, was the European Jewish intelligentsia's historic struggle, from the time of the Jewish Enlightenment until the twentieth century, to defend Jewish culture against that of the dominant Christian society through strategies similar to those employed by the colonized intelligentsia of Asia and Africa.

After 1948, the young state of Israel, like many countries in Asia and Africa, translated the anti-colonialist rhetoric of victimization into a triumphant post-colonial discourse of technical planning and state socialism. Yet colonialist elements were present as well in the treatment of Israel's Arab minority and state confiscation of its land. Israeli territorial conquests in the 1967 war, although fueled mainly by security concerns, evoked powerful feelings of manifest destiny as well as a lust for profit, thus highlighting the colonialist aspects of the Zionist project and causing many of Israel's critics to adopt a longstanding Arab discourse of Zionism as a purely colonialist movement from the start.

Unlike most of the literature on Zionism's relationship with colonialism, which tends to employ comparative models solely in order to incriminate or exculpate Zionist thought and practice, my intent here is to build a two-way street, in which a comparative approach can throw new light on our understanding of not only Zionism but also the historic relationship between colonialism and nationalism throughout the globe. I draw here on some essential texts in post-colonial studies, especially the work of Partha Chatterjee, whose theoretical models of anti-colonial nationalism, although based on the particular case of Bengal, suggest many intriguing points of contiguity between the Zionist project and anti-colonial movements. Dialectically, however, my use of post-colonial texts to deconstruct current conceptions of Zionism's relationship with colonialism will deconstruct the texts themselves, for, I believe, scholars such as Chatterjee are prone to essentialize anti-colonial movements and unjustly deny their grounding in classic European nationalism.[2] In other words, by depicting Zionism as in many ways an anti-colonial movement and Israel as having resembled, at least for its first two decades, a post-colonial state – by placing Zionism in Asia, as it were – I will be re-placing Zionism in Europe, a continent distinguished by not only the great overseas empires of the West but also a sizeable body of colonized, stateless peoples, including Jews.

In this chapter I draw a distinction between post-colonial discourse and post-colonial practice. When first used in the 1950s, the "post-colonial" referred to a historical moment, when Europe's former colonial possessions became independent. Since the 1970s, however, post-colonialism has mutated from a descriptive category into a conceptual framework for critiquing western forms and relations of power. (Thus the de-hyphenization of the term; from the delimited temporal and spatial realm of "the post-colonial world," emphasizing transition, to the diffuse and overarching intellectual field of "post-colonialism") Whereas post-colonial states were frequently the creation of nationalist movements, post-colonialism, according to Robert Young, one of the subject's most eminent scholars, "always operates as a form of internationalism," because nationalism is, in his view, inherently oppressive, and new tri-continental (Asian/African/Latin American) states that adopt European nationalist sensibilities and practices have internalized the evils of the oppressor.[3] I do not share this view, which robs the anti-colonial nationalist movements of the power of judgment, and which, as I argue at the end of the chapter, overlooks nationalism's transcendence of its European origins to become a global vehicle of collective identity.

Modern European colonialism took many forms, the principal ones being settler colonialism, in which substantial numbers of Europeans established permanent communities that became extensions of the homeland; penal colonialism, where Europe's dangerous classes were shipped off to distant terrain (for example Australia); and exploitation colonialism, wherein the natural resources and indigenous population of lands in the New World, Africa, and Asia were harnessed in the service of the motherland or of a private company licensed by the state (for example the British East India Company). The exploitation of native labor, as well as the expropriation of native lands, could occur in all three types of colonialism. The two phenomena were, at times, causally linked, in that expropriation could stimulate the formation of a landless rural population, which then provided cheap labor on plantations and in workshops and factories. On the other hand, the two could develop separately; settlement-colonialism frequently displaced the native from his land so that it might be worked by members of the colonizers' nationality.

It is tempting to classify Zionism as a form of settlement-colonialism, not only because of the large numbers of Jews who immigrated to Palestine but also because of the speed with which they indigenized, that is, became rooted in the land and came to think of it as their native land (as opposed to an abstract, distant object of desire, a "holy land" or "land of their ancestors" to which they would return in messianic days). In this regard the Zionist Yishuv resembled the settlement of the Boers in South Africa or the British colonists in early modern North America. Perhaps the most celebrated exponent of this view in the western world is the late Edward Said, who in a stream of writings decried the Zionists' eagerness to ally with the great colonial powers and the rapidity with which they engulfed, and then extruded, virtually the entire Palestinian nation.[4] A far more nuanced stance was adopted by the French scholar Maxine Rodinson in his thoughtful long essay *Israel: A Colonial-Settler State*, published in 1973. Rodinson displayed considerable sympathy with the Jews' historic attachment to the Land of Israel, and he believed that the aspiration to return to Zion was not, in and of itself, tainted by colonialism. Nor did he identify Zionist courting of the European powers with colonial ambition, since Arab nationalists did exactly the same thing in order to realize their own political aspirations. What made Zionism a form of settler-colonialism, in Rodinson's view, was the simple fact that Palestine was inhabited by an indigenous people and colonized by a European one.[5] Quoting the sociologist René Maunier, Rodinson wrote that: "One can speak of colonization when there is, and by the very fact that there is, *occupation with domination*: when there is, and by the very fact that there is, emigration with legislation."[6] That is, Zionists immigrated to Palestine, dominated it, and then legitimated their domination through legislation such as the Law of Return.

Rodinson contends that Zionism is a form of settler-colonialism but observes that colonialism has run throughout the entirety of human history, and so the only real difference between Zionism and past forms of European colonialism is its relative novelty. This argument is unassailable by dint of its excessive breadth. The period between the birth of Zionism and the birth of the state of Israel corresponded, more or less, to the era when European colonial domination reached its zenith. It is thus not surprising that the debate about Zionism's relationship with colonialism centers around its connections with or divergence from European practices of that period.

Fin-de-siècle European colonialism was fostered by a colonizing state, a key factor missing in the early Zionist movement. Until Israel's establishment in 1948 the various international Zionist agencies and the Zionist institutions of the Yishuv exercised highly limited authority over small portions of Palestine. It is often claimed that, after the collapse of the Ottoman Empire and the establishment of the British Mandate over Palestine, Britain came to play the role of colonizing state. The British Mandatory regime developed Palestine's physical infrastructure, sanctioned mass Jewish immigration, and encouraged the development of Jewish autonomous political and even military institutions.[7] Clearly, without British support the Zionist project would have died in the cradle. Yet Britain's role was inconsistent, vacillating between promoting and throttling the Zionist project. Britain was more a stepfather than a biological parent of the Jewish state. Thus even critics of Zionism such as Daniel Boyarin and Gershon Shafir have acknowledged that the Zionist movement lacked a "mother country" and so defies simplistic association with European settlement-colonialism.[8]

There are apparent parallels between the Zionist movement's nation-building practices and the exploitation and displacement models of colonial practice. The former manifested itself in the heavy reliance upon Arab labor in the Zionist plantation colonies and in certain urban industries. The level of exploitation, however, was exceedingly modest; during the Mandate period only about 5 percent of Palestine's Arabs worked in the Jewish sector, and their earnings made up only 7 percent of the Palestinian Arab national product.[9] Moreover, the use of Arab labor was not necessarily or purely colonial, as throughout the Arab world in the early twentieth century the development of capitalist agriculture tore peasants from their holdings and sent them into agricultural wage labor. Both Arabs and Jews owned citrus groves, and both employed Arab laborers on similar terms. The argument that Zionism aspired from the start to displace the local population points to the Zionist national institutions' assiduous purchase of Arab-owned land and restrictive access to it to Jews alone. Indeed, there are many documented cases, from the turn of the century through the 1930s, of Jewish land purchases causing the displacement of Palestinian peasants, yet the overall dimensions of the phenomenon are difficult to determine, as is the overall importance of displacement as opposed to other factors in the movement of Palestinian laborers from the countryside to the cities during the Mandate period.[10]

Critics of Zionism as a form of displacement colonialism not only point to Jewish land purchases but also claim that from the time of Herzl onward the Zionist movement intended to expel the native Palestinian population. Until the intensification of the Zionist–Palestinian conflict during the mid-1930s, however, there was little discussion, public or private, of systematic removal of Arabs from Jewish-owned land.[11] A discourse of expulsion did not develop even when Zionists explicitly invoked European nationality conflicts as models for their own actions. (Thus, for example, in 1908 the World Zionist Organization (WZO) planned to establish a publicly funded colonization company along the lines of the Prussian Colonization Commission, which sought to strengthen the German presence in Prussian Poland. Zionist bureaucrats blithely cited both the Prussian Commission's colonization of German settlers and Polish countermeasures, such as agricultural co-operatives to assist Polish freeholding peasants, as models of the mobilization of public direction and expertise, on the one hand, and private capital, on the other, for the public good.)[12] The tumultuous events of the years 1936–45 introduced an aggressive, militant tone into Zionist political rhetoric, which did not shy away from a possible "transfer" of Palestinians. But neither this rhetoric nor the mass expulsions that in fact did occur during the 1948 War can be assimilated within a colonialist analytical framework. The war was not a colonial uprising, but rather an existential conflict between two nationalities.

Although the consequences of Zionist settlement up to World War II did not assume the grand dimensions of European colonialism, the Zionist project's means and methods, its underlying sensibilities regarding Palestine and its inhabitants, were shot through with colonial mentalities. Within a few years of its founding in 1897, the WZO tried to assume the role of a colonizing state. It overtly emulated European practices by establishing a colonial bank, funding research and experimentation in tropical agriculture, and supporting capitalist joint-stock companies that, like their counterparts in the service of European imperialism, were hoped to yield, eventually, a profit to their shareholders. The instrumental rationality, bureaucratic procedure, and expectation of sustained profit that characterize modern colonialism (and distinguish it from mere conquest) were all present in the early Zionist project. The WZO's attempts to take on the mantle of the colonizing state, however, failed, primarily due to a lack of means. Moreover, although the officers of the WZO had few qualms about linking their enterprise with European colonialism, their colonization schemes did not call for the exploitation of native labor (as was the case in the African colonial societies sponsored by the Zionist leader Otto Warburg, who hoped to set up profitable plantation colonies in Palestine but assumed that the laborers would be Jewish).

Zionist discourse conformed in many ways to the colonialist and Orientalist sensibilities of *fin-de-siècle* European society. Zionism contained a powerful *mission civilisatrice* to awaken the Middle East from what was believed to be a narcotized Levantine torpor, to shatter the fossilized soil of the Holy Land with European tools and technology. One of the most powerful motifs in Zionist thought, the desertification of Palestine under Arab and Turkish rule and the Zionist mission to make the desert bloom, was shared by many Europeans, who attributed the naturally arid ecology of the Middle East to human malfeasance. French colonialists claimed, for example, that in antiquity Algeria had been the breadbasket of Rome but under Berber rule had become barren and malarial.[13] Moreover, Zionists, like Europeans in general, both romanticized and scorned the Middle East's native peoples. Zionists exalted the Bedouin as the true son of the desert, and some residents of the Yishuv, particularly students, laborers, and guards, dressed in Arab fashion as an expression of their sense of return to reclaim their ancient Middle Eastern patrimony. This sentimental idealization of the noble savage, however, was overlaid by powerful feelings of moral and material superiority. The Palestinian peasant was often perceived by Zionists as an ignoble savage, uncouth and backward. The most benign Zionist impulses to offer Arabs the fruits of western technology and to present a model of bourgeois social relations were imbedded in a project to control, direct, and regulate all affairs in the Land of Israel. This blend of feelings of familial affinity and paternalist superiority was manifested in the Zionist claim that the Palestinian Arabs, or "Arabs of the Land of Israel," as they were called, were the descendants of ancient Hebrews who had been cut off from Jewish civilization and slowly devolved, preserving shards of the ancient Hebrew customs and language.

Such views towards Arabs could be understood in terms of Mary Louise Pratt's concept of the "anti-conquest," "strategies of representation whereby European bourgeois subjects seek to secure their innocence in the very moment that they assert European hegemony."[14] Zionism certainly contained Orientalist elements, and it constructed elaborate moral justifications for its colonization project. At the same time, its discursive framework differed from that of European overseas colonialism in intriguing ways, as, for example, in its assertion of familial propinquity, however distant, with the Arabs. As opposed to Joseph Conrad's nightmarish vision of the corruption of the white man who journeys into the heart of African darkness, Conrad's contemporary, the Hebrew writer Moshe Smilansky, presented Jewish contact with the Bedouin and Druze of Palestine as literally an ennobling experience. In Smilansky's writing, celebration of the Arab must be understood in terms not of western romanticization of the utterly alien noble but rather of Russian depictions of the semi-Asiatic Caucasian Muslim as intrinsically Russian.[15] Of course, the Caucasian Muslim in imperial Russia was, no less than the Palestinian Arab, a colonized figure; what interests us here is the differing strategies of and justifications for domination.

Whereas the topos of the Arab as sexual object figured prominently in Orientalist fantasy (the object was usually female but at times male, as in André Gide's novel *The Immoralist*), the sexualized Arab rarely figured in literature or public speech as an object of Zionist desire.[16] Although there were surely romantic and sexual contacts between Jews and Arabs in early twentieth-century Palestine (this subject requires serious exploration), the issue of miscegenation, the source of such great anxiety and public debate in French, Dutch, and German colonialism, scarcely rippled the waters of Zionist discourse. In early twentieth-century Germany, female colonial activists had to struggle for the legitimization of the woman as a colonizing agent in the form of the settler's wife (as opposed to the native concubine), while in the Zionist movement and the Yishuv the Jewish woman was, from the start, accorded a central role as wife and mother, and, indeed, the socialist Zionist women's movement's struggle to replace that ideal-type with the female pioneer laborer attests to the significance and tenacity of the former.[17] Perhaps the difference between the two situations may be attributed to the fact that German colonialism was primarily an exploitative venture, in which men sought adventure and release from the confines of the domestic sphere, whereas Zionism represented a form of settlement-colonialism, which, as in North America, frequently involved families immigrating as a whole.

Our discussion thus far has focused on the Zionist movement's relation with Palestinian Arabs, with whom Zionists claimed a hazy affinity while asserting their absolute cultural superiority. This claim of propinquity came into much sharper focus when the Zionist leadership and intelligentsia, which was overwhelmingly Ashkenazic, turned its attention to Jews of the Middle East (Mizrahim). Zionists followed in the tracks of the Alliance Israélite Universelle, a Paris-based organization that, in the last third of the nineteenth century, established a network of schools for Jewish youth throughout the Mashrek and Maghreb. As agents of French language and culture in the Middle East, the teachers of the Alliance were suffused with a *mission civilisatrice* very much in keeping with the cultural goals of French colonialism.[18] Ashkenazic Zionists, in turn, considered their Middle Eastern brethren to be degenerate yet improvable "human material," to employ the commonly used term from the interwar period.[19] Those who had been least exposed to western influences (for example the Jews of Yemen) were seen as petrified exemplars of the ancient Hebrews (Galapagos Jews, as it were). Precisely because they were believed to be true Orientals, however, Yemenite Jews were also perceived as "natural laborers" who could compete successfully with Arabs, performing backbreaking agricultural work at low wages. (With this goal in mind, in 1912 the WZO's Palestine Office recruited Yemenite Jews to immigrate to Palestine; a contingent of them labored on the lands of the Kinneret training farm, only to be summarily expelled in 1930 when the land was needed for new immigrants from Eastern Europe.)[20] On the other hand, the highly urbanized Jews of Iraq were perceived as degenerate because of their assimilation into Arab culture and their advanced state of secularization. Thus during the early 1940s Histadrut emissaries in Iraq conceived of the Jews in that land as requiring not only physical rescue but also a physical and spiritual regeneration in the Land of Israel.[21] Throughout the Mandate period, American and European Zionists active in a variety of social-welfare projects (for example the Hadassah Medical Organization) conceived of Palestine's Mizrahi Jews and Arabs alike as socially and culturally backward and in need of the blessings of western civilization.

It has become fashionable to claim that from the Zionist movement's very beginnings the Ashkenazic Zionist stance towards Middle Eastern Jews was pronouncedly colonialist.[22] As I will argue below, there is good reason to make a claim for a colonialist policy by the Israeli state during the period of the great immigration from the Mashrek and Maghreb. Before 1948, however, Zionist institutions had limited abilities to command the fate of Jews in Palestine, and virtually none in the rest of the world. To the extent that colonialist elements suffused the Zionist movement's position towards Mizrahi Jews, these were more cultural than operational. It is certainly possible to employ the term "colonial" to describe not merely physical domination but also cultural hegemony, not governmentality but collective mentality, but if we are to do so then we must be willing to apply this concept to the historic status of European, and not only Mizrahi, Jews as a colonized people. Only then can we understand why Zionism, even when espoused by an Ashkenazic elite and suffused with colonial motifs, represented the ultimate phase of a European Jewish anti-colonial discourse that dated back to the early nineteenth century.

In an essay on colonial practice in *fin-de-siècle* French Indochina and the Dutch East Indies, Ann Stoler writes of the profound anxiety caused to colonial administrators by the phenomenon of miscegenation between European males and native females. The offspring of such unions were said to create an economic problem by producing an underclass of paupers, yet the threat that these children posed to their colonial masters was clearly cultural in nature. A child neglected by his European father but dutifully raised by his native mother was said to have been abandoned, and thus subject to government action, whereas the abandoned children of native fathers were objects of neither concern nor tutelary policy. Children of mixed unions were considered potentially improvable because of their European blood; in fact, if raised as wards of the state, they could form "the bulwark of a future white settler population, acclimatized to the tropics but loyal to the state."[23] In Indochina and the East Indies French and Dutch citizenship were granted to *métis* via an examination of the supplicants' racial fitness, mastery of the colonizer's language and culture, and demonstrated commitment to leave behind the world into which they had been born.

Stoler's description of French and Dutch policies and attitudes towards their colonial subjects can be easily mapped onto attitudes and policies towards Jews in eighteenth- and nineteenth-century Europe. Emancipation was granted on a quid pro quo basis. Cultural and economic regeneration – that is, mastery of the host society's language, the adoption of reigning cultural mores, and a movement from the traditional practice of peddling to livelihoods in crafts and agriculture – were considered either preconditions for citizenship (as in the German states) or immediate and necessary outcomes of the attainment of citizenship (as in France). For Jews in post-Napoleonic Prussian Poland, as for Indo-Europeans in colonial southeast Asia, citizenship was granted on a case-by-case basis, the result of a rigorous yet arbitrary examination procedure. Proposals made in the late nineteenth century by colonial officials to establish agricultural colonies for the regeneration of the Indo-European poor had their parallel in the era of enlightened absolutism, when reformist bureaucrats in Prussia, Austria, and Russia championed, and at times established, colonies to train Jews in productive labor.[24]

Much of the recent literature on the colonial encounter probes the complex reaction of the colonized intelligentsia to the blandishments of the West, the inability to achieve full acceptance, and the simultaneous desire to preserve and transform indigenous cultures. Throughout Asia and Africa, intellectuals compensated for their economic and military inferiority *vis-à-vis* the West by asserting the moral and spiritual superiority of the colonized nation versus the powerful, but allegedly spiritually bankrupt, European powers. For example, in India, Vivekananda's Ramakrishna mission, founded in

1897, refashioned Hinduism into a bulwark against the West, which allegedly inculcated spiritual discipline into its adherents through yoga and meditation, and stimulated national solidarity by preaching the necessity of social action.[25] Here, as well as in such diverse lands as Thailand (Siam), Meiji Japan, and late Ottoman Egypt, the locus of collective identity was presented by intellectuals as found in the realms of culture, religion, and historical commemoration, which could lead to a purification of contemporary ways of thinking and a return to lost glory.

Moreover, colonized intellectuals in various lands claimed that the colonized peoples' material disadvantage was the result of their culture's unjustified and tragic rejection of science and technology, which had been essential elements of the pristine sources of the indigenous culture (for example Islam, Hinduism, Buddhism). Siam's King Rama IV (1851–68) ascribed opposition to scientific inquiry within Buddhism to pollution from Hinduism, whereas in the predominantly Hindu Bengal early Indian nationalists located the source of their technological decline in Islamic influences.[26]

King Rama's distinction between Buddhism's rich spiritual heritage and the cold truths of western science, and his well-tempered statement that each is necessary to human well-being, find their Jewish-historical parallel in the Haskalah, the Jewish variant of the European Enlightenment. One of the Haskalah's pioneering texts, Naphtali Hirsch Wessely's *Words of Peace and Truth* (1782–5), distinguishes between the "torah of God" and the "torah of man" and calls for a new appreciation of the latter in Jewish education. Like Thai, Bengali, and Egyptian intellectuals in the late nineteenth century, Wessely and his fellow adherents of the late eighteenth- and nineteenth-century Haskalah claimed that their religious culture was inherently open to scientific inquiry but had been tainted by superstition. Such arguments were made by maskilim throughout Europe, yet they were particularly prevalent in the German lands, which were home to ideologically rigorous movements for reform within Judaism and for the systematic study of Jewish texts following the norms of western scholarship. In the first half of the 1800s, champions of Reform Judaism attributed the superstitions that allegedly stunted the Jews' worldly knowledge to baleful Christian influences, just as Asian intellectuals besmirched neighboring or competing religions. And, like colonized Asian intellectuals who used western methods to study their civilizations' classic texts, practitioners of the Wissenschaft des Judentums, that is, the study of the Jewish lettered tradition outside the pietist parameters of that tradition, adumbrated Asia's colonized intelligentsia in their compensation for powerlessness by locating the essence of Jewish civilization, and its justification for continued existence, entirely in the realm of spiritual and literary creativity. As Susannah Heschel has argued in her study of Abraham Geiger, the founder of Liberal Judaism in Germany, Geiger's writings on the Pharisaic roots of Jesus's teaching can be interpreted "in [Edward] Said's terms as a revolt of the colonized against Christian hegemony."[27] Geiger, like the mobilized, anti-colonial intellectual, turned a proud and defiant gaze towards the dominator, appropriating his discourse not merely to refute claims to superiority but also to reverse the dominator–dominated power relationship.

The division between body and spirit, between the physical and the metaphysical, that was central to post-Cartesian Christian civilization had worked its way into Jewish culture already in the seventeenth century, stimulating astronomical, medical, and (al)chemical inquiry. The Haskalah, Reform Judaism, and the *Wissenschaft des Judentums*, however, contained a revolutionary and totalizing agenda not found previously in the realms of Jewish thought. The modernizing movements within Judaism claimed the right to abrogate centuries of interpretive tradition and to base faith and practice entirely on a rationalistic reading of ancient authoritative texts. This transformation of Judaism was paralleled in early nineteenth-century India by Rammohan Roy, who invented a laicized, rationalized Hinduism that drew solely on the ancient Hindu scriptures, the Upanishads, and their philosophic commentaries, the Vedanta.[28]

Abraham Geiger dismissed much of rabbinic Judaism as a lifeless husk encasing Judaism's biblical, monotheistic essence, and Leopold Zunz, the greatest of the early exponents of secular Judaic scholarship, excavated the literary riches of the Jewish past to demonstrate its superiority to contemporary arid talmudism. The Indian parallel to the work of these men, a *Wissenschaft des Hinduismus*, if you will, came into its own in the 1870s with the founding by Dayananda Saravati of the Arya Samaj. The Arya Samaj saw in the Vedanta a fixed, textual base for a rationalized Hindu religion. The Arya Samaj presented ancient Vedic religion as monotheistic and egalitarian, far superior to its degenerate Hindu successor, which had allegedly been corrupted by polytheism and the introduction of the caste system.[29] Like the proponents of Jewish *Wissenschaft*, Hindu reformers accepted western scholarly methods, for a rationalized religion depended upon standardized, critical editions of sacred texts.

Among both Jews and Hindus, religious reform and textual scholarship were part of a broad movement for cultural renewal, of which education was an essential part. Like the maskilim in Europe, the Arya Samaj founded schools to educate Indian children as an alternative to the schools of the colonizer, in this case western missionaries. Cultural renewal also sought to rearrange and stabilize gender relationships. According to Partha Chatterjee, Bengali literature in the late nineteenth century contained a strong criticism of the politically emasculated and feminized *babu*, or middle-class male. Misogynistic discourse about women as seducers of and lords over men was a projection of the *babu*'s fears of his own loss of traditional culture and emasculation at the hand of the colonial state. The *babu*, then, had much in common with the *balabat*, the Jewish householder, who was presented in classic Yiddish literature as talkative but impotent, and dominated by bossy females.

Comparing Chatterjee with recent work by the Jewish historians Marion Kaplan and Paula Hyman, we see both Jewish and Indian writers in the late nineteenth century accusing women of leaping to assimilate into the colonizers' culture, thereby neglecting their duties as mothers of the nation and preservers of religious ritual. These accusations were themselves yet another form of projection, for among both Jews and Indians men comprised the bulk of the vanguard undergoing assimilation. Women, largely confined to the home, maintained religious traditions within the intimate sphere of the family while the observance of pubic ritual experienced decline.[30]

An essential component of early Indian and Jewish nationalism was a defensive, secular historiography that posited the continuous existence of a united people (what Benedict Anderson calls a "bound seriality"),[31] whose fall from ancient glory was the result of random chance and human action, not divine will. Traditional Hindu historiography, like the historical consciousness of biblical and rabbinic Judaism, interpreted the course of human events as the result of divine providence, which rewarded and punished the leaders of the faith and people according to their observance of the divine way, be it dharma or halakhah. Although Jewish historical thinking began to secularize in the sixteenth century, in the wake of the expulsion of the Jews from Spain, Hindu scholars were accounting for the Muslim and British conquests of India within this sacred-historical framework as late as the mid-1800s. But in the 1870s Hindu historiography adopted modern western conceptual norms, with the result being a body of writing in many ways parallel to the great works of Jewish historical writing of the age. Heinrich Graetz's magisterial *History of the Jews*, like Tarnicharan Chattopadhyay's *History of India*, blended staggering erudition with proto-nationalist apologetics. Both authors molded history by compartmentalizing it into distinct periods, separated by particular events that became synecdoches for the nation as a whole. History moved from the periphery to the center of consciousness; the nationalist project was presented as an act of restoration as much as one of revolutionary transformation.[32]

The comparisons I am offering between the Jewish and Asian intelligentsia might appear forced because, prior to the rise of Zionism, the former rarely thought of themselves as colonized, but rather as members of a religious minority. Even in Russia, where the status of Jews was hobbled by legal restrictions and governmental policy was often steeped in Judeophobia, maskilim believed themselves to be deeply rooted within their lands of residence and foresaw the day where in Russia, as in most of Central and Western Europe, emancipation would transform Jews into enfranchised citizens and capitalism would make them into prosperous burghers. The sense of confidence in the Jewish future was far greater still in most of the Hapsburg Empire, the German states, and Western Europe. In an environment suffused with such irenicism, one could argue, Jewish intellectuals did not engage in colonial mimicry (to employ Homi Bhabha's celebrated concept);[33] rather, they were no more or less European than their Christian fellow countrymen. There was, however, a clearly apologetic, defensive component in the Haskalah and *Wissenschaft* movements that differentiates

them from their general European counterparts, the Enlightenment and historicism. The popularization of scientific discourse in the Jewish press was far more than an instrument of mass education through the dissemination of useful knowledge; it was seen as a vehicle for the collective transformation of a people psychically stunted by talmudism. Jewish intellectuals in nineteenth-century Europe may have felt that time was on their side, but they were nonetheless engaged in a vigorous campaign to refashion Judaism, not merely to be accepted into European society, but also to protect Jewish life from the blandishments of both Christianity and secularism, to engage in a carefully thought-out process of imitation in order to prevent assimilation. The material conditions of life for European Jews and Asians differed greatly, as did the relations of power with the European hegemonic powers, but the thought processes of Jewish and Asian intellectuals were similar, including those that led to the development of nationalist ideologies. It is no surprise, then, that aspects of Zionism resemble anti-colonial national movements, although there were spectacular differences as well.

Partha Chatterjee has traced the transition in nineteenth-century Bengali thought between the rationalist and universalist trends of Hindu reform movements and the rejection of those trends late in the century by an anti-rational, mystical glorification of the Indian national spirit. For example, the lower-caste mystic Ramakrishna, who became the object of a cult in the 1880s, glorified the "ancient Hindu national ideal" of ecstatic asceticism.[34] Ramakrishna's emphasis on myth rather than rationality, and on myth's power to fuel nationalistic sentiment, found its counterpart in a major stream of Zionist ideology, beginning with Micha Berdichevsky and finding its most scholarly exponent in Gershom Scholem, who rejected the rationalism of the *Wissenschaft des Judentums* and embraced kabbalah as the primary manifestation throughout the ages of Jewish vitalist spirit.

As the late Amos Funkenstein observed, the Zionist project was fueled by two contradictory conceptions of human nature, romantic and materialist. The former defined man as ineffable, spontaneous spirit, and the latter operated within grooves cut by economic laws, "stychic" social processes (to use Ber Borochov's terminology), and a search for "human material" to be shaped by Zionist apparatchiks into a productive laboring nation.[35] The nationalization of the masses had to be rationally planned even when it involved stoking irrational collective feeling. Thus anti-colonial movements, and the post-colonial states that succeeded them, featured aspects of hyper-rational, utopian planning while pooling reservoirs of tribal solidarity and fury against the colonizer.

Consider the case of women's suffrage, which was the subject of almost two centuries of debate in the West and which only came to France and Switzerland after World War II. As Sylvia Walby has noted, post-colonial states have granted women the franchise at the time of the states' establishment. Political citizenship is granted to all adults at the time of state-creation as an expression of a populist sentiment and a legitimization of the overthrow of non-representative colonial rule. As Chatterjee writes of India, nationalists asserted that the entire people had been nationalized; that is, vested with a distinct and unifying Indianness. The entire nation, having been feminized by the colonial power, was to be emancipated in one fell swoop.[36] This conceptual framework is of benefit for the study of Zionism, for it helps account for the WZO's early granting of voting rights to women (for the second Zionist Congress of 1898, at a time when only New Zealand had national female suffrage) and the passion with which all but ultra-Orthodox members of the Yishuv advocated women's suffrage after World War I.

State-building in the post-colonial world demands direction, planning, and regulation. Chatterjee's important essay on the role of planning and technical expertise in modern Indian nationalism helps us to pinpoint the point of departure between Zionism and anti-colonial movements, and between Israel and post-colonial states.[37] For Chatterjee, economic planning, like the woman's suffrage mentioned above, is a form of state legitimization, through which the state appears to rise above individual interests and promotes a Gramscian "passive revolution" in which modest reforms are accomplished but pre-capitalist elites are not annihilated. Economic planning is outside of the politics of the state but deeply imbricated with it. For most Third World countries, India included, such planning has focused primarily on industrialization, with agriculture more likely to be left to the private sector.

The comparisons with the situation of the Jews in the twentieth century are striking. For the Jews, there has been, even after the creation of the state of Israel and certainly before it, no unifying state to orchestrate economic development. Yet world Jewry has formed a unit more cohesive than an ethnic group or stateless nationality. Thanks to their economic and philanthropic elite (often one and the same), Jews the world over have been joined up into a quasi-polity, whose members, unlike those of a state, cannot be confidently tallied up and located in a particular space. Rather, this entity resembles, to use another of Benedict Anderson's terms, an "unbound seriality," borderless but finite. Nor did twentieth-century Jewry have to contend with pre-capitalist elites cluttering up the developmental landscape. Indeed, the Jews' elites have been among the West's princes of capitalism.

During the first half of the twentieth century, the Zionist movement created a proto-state, in which planning was indeed a form of legitimization, of imagining the nation by asserting the authority to set the course of the nation-building enterprise. Like post-colonial states, the Zionist movement and early state of Israel venerated technical expertise; the engineer, along with the farmer and warrior, was part of the pantheon of Zionist heroes. In Zionism, however, the position of the colonial state in Third World developmental nationalism was replaced by an opponent as amorphous and unbounded as the Jews themselves: the diaspora, which had allegedly distorted the healthy political, economic, and spiritual structures of ancient Israel and had rendered the Jews dysfunctional.

Because Jews have constituted an unbounded nation, Zionists were not the only agents of Jewish social engineering in the last century. During the formative decades of the Yishuv, a number of international Jewish philanthropic organizations, often better funded than the Zionists, attempted mass colonization of Jews in lands as far flung as Argentina and Ukraine. Zionism's developmental ethos and its program of massive Jewish social and economic change appealed to Jewish philanthropies of virtually every stripe. Thus in 1929 non-Zionists in the United States were mobilized to serve Zionist political goals through the expanded Jewish Agency for Palestine, while the Yishuv's material needs were attended to during the interwar period by organizations such as the Palestine Economic Corporation, which received much of its funding from the New York-based Joint Distribution Committee. Both Zionists and the array of non-Zionist Jewish philanthropies shared an eccentric developmental agenda that focused, unlike the case in post-colonial states, on agricultural rather than industrial planning. The reason for this reversal was ostensibly because the Jews' particular concentration in urban occupations, particularly commerce, and the economic needs of the sites of Jewish social engineering (for the Jewish Colonization Association, the Argentinean pampas; for the Joint Distribution Committee, Crimea and the Ukraine; for the Zionists, Palestine) demanded the creation of a class of Jewish agriculturalists.

Much of the motivation behind the agrarian orientation of the agents of Jewish social engineering, however, was ideological – apologetic, romantic, or socialist. After all, contemporary Israel has become exactly what Revisionist Zionists, whose economic views differed sharply from not only Labor Zionism but also most Jewish philanthropies, called for: an industrialized city-state that imports raw goods and cheap labor and exports high-technology products. Thus the motives behind the Zionist project had little in common with those of western settlement-colonialism but also did not fit well with the developmental world-view of post-colonial state-building.

Our discussion demonstrates that at a certain point comparisons between Zionism, on the one hand, and colonialism or post-colonial states, on the other, are no longer valuable except as tools for highlighting the eccentric, distinctive qualities of the Zionist project on the world stage. Attempts to force the Zionist project into Chatterjee's theoretical framework of an anti-colonial nationalism and post-colonial state yield valuable new ways of perceiving Israel, yet ultimately they fall short, not only because of Zionism's unique features, but also because Chatterjee fails to satisfactorily distinguish anti-colonial nationalism and post-colonial policy from their European predecessors, which are, in fact, Zionism's true parents.

Chatterjee's desire to essentialize the colonized nation leads him to juxtapose western, liberal politics, allegedly based on the mechanistic principals of majority rule and legitimized by atomized, individual voters, and what he claims is the consensus-based politics of post-colonial states.[38] In fact, a politics of consensus characterized many modern European states, including Imperial Germany, in which the chancellor and cabinet were not responsible to parliament, and the Italian kingdom, which was managed through a constant process of give and take between members of a minuscule political and economic elite. The failure of the international Zionist movement or the Yishuv's representative bodies during the interwar period to function as paragons of representative democracy, therefore, does not in any way remove the Zionist project from mainstream *fin-de-siècle* European statecraft, let alone the rough and tumble world of politics among socialists and national minorities in Eastern Europe.

Chatterjee attempts to refute Anderson's claim that the modern nation-state is a western conceptual category that predetermined the form and content of anti-colonial collective identities. Chatterjee posits a distinction between western and post-colonial states, claiming that the former, having long performed their national identities through the free exercise of power, have been sufficiently secure in their identities as to leave the realms of education, religion, and familial affairs to the private realm. Postcolonial states, on the other hand, have been forced to make such area matters central to state policy, for these had formed the core of the colonized people's identity during the period of struggle with the West.[39] This distinction, of course, has not historically existed; the modern state has been an increasingly invasive entity from the days of absolutism through the era of social-welfare states in the mid-twentieth century. Moreover, virtually all forms of European nationalism have stressed the cultural uniqueness of the people and the obligation of the state, or, in the case of stateless peoples, the intelligentsia, to preserve and promote the national culture.

Zionism's *mission civilisatrice* was directed primarily at Jews, not the indigenous Arabs of Palestine. It was not primarily a manifestation of a colonial will to power; nor was it merely a response to centuries of gentile criticisms of Jewish social and economic behavior. As a European nationalist movement, Zionism could not help but have a powerful pedagogic and developmental dynamic. In the late eighteenth century, German states expected Jews to undergo, as the bureaucrat Christian Friedrich Wilhelm von Dohm put it, "civil improvement," but the same expectations were held for other social groups considered to be unproductive. Hence the appearance in Germany in the 1780s of books with titles such as *On the Civil Improvement of Women* and *On the Civil Improvement of Monks.* Similarly, the demand upon the Jews in revolutionary France to undergo "regeneration" had at first been applied to the people of France as a whole, as part of the revolutionary project to forge a homogeneous French nation, language, and culture.[40] A century later, French Jewry's ongoing efforts to fully acculturate were paralleled by the Third Republic's gradual transformation of, to cite Eugene Weber's memorable phrase, "peasants into Frenchmen." The Zionist aim of transforming "Jews into Israelis" was unique not so much in the project of nationalization as in its overwhelming difficulty, in that the nationalization of the Jews demanded the rapid and laborious creation of its own preconditions, for example the presence of a population *in situ*, a rudimentary national economy, and a body of indigenous folk culture.

Chatterjee depicts the historian as the craftsman of the modern Indian nation, but of course the same can be said of any land in nineteenth-century Europe. Augustin Thierry and François Guizot in France, Johann Gustav Droysen and Heinrich von Treitschke in Germany, Pasquale Villari and Gioacchino Volpe in Italy, all claimed to engage in a scholarly enterprise, based on a careful accumulation of evidence and free of prejudgments, yet still compelled, in Villari's words, not by "merely a scientific need, but a moral duty" to demonstrate the historical roots of national unification.[41] (How rare was Benedeto Croce's tart statement of 1916 that "the history of Italy is not ancient or centuries old but *recent*, not outstanding but *modest*, not radiant but *labored*."[42]) Zionist ideology was well served by the Jews' unusually high level of textual production and by the long history of Jewish communal autonomy, which provided Zionist historians such as Ben-Zion Dinur ample evidence, reproduced in his multi-volume anthology *Yisrael Bagolah* (Israel in Exile), that the Jewish collectivity had, throughout the historic depth and geographic breadth of the diaspora, comprised a coherent national body, which, through Zionism, was merely fulfilling its long-standing and inevitable destiny. Although Villari's object of study on the other hand was a predominantly peasant culture, he, too, combed through the past to locate manifestations of the united *Volksgeist*, although in his case the evidence came largely from the realm of folk customs and lore.

The origins of modern European nationalism are steeped in controversy, as classic views emphasizing the centrality of nationalist ideology, created and disseminated by narrow intellectual elites, have been steadily replaced by a focus on socioeconomic transformation, uneven economic development, and the reshaping of pre-existing collective identities as the prime sources of popular nationalist sentiment. Nationalism may well have had eighteenth-century manifestations outside of Europe, as Anderson has argued of the socially frustrated and independent-minded "creole pioneers" of Latin America. Even within Europe nationalist sensibility could emerge from what was essentially a political conflict between metropole and creoles, as in Ireland at the time of the Act of Union, when Anglo-Irish landowners claimed to be true Irishmen, the natural-born stewards of the indigenous thralls. But it was precisely this sort of political conflict that stimulated the European intelligentsia to formulate nationalist ideology as early as the sixteenth century, and to frame the cult of national essence within issues of cultural production. Thus in Elizabethan England the unparalleled beauty of the English language and the unassailable virtue of English liberty were totally intertwined.[43] French nationalism, in turn, equated collective identity, morality, and culture, and featured a defensive ethos in which England was perceived as the dominant enemy. German nationalism emerged as a response to French cultural and political hegemony during the Napoleonic era, and so the chemical equation for a defensive nationalist ideology spread eastward and southward throughout the European continent.

Scholars in post-colonial studies strive to divorce the politics of the colonized from that of their colonizers. Chatterjee has devoted a dense, rich monograph (*Nationalist Thought and the Colonial World: A Derivative Discourse?*) to just this project, setting himself at the outset against the classic work of Elie Kedourie, who pronounced nationality theory to have been entirely, and uniquely, European in origin and to remain, in Chatterjee's words, "a prisoner of the European intellectual fashions," incapable of functioning as an autonomous discourse.[44] Yet, with the powerful exception of Mohandas Gandhi, the nationalist ideologues and political leaders who fill the pages of this book all espouse ideas with European equivalents, and, at many times, European roots. Throughout the book, Chatterjee intimates that the problematic of nationalism lies in bourgeois modernity as such, and that anti-colonial nationalisms, even while challenging "the colonial claim to political domination, . . . also accepted the very intellectual premises of 'modernity' upon which colonial domination was based."[45] Dipesh Chakrabarty, another post-colonial theorist working on modern India, finds that the only way to escape from the tyranny of European thinking, or, as he puts it, to "provincialize Europe," is to divest oneself of the nationalist project altogether, and by extension from modern historicism, whose developmental dynamic and homogenizing yet exclusivist forms of classification manifest themselves in and are sustained by nationalist sentiment. Chakrabarty concedes, however, the improbability of his project. With a Derridean flourish, he writes:

> the project of provincializing Europe must realize itself within its own impossibility. . . . This is a history that will attempt the impossible: to look towards its own death by tracing that which resists and escapes the best human effort at translation across cultural and other semiotic systems, so that the world may once again be imagined as radically heterogeneous.[46]

Chakrabarty's project is not only "impossible," it is elitist, for it denies the legitimacy of the self-consciousness of hundreds of millions of humans across the globe. It is also naïve for assuming that "radical heterogeneity" is consonant with legitimacy and authenticity. And here we come to the core of my argument. The fact that nationalism was a European cultural invention does not delegitimize or subordinate extra-European nationalist movements any more than modern mathematics in the West has been tainted by its dependence on the medieval Islamic invention of algebra. As in math and science, so too in the realms of philosophy and sensibility certain concepts enter global circulation and become fixtures in human consciousness. One may reject the existence of universal truths or beliefs but acknowledge that substantial portions of humanity share certain conceptual categories and employ similar methods for structuring reality and locating meaning. For much of the population of the globe over the past century, nationalism has functioned as an algebra of modernity, isolating and bringing to light the factors of ethnic solidarity, and then initiating *al-jabr*, the reunion of broken parts. Jews are but one of many dependent variables in this global equation, to which Zionism is one of many possible solutions.

Thus far I have set Zionism against the background of colonialism, anti-colonial movements, and post-colonial states. I have argued that Zionism is not merely a subset of the first and can, like the latter two, be simplified and rendered largely congruent with European nationalism. Zionism was a product of the age of imperialism; its adherents shared a number of common sensibilities with European advocates of colonial expansion in the Middle East. Yet the movement was more than a form of colonial practice. Enmeshed in a matrix of religious sensibility, political ideology, and historic circumstance, Zionism realized itself in the Middle East, an area chosen not for its strategic value, natural resources, or productive capabilities, but rather because of what Jews believed to be historic, religious, and cultural ties to the area known to them as the Land of Israel. To be sure, Zionism's call for a persecuted religious minority to build a new society in a distant land resembled the ideology of the Puritans, who spearheaded settler-colonialism in what would become the United States, but, whereas the Puritans saw North America as a *tabula rasa* upon which a new Jerusalem could be inscribed, Zionism was based in concepts of return, restoration and re-inscription. The fact that these concepts were social constructions of a particular time and place (nineteenth-century Europe), that they represented a profound rupture with traditional Jewish conceptions of the Land of Israel, and that Jewish political and settlement activism assaulted the longstanding Jewish discourse of eventual redemption in messianic time does not alter the assumptions of continuity and the claims of return inherent in Zionist ideology and sincerely held by its exponents. Finally, because Zionism's *mission civilisatrice* was directed almost entirely inward, to the Jews themselves, Zionism lacked the evangelical qualities of European colonialism in North America, Asia, and Africa, where conversion of the heathen to Christianity served as a justification, consequence, and, at times, a cause of colonial expansion.

Anti-colonialism's emphasis on cultural renewal, akin to cultural nationalism in nineteenth-century Poland, Bohemia, Ireland, and many other European lands, had its Jewish equivalent in the Haskalah and *Wissenschaft des Judentums*. These movements, which often denied Jewish national distinctiveness, were not Zionist despite themselves, playing the role of unwitting soldiers in a teleological march to full-blown nationalism. The Haskalah and *Wissenschaft des Judentums* were necessary but hardly sufficient preconditions for Zionism. Without challenges to emancipation in the West and brutal, state-sanctioned antisemitism in the East, Zionism would have been stillborn, just as, say, modern Thai nationalism would not have developed from its mid-nineteenth-century Buddhist reformist roots had France not seized lands traditionally under Siamese jurisdiction in the Mekong River valley.

The Arab Revolt of the late 1930s transformed the Palestinian Arab in the Zionist imagination from a natural part of the landscape into a coherent, hostile political force, an enemy that would have to be vanquished in the struggle to establish a Jewish state. During the 1948 War, hundreds of thousands of Palestinian Arabs were compelled to leave their homes, and after the war the Israeli state prevented the return of refugees, carried out massive expropriations of Arab land, and subjected the Galilee's Arabs to harsh military rule. Palestine was but one of many places on the globe in the mid-twentieth century where indigenous nationalities were expelled in the wake of state-creation. (The partition of India led to the forced migration of some 14 million souls. Ethnic cleansing and land confiscation/redistribution were widely practiced in post-1945 Eastern European successor states, and more than 10 million ethnic Germans were expelled from the Soviet Union.) Thus the most controversial aspects of Israeli actions towards Palestinians during the 1948 War and its aftermath were not uniquely colonial. A colonial sensibility may, however, be detected in the young Israeli state's educational policies towards its Arab population, in that a curriculum steeped in Hebrew literature, Jewish history, and Zionist ideology was imposed on to the defeated native population. Moreover, Israeli Palestinians, like other colonized peoples, responded by engaging in a complex process of refraction and manipulation of the hegemonic culture and political system (what Mary Louise Pratt has termed "transculturation"), leading to the creation of new forms of collective consciousness.

The early years of the Israeli state brought to the fore a rather different form of Zionist colonial discourse, this time directed towards Jewish immigrants from the Middle East and North Africa. As mentioned above, already during the Mandate period European and North American Zionist leaders had looked upon the small Oriental Jewish community of Palestine as culturally backward and had treated Middle Eastern Jews as a ready source of manpower that could compete with cheap Arab labor. With the mass immigration after 1949 of Jews from the Middle East and North Africa, a new colonialist dimension was added to Ashkenazic hegemony over and discrimination against Middle Eastern Jews. In the 1950s the Ashkenazic governing elite invented "Oriental" (Mizrahi) Jews as a coherent ethnic category; Jewish communities of diverse provenance, from Morocco to Iran, were sewn into a single ethnic collective defined solely by their origins in the lands of Islam.[47] The colonialist aspect of this action lies in the European colonial state's historic practice of hardening and standardizing borders, both territorial and ethnic. That is, just as the colonial state drew borders that threw together historically antagonistic collectives into a single polity, so it institutionalized difference between ethnic groups. As Mahmood

Mamdani has written of the Rwandan genocide, although prior to Belgian colonial rule cultural distinctions between Hutu and Tutsi certainly existed, the Belgians exaggerated, hardened, and rendered those distinctions impermeable through a construction of the Tutsi as racially distinct from and superior to the Hutu, and thus worthy of a favorable educational policy that groomed them for the colonial administrative elite. In the case of the Mizrahi Jews, the Israeli Ashkenazic elite experimented with ethnic fusion rather than fission, amalgamation rather than differentiation, but the result was the same: the creation of an essentialized, naturalized Other. As Mamdani puts it,

> [T]here is no middle ground, no continuum, between polarized identities. Polarized identities give rise to a kind of political difference where you must be either one or the other. You cannot partake of both. The difference becomes binary, not simply in law but in political life. It sustains no ambiguity.[48]

The last words of the quotation from Mamdani point to the limitation as well as applicability of a colonial model to the Ashkenazic–Mizrahi dichotomy in recent Israeli history. Although discrimination against Mizrahi Jews is still a prominent feature of Israeli society, it has declined over time; and as the uniform, statist political culture of David Ben-Gurion's Israel has collapsed into a bric-a-brac of separate subcultures, ethnic difference, not only between Ashkenazic and Mizrahi Jews, but also within these blocks, is flourishing. More than a half-century of life in Israel has effectively destroyed the Arab–Jewish culture of the Maghrebi/Mashreki diaspora but has engendered new forms of Mizrahi political activism and cultural creativity. However problematic the position of "Mizrahiness" may continue to be in Israel, the primary site of colonial discourse in contemporary Israel is not south Tel Aviv, but the Occupied Territories, for after the 1967 war Israel's relationship with the Arab minority changed to a *bona fide* form of colonialism. The demographic balance between occupier and occupied tilted increasingly towards the latter, Israel gained substantial economic profit from the Occupation, and its military and security forces brutally combated Palestinian nationalism in a fashion similar to French rule in pre-Independence Algeria. Perhaps even more important, from the late 1970s onward Jews were encouraged to move into the Occupied Territories as state-sponsored settlers, living as a minuscule minority of privileged colonists in areas that remained, unlike post-1948 Israel, overwhelmingly Arab.

Israelis justified the conquest of eastern Jerusalem and the West Bank via arguments about the religious and historical right of Jews to sovereignty over their alleged ancient biblical patrimony. Moreover, the seizure of the Sinai Peninsula, Gaza Strip, and the Golan Heights was attributed to *bona fide* security concerns. The act of conquest was arguably not motivated by a desire to subjugate a people and expropriate its land, but the speed with which the Palestinian labor force and market became tools for Israeli economic exploitation, the harshness of the Israeli military occupation, and the sheer numbers of Arabs brought under Israeli control quickly created a colonial regime in the Occupied Territories.[49] Indeed, one could argue that post-1967 Israel became not only a colonial state but also an imperial one, the difference being that imperialist ideology, which emerged in late nineteenth-century Europe, posited that the nation depended for its survival upon territorial expansion and that empire was an indivisible extension of the nation.[50]

Classic Zionism and its ideological underpinnings grew out of, yet departed significantly from, European high imperialism and the Orientalist sensibilities that justified it. After 1967, however, Israel underwent a rapid evolution into a colonial state. We would be well served, therefore, to consider the importance of ruptures as well as continuities within the fabric of Israeli history when evaluating the relationship between Zionism and colonialism. Similarly, we must be sensitive to Zionism's multi-vocality, its capacity (present in all nationalist ideologies) to function within discourses of both power and powerlessness, national liberation and ethnic exclusion. The blinkered passion that leads Jewish activists to identify Zionism as a movement of national liberation and to whitewash its oppressive and racist qualities finds its counterpart in the overwrought, almost campy tone of anti-Israel discourse, within academia as well as outside of it. (For example, Columbia University's Joseph Massad, who brooks no comparison between Zionism and Afro-Asian nationalisms, reduces the infinitely varied aspirations of millions of individuals caught up in the Zionist project to an act of sexual conquest intended to deflower the Holy Land, inseminate it with western seed, and emasculate the Arab and Mizrahi Jew alike.)[51] Surely scholars can set an example for their students and the public by shunning the use of the word "colonial" as universal pejorative akin to "fascism" during the heyday of the student movements of the 1960s and 1970s. Let us understand colonialism to be no more or less than a form of power, and the colonized as subjects of various forms of domination, without making facile identifications between power relations and moral qualities. Let us approach the questions "Is Zionism a colonial movement?" and "Is Israel a colonial state?" as an invitation to serious reflection, open to all possibilities, carried out according to the most stringent academic standards, albeit fraught with implications that reach far beyond the walls of academia to other walls, which run through the heart of Israel and Palestine.

6 Antisemites on Zionism

From indifference to obsession

In his classic Zionist manifesto *The Jewish State* (1896), Theodor Herzl claimed that the "Jewish Question" was:

> neither a social nor religious one, even if it at times takes on these or other colorings. It is a national question, and in order to solve it, we must make it into an international political question, which will be managed through counsel with the civilized nations of the globe.[1]

Herzl believed that the antisemitism of his day contained certain elements of what he called "legitimate self-defense," for emancipated Jews were particularly well suited for commerce and the professions, thus creating "fierce competition" with bourgeois gentiles. Economic issues, however, were, in Herzl's view, epiphenomenal, for no matter how Jews earned their livelihood, no matter how greatly they contributed to the wealth and welfare of the lands in which they lived, they were decried as strangers and parasites. Thus for Herzl, as for millions of Jews from his time to our own, Zionism has appeared to be a rational response to an irrational and ineradicable form of prejudice.

Herzl believed that antisemites themselves would appreciate the desirability and feasibility of the Zionist project and would gladly help ensure a smooth transfer of unwanted Jews from Europe to Palestine. In fact, however, most antisemitic ideologues in *fin-de-siècle* Europe were indifferent to or dismissive of Zionism. Believing that Jews were incorrigibly dishonorable and work-shy, antisemites considered Zionism to be at best an impracticable fantasy, as Jews would not willingly leave the fleshpots of the West to take on the arduous task of rebuilding their ancient Oriental homeland. At worst, Zionism was thought to represent yet another tentacle in the vast Jewish conspiracy to extend financial and political control over the entire globe. Over the period 1880–1940, as antisemitism became a mobilizing, all-embracing ideology in much of Europe, the latter view gained prominence, although the process was gradual, uneven, and specific to certain countries.

Over the same period, the Arab world witnessed an eruption of anti-colonial and nationalist sentiment, often directed against the Zionist project.

Whereas Zionism was peripheral to European antisemitism, it was central to Arab sensibilities about Judaism and Jews. In both environments antisemitism was a response to apparently inexplicable upheavals and an expression of virulent *ressentiment*, yet the differing function of Zionism in antisemitic discourse in Europe and the Middle East suggests the need to draw a distinction between systemic intolerance, aggravated by socio-economic crisis, and political strife, driven by discrete events and policies. To employ a medical metaphor – quite appropriate, since all forms of antisemitism are pathological – European antisemitism may be compared to a psychosomatic illness, whereas its Arab counterpart more closely resembles a toxic allergic reaction. The former originated in fantasy yet crippled the entire body politic; the latter has been a debilitating, even fatal, response to a genuine substance.

Whereas most of the literature on the relationship between antisemitism and anti-Zionism focuses on contemporary developments, there is much to be gained through a historical approach, through grasping underlying assumptions and visceral feelings about Zionism when they were first expressed, before they were affected by contingencies and rapidly changing events on the ground. Historical developments could either mitigate or intensify anti-Jewish feeling. An example of the former would be the temporary alliance between Zionism and Nazism in the guise of the Transfer Agreement of the 1930s, which facilitated German-Jewish emigration to Palestine. The power of events to deepen antisemitic grooves is demonstrated in the Arab world, where Israel's military victories in 1948, 1956, and 1967 generated a tidal wave of anger and compelled a search for explanations for the Arabs' ignominious defeat in the arcane realms of antisemitic fantasy. In the early 1900s, however, and particularly after the proclamation of the Balfour Declaration in 1917 and the rapid growth of the Jewish National Home thereafter, Zionism was a sufficiently powerful presence on the international scene and within Palestine itself to command attention, without being so influential that it had to be accorded de facto acceptance or utterly demonized.

This chapter focuses primarily on Europe, and it does so for two reasons: I have some expertise in the area; and, despite the vast literature on the history of European antisemitism, its conceptual stance *vis-à-vis* Zionism has, surprisingly, not been properly elucidated. The discussion of Arab antisemitism and anti-Zionism is briefer and more synthetic, but it is placed within a comparative analytical framework whose novel features will, I hope, stimulate experts in the modern Middle East to further, fuller reflection on the subject.

Classic, nineteenth-century antisemitism identified the Jew with modern capitalism and the rapid transformation of society and culture that came in its wake. Ancient and medieval tropes of Jewish avarice, murderous hatred of gentiles, and black-magical practices mutated into the modern stereotype of an international Jewish conspiracy. Tellingly, the myth of a global Jewish financial cabal flourished among early socialist thinkers in France and Germany during the 1840s, a decade of economic turmoil due in part to the impact of industrialization on the peasants and artisans who constituted the bulk of the population. The metonymic association between Jew and capitalism, and by extension with modernity as such, was a driving force behind late nineteenth-century political antisemitism, described appositely by the German socialist leader August Bebel as "the socialism of the stupid man."

Intriguingly, the discourse on Jewish restoration to Palestine, a discourse that intensified with the writings of the former socialist Moses Hess in the 1860s and, of course, with the establishment of the Zionist movement in the 1880s, attracted little sustained attention from antisemitic ideologues. To be sure, one can find scattered statements in writings on the "Jewish Question" dating back to the Enlightenment about shipping Jews out of Europe and back to Palestine. Scholars have painstakingly accumulated such statements by the likes of Johann Gottfried von Herder, Johann Gottlieb Fichte, Pierre-Joseph Proudhon, Heinrich von Treitschke, and Adolph Stöcker, among others, but they have failed to note that these utterances were merely barbed quips or enraged outbursts, and rarely led to a sustained engagement with Zionism even after Theodor Herzl brought it on to the stage of public opinion.

One apparent exception was the Hungarian antisemitic activist Györö Istóczy, who is the subject of a recent biography by Andrew Handler, provocatively titled *An Early Blueprint for Zionism*. Handler draws the title from a speech of 1878 on "The Restoration of the Jewish State in Palestine" delivered by Istóczy from the floor of the Hungarian Diet of which he was an elected member. Reflecting an anti-Russian and pro-Turkish sentiment as much as an antisemitic world-view, Istóczy claimed that such a state would revive "the enfeebled and backward East" by introducing Jewish wealth and energy, "a vigorous, powerful and new element and an influential ingredient of civilization."[2] Istóczy offered few specifics as to how this plan would be implemented, and subsequent to the speech Istóczy soon let the matter drop, as it encountered strong disapproval from his fellow parliamentarians. Thus this "early blueprint" for Zionism was, in fact, quite sketchy and faded quickly. For the next twenty years, Istóczy pursued the usual antisemitic agenda of attacking alleged Jewish domination in finance, commerce, and journalism within Europe. It is true that in 1906 he began to speak in support of the now-established political Zionist movement, but by 1911 he had lost interest, largely due to the Young Turk government's opposition to massive Jewish immigration to Palestine.[3]

By and large, antisemitic ideologues of the *fin de siècle* paid Zionism little heed, and, when they did think about it, dismissed it as a trick perpetrated by the agents of the international Jewish conspiracy. In the French journalist Edouard Drumont, perhaps the most successful antisemitic scribbler of the period, we have the interesting case of an antisemite whose interest in

Zionism waxed and waned, fading away altogether when Drumont decided that Zionism did not stand a chance against its rivals, assimilationist and plutocratic Jews, who also happened to be, in Drumont's view, the greatest threats to the world as a whole.

Drumont's daily newspaper *La Libre Parole* greeted the First Zionist Congress of 1897 with great fanfare. Apparently confirming Herzl's view that antisemites and Zionists would find a meeting of minds and form a productive collaboration, the newspaper wrote, in its customary sneering tone:

> Not only does [*La Libre Parole*] offer, freely and enthusiastically, publicity for the [Zionist] colonists, but if it were ever – an inconceivable thing – a question of money that caused the Jews to hesitate, it takes upon itself the commitment to take up a subscription whose immense success is not in doubt.[4]

Yet right from the start Drumont saw a snake in the Zionist garden, Jewish "*haute banque*," that cabal of powerful Jewish financiers whose economic interests depended on the maintenance of a vast global Jewish network and would thus be harmed by the mass movement of Jews to Palestine.[5]

A decade later, as the Zionist movement appeared to shake off the lethargy that had gripped the movement since Herzl's death in 1904, Drumont devoted considerable energy to drumming up antisemitic support for Zionism. At the time of the Eighth Zionist Congress in 1907, Drumont wrote that Zionism represented the "future of the Jewish Question and, consequently, the future of humanity as a whole." Were the Jews removed from Europe to Palestine, "this Jewish Question, which ... dominates all human affairs, including the Social Question, would be resolved, at least for the time being, and the world would finally know a period of calm and relative security." Drumont even expressed admiration for Zionists, whom he contrasted favorably with their opponents:

> The Jew who aspires to reconstitute a homeland is worthy of esteem. The Jew who destroys the homeland of others is worthy of every kind of scorn. The Jew who wants to have a flag and a religion is a virtuous Jew, and we will never proffer against him any hurtful word. ... We have therefore all sorts of reasons to prefer the Zionist Jews over those arrogant Hebrews who aspire not only to involve themselves in our affairs but also to impose their ideas and their will upon us, who treat us in our own homeland as representatives of an inferior race, as vanquished and pariahs.[6]

Drumont and his contributing journalists consistently praised Herzl, and especially Max Nordau, for his fiery and unapologetic Jewish nationalism, while they pilloried the principled assimilationism of French-Jewish notables such as Joseph Reinach and Emile Cahen, editor of *Les Archives israélites*.

By 1913, however, Drumont had changed his tune. On the eve of the Eleventh Zionist Congress, Drumont warned darkly that "this conference will probably be the last, and this racket will have sounded Zionism's death-knell."[7] Reproducing verbatim large sections from his 1907 articles on the subject, Drumont added a new twist: The "great Jews" Herzl and Nordau have been vanquished by the combined forces of assimilationists and Jewish high finance. Drumont accused the former of shifting the WZO's focus away from international diplomacy, aimed at obtaining a Jewish homeland secured by public law, and enmeshing the movement in *Gegenwartsarbeit*, political and cultural activity in the diaspora. Even worse, according to Drumont, was the work of "the great Jews, the aristocrats of banking," who, like Maurice de Hirsch, had always been hostile to Zionism, and who had now created Territorialism:

> It is no longer a matter of reconstituting in Palestine or elsewhere a Jewish nation having its land, its flag and its religion, but only of creating Jewish colonies for the use of poor and miserable Jews who would go establish themselves in distant territories. During this time, the ambitious Jews, having pushed from view their shabby brethren, would enjoy, more than ever, the unquestioned authority and enormous power that they wield in the country where, as in France, they have become the masters and the rulers.[8]

It matters little that Drumont was wrong on both points – both *Gegenwartsarbeit* and Territorialism developed from within the heart of the Zionist movement – rather, the key here is that Drumont placed the contest between Zionism and its enemies within sturdy and venerable antisemitic frameworks of conspiracy led by Jewish plutocrats and cultural domination by assimilated Jewish intellectuals. Drumont's views on Zionism were not influenced by, nor did they influence, his general antisemitic world-view. Drumont was willing to endorse Zionism if it appeared to confirm his pre-existing views that Jewish nationhood was ineradicable, but at the blink of an eye he was quite willing to disown it, especially since on the eve of and during World War I Zionist goals increasingly appeared to conflict with French imperial interests and the sensibilities of Roman Catholics in the Middle East.[9]

As we expand our chronological horizon into the twentieth century, it appears that in France, Zionism, although occasionally applauded or derided, appears to have been peripheral to the antisemitic imagination. Adulatory literature written in France about Drumont in the decades following his death – literature that includes generous extracts from his work – does not make so much as a mention of Zionism. Such writing does, however, faithfully reproduce Drumont's own *idées fixes* about Jewish responsibility for the corruption, social upheaval, and financial scandals that were making life hell for the little man.[10] More important, during France's darkest and most shameful hours in World War II the Vichy regime devoted little time and effort to the issue of Zionism, and when the matter did come up attitudes were instrumental, based on the needs of the moment. In 1943, when a German victory no longer seemed assured and the mass deportations of Jews were provoking considerable discontent in France, the Vichy regime toyed with pro-Zionist proposals to facilitate mass Jewish emigration to Palestine and endorse the creation of a Jewish state. Unlike the Nazis, who had come out clearly against Jewish statehood at the time of the Partition Controversy of 1937 and put an end to Jewish emigration to Palestine in 1940 as part of the transition from a policy of mass expulsion to one of genocide, Vichy leaders, admittedly steeped in antisemitic yearnings to rid France of the Jews, were willing to ponder what the chief of Marshal Pétain's civilian staff called "the only truly effectual solution [to the Jewish Question] that is both completely humane and Christian."[11]

Similarly, Italian fascism adopted an instrumental approach to Zionism, opposing it when it clashed with Catholic interests or appeared to be a tool of British expansionism in the eastern Mediterranean, and embracing it when it was thought that Zionists might sever their alliance with Britain and turn to Italy as their protector. This flexibility reflected the ambiguous legacy of Italian antisemitism in the post-unification era. On the one hand, Italian Catholicism could espouse no less fierce an antisemitism than its French counterpart, as seen in the stridently Judeophobic Vatican periodical *La Civiltà cattolica*, which argued that the Jewish religion was corrupt, materialistic, and long superseded by Christianity, and that the Jews comprised

> [a]n ambiguous nation, because, at the same time, it [the Jewish community] is the same and the Other, as the other nations of the world where they have settled: [they are] Jewish Italians, French, Germans, English, Americans, Rumanians, and Poles, that is to say, the Jews enjoy dual nationality. It seems that they carry "a harvest of" advantages to the country where they sit, and that the country will reap these advantages, their financial skills and intelligence. But these advantages are, directly or indirectly, consciously or unconsciously, used methodically to get the upper hand and secure power for the Jewish nation, controlling high finance so that more or less veiled, they will control everybody.[12]

Nonetheless, due to the relative strength of the secular Italian state *vis-à-vis* the vanquished Church, antisemitism did not become a political force in the early twentieth century. The Italian kingdom, with its Jewish cabinet ministers, mayors and prime minister, was a country with many Dreyfuses yet no Dreyfus Affair.

Ironically, the relative weakness of political antisemitism in early twentieth-century Italy made possible a more serious and pragmatic engagement with Zionism than was the case in France, where Zionism's political program was engulfed by the antisemitic fog generated by the Dreyfus Affair. Accordingly, during the early years of Mussolini's rule there were numerous meetings between Mussolini and the leaders of Italian and international Zionism, and, although in the late 1920s Mussolini unhesitatingly turned against Zionism in order to satisfy the interests of the Vatican, with which he negotiated a Concordat in 1929, in the early 1930s Mussolini once again announced a favorable stance towards Zionism, inviting the WZO to convene in Italy and hoping (rather improbably) that pro-Italian Jewish immigrants to Palestine could gain sufficient influence to overturn the British Mandate.[13]

In Germany, by contrast, from the 1870s onward antisemites were wont to judge Zionism more harshly, as a manifestation of ongoing global Jewish chicanery. Wilhelm Marr, who is credited with coining the term "antisemitism" in the late 1870s, wrote here and there throughout the 1880s about shipping all of Europe's Jews to Palestine, where they could put their boundless energy and resources to work in creating a model polity, a *Musterstaat*. Yet this relatively sanguine attitude did not survive the passage of time, as Marr's antisemitic world-view grew ever darker and more bitter. Marr wrote at the time of the First Zionist Congress of 1897 that "the entire matter is a foul Jewish swindle, in order to divert the attention of the European peoples from the Jewish problem."[14] Marr did not elaborate on his opposition to Zionism, for, as with Drumont and the other antisemites we have analyzed thus far, Zionism was far from central to Marr's concerns.

The logical connection between conspiratorial antisemitism and an adamant rejection of Zionism may be found in the work of Marr's contemporary Eugen Dühring, author of what was perhaps the most relentlessly brutal antisemitic tract of the late nineteenth century, *The Jewish Question as a Question of Racial Noxiousness for the Existence, Morals and Culture of Nations* (1881). This book, which went through six editions up to 1930, offers an opportunity to observe how an acutely intelligent but deranged individual responded to Zionism as the movement gained prominence from the 1880s through the end of World War I. We see that it was precisely the depth of Dühring's antisemitism that prevented him from taking Zionism seriously and considering it outside of the prepackaged framework of a Jewish financial and cultural stranglehold over all of Europe. In the 1892 edition, Dühring devotes over seventy pages to elaborately detailed "solutions" to the Jewish Problem – solutions including reducing the numbers of Jews in, or barring them altogether from, the civil service, professions, journalism, and teaching; and laying punitive taxes on Jewish-owned banks and other enterprises. In short, Dühring advocates the de-emancipation of European Jewry. Claiming that the Jews are racially incorrigible, Dühring dismisses Zionism in a couple of paragraphs, beginning with the following observation:

> Moreover I do not believe that the Jews, if they were to really unite in a territory, be it a Jewish colony in Palestine or some other settlement, would be prevented from renewing their obtrusive nomadism. Nomadism is their world-historical natural condition. Without it and alone among themselves they would eat one another alive, for other peoples would not be among them. Such a thing as a Jewish state would mean the destruction of the Jews by the Jews.[15]

Thus Jews would always prefer, Dühring goes on to argue, living under the most oppressive conditions among gentiles rather than among their own kind.

As Dühring aged, his language grew ever more bilious and threatening. In the posthumously published 1930 edition of the work, incorporating changes and additions made by the author ten years before, Dühring claimed that throughout history no political force had been able to contain the Jewish menace. The Roman conquest of Palestine merely spread the Jewish disease into the diaspora, expulsion decrees in medieval Europe were ineffective, and ghettoization served only to strengthen Jewish solidarity. In turn, today's Zionists sought to dupe honest Europeans, who would like to see the Jews leave for Palestine, by selling them shares in various Zionist enterprises, all designed to enrich their Jewish directors. Moreover, a Jewish state, even if one were to be established, would only accentuate Jewish power; the Jewish snake that encircled the globe would now have a head:

> This would entail pushing history back, thereby making necessary something like a second Roman clearing action. It would mean going back to the beginning, where the matter would be brought to an end in an entirely different and far more comprehensive sense. (*Es hiesse zum Anfang zurückzukehren, wo in einem ganz andern und weit durchgreifenderen Sinne ein Ende zu machen ist*.)[16]

A chilling, and prescient, threat indeed, yet one made in passing, via a few sentences, after which Dühring returns to his favorite themes of Jewish control over most aspects of politics, economics, and culture in the western world.

The significance of Dühring's text lies not only in what he says but also in the popularity and durability of his book and the apparently paradoxical combination of a lack of serious interest in Zionism and a blanket condemnation of it. One encounters a similar case in the writings of Theodor Fritsch, whose *Antisemites' Catechism*, also published under the title *Handbook of the Jewish Problem*, went through thirty-six editions and a total print run of 155,000 copies between 1886, when it first appeared, and 1934, a year after Fritsch's death.

Although the book was expanded considerably over time, its basic structure remained intact. First came an overview of the allegedly noxious role played by Jews throughout history from antiquity to the present, then a chapter of

citations from contemporary Jewish writers attesting to the Jews' status as a separate nationality, followed by a chapter on the Jewish presence in malevolent secret societies. First and foremost among them were the Alliance Israélite Universelle (in fact, a philanthropic, educational and lobbying organization established in Paris in 1860) and the Russian *kahal*, an imaginary network of Russian-Jewish communities, as dreamed up by the Russian convert Iakov Brafman in a notorious book of 1868. The 1907 edition of Fritsch's book does not even mention Zionism in its chapter on Jewish secret societies, although the Anglo-Jewish Association (whose purview was similar to that of the Alliance) is singled out for condemnation, along with that venerable object of antisemitic fantasy Freemasonry. In the chapter of statements by Jews claiming a unique national identity, most of the statements are from anti-Zionists, such as the Viennese Orthodox rabbi Leopold Kohn, or individuals who were or may have been Zionists but are not identified as such (for example the American rabbi Bernhardt Felsenthal). There is abundant, albeit wildly inaccurate, analysis of the socio-economic situation and political life of the Jews in Germany's neighboring lands, but no treatment of the Zionist movement, its diplomatic activities, or events on the ground in Palestine.[17]

In the 1934 edition, the chapter on "Jewish Organizations and Parties" expanded to include material on a vast array of Jewish political bodies, and Zionism finally received its own subsection, but it only amounted to two pages out of more than 500 in the book, and "Zionism" does not appear in the otherwise exhaustive index. Fritsch induces a frisson of fear as he details the evil deeds of the shadowy Russian-Jewish *kahal* or the omnipotent Alliance, "the central node for the realization of all Jewish special interests, implementing on any occasion the power of the whole of Jewry," and which has been responsible for everything from agitation on behalf of Captain Alfred Dreyfus to rallies for the condemned Italian-American anarchists Sacco and Vanzetti. Zionism, on the other hand, is dismissed out of hand: Herzl and Nordau were frauds, lacking in imagination or ability; and the Zionist project would have been stillborn had it not been for wartime collusion between the British government and the Rothschilds, by which a promise of a Jewish National Home in Palestine was made in return for international Jewish assistance to defeat Germany. Intriguingly, Fritsch does not credit the Zionists with the power and influence that one might expect from a virulent antisemite. Fritsch focuses instead on the British, who, he claims, have no intention of allowing a Jewish state to be set up in Palestine, as it would conflict with their imperial interests. Besides, Palestine is too small and its economy too undeveloped to accommodate large numbers of Jews, and the current Jewish community in Palestine is mostly urban, and hence no less corrupt and parasitical than its diaspora counterpart. The only good thing about Zionism, concludes Fritsch, is that it has "transformed previously in large measure inactive and apolitical Arabs into convinced opponents of the Jews."[18]

Like any antisemitic ideologue, Dühring and Fritsch had to simultaneously fabricate falsehood and deny reality. Not only did they demonize Zionist international diplomatic and fundraising activity, they also ignored the growth of the Jewish National Home, which was rooted in notions of Jewish bodily and cultural renewal. Like ultraviolet light, invisible to the naked eye, many aspects of the Zionist project simply could not be perceived within the optical field of antisemitism. One encounters precisely this sort of conceptual blindness in the somewhat more genteel, but no more palatable, tome by Houston Stewart Chamberlain, *The Foundations of the Nineteenth Century* (1899). In the midst of a massive (and highly negative) historical analysis of Judaism and Jews comes a remarkable observation that the Hebrew language died out 400 years before Christ. (Apparently Chamberlain knew nothing about rabbinic literature.) Moreover,

> Its adoption many centuries later was artificial and with the object of separating the Jews from their hosts in Europe. ... The absolute lack of feeling for language among the Jews today is explained by the fact that they are at home in no language – for a dead language cannot receive new life by command – and the Hebrew idiom is as much abused by them as any other.[19]

Thus when a Jew speaks Hebrew he does not speak Hebrew, just as a laboring Jew in a Palestinian vineyard does not truly labor. For these antisemites, Zionism is nothing but smoke and mirrors, and the only appropriate response is to conjure it away.

An association between Zionism and Jewish criminality became central to Nazi ideology, pioneered by Alfred Rosenberg, who claimed in 1922 that Zionism was an anti-German movement that drew support from reactionary capitalists (the Rothschilds) and Communists ("Jewish" Bolsheviks) alike. Drawing on Rosenberg and Dühring, Adolf Hitler, writing in *Mein Kampf*, would claim that Jews had no intention or ability to construct a legitimate state in Palestine, but rather wished to make it into a clearing house for their international economic swindling operations. "[E]ndowed with sovereign rights and removed from the intervention of other states," a Jewish state would become "a haven for convicted scoundrels and a university for budding crooks."[20] (Thus the intellectual pedigree of the notorious contemporary Holocaust denier Ernst Zundel's characterization of Israel as "a gangster enclave in the Middle East.")[21]

Even in Nazi ideology, however, Zionism was little more than an addendum to a well-worn diatribe against international Jewish political machinations and inveterate malevolence. The presence of the Zionist movement did not substantively add to or detract from pre-existing modes of antisemitic sensibility. The conceptual irrelevance of Zionism behind modern European antisemitism is demonstrated all the more clearly by the most significant text in the history of twentieth-century antisemitism, *The Protocols of the Elders of Zion*.

The precise authorship of the *Protocols* remains obscure, but scholars concur that the work was written by agents of the Russian secret police in Paris at the turn of the last century. The *Protocols* were the most notorious expression of Jewish conspiracy theory, which originated among opponents of the Enlightenment and French Revolution. Specifically, the *Protocols* were inspired by Hermann Goedsche's novel *Biarritz* (1868), a section of which depicts the assembly of a Jewish cabal at a Prague cemetery. Much of the *Protocols*' text, however, was plagiarized from a second, wholly innocuous work, Maurice Joly's *A Dialogue in Hell* (1864), which employed a fictional dialogue between the philosophers Machiavelli and Montesquieu in order to satirize the authoritarian rule of the French emperor Napoleon III. The authors of the *Protocols* lifted many of Machiavelli's speeches verbatim and put them into the mouths of Jewish conspirators. Yet the authors of the *Protocols* transmuted Joly's text while plagiarizing it, in that Joly presented Machiavelli as a cynical realist, whereas the *Protocols* depict the Jews as the embodiment of preternatural, all-consuming evil.[22]

Antisemitism in *fin-de-siècle* western and central Europe could be a form of lower-middle-class protest; in Germany and Austria, it took the form of "Christian Socialism" and nourished the populist demagoguery of Vienna's mayor Karl Lueger. In Russia, on the other hand, antisemitism was often reactionary, a rejection of modernity in any form and a paean to rigid hierarchical rule by a hereditary nobility. These sentiments pervade the *Protocols*, which were written primarily in order to sabotage Russia's halting moves towards economic modernization by associating liberalization with Jewish conspiracy. The link between Russia, reaction, and the *Protocols* was strengthened by their publication in St. Petersburg in 1903. The *Protocols* were disseminated throughout Russia by members of the ultra-rightist Black Hundreds, and Tsar Nicholas and Tsarina Alexandra commanded that Orthodox priests declaim the *Protocols* in the churches of Moscow.[23]

In its early editions a variety of origins were attributed to the *Protocols*, and only after World War I do we see a popularization and routinization of the claim that they transcribe deliberations from the First Zionist Congress. The references to Herzl and the Congress come at the very beginning of the texts, and nothing in the text of the *Protocols* itself touches upon Zionism, although the *Protocols* were forged at the time of the beginnings of political Zionism in the late 1890s. Significantly, in editions of the *Protocols* issued before 1917 the international Jewish body referred to most often as generating the text is the Alliance. (A spectacular, but anomalous exception was the work of the Russian reactionary Paquita de Shishmareff, who, writing under the pseudonym L. Fry, claimed that the Zionist intellectual Ahad Ha-Am had penned the *Protocols*.)[24] Just as the internationalist dimension of the Alliance's name and activities stoked the antisemitic imagination of the *fin de siècle*, so could the increased visibility of the Zionist movement in the wake of the Balfour Declaration and establishment of the British Mandate over Palestine encourage antisemites to interpret the Basel Congress as, citing Norman Cohn, "a giant stride towards Jewish world-domination."[25] But the actual Zionist program, enunciated at Basel in 1897 and legitimized in part by the British in 1917 and 1920, of creating a Jewish National Home in Palestine is overlooked in the interwar editions of the *Protocols*. Even the notorious paraphrase of the *Protocols* serialized in Henry Ford's *Dearborn Independent* in 1920, which claims that the Sixth Zionist Congress predicted the outbreak of world war and that the Zionist movement represents the tip of an iceberg of international Jewish power, only engages issues relating to Jewish political activity in interwar Europe, specifically the minority rights treaties, which allegedly singled Jews out for favorable treatment.[26]

To sum up, Zionism did not exist as a discrete phenomenon in the minds of European antisemites during the half-century prior to the Holocaust. It was merely a placeholder for a host of conspiratorial fantasies that were rooted deep in the nineteenth century and in a search for an identifiable agent responsible for the bewildering social and political transformations sweeping Europe like a storm. Jews were of course only occasional representatives, rather than creators or agents, of these processes, as the antisemite's Jew was little more than a reflection and reification of European society itself. Granted, although European antisemitism was riddled with contradictions and highly irrational, it was not wholly illogical. It attributed to the Jew only selected attributes of the human psyche, such as arrogance, cupidity, and a thirst for power. The antisemite's Jew was not stupid, brutish, or enslaved to passion. Bridging the clashing stereotypes of the Jewish capitalist and Communist was an underlying and unifying reality: the Jews' historic prominence in the economy's distributive sector and as agents of economic change. Even so, the visibility of Jews in commerce and the medical and legal professions was a symptom, not a cause, of a capitalist economic order with a meritocratic impetus and a permeable elite. The "Jewish Question" in modern Europe did not amount to anything more than a deceptively tangible avatar of the "social question." Zionism as an ideology and political movement did not impinge upon the lives of Europeans as did other forces associated with Jews, such as capitalism, Bolshevism, or cultural modernism.

The function of Zionism in modern Arab antisemitism is radically different from its European counterpart. Simply put, whereas European antisemites regarded Zionism as a manifestation of Judaism, in the Middle East Jews and Judaism have, for the past century or more, been defined in terms of Zionism. We may take as a starting point the argument made in 1978 by Yehoshafat Harkabi, an Israeli scholar of the modern Arab world and Israeli security policy, that Arab antisemitism was the product of a specific political conflict – the century-long struggle with the Zionist movement, the Yishuv (pre-state Jewish community in Palestine) and the state of Israel – as opposed to the Islamic religious tradition as such or a fundamental inability of Islamic lands to tolerate Jews in their midst.[27] In an earlier work, Harkabi had documented at considerable length the extent of

Judeophobic fantasy in the Arab world, and he made no effort now to deny or belittle the findings from his previous research.[28] But Harkabi came to question the value of cataloging hostile statements about Israel or Jews without taking into account the historical circumstances in which they emerged or noting, as one could see during the era of the Camp David Peace Accords, that the same government directives that stoked antisemitic rhetoric could also staunch it, and that Arab attitudes towards Israel were shaped as much by specific Israeli policies and actions as by inherited, pervasive antisemitic stereotypes.

Harkabi's argument and my own here are not to be confused with that of post-1948 Arab propagandists who have presented the history of the Jews in the lands of Islam as uniformly stable and prosperous, blessed by Islam's enlightened and tolerant attitude towards its protected minorities, an attitude overturned solely by the injustices and cruelties against Arabs perpetrated by the state of Israel.[29] Obviously, the fate of Jews in *dar al-Islam* has been often an unhappy one, molded in part by the Judeophobic motifs that are imbedded in Islam's foundational texts. In addition to the Koran's many polemical comments about Jews and its accounts of Jewish treachery against Mohammed, a traditional biography of Mohammed attributes his death to poisoning by a Jewish woman, and an equally venerable historical text claims that Shi'ism, which sundered Islamic unity, was instigated by a Yemenite Jew.[30] Such texts, however, mean little when not considered in the context of medieval Jewish life in the lands of Islam, where despite constant discrimination the Jews lived in greater security, and were far less often the subject of chimeric fantasy, than in Europe, where persecutions and expulsions of Jews often followed accusations of ritual murder, desecration of the sacred host, and consorting with the Devil. As Mark Cohen has argued convincingly in his comparative history of Jewish life in medieval Christendom and *dar al-Islam*, in the latter acts of expulsion and forced conversion were highly exceptional.[31] Today, many critics of Muslim antisemitism place great stock in Moses Maimonides's celebrated *Letter to the Jews of Yemen* (1172), in which the renowned scholar claimed that the lot of Jews had been far worse under Muslim than Christian rule. Yet this was a *cri de coeur* issued in a time of extreme, and atypical, persecution.

In the nineteenth century notions of a Jewish international political and financial conspiracy were exported to the Middle East, largely via French and Francophone Christian clerics. Intriguingly, however, during the late Ottoman era Arab opposition to Zionism was not necessarily antisemitic. Palestinian Arabs expressed rational fears of displacement from a land in which they had long been resident, and Ottoman officials worried about the creation in the empire of a new minority problem akin to that presented by the Armenians.[32] Intellectuals in Egypt and Syria conceived of Jews in complex ways, combining a realistic assessment of the Zionist movement's accomplishments with an exaggerated belief in Jewish power. For example, the *fin-de-siècle* Muslim reformer Rashid Ridha, who followed the Dreyfus

Affair carefully and denounced antisemitism in print, wrote in 1899 that Muslims and Arabs would be wise to emulate Jewish solidarity, which had allowed them to preserve their language and culture despite many centuries of dispersion. Moreover, the Jews deserved praise for having adopted scientific knowledge and accumulated great wealth. The Jews, wrote Ridha, "lack nothing but sovereign power in order to become the greatest nation on the face of the earth, an objective they pursue in a normal manner. One Jew [Herzl] is now more respected than an Oriental monarch [Ottoman sultan Abdul Hamid]."[33] There are obvious shades of hostility and exaggeration in Ridha's image of Jews as comprising a unified, wealthy, and powerful collective, but his concern was the reality presented by the immigration of tens of thousands of Jews into Palestine, not, as in the case of European antisemitism, broad social transformations in which Jews played no significant causal role.

The secular Arab nationalist Najib Azuri, writing in 1905 in his classic work *Le Reveil de la nation arabe*, described Jews as a people engaged in a concerted drive to establish a state in what they perceived to be their homeland. "On the final outcome of this struggle," Azuri noted darkly (and, one hopes, not presciently), "between these two peoples, representing two opposing principles, will depend the destiny of the entire world."[34] Azuri's casual reference to Jews as a people points out an interesting distinction between early twentieth-century Arab anti-Zionism, on the one hand, and both European antisemitism and later forms of Arab anti-Zionism, on the other. It was a staple of European antisemitism that Judaism comprised both a nation and a religion. Unlike European antisemitism, which imagined Jews to constitute an unassimilable and noxious nation, defying the quid pro quo of assimilation for emancipation, in the decades after Azuri Arab propaganda had to develop an opposite argument that the Jews did not constitute even a retrograde nation, for to admit as much might open the way to accepting the legitimacy of the principles of Zionism.

In the twentieth-century Arab world, the interlacing of antisemitic motifs with opposition to Zionism occurred in a direct response to increased Jewish immigration to Palestine. It is no coincidence that the *Protocols of the Elders of Zion* first appeared in Arabic in 1925, during the fourth, and largest yet, wave of Zionist immigration to Palestine. (The translation, from the French, was the work of a Catholic priest, Antoine Yamin, in Egypt.) The following year, an article in a periodical of the Jerusalem Latin Patriarchate announced the presence of the Arabic translation of the *Protocols* and urged the faithful to read them in order to understand what the Zionists had in store for Palestine. During the disturbances of the years 1928–9, Haj Amin al-Husayni, the mufti of Jerusalem, publicized portions of the *Protocols* in connection with alleged Jewish plots to conquer the Temple Mount. Thus, although the translation was done by a Christian cleric and was infused with European antisemitic sensibilities, the text was immediately introduced into the context of the new and unique political conflict between Arabs and Jews for control over Palestine.[35]

To be sure, during the interwar period Arab antisemitism was nourished by sources outside of Palestine. The rapid social mobility and prominence of Jews in Middle Eastern lands under colonial rule, and the economic and administrative links between Jews and colonial regimes, instilled a powerful antisemitic element into Arab nationalism, for which Jews served as metonymic representations of the West. In some instances, as in Iraq during World War II, German political and intellectual influences catalyzed pro-Nazi nationalist movements that imbibed racial antisemitism from its most potent source. A ruthless dedication to creating a culturally homogeneous Arab nation led in Iraq to the massacre of thousands of Assyrian Christians in 1933 and of some 400 Jews during the *Farhoud* of 1941.[36] During the 1930s and 1940s, Middle Eastern antisemitism was strengthened further by the increasing popularity of socialism and communism among Arab intellectuals. Jews were defined by the Arab Left as in league with their fascist persecutors, while royalists and fascist sympathizers leapt to wild conclusions from the disproportionate involvement of Jews in the communist parties in Egypt and Iraq. The important common element behind these contradictory expressions of Arab antisemitism during the interwar period was the adoption of common European views of the Jew as universal solvent, the destroyer of social order and bringer of chaos, housed in both the left and right ends of the political and economic spectrum. Arab antisemitism even adopted European notions of preternatural Jewish sexual powers. The secular and socialist-inspired youth so visible among the Zionist immigrants prompted Arab accusations that Jews were sexually promiscuous as well as carriers of Bolshevism – indeed the Arab word for "communist" was "*ibahi*," "permissive."[37]

Nonetheless, up to 1948 Arab antisemitism did not routinely function, as it did in Europe, as a totally unbounded discourse, attributing every ill of modern humanity to Jewish influence. And within Palestine itself antisemitism grew directly out of conflict with the Zionist movement and its gradual, yet purposeful settlement of the country. The dominant tone was set as early as 1920, when in a play entitled *The Ruin of Palestine*, performed in Nablus, the comely daughter of a Jewish tavern keeper seduced two wealthy Arabs, coaxed out of them their money and even the deeds to their properties, leaving the Arabs with no resource other than suicide, before which they wailed, "[T]he country is ruined, the Jews have robbed us of our land and honor!"[38]

Our focus thus far on the period before 1948 sharpens our perception of the novel qualities of Arab antisemitic discourse generated since the creation of the state of Israel. As opposed to traditional Muslim Judeophobia, post-1948 Arab antisemitism featured a transition from a view of the Jew as weak and degraded to a belief in Jewish global power. Traditional Islam scorned the Jew; post-1948 Arab antisemitism has blended contempt with fear. The fear stems from the apparent inability of Arabs to stop what has seemed to them to be a gradual, yet carefully planned and executed, Jewish takeover of Palestine, a land whose sanctity and significance have grown in the face of what appears to be a repetition of the Crusades, a European assault against the heartland of the Islamic world. The growth of a secular Arab nationalism, uniting Christians and Muslims in a common battle against western colonialism, has expanded the purview of this alleged new crusade from a Muslim Holy Land to the Middle East as a whole. Older forms of contempt for Jews have, in recent decades, taken the form of the widespread view that, humiliating though it was to be subjugated by Christian Europe, it has been all the more galling to witness Palestine falling under the rule of Jews.

Indeed, the trope of assaulted Arab dignity is perhaps the most common theme in contemporary Arab antisemitism. Western pundits are wont to attribute this discourse to an atavistic shame culture, in which codes of personal honor, particularly male honor, bind a rigid socio-religious hierarchy that privileges status over achievement and resists the formation of a liberal, inclusive, egalitarian, and democratic western-style civil society. It is not my brief to determine if such views are accurate or are the product of facile Orientalist fantasies. What is clear, however, is that the discourse on dignity in the Middle East stems primarily from a sense of overwhelming helplessness rather than merely wounded pride. However much the Arab powers may have bickered over the fate of Palestine during the 1940s, the loss of Palestine to a Jewish state was seen as the defining catastrophic event of the era, or, as Constantine Zurayk described it in 1956, *al-naqba* (the disaster), a term that gained universal currency in decades to come:

> The defeat of the Arabs in Palestine is no simple setback or light, passing evil. It is a disaster in every sense of the word and one of the harshest trials and tribulations with which the Arabs have been afflicted throughout their long history – a history marked by numerous trials and tribulations.[39]

Regardless of how one apportions responsibility for *al-naqba*, the conquest of the West Bank and Gaza in 1967, the ensuing occupation of those territories, and the steady settlement of Jews therein, all of these phenomena are historical realities, as is Israel's close relationship – particularly since 1967 – with the United States, which is widely seen in the Middle East as the last remaining great colonial power. There is an immeasurable gap between this scenario and that of modern Europe, where Jews as a collective wielded no power, conquered no land, expelled no family from its home.

There are strains of post-1948 Arab antisemitism that absorbed the Manichean qualities of Nazism, elevating the Jew into a global, even cosmic, evil, which must be annihilated, not only within Palestine but wherever he may be found. Such viewpoints are espoused vigorously by Muslim fundamentalists in many lands. They trace their intellectual pedigree to Sayyid Qutb, the intellectual father of the Muslim Brotherhood, who, while in Egyptian prisons during the 1950s, embroidered a European-style antisemitism into his massive commentary on the Koran. Qutb's antisemitism was ontological, perceiving Jews as incorrigibly evil and associated with all the world's ills, including capitalism, communism, atheism, materialism, and modernism.[40] During the 1960s, Qutb, like fundamentalist leaders elsewhere in the Middle East, devoted most of his effort to toppling secular Arab leaders. Developments over a period of fifteen years – the 1967 war, the Sadat peace initiative, the Iranian Revolution, and Israel's invasion of Lebanon – transformed Muslim fundamentalism, causing anti-Zionism, according to Emmanuel Sivan, to "take pride of place, presented as the modern-day incarnation of the authentically Islamic hostility to the Jews."[41]

Nonetheless, the older, Palestinocentric streak in Arab antisemitism lives on in our own day, as in the 2002 Egyptian television series *Horseman without a Horse*, which is based in part on the *Protocols of the Elders of Zion* but in which the Jewish conspiracy to control the world is replaced by a specific plot to take control of Palestine. Moreover, it is significant that the *Protocols* come in and out of fashion in Egypt; they were popular under Nasser but fell out of circulation in the wake of Camp David, only to return after the failure of the Oslo Peace Accords. Arab antisemitism in any form is repugnant, but those forms that wax and wane in response to developments in Arab–Israeli relations are qualitatively different from the Manicheanism of extremist Muslim fundamentalists who, no less than the Nazis, imagine Jews as literally the handmaids of Satan and call for their eradication from the face of the globe. It is essential to draw a clear distinction between these two different forms of antisemitism, one of which may be malleable, subject to change in a dynamic and constructive political environment, while the other kind is incurable and must be confronted with unequivocal condemnation, isolation, and, when necessary, forceful suppression.

This chapter's comparative framework will not please those who see European and Arab antisemitism as of a piece and who associate anti-Zionism with antisemitism *tout court*. Some of my critics have responded with a comparison of their own, claiming that Jews in modern times have featured an exaggerated, perhaps unique, capacity for self-criticism and that this practice has led Jews, particularly Jewish intellectuals, whether in nineteenth-century Germany or early twenty-first-century North America and Israel, to internalize antisemitic assaults against them and to labor in vain to ingratiate themselves with their persecutors. The frequently cited example of nineteenth-century German Jews relates a pathetic tale of individuals who responded to antisemitic accusations of Jewish vulgarity and parasitism by encouraging circumspect public behavior, the utmost probity in business affairs, and the promotion of reputable, honorable occupations in crafts among poor Jewish youth. Of course, nothing German Jews did could possibly mitigate antisemitism, let alone assuage the genocidal fury of the Nazis. Similarly, argue many staunch supporters of Israel today, leftist

Israelis and their counterparts in the Jewish diaspora are urging that Israel make massive, and ultimately self-destructive, territorial and political sacrifices in an illusory pursuit of peace. According to this pessimistic world-view, for most Arabs peace can only come in the wake of Israel's destruction, either spectacularly, by force, or gradually, through its transformation into a bi-national state, whose Jewish component would over time be overwhelmed by a rapidly growing Arab population, and whose Jewish character would accordingly fade away.

I respond to this objection by noting that Israel, unlike the Jewish global conspiracy of the European antisemitic imagination, does exist. Precisely because Arab antisemitism's fantasies are far more thoroughly grounded in reality than those of their European predecessors, a necessary, although admittedly insufficient, precondition for deconstructing those fantasies will be a radical transformation of Israel's borders and policies towards Arabs both within and outside of the state. As Yehoshafat Harkabi wrote in the wake of the Camp David Summit, "It is not the change of images ... which will lead to peace, but peace which will lead to the change of images."[42] Unlike the decline of antisemitism in post-1945 Europe, which was not the work of Jews but rather the result of the crimes and guilt of European society as a whole, in the Middle East Jews are obliged to make fateful political decisions in the hopes that such decisions will stimulate equally constructive action on the part of Israel's neighbors and the Palestinians under Israeli control, that these multilateral actions will in fact lead to peace, and that peace will lead to a change of Arab images of Jews. This time around, antisemitism grows out of a political conflict in which Jews are empowered actors, not figments of the imagination. For this reason, although the chances for accommodation between Israel and the Arab world often appear slim, conditions are vastly more favorable than in pre-World War II Europe, not simply because the Jewish state possesses military power, but also because it has the capacity to take actions that can subvert the *raison d'être* of Arab antisemitism.

Part III

Zionism as a technology

7 Zionism as a form of Jewish social policy

A melding of state and civil society took place in much of the western world in the latter part of the nineteenth century. According to Jürgen Habermas's classic formulation, the liberal-constitutional state which had developed over the previous two centuries had not intervened in economic and family life, that is, the spheres of commodity production and social reproduction. But by the *fin de siècle* the state was an invasive presence in the spheres of economics, education, and social and family welfare.[1]

Although Habermas's characterization of the liberal society of the turn of the nineteenth century is idealized, even ahistorical, his depiction of the fusion of state and civil society at the turn of the twentieth does successfully illustrate the origins of modern social policy, that is, the mobilization of public resources and administrative expertise for the material benefit of the populace as a whole. Moreover, just as the melding of state and civil society – the realms of public administration and economic life – engendered modern social policy, so a simultaneous intertwining of the institutional-administrative and socio-economic aspects of Jewish society produced a particularly Jewish social policy. Even when and where liberalism enjoyed its greatest hegemony in Europe, the nineteenth-century Jewish community as a legal entity had never dissolved, and the provision of charity had remained one of the community's most important functions in the eyes of the host society. From the 1860s, collective social action on the communal and eventually on a national and even international level assumed an ever greater scope. The poverty, persecution, and migration of Eastern European Jewry became the cynosure of Jewish institutional life in Western and Central Europe as well as the United States. The Jewish leadership elite devoted itself to solving the "Jewish Problem" through concerted action that would produce, it was hoped, a coherent and effective social policy. As we shall see in this chapter, the Zionist movement's diagnosis of Jewish socio-economic dysfunction, its prescribed therapy of social engineering, much of its institutional structure, and many of its operative sensibilities derived from and operated within the larger universe of modern Jewish social policy.[2]

The "Jewish Problem/Question": a discursive analysis

Before analyzing attempts by Jews to solve the "Jewish Problem," we need to take a close look at this term and its synonym, the "Jewish Question," for within them lie a host of assumptions that account for the very existence of an independent Jewish social policy.

Scholars who have written on the origin, meaning, and development of the term "the Jewish Question" have presented it as originating in a political, rather than a socio-economic, context. Moreover, they have focused on its usage in Germany as opposed to other lands. Jacob Toury observed that the phrase "*Die Judenfrage*" gained currency in Germany only in the early 1840s, after decades of gradual improvement in the socio-economic status of German Jewry. *Die Judenfrage* was employed by gentiles not to decry Jewish poverty or other forms of economic dysfunction, but rather to express unwillingness to admit a body which was still seen as a corporation into an imagined, homogeneous German nation. Similarly, Peter Pulzer has offered a conceptual distinction between the "Jewish Question" in Imperial Germany and antisemitism. The former, he claims, was a political issue, reflecting unresolved tensions in the Second Empire between confessional and national identity. Germany's failure to clearly define the criteria for citizenship and political integration left the status of the Jews open to public debate and thus opened the way to a political antisemitic movement.[3]

True, the term "the Jewish Question" did originate in Germany, although after mid-century it began to crop up in France and the English-speaking world as well. Moreover, although the term operated within the particular matrix of the Jews' political relationship with the lands in which they lived, the term nonetheless shares certain features in common with other linguistic forms in which, throughout the nineteenth century, the words "problem" or "question" were attached to various sources of social anxiety. A hegemonic elite or dominant majority group which discriminated against a subaltern or minority group called the latter a "problem," suggesting that it was mainly responsible for its own disabilities. Thus the constant invocation from the mid-nineteenth century of the "Social Question," that is, the misery of the pauperized and proletarianized lower orders and the threat they posed to bourgeois society, and the "Negro Question," that is, the debate over the fate of slavery.[4] The "Women's Question" throughout Europe and the "Irish Question" in England employed a similar taxonomy of dysfunction. In all these cases, the anxiety-producing groups were thought to be immature and irrational (workers, women, blacks, Irish), and so it was the responsibility of the reform-minded among the dominators to formulate and implement solutions, that is, to provide guidance, the obedient following of which was a sign of the anxiety-provoking group's worthiness for civil improvement.

Conceptualizations of the "Jewish Question" partially fit into this framework, yet the "Jewish Question" possessed unique features. Unlike the other groups mentioned above, Jews were thought to be fully capable of taking care of themselves. True, from the time of the Enlightenment until 1848, programs for Jewish civil improvement in Germany possessed a strong tutelary quality, but this was not the case in Western Europe, and, besides, even in Germany the tutelary quality faded in the second half of the century. In the late 1800s, as the immiseration of Eastern European Jewry deepened and emigration of Jews from Eastern Europe to the West skyrocketed, the Jews of Western and Central Europe were left to solve this massive social problem with little assistance from the state or other public sources of aid. Throughout the centuries, European Jewry had always cared for its own poor and was expected to continue doing so, this despite the removal in the modern era of virtually all the other functions of the traditional autonomous community. In general, Jewish activists welcomed this arrangement, partly to maintain Jewish communal institutions, and thereby collective identity, and partly to prevent the Jewish poor from embarrassing middle-class Jews and stimulating antisemitism.

Thus the nineteenth-century "Jewish Problem" was social as well as political. In turn, Jews who tried to solve the "problem" did not make a clear distinction between political action (lobbying world leaders, appealing to international public opinion) and social welfare work (establishing schools and vocational educational programs, relief and reconstruction, aid to immigrants). Therefore, as we shall now see, in the realms of both politics and social policy the Zionist movement was imbedded in a much larger project of Jewish rescue and renewal.

Zionism and Jewish politics: structural comparisons

The term "Jewish politics" can mean many things. From the late nineteenth century to the Holocaust, Jewish political organizations and parties flourished in Central and Eastern Europe. Spanning the ideological spectrum from ultra-Orthodoxy to Liberalism and from various forms of nationalism, including Zionism, to anti-Zionist socialism, these organizations (for example the Bund and Centralverein deutscher Staatsbürger jüdischen Glaubens) sought to advance the political, economic, and cultural interests of the Jews in the lands in which they lived. Another type of Jewish political organization, limited to the United States and those European countries whose Jewish populations had benefited from legal emancipation, aimed at improving the situation of unemancipated and persecuted Jews living in Rumania and the Russian and Ottoman Empires. These bodies included the Anglo-Jewish Association, Alliance Israélite Universelle, Hilfsverein der deutschen Juden, and Israelitische Allianz zu Wien.

In his brilliant essay on modern Jewish politics, Ezra Mendelsohn analyzes Zionism within the context of the first type of political organization; that is, he explains Zionism as a diaspora political movement which, in certain circumstances and geographic regions, was able to appeal to the hearts and minds of the Jewish masses more successfully than its rivals such as the

Bund, the Folkists, or the Agudat Yisrael.[5] Mendelsohn's analysis does not, however, incorporate the second type of organization, whose Zionist parallel would be not nationally based parties or pioneering organizations like He-Halutz so much as the WZO itself. Although the WZO's constituent federations (for example Mizrachi, Po'alei Tsiyon) engaged in political activity in the diaspora, in the eyes of the WZO leadership "politics" entailed, first and foremost, international diplomacy, influencing Great Power policies, and establishing a foothold in territory separate from the WZO's European base. Our concern here, therefore, is international not domestic Jewish politics; the politics of the WZO and not of Zionist parties within various lands, and the relationship between international Jewish politics and social policy.

All agents of international Jewish politics, the WZO included, envisioned a mutually beneficial relationship with the government of the state that housed the organization in question. The Alliance and the Hilfsverein, for example, claimed a consonance of interests between themselves and those of France and Germany, respectively. Paul Nathan, secretary of the Hilfsverein, observed that Germany's desire to expand its sphere of economic influence in the Ottoman Empire matched the Hilfsverein's philanthropic interest in the well-being of Palestinian Jewry.[6] Agents of international Jewish politics were not, as Zionist propagandists put it, merely currying favor with their host governments in order to enhance their status in the eyes of the gentiles; rather, they were following a stratagem, displayed most clearly by the WZO itself, of claiming a symbiotic relationship between the political interests of the Jews and of a certain Great Power or concert of them. The Alliance appealed to the *mission civilisatrice* of French imperialism in order to carry out a *mission civilisatrice israélite* of its own design.[7] What difference is there between this approach and Theodor Herzl's claim that the Zionists would manage the Ottoman Empire's finances, or Chaim Weizmann's depiction to the British of the Yishuv as Cerberus, zealously guarding the eastern approach to the Suez Canal?

Herzl carried out diplomatic activity largely on his own initiative, as did Weizmann during World War I. Nonetheless, these individuals claimed to speak for a well-organized international movement with a mass membership base. With some 217,000 members by 1913 and 844,000 by 1933, the WZO was the world's largest Jewish political organization.[8] Yet these numbers should not obscure the admittedly smaller, but still significant, membership base and international appeal of other agents of international Jewish politics. In 1885 the Alliance claimed more than 30,000 members. Some 20,000 individuals voted in the 1911 Alliance's central committee elections. The Hilfsverein numbered 10,000 members on the eve of World War I.[9] The Allianz zu Wien was smaller; at its peak its membership did not pass 4,500, but it was a highly cosmopolitan organization, with branches extending into every nook and cranny of the multinational and massive Hapsburg Empire.[10]

The Allianz zu Wien, Anglo-Jewish Association, and Hilfsverein all owed their existence in part to a desire by Jewish activists of various nationalities to free themselves of the hegemony of the Alliance. At the same time, the Alliance retained an international appeal (in the 1880s, 60 percent of the Alliance membership was not French), and close administrative and institutional ties linked the Alliance with its ostensible rivals. For example, the Deutsche Conferenz Gemeinschaft, formed in 1906, consisted of the German membership of the Alliance central committee. Berthold Timmendorfer, vice-president of the Hilfsverein, was also president of the Deutsche Conferenz Gemeinschaft.[11] Moreover, as we shall see below, most of the agents of Jewish politics sought to work in concert when addressing social-political issues such as the plight of Eastern European Jewry and its mass movement westward. Thus, despite the obvious discontinuities between them, there are important semantic connections between the Alliance's Hebrew name, Kol Yisrael Haverim (All Israel are comrades) and Herzl's celebrated proclamation in *The Jewish State* that "we are a people – one people."

True, large memberships and international co-operation did not necessarily translate into democratic management. Agencies of international Jewish politics were, by and large, oligarchic and plutocratic, and in this sense the WZO was something of an exception. The management style of organizations that devoted themselves purely to Jewish social policy was particularly oligarchic. For example, although the American Jewish Joint Distribution Committee (hereafter, the Joint) featured a complex organizational structure which reached down to local communities, policy was made entirely by a handful of the wealthiest Jewish men in America; as Louis Marshall said, "The work was so conducted that we would dispose of millions of dollars without a vote being taken."[12] The Jewish Colonization Association (JCA), the wealthiest Jewish philanthropy in Europe, was managed by a board of directors and a salaried bureaucracy and drew its funds entirely from the estate of the railway magnate Maurice de Hirsch.[13] According to longtime JCA official Emil Meyerson, "his board was not sensitive to public opinion . . . it enjoyed perfect immunity from any and all attacks by the Jewish press. . . . [and it] was not only autocratic and bureaucratic, but also plutocratic."[14] Both the Joint and the JCA looked with suspicion upon Eastern European Jews in general and Jewish socialists in Eastern Europe in particular. In correspondence between the two organizations, "worker" and "democrat" were used interchangeably, and both had negative connotations.[15]

The Joint and JCA also disliked Orthodoxy and strove to ward off rabbinic influence over their actions. Bernard Kahn, the omnicompetent director of the Joint's European activities, wanted to shoulder the Orthodox away from any leadership role in the Joint's post-World War I activities for economic reconstruction. He claimed that Orthodox Jews could never support the Joint's innovative credit co-operative schemes because of Mosaic prohibitions against the lending of money at interest.[16] Kahn's hostile and uninformed comment nicely illustrates that modern Jewish politics and social politics was, by and large, a secular affair. (The Agudat Yisrael constitutes, of course, a vital exception.) Jewish political leaders were frequently, like Herzl or Nathan, assimilated Jews who sought to accomplish in the sphere of Jewish politics what they could not in the gentile world. Extreme Orthodox Jews opposed the Alliance, Hilfsverein, and WZO as vehicles of assimilation, largely because of the agencies' common agenda to submit the Yishuv to a socio-economic sea-change involving weaning the Yishuv from charity (*halukkah*), introducing western education, and occupationally restructuring the Yishuv population. This view affected even the German Neo-Orthodox, who had been deeply influenced by the Haskalah. In the 1870s, Sampson Raphael Hirsch claimed that Yishuv society did not need to be reformed, that productivization projects were impracticable, and that control over *halukkah* should stay in the hands of the Yishuv's rabbinic leadership. *Der Israelit*, the newspaper of the Frankfurt Neo-Orthodox, maintained a hostility to groups like the Hilfsverein well into the twentieth century.

Those Orthodox Jews who became involved in organizations like the WZO, Hilfsverein, and Alliance were able to compartmentalize their religious sensibilities and justify their involvement in secular affairs in humanitarian terms. The historian Ehud Luz has examined the impact of this way of thinking on the founders of the religious-Zionist organization Mizrachi, but it can also account for Rabbi Esriel Hildesheimer's support for the Alliance and various German-Jewish secular philanthropies or the leadership role of *grand rabbin* Zadoc Kahn in the Alliance. Moreover, both men accepted as valid the Haskalah's critique of Jewish economic dysfunction, particularly in Palestine, though Hildesheimer, in keeping with traditional Jewish attitudes towards charity, shunned the harsh, Social Darwinist language of the secular Jewish organizations and took a more generous stand on offering aid to the infirm and unproductive.[17]

It was in Palestine that the greatest amount of agreement between Zionists and other agents of international Jewish politics could be found. This statement might sound odd, given the celebrated history of conflict between the WZO and organizations such as the Alliance or Hilfsverein. But numerous areas of concord, co-operation, and overlap existed between the WZO and its ostensible rivals in the field of *social* policy, for example education and agricultural settlement. Assimilationist political organizations may have considered Zionism illegitimate, a bar sinister to be kept off their patriotic coats of arms, but nonetheless they maintained a deep, if not always clearly articulated, attachment to Eretz Israel, their natural parent.

Zionism, Jewish social policy, and the Yishuv

The Yishuv, in particular its rural sector, owed its existence to non-Zionist sources. The founding of the agricultural school Mikveh Israel in 1870 marked the beginning of the Alliance's Palestinian activity. Close connections developed between the Alliance, the administration established by Edmond de Rothschild over the fledgling First Aliyah settlements in the 1880s, and the JCA. In 1896 the JCA became involved in Palestine and in 1900 a separate section within the JCA, the Commission Palestinienne (CP), took over the administration of the Rothschild colonies. In 1913 the CP became a more autonomous agency, and in 1924, under the presidency of Edmond's son, James, it broke away from the JCA altogether and became the Palestine Jewish Colonization Association, or PICA. In 1914, the JCA and CP held more than half of the Yishuv's rural real estate; in 1936, JCA/PICA holdings amounted to one-third of the rural Yishuv.[18]

At the turn of the century, the JCA's managerial board contained both opponents of and zealous enthusiasts for colonization in Palestine. During the decade after 1896 the enthusiasts, led by Zadoc Kahn and Narcisse Leven, JCA president, won the day. Leven and Kahn were explicitly Zionist; they had been leaders of the Paris Choveve Tsiyon, in which the director of the CP, Emil Meyerson, was also active during the 1890s. Levin and Meyerson drew up plans for Jewish colonization and instructed the JCA's man in Palestine, Joseph Niégo, to purchase sizeable tracts in the Galilee. Meyerson hoped to demonstrate the superiority of Palestine over Argentina as a site for colonization, and he, like Niégo, favored the gradual development of a sizeable Jewish presence in the Palestinian countryside.[19] After World War I, Meyerson and Louis Oungré, director-general of the JCA, expressed smug satisfaction with the JCA's accomplishments; they observed ironically that due to the constraints of political Zionism, the WZO "took no interest for many years" in colonization, and that it was the colonies set up or administered by the JCA that had enabled political Zionism to achieve its greatest triumph, the Balfour Declaration.[20]

There were also close personal and institutional links between Zionism and the most effective agent of Jewish social policy during the interwar era, the Joint Distribution Committee. Bernard Kahn (1876–1955), manager of the Joint's European operations during much of the interwar period, had worked before the war as secretary of the Hilfsverein, where he was involved, among other things, with the construction of the Haifa *Technikum*, a source of great controversy between the Hilfsverein and the WZO. But before going to work for the Hilfsverein, Kahn had been an avowed Zionist and a delegate to the Fifth and Sixth Zionist Congresses. A series of lectures which he delivered in Munich over the years 1901–3 expressed a deep attachment to cultural Zionism.[21] While employed at the Joint, Kahn sat on the boards of directors of the Palestine Economic Corporation and Keren Hayesod and on the non-Zionist portion of the JA Executive. Clearly, Kahn was devoted to the Yishuv, even if he built his career outside a formal Zionist framework.[22]

The Joint paid considerable attention to Palestine, both in the form of Reconstruction activity and support for the Palestine Economic Corporation, which invested in a wide variety of business enterprises and public works. The Yishuv, only a few scores of thousands strong, received more than 10 percent of the Joint's worldwide distributions to millions of Jews over the period 1914–28.[23] Yet relations between the WZO and the Joint were often tense, and Chaim Weizmann's efforts throughout the 1920s to attract the Joint's plutocratic leaders into an enlarged Jewish Agency aroused considerable opposition in Zionist circles. Zionists were enraged by the Joint's heavy investments in the Agro-Joint, a colonization venture in the Crimea and Ukraine. The Agro-Joint, like the JCA's Argentinean colonies, appeared to Zionists as a sign of equivocation towards or outright rejection of the only authentic and feasible solution to the "Jewish Problem." Zionism demanded exclusivity and total commitment.

Unlike other recipients of the Joint's largesse, members of the Yishuv, according to David De Sola Pool, director of the Joint's Reconstruction activity in postwar Palestine, believed that "it is the *duty* of outside Jewry to send them money for them to distribute and used [sic] as they see fit."[24] No matter how strong the commitment of agencies like the JCA or Joint to the Yishuv, essential differences existed between the philanthropies, which were hierarchical, oligarchic, and plutocratic, and the anti-authoritarian, egalitarian, and politicized factions that comprised the Yishuv. As De Sola Pool complained, not only was the Yishuv wretchedly poor, it contained no reliable persons in whose hands Joint funds could be left, because no one, from the ultra-Orthodox to the barefoot pioneer laborers, stands "above party and narrower interests." Epitomizing the Brahmin spirit of the Joint, De Sola Pool observed mournfully that the Yishuv had no class of "leisured and disinterested men needed to constitute the directors of public institutions."[25]

Clearly, there were significant differences between the Zionists and the other agents of Jewish social policy in the conception and envisioned solution of the "Jewish Problem." The interesting case of the young Bernard Kahn aside, non-Zionist philanthropists rarely articulated the existence of a "problem of Judaism," that is, a cultural or spiritual crisis among the Jews. This notion was, of course, central to cultural Zionism. And while both Zionists and non-Zionists agreed that there was a political "problem of the Jews," non-Zionists, no matter how attached and committed to the development of the Yishuv, balked at the proclaimed goal of the attainment of Jewish sovereignty over Palestine. Finally, just as the WZO's politics was a more public affair than that of other international Jewish organizations, so Zionist social policy breathed an unusually democratic, even radical spirit.[26] Yet, despite all these differences, Zionists and activists in non-Zionist international Jewish organizations shared many common assumptions about the "Jewish Problem": not merely the idea of Palestine as a solution to the problem, but rather, as we shall see, an entire array of social and economic sensibilities.

Zionism and Jewish social policy: conceptual and operative similarities

Bourgeois society stigmatized poverty as a sign of moral degeneration. The indiscriminate giving of alms was seen as a stimulus to profligacy. Jewish social policy's careful selection of those worthy of aid, strict supervision, and unceasing moral education of its beneficiaries clearly reflected current bourgeois conceptions of the relationship between industry and morality and of the need for a tutelary relationship between benefactor and beneficiary. Such thinking stimulated efforts by Western European Jews throughout the nineteenth century to wean poor Jewish youths away from peddling and train them instead in crafts and, at times, agriculture.[27] From 1870, these concepts motivated Jewish social policy in Palestine, which Western European Jewish activists viewed as both a Holy Land and a sink of poverty, to be reformed, like the European Jewish *Lumpenproletariat*, through education, vocational training, and close supervision.[28]

Yet Jewish social policy, in Palestine and elsewhere, differed from its general counterpart in that fear was not one of its prime motivations. Throughout the nineteenth century, Jewish philanthropists and communal activists in Germany, although quick to bemoan the extent of Jewish poverty, denied the existence of a Jewish dangerous class threatening to attack the "educated, upper classes."[29] In England as well as Germany, the escalating crisis of Eastern European Jewry from the 1860s rarely instilled into Jewish philanthropists a dread of physical abuse by their beneficiaries.[30] Embarrassment and worry about gentile reactions to the presence of the Jewish poor, on the other hand, were important motive forces behind the development of Jewish social policy at the *fin de siècle*.[31] Over the period 1881–1914, the flood of Eastern European Jewish refugees seeking passage to points west aroused worry lest the refugees became a public charge, and Jewish philanthropies, in Europe as well as the United States, agreed that only the young and healthy should be allowed to make the Atlantic trek. Anglo-, German-, and Austrian-Jewish philanthropies repatriated scores of thousands of Russian Jews deemed unworthy of emigration.[32] Joseph Ritter von Wertheimer, founder of the Allianz zu Wien, compared these unfortunates to the generation of the desert, intractable and uneducable.[33] The Darwinistic culling of humanity which was practiced by the emigration assistance programs was even more apparent in the Argentinean and Palestinian colonies of the JCA, which invested great effort locating what Emil Meyerson called "selected human material": sturdy, resourceful, and independent.[34]

Zionism fits well into the cultural matrix which we have just outlined. Mainstream Zionist thinking reflected much of general Jewish social policy's sense of embarrassment and shame, its internalization of economic antisemitism and its desire to demonstrate to the gentiles that Jews are not inveterate *shnorrers*. This point may be nicely illustrated by comparing Arthur Ruppin, the WZO's chief technocrat through the 1920s, and James Rosenberg, a leader of the Joint whose pet project was the Agro-Joint. As youths, both men endured antisemitic taunts and in large measure accepted as true claims that Jews tended to be crass, venal, and parasitic. Both were confirmed racialists who longed to bring about an esthetic as well as economic improvement of the Jews. As a youth, Ruppin aspired to join an antisemitic German political party; the mature Rosenberg deliberately purchased Ford tractors for the Joint's Russian work in order to prove to Henry Ford, America's most influential antisemite, that Jews could successfully work the soil.[35]

On a more pleasant note, Zionist social policies, like those of the non-Zionist philanthropies, had little to do with any concept of an imminent Red Peril. Even before World War I, the WZO formed close relations with the Yishuv's labor movement, and although bourgeois and, later, Revisionist Zionists attacked this alliance, even Labor's staunchest enemies rarely spoke of a forthcoming massacre of the Yishuv's middle class. What is more, until the 1930s the Zionist labor movement and its bureaucratic allies in the WZO agreed that emigration, although a matter to be left entirely in the hands of the Zionists, rather than any external authority, must be selective, with careful consideration of the quality of the "human material" (*homer enushi*, *Menschenmaterial*) seeking entrance into the Jewish National Home. For the Zionists, as for the other vehicles of Jewish social policy, the phrase "human material" had numerous conceptual echoes, evoking notions of human meliorability and malleability, yet also of the power of degenerate material to destroy a fragile and precious undertaking; of the essentiality of a Pygmalion to mold the material into its proper shape and the ambiguity of the "material's" freedom of agency.[36] For the Zionists, as for the other agents of Jewish social policy, immigration was not necessarily a universal right; it needed to be regulated, adjusted to the absorptive capacity of the destination (be it Palestine during the Ottoman or early Mandate periods or the United States at the *fin de siècle*), and suited to the long-term economic interests of the new homeland.[37]

Jewish social policy was social engineering, an attempt to create a blueprint for a new type of Jew, both in the diaspora and in Palestine. Throughout the western world, the makers of Jewish social policy strove for rationality, planning, and centralization. Between 1869 and 1882, six international assemblies of Jewish political and philanthropic organizations were held to organize Eastern European Jewish emigration to the West. The 1903 Kishinev Pogrom spurred another round of internationally co-ordinated relief activity and emigration assistance.[38] Within a few years of being authorized to operate within the Russian Empire, the JCA undertook systematic statistical studies of rural Russian Jewry; these studies formed the basis of its extensive program of vocational education and technology transfer.[39] For Maurice de Hirsch, the JCA's creator, "planning" entailed not merely the rationalization of aid-distribution but rather a full-blown program for mass colonization in Argentina. In 1891, Hirsch formulated a vision of Jewish social engineering no less audacious than Herzl's celebrated manifesto *The Jewish State*, written four years later. Hirsch called for the movement of 3.5 million Jews out of Russia over twenty-five years. Like Herzl, Hirsch argued that the migration, settlement, and vocational training of these millions of Jews were to be carefully orchestrated and to be carried out with full and public approval from the suzerain. "One cannot," said Hirsch, "start colonizing haphazardly, and the movement should be preceded by a preliminary serious and careful investigation." These lines, which could easily have come from Herzl, were penned by Hirsch, who wrote them with reference to Palestine, which he believed to be unsuitable for mass colonization.[40]

Social engineering demands direction – not charismatic leadership or military command so much as technical administration. From its inception, the Zionist movement was steeped in a cult of technical expertise. Herzl's writings abound with Jules Verne-like technological wonders and paeans to their makers. From the turn of the century, the WZO developed a technocratic elite with considerable policy-making powers, and during the Mandate period the technical expert was absorbed into the Yishuv's pantheon of heroes, alongside the farmer, laborer, and warrior.[41] Other forms of Jewish social policy were, if anything, even more in thrall to technocracy because they lacked the democratic structure of the WZO and the anti-authoritarian ethos of the Yishuv's labor movement. Hirsch relied heavily on commissions of experts before approving the Argentinean project, and his principle objection to the Russian Choveve Tsiyon's Palestinian activity was their failure to employ experts to perform a feasibility study.[42] Similarly, within the Joint Distribution Committee Bernard Kahn and Joseph Rosen, director of the Agro-Joint in Russia, wielded wide-ranging policy-making powers. Rosen, a distinguished Russian agronomist with a revolutionary background, enchanted Felix Warburg and the Joint's other Croesuses with his scientific knowledge, good relations with the Soviet authorities, and intensity, even severity, of character.[43]

In one of the great ironies of Zionist history, the Joint's adoration of technical expertise both helped set off a major crisis in the WZO's relations with non-Zionist Jewish philanthropists and provided a solution to that crisis. The Agro-Joint's activities in Crimea and the Ukraine provoked outrage among Zionist activists who despaired at seeing millions of dollars poured into the Soviet Union when that money, they felt, should be going to support the Zionist project. While WZO President Chaim Weizmann labored to win over the likes of Louis Marshall and Felix Warburg to an enlarged Jewish Agency, American Zionist leaders deeply offended these pillars of the Joint by denouncing them as anti-Jewish, anti-British, and even pro-Bolshevik. Seeking a solution to the crisis, Weizmann suggested that Rosen be sent to Palestine to inspect the land and prepare recommendations for its rational development. The proposal was the balm of Gilead; Marshall accepted it immediately. Rosen did not serve on the commission, but other noted authorities did, and Marshall agreed to accept the expansion of the Jewish Agency upon submission of the committee report (few of whose recommendations were, in fact, followed).[44]

Ideally, Jewish social policy – planned, centralized, well funded, and guided by competent experts – was to solve the "Jewish Problem" through one of three ways: improvement of the social and political position of Eastern European Jews *in situ*, limited assisted emigration of skilled workers to economically advanced regions like the eastern United States, and mass agricultural colonization in thinly populated territories such as Argentina, the western United States, or Palestine (if one accepts conventional Zionist views of the land as a *Raum ohne Volk*). In fact, none of these three scenarios worked out as planned, not for lack of will or vision, but rather for lack of resources in the face of what had become, as early as the end of the 1860s, an unstoppable sea of refugees which overwhelmed the relatively prosperous Jewish communities of Western and Central Europe.[45]

The flood of refugees created a sense of deep crisis and impending catastrophe. The ominous tone that characterizes Zionist discourse from Pinsker on was part and parcel of modern Jewish social policy as a whole. So was the feeling of bearing sole responsibility for the treatment of the "Jewish Problem," a burden which the Jews' host societies did not wish to assume and which, they believed, wealthy Jews were perfectly capable of handling on their own. It is a staple of Zionist historiography that the founding fathers of Zionism understood, and Jewish assimilationists did not, that antisemitism was indelible and that there was no alternative to a mass emigration of Jews from Europe. But this view is not accurate. It is true that most Jewish political activity up to around 1900 was aimed at improving the conditions of Jewish life *in situ*. On the level of social policy, Jewish organizations set up schools and vocational education programs in Eastern Europe and the Middle East so that children from pauperized Jewish families might have a livelihood. The Jewish philanthropies, however, were anything but irenic about the future of Jewish life throughout much of the diaspora. In 1870, Narcisse Leven spoke of the impossibility of continued Jewish life in Russia: the railroads were destroying the Jewish commercial network based on small-scale peddling; there were too many Jewish laborers and craftsmen in the Pale, and agriculture was forbidden to them. Large-scale emigration to the United States was a welcome solution to this pressing problem.[46] In the early 1880s, the flood of Eastern European Jewish refugees in Brody led Charles Netter, the Alliance's man on the scene, to write that antisemitism was unstoppable, that mass emigration had only begun, and that it was the responsibility of western Jewry to organize and rationalize this great wave of humanity.[47]

At the same time that Netter penned these lines, the leaders of the Allianz zu Wien were sadly observing the limited ability of Jewish politics to improve the situation of the Jews of Rumania, whose government blithely ignored the commitments which, thanks to Jewish lobbying, had been imposed upon it by the Congress of Berlin. Two decades later, the Kishinev Pogrom sent a shudder through not only the Zionist movement but also the Jewish political and philanthropic network as a whole. In the face of catastrophe, agencies like the Hilfsverein and Allianz zu Wien set aside their programs for the gradual socio-economic transformation of Eastern

European Jews and hurriedly mobilized massive fundraising drives for relief and emigration assistance. By 1910, the Vienna Allianz had despaired altogether of the power of Jewish politics to secure the future of Eastern European Jewry; its annual report observed darkly that just as Russia's "rape of Finland" had failed to provoke substantial opposition from international public opinion, neither would Russia's oppression of the Jews.[48]

The pressure of events, combined with a lack of funds, meant that there was neither the time nor the money to plan and implement a comprehensive Jewish social policy; instead, Jewish aid agencies jumped from one stop-gap measure to the next: immigration assistance, relief efforts, and reconstruction activities in areas ravaged by war, disease, and pogroms. The sense of urgency, and the amounts expended, increased greatly after World War I. Most emigration, both before and after the war, took place spontaneously and without philanthropic guidance or assistance. For example, between 1903 and 1907 the Hilfsverein assisted the transmigration of 60,000 Eastern European Jews, less than 10 percent of the total number of Jewish emigrants over that period.[49] In Argentina, most Jewish emigration from the 1890s through the 1930s took place outside of the framework of the JCA's colonization program. Similarly, during the Ottoman and early Mandate periods, the bulk of Jewish emigration to Palestine took place without significant support from the WZO, whose shoestring immigration and settlement budget was committed largely to rural co-operative settlements, home to only 5 percent of the Yishuv's population.[50] Much as the officers of the WZO strove to formulate grand plans for the development of the country, little could be done in the face of the worsening crisis of Eastern European Jewry, strife with the Palestinian Arabs, painfully slow fundraising efforts, and the fickleness of Palestine's suzerain, be it Turkey or Britain.

Better prospects for planned colonization reigned in projects sponsored by non-Zionist philanthropies that had more money than the WZO and operated in less flammable environments. The JCA had managed by 1911 to settle 19,000 Jews on the Argentinean pampas, 50 percent more than the number of Jews in agricultural colonies in Palestine at the time.[51] But the Argentinean project eventually failed because of the attraction of Argentina's booming cities and the lack of a social or political ideal that could compensate Jewish immigrants for the enormous difficulties of agricultural life. If a non-Zionist colonization project was to work, it required not only a favorable attitude from the territorial suzerain but also a large pool of potential colonists already *in situ* and without any attractive options to life as farmers.

The one case in the history of Jewish social policy where this constellation of factors appeared to operate was the work of the Agro-Joint in the USSR. Therefore this subject, as neglected as it is fascinating, deserves our special attention.

Active between 1924 and 1938, the Agro-Joint spent over $16 million, more than the entire WZO immigration and colonization budget for the period. The project enjoyed many other advantages over its Zionist counterpart: whereas the Zionists had to pay dearly for the land they bought, vast tracts – over 1 million acres in Ukraine and the Crimea – were leased out to Jewish settlers at no or a nominal charge. The settlers had access to copious and free supplies of lumber, reduced rates for the transportation of agricultural produce and machinery, and exemption from conscription.[52] What is more, the USSR was home to hundreds of thousands of *déclassé* (*lishentsy*) Jewish petty tradesmen who, being neither workers nor peasants, had been deprived of civil rights by the Bolshevik government and were desperate for a livelihood that would return them to full citizenship. Finally, the Soviet government appeared to welcome the Agro-Joint's involvement as a source of hard currency and a means of increasing agricultural production and solving the problem of the *lishentsy* Jews.[53]

The Agro-Joint operated in a wholly depoliticized and hierarchical atmosphere. True, some of the colonies had been founded by Zionists; Tel Chai, a collective settlement founded in 1922 by Hehalutz, was, according to Bernard Kahn, "in a certain sense the mother-colony of all the Jewish colonies in the Crimea." There were other Zionist colonies, such as nearby Mishmar (a split-off from Tel Chai), run as a moshav rather than a kibbutz, and another collective, Haklaj.[54] But these Zionist colonies account for only a few hundred souls, whereas the Agro-Joint actively assisted the settlement of some 60,000 Jews on the soil. Unlike the Yishuv, whose agricultural population made considerable demands on the WZO, the Agro-Joint's colonists had no say in the management of the operation or the disbursement of resources. Policy was made by Rosen and his staff of some 3,000 technicians of various sorts.[55] Rosen was a strict manager, disciplining or rewarding settlers as he saw fit.

For the leaders of the Joint, the Agro-Joint and the enlarged Jewish Agency were part of a greater whole, a vast solution to the Eastern European "Jewish Problem."[56] Thus the rapprochement between the WZO and the Croesuses of American Jewry occurred precisely as the latter were intensifying their involvement in the Soviet Union; in 1928, at Rosen's initiative, they established the American Society for Farm Settlements in Russia, which, within five years, had raised almost $5 million, most of this coming from Sears–Roebuck founder Julius Rosenwald and Warburg himself.[57] Zionists considered this action an act of folly and a sign of craven assimilationism. But it was endorsed enthusiastically by the likes of Bernard Kahn, no enemy of Zionism, who, when the Agro-Joint was starting up, cabled his superiors that "Jewish settling on land Russia is most important reconstructive work we can do [sic]. … This new agricultural movement among Russian Jews has in my opinion no equal in Jewish history and cannot be measured by any other colonization experience."[58]

The Zionists were right in accusing the Agro-Joint of placing too much faith in the goodwill of the Soviet government. Soviet policy towards the Agro-Joint was informed by antisemitism, suspicion, and exaggerated notions of American-Jewish wealth. At first, Ukrainian authorities were willing to accept a limited number of Jewish colonists, mainly in the hope that the settlements would pull Jews out of the Ukraine's cities, thereby fostering the creation of a Ukrainian urban professional and managerial class. But by 1926 Ukrainian attitudes towards the Agro-Joint had become solidly adversarial. Soviet authorities switched the Agro-Joint's focus to Crimea, although stiff opposition came from Crimean Communist Party officials as well as the indigenous Crimean Tatars, who felt that their land was being overrun by foreigners, first Russians, and now Jews.[59] Champions of the Agro-Joint were wont to claim that their project was superior to that of the Zionists because the Russian territories, unlike Palestine, were thinly populated and lacked a hostile indigenous population. But this was not the case.

A deadly combination of antisemitism and massive economic change in the Soviet Union ensured that the path blazed by the Agro-Joint would lead to oblivion. Under Stalin, agricultural collectivization and industrialization made farming unattractive to Jews, who swarmed to cities to become technicians, scientists, and administrators in factory life. In the mid-1930s Stalin's purges wiped out most of the Agro-Joint staff; in 1941 the German army annihilated the agricultural colonies themselves.[60] Too late, Rosen became a Territorialist; he realized that control over Jewish immigration to and settlement in any territory must be entirely in the hands of Jews. He toyed with the idea of transferring Palestine's Arabs to British Guiana and making Palestine into a purely Jewish territory "in spite of the fact that Palestine could never be expected to be a peaceful country, being as it is located in a pivotal position and at the crossroads of the three religions."[61] But this thoroughly assimilated Jew, who, in a life of ceaseless labor to solve the "Jewish Problem," had studiously avoided any involvement in or even mention of Palestine, did not turn his gaze towards the Middle East. Instead he tried to develop a Jewish colony in British Guiana, and then in the Dominican Republic, where he had a stroke, after which he lingered in agony until his death in 1949.

The Agro-Joint did not solve the problem of Jewish persecution, poverty, and economic marginalization. Nor did any other form of Jewish social policy active in the diaspora. But in the 1930s it was not clear that the Zionist movement would necessarily reach a better result; the Yishuv could not feed or sustain itself, and it depended heavily on Arab labor. The significance of Jewish social policy over the period examined in this chapter lies not only in its accomplishments but also in its effect on those who worked within its network; that is, we must look at the founders and benefactors as well as the beneficiaries.

The "Jewish Problem" weighed heavily on the minds of the architects of Jewish social policy. Conceptions of the problem and solutions to it did vary, but there is a sufficient family resemblance between the various individuals whom we have analyzed in this chapter so as to claim the existence of an international community of Jewish activists united by a sense of political and economic crisis. The activists agreed that Jews would have to solve the problem alone and that they would do so through an international mobilization of Jewish capital and expertise. According to this activist world-view, Jewish leadership could no longer be limited to spiritual or communal affairs alone; the socio-economic fabric of *klal Yisrael* was in tatters, and the Jews' public responsibilities perforce extended into the private sphere of family and economic life.

The work of the WZO, Joint, and other Jewish organizations during the 1920s represented the fulfillment of a process that had begun some seventy years previously. In 1854, the conservative rabbinic leader Zecharias Frankel claimed that philanthropic activity in Palestine would be a source of benefit to Middle Eastern Jewry as a whole and, in addition, "a central point [which] alone can arrange the link between occidental Jews and those scattered across Asia."[62] At around the same time, the influential Reform rabbi Ludwig Philippson spoke of international Jewish activity on behalf of Palestinian and Eastern European Jewry as a source of solidarity among the increasingly secularized and culturally divided Jews of the western world. The founders of the Alliance Israélite Universelle held similar views; Palestine held pride of place in a vision of international Jewish unity through philanthropic activity. In 1869, at a meeting of the leadership of the Alliance and German-Jewish communities, Alliance president Adolphe Crémieux embraced Morritz Lazarus, the German-Jewish scholar and activist, and exclaimed, "At this moment we are not French or Germans – we are Jews!"[63]

From the 1870s through World War I, Jewish philanthropies displayed high levels of mutual co-operation and a sense of common purpose, although there were, as happens in any assemblage of institutions, inevitable rivalries and struggles for hegemony. In the 1920s, however hostile Zionists may have been to the Agro-Joint, they appreciated the consciousness-raising potential of Jewish social policy: In Weimar Germany, for example, Zionists cheered the establishment of a unified national network of Jewish social policy, the *Zentralwohlfahrtsstelle*, which they saw as a vehicle of Jewish national unity.[64]

Social policy remains an essential component of contemporary Jewish life. It provides material aid to the beneficiaries and a sense of collective identity to the benefactors. There remains the potential for conflict between various petitioners for aid, thus the controversies throughout the later 1990s surrounding the diversion of United Jewish Appeal funds, formerly earmarked for the Jewish Agency, to local federations in the United States or to other beneficiaries in Israel (including, ironically, the Joint Distribution Committee, the Jewish Agency's historic nemesis). The difference between contemporary Jewish social policy and its earlier counterpart is that since the end of World War II the "Jewish Problem" has undergone a conceptual sea-change. Although political persecution and economic want still motivate donors, the notion of economic dysfunction, that is, of a malformed Jewish occupational profile that must be changed through "productivization," has almost entirely faded away. The horrors of Nazi persecution and the Holocaust have blocked the internalization by Jews of economic antisemitism. The idealization of physical labor and primary production, central to earlier forms of Jewish social thought, could not survive in a world where smallholding farming has given way to impersonal agribusiness and where services and high-technology industry have supplanted heavy industrial production as the leading economic sectors. Jewish activists in the contemporary world still operate in a mental universe of constant crisis, but the dangers are more political (threats to the state of Israel) and demographic (the corrosive effects of assimilation and intermarriage) than economic.

Over the past five years, the second Palestinian Intifada, the September 11, 2001, terrorist attacks against the United States and the Iraq War have stimulated a revival of antisemitism in Europe and a further strengthening of it in the Middle East. This antisemitism is often referred to by pundits as "new," meaning that it has awoken after several decades of post-Holocaust dormancy, and that it justifies hating Jews in terms of the alleged misdeeds of the state of Israel rather than the loci of pre-1945 antisemitism, which were the Jews' religious beliefs and practices, economic behavior, and position in society. Intriguingly, however worrisome antisemitism may be in our own day, the term "the Jewish Question" has fallen out of use, and it has done so because the antisemitic cognitive framework that conceived of the Jews as constituting a specific socio-political problem is no longer a part of mainstream sensibility in the western world. In turn, although a particularly Jewish social policy continues to operate, no one in the western world charged with managing social welfare expects the Jews to bear the entire burden of caring for their own kind. Jews will always have problems – grave, even existential ones – but the "Jewish Problem" as it was conceived in pre-Holocaust Europe no longer exists.

8 Technical expertise and the construction of the rural Yishuv

The Zionist movement revered technical expertise as an essential tool for the construction of a Jewish homeland. Throughout the formative decades of the Yishuv, however, there was disagreement within the Zionist movement about the role that technical experts should play in the Zionist leadership. The dominant view, developed by members of the Yishuv's labor movement, and accepted by key officials in the WZO, relegated experts to an advisory role to the political leadership. A minority view, associated most closely with the American Zionist leader Louis Brandeis and his supporters, held that the construction of the Jewish homeland should be entrusted to expert managers and technicians, who would operate without consideration for political ideologies or interests.

The intellectual roots of the first view lay in *fin-de-siècle* political economy, which viewed science as an indispensable tool of state power. Exponents of Zionist political economy saw the WZO as a government with the responsibility to direct and, where needed, to fund the nation-building enterprise in Palestine. The directors of the WZO's colonization institutions saw in the Yishuv's agricultural sector the backbone of the future Jewish national economy and considered it less able than the urban and industrial sectors to develop without financial and technical assistance from public sources. The principal beneficiaries of assistance from the WZO, youthful pioneer laborers from Eastern Europe, shared the WZO's reverence for technical knowledge but distrusted technicians, whom they suspected of plotting to limit the workers' freedom of action and rule over them in a dictatorial fashion. In the eyes of the pioneer laborers, a technician should not lead, but rather make vital resources and information available to the workers to use as they saw fit. Key figures in the WZO's settlement institutions accepted this subordinate status for the technician, and employed technical experts to guide, rather than direct, the labor movement in the construction of *hityashvut ovedet*: publicly funded, co-operative agricultural settlement based on autonomous labor.[1]

The Zionist labor movement's anti-professional, autodidactic, and politicized technical ethos was the object of constant criticism in the Yishuv and the WZO. From its beginning, the Zionist movement featured an alternative conception of technical expertise, drawn more from business economics than political economy and tending to favor as its model the corporation rather than the state. This approach, taken by non-Zionist vehicles of Jewish social policy such as the American Jewish Joint Distribution Committee (JDC), was characterized by a yearning for businesslike methods and efficiency, as well as the conviction that apolitical experts should direct economic activity. In the Zionist movement, this position was most popular during the 1920s, and for a brief period its champions wielded influence over the WZO's settlement institutions. But as a result of the tumultuous events of the years 1929–39 the Zionist settlement enterprise fused politics and economics tightly together. Technical expertise was mobilized to serve the political and military leadership of the Yishuv.

In both the political-economic and business-economic approaches to Zionist colonization, the concept of technical expertise included administrative and managerial skill as well as applied scientific knowledge. It has been a common view throughout the twentieth century that managerial and scientific knowledge exist in symbiosis; industrial experts create technology, but experts in the policy sciences implement it. When used in this chapter, therefore, the term "technical expertise" refers to all forms of instrumentally rational behavior informed by specialized knowledge.[2]

Science, Jewish social policy, and Zionism

Nineteenth-century Europe exuded technophilia, an optimism about the ability of *homo faber* to manipulate his environment for the betterment of all humanity. The impact of the European technical ethos on Jewish sensibilities, however, was limited. True, the Jewish press reported extensively on scientific innovation, but it did so as part of a general program of disseminating enlightenment and promoting an emancipationist ideology. Not many Jews, even in relatively open western European societies, pursued advanced technical careers other than the practice of medicine. In Germany, a country whose Jewish population was occupationally diverse and socially mobile, in 1907 only 1 percent of the Jewish labor force worked in second Industrial Revolution fields such as the electrical and chemical industries.[3] Unlike medicine, engineering and chemistry were not easily practiced through self-employment, but rather were practiced through large firms and government agencies, often bastions of antisemitism.[4] Moreover, for all the lip-service paid to the practical sciences in *fin-de-siècle* Germany, engineers' salaries were not high, nor were engineers, who lacked a classical education, readily welcomed into the *Bildungsbürgertum*.[5] So, even if available, a technical occupation did not offer the sort of income and status that would appeal to a socially mobile Jew.

To be sure, there were Jewish pioneers in the European electrochemical industry (for example Emil Rathenau, founder of the German Allgemeine Elektrizitäts-Gesellschaft, and the light-bulb magnate and Zionist leader

Johann Kremenetzky). Russian Jews enrolled at Central European technical institutions, and there were a number of celebrated Jewish mathematicians, chemists, and physicists on university faculties.[6] But not only were such people the smallest of minorities among the Jews, they did not represent a leadership force within the Jewish community itself. From the mid-1800s to World War I, Jewish leadership came primarily from businessmen, with doctors and lawyers entering the leadership ranks in increasing numbers with time.

Even though modern Jewish society did not participate fully in the cult of scientific knowledge, technical occupations had a symbolic value for Jewish communal activists, who saw them, along with crafts and agriculture, as more respectable and economically secure than commerce, the Jews' traditional livelihood. Moreover, Jewish leaders acknowledged the importance of managerial and economic expertise in formulating a comprehensive policy to handle Jewish poverty and vagrancy, problems ever-present in Jewish society but aggravated by the mass movement, beginning in the late 1860s, of impoverished Jews from Eastern to Western Europe. In Germany, Jewish philanthropic activists came under the influence of social Darwinism and sociological theory; some had advanced training in economics or political economy. Placing a new emphasis on Jewish uniqueness as well as commonality with the host society, the activists claimed that the Jews comprised a "national body" (*Volkskörper*) which had to act collectively, through communally generated social policy, to solve its ostensibly unique economic problems. Acting in this spirit, Jewish relief societies such as the Hilfsverein der deutschen Juden employed, and at times pioneered, new organizational methods for inspecting applicants for aid, arranging transport abroad, and providing social-welfare services for those who stayed in Europe.[7]

After 1914 the purview of modern Jewish social policy, and with it its degree of professionalization, increased markedly. The JDC provided wartime relief to Eastern Europe's ravaged Jewish communities and, after the armistice, undertook their reconstruction. It did so, according to official histories of the organization, by establishing "a group of efficient social engineers, experts in welfare work and relief, men and women trained in medical sanitation, migration, child care, cultural and economic affairs."[8] In Russia, the American Jewish Joint Agricultural Corporation, known as the Agro-Joint, along with the London-based Jewish Colonization Association (JCA), fielded a staff of agronomists and machinists in a massive effort to transform *déclassé* Russian Jews into respected agriculturalists.[9]

Non-Zionist philanthropies active in Ottoman and Mandate Palestine operated with a similar concern for technical development. The Alliance Israélite Universelle, which established the agricultural school Mikveh Israel near Jaffa in 1870, was the first organization to employ agronomists in the service of Jewish agriculture. The settlement enterprise of Baron Edmond de Rothschild, entrusted in 1900 to the JCA and transferred in 1924 to the independent Palestine Jewish Colonization Association (PICA), invested vast sums in agricultural technology and imported a host of agronomists and other technicians. Scientific experts, however, played a negligible leadership role in these enterprises, which were directed by wealthy Jewish financiers and a professional administrative staff. Moreover, these philanthropies respected scientific knowledge for its practical benefits alone, and did not invoke it as a source of authority or an inspiration for a broad social vision.[10]

In the Zionist movement, on the other hand, technology served ideological as well as practical ends. Zionist ideology was strongly utopian. Beginning with Saint-Simonian dithyrambs about the transformative power of science and industry, and culminating in the fantastic *Zukunftsromane* of the *fin de siècle*, nineteenth-century utopianism epitomized the liberal view of man as a meliorating force and a meliorable object.[11] The wonders of modern science figure prominently in Zionist speculation, not only in Theodor Herzl's celebrated utopian novel *Altneuland* but also in other Zionist fantasies dating back to the early 1880s.[12] In these fantasies, a veneration for technology in the narrow sense of the word, as applied natural and industrial science, overlapped with an appreciation for technology in its broader sense, as social engineering. In the case of Herzl the latter led to the former; his programmatic work *The Jewish State*, a blueprint for a carefully planned, mass colonization of Palestine, was written several years before the technophilic *Altneuland*.

Moreover, the Zionist movement was overtly political, and it shared the universal belief from the late nineteenth century to our own time that science is an essential tool for the realization of state power. Political Zionism was the child of the age of imperialism, an era defined not only as one of European global conquest but, more profoundly, as a time of rapid technological change which enabled that expansion as well as vast increases in the productive capacity of the national economies of Europe.[13] For Herzl, the fortunes of Zionism were linked to science not only because the WZO confronted vast technical challenges in colonizing Palestine but because it was engaged in an inherently political venture. Herzl's views were shared even by many of his opponents in the camp of the so-called "practical" Zionists, advocates of immediate settlement activity. Otto Warburg, the most distinguished figure in the practical camp, was a university professor of botany and a scientific adviser in the German colonial service. In the year before Herzl's death, and for three years thereafter, Warburg and a group of supporters sponsored scientific exploration in Palestine and published widely on the relationship between Zionism and European imperialist ventures in the Middle East.[14]

During the first decade of the WZO's settlement activity, from 1908 to 1918, ineffective leadership in Europe and a power vacuum in the Yishuv made possible the domination over settlement policy by Arthur Ruppin, a technical expert in the broad, social-scientific sense of the word. A political economist, Ruppin brought to the WZO the statist and agrarian orientation of German political economy of the *fin de siècle.* He developed the first institutions for publicly funded Zionist settlement, and he forged an alliance between the WZO and the Yishuv's pioneer laborers.[15] But Ruppin's power was short lived; during the course of World War I both the WZO and the Yishuv produced formidable political elites which formed complex relations, both symbiotic and antagonistic, with Zionism's technocrats during the post-Balfour era. It is to this time, when the Yishuv developed from infancy to maturity, that we now turn.

The technical ethos of Labor Zionism

During the Mandate period, technocrats did not run the WZO or the Yishuv, but they were far from powerless figures. Zionist leaders relied on expert advice and legitimized policy decisions by invoking expert opinion. Competing elites within the Zionist leadership employed their own fleets of technicians, each offering expert testimony about the virtues of one approach to the colonization of Palestine and the failings of others. The most powerful claimants to political leadership came from the Yishuv's labor movement, whose cadres of technical experts developed a compelling, and ultimately victorious, technical ethos.

It is striking that throughout most of the 1920s the Yishuv's workers' movement, only a small segment of Palestinian Jewry and without significant financial backing abroad, exerted considerable influence in an international Jewish organization run and largely sustained by middle-class Jews. One important provider of Labor's access to power was Ruppin, who from the time of his arrival in Palestine had sympathized with the pioneer laborers' aspirations and had supported their experiments in collective settlement. Labor-oriented agronomists who played key roles in settlement planning during the 1920s, men like Yitzhak Wilkansky of Ha-Po'el Ha-Tsa'ir (The young worker) and Akiva Ettinger of Ahdut ha-'Avodah (United Labor), had been brought into the WZO by Ruppin before the war. After 1918 Ruppin continued to be the WZO's most distinguished technocrat; he began the decade as director of the Colonization Department of the Palestine Zionist Executive (PZE)[16] and was governor of Bank ha-Po'alim (the Workers' Bank). But, as mentioned above, Ruppin never regained the authority he had enjoyed prior to the war. The PZE was a cumbersome affair, with some 120 salaried employees, 28 of whom worked for the Colonization Department alone. This bureaucratic thicket was a constant source of frustration for Ruppin, who looked back nostalgically to the days of the cozy, pre-war, Palestine Office.[17] Tired of inefficiency, constant criticism, and a series of shoestring budgets, which made any kind of systematic colonization impossible, Ruppin resigned from the PZE in 1925. Although he returned to the PZE in 1929, serving nearly continuously until his death in 1943, Ruppin's status became that of a *primus inter pares.*

As Ruppin's influence waned, the labor movement produced its own technicians who worked with, and at times around, Ruppin in the promotion of *hityashvut ovedet* (co-operative settlement on public land). Between the end of the war and 1924, the period of the Third Aliya, the third wave of Zionist immigration to Palestine, Ettinger directed the Agricultural Department, the most important unit within the PZE's Colonization Department. In 1921, when the PZE set up a co-ordinating body known as the Va'ad Hakla'i (Agricultural Committee), five of its seven members were affiliated with the workers' movement or supportive of its aspirations and methods.[18] Between 1924 and 1927, when much of the Fourth Aliya rolled towards Palestine, direction of the Colonization Department fell to the engineer Shlomo Kaplansky, a leader in Ahdut ha-'Avodah and the international Po'alei Tsiyon (Workers of Zion).

How do we account for the overwhelming presence of the Zionist labor movement in the WZO's settlement institutions? One could present purely pragmatic reasons: the Yishuv needed an agricultural sector, the workers' movement was the only source of agricultural laborers, and the labor-oriented technicians provided badly needed agricultural know-how. But *hityashvut ovedet* was far from being the only possible settlement paradigm, and the Labor Zionist technicians were not the only experts available to the WZO. The answer to our question lies in part in the dynamism and stamina of the workers' movement's activists, technicians no less than political leaders. Moreover, there was sufficient common ideological ground between the bourgeois WZO leadership and the workers' movement to make possible a situation in which the WZO spent the bulk of its colonization budget on *hityashvut ovedet* in its various forms.

There was a widespread, though not total, consensus within the Zionist movement that a healthy Jewish national economy required a strong agricultural sector. And given the economic advantages offered by cheap and plentiful Arab labor, a Jewish agricultural workforce could flourish only on publicly owned lands that excluded Arab labor on principle. Thus the Labor Zionist agronomist Wilkansky argued that public land ownership and Hebrew labor were "not a dictate of the higher morality but of stern necessity"; the co-operative farm constituted "a measure of national self-defense."[19] Nonetheless, *hityashvut ovedet* was appreciated as far more than a political necessity. Zionists from all sides of the political spectrum shared the view, popular throughout postwar Europe and in progressive circles in the United States, that some degree of nationalization of natural resources and heavy industry was socially beneficial. An interest in social reform and efficiency led Louis Brandeis and his supporters in the American Zionist movement to favor a strong co-operative sector in the Yishuv as well as the nationalization of economic enterprises, such as utilities, that would otherwise become private monopolies.[20]

A more controversial aspect of *hityashvut ovedet* was the collective structure of the kibbutz. This characteristic resulted in part from the ideological affinities of some of the young pioneers, and in part from the constant pressure of landless agricultural laborers roaming around Palestine, in need of settlement via the quickest and cheapest means possible.[21] The collective was considered economically and socially unfeasible by bourgeois Zionists who preferred another form of *hityashvut ovedet*, the moshav, which combined individual smallholdings with co-operative purchase, sale, and administration. Nonetheless, the collective could and did appeal to many an influential Zionist outside of the workers' movement. The most moving example of bourgeois Zionist sympathy for the collective comes from Ruppin, whose private writings during the interwar period expressed an ongoing, albeit unrequited and increasingly frustrated, passion for a radical reconstruction of Jewish society.[22]

Ideologies influenced not only the broad contours of settlement policy but also highly technical matters which, one might think, would have been decided according to value-free criteria alone. For example, Akiva Ettinger was passionately devoted to the establishment of hill settlements, and he considered the founding of Kiryat Anavim in the Judean hills (1920) one of his greatest achievements. His reasons were in part eminently practical: hill settlements had obvious strategic value, and they could in time become population centers, thereby enabling the Jewish population to move beyond Palestine's coastal plain and inland valleys. But the vision of Jewish farmers laboring in terraced fields enraptured him. Although the task was difficult, he wrote,

> I surely knew that the labor invested in the hills would not be in vain. Our ancestors, hill dwellers they, knew how to adapt to the climate and the land. They knew how to deal with the run-off that sweeps away the soil to the lowlands. They cleared their fields and vineyards of stones and terraced them with sophisticated stone terraces. In the hills our people produced its culture, its eternal creations.[23]

An even more complex mix of romantic and pragmatic thinking lay behind the WZO technical corps' approach to irrigation. Before the mid-1920s the agricultural technicians displayed little enthusiasm for irrigated farming. The sheer expense of irrigation and its complex technological requirements were important reasons for this attitude. But these arguments aside, irrigation had only limited appeal for Ettinger and none for Wilkanksy. The agricultural models available to them – Eastern European peasants, Palestinian *fellahin*, and farmers in the German Templer colonies in Palestine – engaged in dry farming alone. Irrigation was successfully used for citriculture in the Yishuv's plantation colonies, but this very success tainted irrigation with a capitalist ethos which the WZO's technicians abhorred.[24] In the mid-1920s, Kaplansky did lead the Settlement Department into serious experimentation with irrigation. Shlomo Zemach, director of the extension service of the WZO's Agricultural Experiment Station, offered instruction in irrigation and established experimental irrigated fields in some of the Galilean settlements.[25] Significantly, ideologies played as important a role in the new enthusiasm about irrigation as in the earlier coolness towards it. Irrigation was essential for the cultivation of fodder crops, which in turn supported dairy farming, which the settlement technicians decided was the hallmark of an advanced agricultural economy as well as a way to make the kibbutz and moshav viable without dependence on plantation crops.[26]

The ideologies at work behind the application of technical knowledge influenced the production of that knowledge as well. On the one hand, because of the high status of agriculture in Zionist thought, agronomy was a highly respected discipline, and agricultural scientists were eager to serve the Yishuv despite low salaries.[27] On the other hand, although the pioneer laborers of the Second and Third Aliyot venerated technical expertise, they were highly suspicious of experts, who were assumed, until proven otherwise, to be administrators determined to rule autocratically. Moreover, Labor Zionism's obsessive pragmatism, its cult of practical knowledge and deprecation of learning disconnected from life experience, caused the workers to doubt the value of a formal agronomic education. Shlomo Zemach writes of the frosty reception he received from the workers at Tel Yosef when he began work for the extension service:

> The word "agronomist" was not respected in those days in Palestine; . . . people with that name were not really tied to agriculture. They were afraid to come near a horse or a stable; their advice came from books, and it was no good.[28]

Although this evaluation was not just, it is true that the technicians were likely to be only somewhat more agriculturally literate than the settlers and laborers, for the technicians often received only a limited, practical training in Europe and had little research experience and prior exposure to agricultural conditions in Palestine.[29]

As a result of this tension between experts and their ostensible beneficiaries, researchers at the central Experiment Station at Ben Shemen did not merely project agricultural knowledge out towards the rural communities. Rather, knowledge spread through the Yishuv through a process of diffusion, the result of constant interaction between technicians in the extension service and the settlers themselves.[30] Technical expertise did not justify elitism. Zemach observed that "under no circumstances can instruction become administration. Everything is to be done via co-operation and agreement between the instructors and the settlers."[31] Zionist technical expertise flourished in a highly democratized and politicized context, a state of "civic equality in the relationship of scientists and lay people."[32]

The ethos of Zionist agricultural research found its most eloquent spokesman in Wilkansky, the Experiment Station's director. Wilkansky's technical writings were steeped in an odd brew of anti-industrialism and technophilia. According to Wilkansky, industrial science enslaves, whereas agricultural science liberates. Industrial technology can be captured, hidden, and monopolized for the benefit of a select few. But this is not the case with agricultural knowledge; once a new type of seed or strain of livestock enters the gene pool it becomes part of the public domain, and it benefits the entire rural community. Biological inquiry empowers the scientist as well as the farmer, for the scientist experiences the pleasure of working at a genuine craft, practiced with small, fine instruments. Mechanization, on the other hand, should not be introduced into agriculture. Not only is it socially regressive, fostering the creation of a dispirited rural proletariat; it is also technologically anachronistic, for the intensively farmed smallholding is more efficient than the large estate.[33]

Wilkansky's romanticism, agrarianism, and commitment to the diffusion of useful knowledge endeared him to the Yishuv's workers' movement, of which he was a member. But even Wilkansky was never completely comfortable in the anti-authoritarian atmosphere of the Labor community. Writing in a wistful tone, Wilkansky noted that administered farms cannot succeed in the Yishuv because Jewish workers do not "possess a single one of the qualities of the born agricultural laborer." Unlike peasants, they refuse to "subordinate their will" and "work automatically." Perhaps recalling his own pre-war days as manager of the WZO's properties at Ben Shemen and Hulda, Wilkansky observed that, whereas in any other land the worker sees himself as replaceable and heeds the foreman's orders lest he be sacked, in the Yishuv it is the manager who is under stress, with laborers constantly breathing down his neck and taking credit for the manager's innovations.[34] This environment accounts for Wilkansky's loose management style at the Experiment Station, which he adopted after trying unsuccessfully to run the station in a highly centralized, bureaucratic fashion.[35]

It is not coincidental that Wilkansky worked primarily as a researcher, consultant, and educator, and did not hold a policy-making position in the Zionist settlement apparatus. The directors of settlement policy through much of the 1920s, Ruppin, Ettinger, and Kaplansky, gained access to directorial positions at least in part because the workers' organizations supported them, and they did so because these technocrats accepted the settlers' demands for maximum autonomy in settlement management. Ruppin wrote in his diary that his chief merit, according to one pioneer laborer, was that "I did not meddle with the workers' aspirations for new social forms in the style of earlier 'administrators' as a know-it-all, but rather I gave them the opportunity for natural development."[36] Crucial developments of the period of the Third Aliya, such as the founding of the first moshav and kibbutz, resulted from the initiatives of agricultural laborers (Eliezer Joffe for the moshav and Shlomo Lavi for the kibbutz); Ettinger and Ruppin embraced these initiatives and lobbied the WZO to fund them.[37] And in 1924, when the laborers lost faith in Ettinger's ability to defend their cause against mounting criticism within the WZO of workers' settlement, Ettinger resigned his position and Kaplansky took his place.[38]

Although Kaplansky assumed office during a period of grave financial crisis, the accession of a veteran leader of Ahdut ha-'Avodah and the international Po'alei Tsiyon to the directorship of the Settlement Department represented a victory for the Yishuv's workers' movement. Kaplansky was a complex figure; although he was primarily a political activist, he was an engineer by training and had substantive knowledge of as well as interest in technical issues. An experienced member of the WZO's Financial Council, Kaplansky was able to defend workers' settlement in sober, businesslike prose heavily seasoned with statistics, charts, and graphs.[39] Acting according to his dual nature, Kaplansky ferreted out cost overruns and other financial irregularities in settlements, only to let the offending parties off with a warning and funnel more public funds into them.[40]

In the case of Zionism's settlement technocrats, leadership largely involved representing the interests of the organized workers in the Yishuv and the funding instruments in Europe. This is not to say that the technical experts did not lead at all. There were certain areas of technical decision-making in which the settlement experts took the initiative and strongly influenced the development of the rural Yishuv. The emphasis on dairy farming and the introduction of certain crops, such as table grapes and bananas, was the work of Ettinger.[41] Research done at the Experiment Station produced valuable knowledge regarding all aspects of crop and dairy farming.[42] Under Kaplansky's direction, the Settlement Department added a building sub-department, which replaced temporary with permanent housing and lowered construction costs through the standardization of building practices.[43] In 1927, Wilkansky's opposition to mechanization notwithstanding, the Settlement Department began studying farm machine use and repair, and by 1931 it was supplying gasoline-driven tractors and combines to the Jezreel Valley settlements.[44] Finally, the great public works projects undertaken by the Jewish National Fund (JNF) – afforestation, drainage, and the provision of fresh water to settlements – were formulated by Ettinger, who directed the JNF's Lands Authority throughout the 1920s, and his successor, Yosef Weitz.[45]

Impressive though these accomplishments were, the WZO settlement technicians operated in a never-ending storm of criticism of their actions and methods. From the time the WZO took its first steps towards colonization activity in 1903, fiscal conservatives in the WZO's financial institutions decried the use of public funds for risky and unprofitable settlement experiments. Even before World War I, collective settlements came under fire for their consumption of public funds and subordination of economic to social goals.[46] Throughout much of the 1920s there was ongoing tension between the WZO's Settlement and Financial Departments, with the latter accusing the former of wasteful spending on social experiments of dubious value.

After World War I, fiscal conservatives found a champion in Louis Brandeis, who called for a businesslike and efficient colonization to be carried out by independent agencies run by expert managers. According to Brandeis, the managers and the agencies they directed should be free of political ideology and serve no political interests. The Brandeisian notion of the expert was technocratic in the classic sense of the word – empowered, apolitical, and businesslike, along the lines of the efficiency-minded "production engineers" of the American sociological imagination of the early twentieth century. Brandeis's businesslike approach was not capitalist; he recognized the need for public institutions to create the infrastructure of the Yishuv's national economy. But Brandeis shared the popular American view that the goal of philanthropy, the promotion of economic independence, could only be reached if philanthropies employed the same professional and efficient management that characterized profit-making enterprises.[47]

The Brandeis camp's bid for power in the American and international Zionist movement was defeated, but Brandeis's economic views lived on in the leadership of the non-Zionist section of the enlarged Jewish Agency (JA). During the negotiations leading up the establishment of the agency in 1929, Brandeis met with the American Jewish financier Felix Warburg, who requested Brandeis's guidance on Zionist affairs.[48] Warburg communicated to WZO President Chaim Weizmann a plan for the administration of the Zionist enterprise similar to that of the JDC, of which Warburg was director. Warburg envisioned the WZO and JA as a single corporation, in which the JA Council would be the managing board, passing on instructions to the Zionist Executive, which would become a body of expert officials without policy-making powers.[49]

Some elements of the American technocratic program were in fact implemented in the WZO. Shaken by a financial crisis in the Yishuv and a drastic drop in WZO revenues, in 1927 the WZO created an executive without Labor representation. Control over colonization passed to the attorney Harry Sacher, who strove to make the best use of the WZO's paltry resources by cutting the settlement apparatus' payroll and concentrating expenditures in selected programs for the long-term improvement of the existing colonies. In his efforts he was aided by a new director of the Agricultural Department, the equally businesslike accountant Eliezer Bavli.[50] Other than its apolitical quality and attention to accountability, however, there was little similarity between the "Sacher regime" and Warburg's corporate vision. Sacher, an ardent Zionist and longtime ally of Weizmann, was not on good terms with Warburg.[51] Aside from business savvy, Sacher brought little in the way of new forms of expertise into the WZO's colonization operations. Sacher's agricultural experts were Wilkansky, Zemach, and David Stern, all veteran members of the labor movement, although the most important of them, Wilkansky, was admittedly more cautious than many of his peers, favoring a protracted period of scientific experimentation and planning prior to mass settlement.[52]

This is not to say that the Yishuv lacked technical experts without a Labor orientation. Bourgeois Zionists found their most reliable ally in the agronomist Selig Soskin,[53] whose capitalist agricultural scheme was the subject of furious debate at the 1921 and 1925 Zionist Congresses. Whereas the Labor Zionist agricultural ideal was one of self-sufficiency, with dairy and poultry farming having pride of place in a farm economy based on cereal and fodder crops, Soskin derided the striving for autarky as misguided and the emphasis on dairy farming as, literally, a sacred cow. Seeing Palestine as an integral part of a world market, Soskin argued that the Yishuv should focus all its efforts on the production of luxury crops, such as bananas, oranges, and tomatoes, for export to Europe. Grain, dairy products, and eggs could be imported from abroad for far less cost than their production price in Palestine.[54]

Other experts stressed alleged flaws in the organizational structure of collective settlement. In 1926 the WZO solicited the views of Solomon Dyk, an agronomist whose hostility to the workers' movement and the collective was well known.[55] Dyk's report condemned the collective settlements' lack of permanent, professional management as well as their refusal to link wage levels with productivity. Similar charges of inefficiency and recommendations that the collective system be dismantled were made in 1928, when, as part of the preparations for the enlargement of the JA, the Palestine Joint Survey Commission sponsored a massive report by a team of internationally renowned experts headed up by Dr. Elwood Mead of the US Department of the Interior.[56]

The WZO's technicians responded to these hostile experts by claiming that the critics did not understand the peculiar physical challenges of the Palestinian ecology or the psychological dimensions of the Jewish return to the soil. Over and over again, technicians supportive of Labor Zionism attacked "foreign authorities" who, after making a superficial tour of Palestine, dictated policies forcing Zionist colonization into the iron framework of their previous experience.[57] Wilkansky purported to know the Land of Israel more intimately than his rival Soskin; combining the romantic and pragmatic motifs in Labor Zionist ideology, he blended biblical descriptions of cereal culture and dry farming with voluminous data from his own years of practical experience to discredit Soskin's plan.[58] Countering Dyk's criticism of collectives, Kaplansky noted that, despite their formal lack of a hierarchical administration, in fact each kibbutz tended to develop a leadership group which, through popular consensus, ran its operations year after year.[59] For Ruppin, the main problem with the Mead report was not empirical error so much as insensitivity; couched purely in abstract, economic terms, the report neglected the aspirations of the workers without whom there would be no rural Yishuv.[60] For the WZO settlement technicians, the belief that "outside experts" could not fathom the collective psychology of the workers disqualified the opinions not only of a gentile like Mead, but also of Jews like Soskin or Dyk, who neither had mastered

Hebrew nor had any common cultural frame of reference with the agricultural workers.[61]

As it turned out, critics of Zionist colonization policy during the 1920s had little long-term impact. Their alternative approaches conflicted with the WZO political leadership's view of the movement's essential interests. In case of a clash between purely economic and political economic considerations, the latter won out. In Weizmann's view, the WZO was a government, not a corporation; it sought long-term national goals such as the acquisition of contiguous territory and the entrenchment of Hebrew labor in all sectors of the Yishuv's economy. Although Weizmann fully supported Sacher's entry into the Zionist Executive, he quickly grew irritated with his old ally, accusing Sacher of detrimental penny-pinching in matters like the purchase of land in the Haifa Bay area, which Weizmann felt must come under public control and was too important "to be swallowed up by a capitalist concern".[62] Weizmann claimed to have initiated the idea for the Joint Palestine Survey Commission, but he was quick to dismiss the Mead report, invoking all the arguments used by Ruppin and his colleagues.[63]

Ironically, although Zionist settlement technicians were perceived by their critics as single-mindedly promoting the interests of the workers' movement, the political leadership of the labor movement could be harshly critical of the technician's activities. Technicians were caught in the crossfire between the movement's opposing camps; several of the technicians, Wilkansky among them, belonged to Ha-Po'el Ha-Tsa'ir, a party opposed to Ahdut ha-'Avodah's collectivism and striving to centralize power within its own political machine. Exuding a fiery, romantic individualism, Wilkansky, like his party comrade Eliezer Joffe, cast his lot with the moshav rather than the kibbutz, believing that the former guaranteed "personal freedom in creation," while the latter threatened to stifle it.[64] Indeed, the leadership of Ahdut ha-'Avodah did, at the beginning of the 1920s, express a preference for the collectivist kibbutz.[65] Ettinger and Kaplansky belonged to Ahdut ha-'Avodah and vigorously promoted the kibbutz, but still the party did not treat them kindly. Ettinger, we saw above, resigned the directorship of the Settlement Department after losing the political support of the workers' movement in 1924. His successor, Kaplansky, faced assaults on his freedom of action by Ben-Gurion, who, as leader of Ahdut ha-'Avodah, pressured Kaplansky to resign from the PZE in protest against insufficient funding for workers' settlement.[66]

By the mid-1920s the Histadrut leadership, and especially its members from Ahdut ha-'Avodah, had developed an urban orientation in response to the fact that its membership and power base lay in the city, not the countryside. Agricultural settlement was seen as but one vehicle for the realization of the Labor Zionist vision.[67] Nonetheless, *hityashvut ovedet* was understood to be an integral part of the Yishuv, and the Labor leadership was unwilling to entrust it to anyone, even an ally, in the WZO. No sooner had the Histadrut been created in 1920 than it began to seek control over workers' settlement through the Vaad Haklai, an advisory group appointed by the PZE, and the Histadrut's own section on agricultural affairs, the Merkaz Hakla'i. The Merkaz Hakla'i was headed by Abraham Harzfeld, a laborer with no formal agricultural training and a long history of organizing and mediating activity going back to his arrival in Palestine shortly before World War I. As director of the Merkaz Hakla'i, Harzfeld successfully lobbied the JNF to purchase lands for workers' villages and won for the Merkaz the authority to allocate purchased lands to settlement groups.[68] The growing role of the Merkaz paralleled the many other Histadrut activities which, relying on WZO funding, were embodied in Hevrat Ovdim (Society of Workers), an umbrella organization created by the Histadrut in 1923, and whose subsidiaries controlled virtually all aspects of the labor economy. An equally significant sign of the Histadrut's growing control over the rural Yishuv's development was its decision in 1930 to take the initiative in the creation of a water-supply network for Jezreel Valley settlements. Levi Eshkol (Shkolnik), then of the Merkaz Hakla'i, took on the project, and seven years later became the first director of the national water company Mekorot.[69]

The ascent of Histadrut apparatchiks such as Harzfeld and Eshkol in the making of settlement policy marked a generational change in the make-up and characteristics of Zionist technical corps. The old guard, formally educated and trained in Europe, had entered the Zionist movement before World War I, a time when the rural Yishuv was undeveloped and its agricultural workforce largely adolescent. By the mid-1920s the youthful autodidacts of the Second Aliya had matured sufficiently to be in a position to become guiding technical experts in the Yishuv. This power shift, progressing gradually through the 1920s, accelerated suddenly in the mid-1930s as the result of two unconnected but coterminous events: Labor's conquest of the WZO and the Arab Revolt in Palestine. After its removal from the PZE in 1927, Labor began a political campaign that culminated in 1935 with Labor as the dominant faction in the Zionist Congress. Ben-Gurion was elected chairman of the PZE and the JA Executive, "thus ensuring," according to the historian Henry Near, "full political backing for the foundation of kibbutzim and moshavim alike."[70] The following year, rebellion by Palestinian Arabs threw the Yishuv into turmoil, stimulating heightened interest in the strategic value of *hityashvut ovedet* as well as its ability to supply produce to a growing population with uncertain access to Arab sources. A melding of political, military, and technical considerations occurred within Zionist colonization policy, and experts formerly devoted to the construction of a Zionist utopia now took on the tasks of a corps of military engineers.

Strategic planning and the birth of the state

The shift from a settlement program based on social and economic considerations to one centered around strategic concerns began after the 1929

Arab riots in the Yishuv. In response to the riots the Zionist settlement agencies set out to create a contiguous bloc of Jewish territory in the coastal plain, the population center of the Yishuv. After the Peel Commission recommended the partition of Palestine in 1937, the settlement agencies also moved to acquire land in the Galilee, Beit Shean Valley, and Negev in order either to forestall partition or to assure the maximum possible borders should it occur. The term used to describe this two-pronged strategy was "consolidation," which during the 1920s had referred to the economic stabilization of the settlements. In this environment, the Political Department of the JA and its director, Moshe Sharett (Shertok), came to play the central role in settlement policy. Sharett sponsored the expansion of the Yishuv beyond the "N" formed by settlement in the coastal plain, Jezreel Valley, and eastern Galilee. The policy of expansion was vigorously promoted after World War II by the new head of the Settlement Department, Levi Eshkol, who placed a particular emphasis on gaining the Negev for the Jewish state.[71]

During this period of strife the Yishuv developed a new type of technician, exemplified by Yosef Weitz, director of the JNF's Lands Authority, and Yosef Avidar (Rokhel), director of the Haganah's Technical Department. Unlike the formally trained agronomists of the pre-war generation, Weitz and Avidar were part of the generation of autodidacts who began life in Palestine as laborers. Whereas the earlier cohort of settlement experts had dabbled in strategic thinking, the latter lived for it. Immediately after the establishment of the first Tower and Stockade settlement, Tel Amal, in 1936, Weitz forcefully championed the widespread application of this format, which, given its rapid mobilization, use of prefabricated structures, and provisions for military defense, was an ideal instrument for establishing a Jewish presence in isolated rural areas. Weitz worked closely with the leadership of the Haganah in the establishment of Tower and Stockade settlements, several of which, including Hanita in the western Galilee and Dafna in the Huleh valley, were planned by Avidar.[72]

A dyed-in-the-wool soldier, Avidar, along with Weitz and the military expert Raphael Lev, drew up an influential long-term plan for the Yishuv's rural development in 1943. Taking only strategic goals into consideration, the plan made no provision for any agricultural format other than *hityashvut ovedet*. It took for granted that the tightly knit kibbutz was strategically superior and should be the settlement of choice in any isolated region, with the moshav being used in more established regions.[73] In a Yishuv pummeled by rebellion and threatened by war, there was no place for the economic arguments for and against the kibbutz that had so engaged the Zionist movement during the 1920s.

Not all the settlement technicians of the period after 1936 approved of the new direction of Zionist settlement policy. Ruppin opposed the tactic of expansion, arguing that it was too costly. Like his colleagues in the Zionist leadership, Ruppin had a political agenda, albeit opposed to that of his peers: he favored an even smaller Jewish commonwealth than that proposed by the Peel Commission, so as to lessen the number of Arabs who would come under Jewish rule.[74] But Ruppin, the architect of Zionist settlement in the past, had ceased to lead; for all his gifts, he was not a tactician, and in the era of militant Zionism leaders were called upon to think strategically as well as constructively. Weitz, on the other hand, was in tune with the new spirit of the era. Although his actual influence over policy is a highly controversial issue, it is clear that Weitz took an interest in planning the transfer of Arabs from what would become Jewish territory and advocated the expulsion of Arabs from sensitive rural areas during Israel's War of Independence.[75]

Weitz was the archetypal technician for the era of militant Zionism. The new breed of experts were planners and administrators who, like the political and military leaders whom they served, considered strategic thinking an inherent component of the constructive Zionist project. New emphases on the military value of *hityashvut ovedet* blended with older beliefs in its political-economic virtues. The new corps of settlement planners possessed technical knowledge, necessary for the tasks they undertook, but it was not knowledge *per se* that legitimized them as leaders in the eyes of their comrades. Rather, it was the process by which that knowledge had been acquired – practically, informally, and entirely within the framework of the Labor Zionist community – and the correspondence between the planners' agenda and the political goals of the Labor leadership.

In the newly born state of Israel, technical expertise was placed in the service of a world-view that blended *raison d'état*, nationalism, and socialism into an indivisible whole. The principal symbol of the Zionist enterprise, the pioneer laborer, was portrayed not only as tough and zealous but also as technically resourceful. The technically skilled pioneer assured a decent standard of living for himself while providing essential foodstuffs and industrial products for the embattled nation. The leaders of Labor Zionism, like their counterparts in revolutionary movements throughout the globe, believed that harnessing the creative powers of technology was an essential step towards the realization of socialism.[76] For all these reasons, the Labor Zionist technician was accorded an important role in the construction of a socialist Hebrew republic.

Modern Jewish social policy developed prior to and parallel with the Zionist movement. Like the WZO, the vehicles of Jewish social policy featured corps of experts able to develop and implement technology for the collective good of the Jewish people. But the Zionist movement was unique in its politicization of the technical, its subordination of expertise to the goal of constructing an autonomous polity. Also unique was the Zionist adoration of applied science and its practitioner, a Promethean figure who did not view technical knowledge as hermetic or esoteric, but rather as the common possession of the Hebrew nation, the means for its reconstruction in the Land of Israel.

Part IV

From Jewish to Israeli culture

9 The continuity of subversion

Hebrew satire in Mandate Palestine

Satirical literature attempts to subvert a cultural system through the manipulation of its foundational symbols. It rests on the assumption that the reader is familiar with these symbols' conventional signification, and that he or she also possesses deep knowledge of the cultural system being mocked. This statement holds true for modern Jewish satire, which originated among traditionally educated adherents of the Jewish Enlightenment in late eighteenth-century Eastern Europe and flourished throughout the 1800s. When exported in the early twentieth century to Palestine, this subversive tradition took the form of parodies of traditional texts such as the Passover Haggadah, produced in the secular atmosphere of Tel Aviv and the kibbutzim.

This chapter sets Hebrew satirical literature produced in interwar Palestine against the backdrop of its European predecessors. Changes in the form and content of parodies of sacred Jewish texts nicely demonstrate the transition in the first half of the twentieth century from Jewish to Israeli culture. From the turn of the century through the 1930s, Palestine's Jewish community (the Yishuv) was a liminal zone in which a catalytic, yet ephemeral, coming together of Judaic erudition and a freethinking spirit engendered a Zionist secular culture. The principal texts analyzed here are Isaak Meir Dick's *Masekhet 'Aniyut* of 1844, as an example of learned parody from the period of the Jewish Englightenment (Haskalah); Kadish Yehuda Silman's *Bava Tekhnika* of 1913, to demonstrate the continuation of the Haskalah tradition in the early years of the new Yishuv; and several satiric haggadot published in Palestine during the 1920s and 1930s.

My analysis is informed by the anthropologist Mary Douglas's seminal essay on the joke, which she defines as

> a play upon form. It brings into relation disparate elements in such a way that one accepted pattern is challenged by the appearance of another, which in some way was challenged by the first. . . . The joke merely affords opportunity for realizing that an accepted pattern has no necessity. Its excitement lies in the suggestion that any particular ordering of experience may be arbitrary and subjective. It is frivolous

in that is produces no real alternative, only an exhilarating sense of freedom from form in general.[1]

Thus a joke is predicated upon the existence of a dominant pattern of relations, which is then challenged. The "essence of the joke is that something formal is attacked by something informal, something organized and controlled, by something vital, energetic."[2] The joke is the antithesis of the religious rite, for the latter imposes an order that the former strives to dissolve.[3]

The significance of Douglas's remarks lies in the close association between modern Jewish satire and the parody of hallowed texts. In the Yishuv the Passover Haggadah was the most common target of satirical parody. The reading of the Haggadah is an ancient domestic rite – a seder, literally a fixed order, that unifies all Jewish experience across time and space into a fixed narrative. The frequency and ease with which that narrative order was subverted by Hebrew satirists, the sort of Jewish literacy that was required for the production and consumption of these acts of literary subversion, and the question whether these parodies offered a new collective narrative in place of that which was dissolved, will be explored below.

Parody is a vast and amorphous genre, which in recent years has attracted considerable attention from literary critics influenced by postmodern concerns with intertextuality and self-referentiality. Contemporary theories of parody owe much to the interwar writings of Mikhail Bakhtin, who was intrigued by parody's heteroglossia – that is, its performance of multiple discursive modes within a single linguistic system – and who celebrated parody's Carnivalesque, subversive qualities. Contemporary scholars maintain and refine Bakhtin's analysis of parody as multi-voiced; some emphasize parody's qualities as a form of meta-fiction, commenting upon literary forms, while others see in parody a *locus classicus* for challenging the notion of textual authorship. One of the chief areas of disagreement between scholars is parody's relationship with humor, ridicule, and subversion. Linda Hutcheon questions these associations, preferring to see parody as "repetition with critical distance," an ironic but by no means necessarily satirical imitation of an established cultural production or practice. Simon Dentith, on the other hand, insists that parody always possesses a polemical quality, even if it is acting as a socially conservative force, criticizing innovation by lampooning the form and content of its expression.[4]

In this chapter I have blended various literary critics' approaches to formulate a theoretical framework that fits the particular conditions of Jewish parody. Most literary analyses of parody focus on ancient and modern secular texts, be they the plays of Aristophanes or the novels of Cervantes and Fielding. Well into the twentieth century, however, the target of Jewish parody (or the "hypotext," in Gerard Genette's terminology) was often a sacred text, even if the author of the parody (the "hypertext") was far removed from the hypotext's cultural universe. We may borrow an important concept, however, from the literature on parody in the western world: the notion of parody as flourishing in societies dominated by a textual tradition yet challenging it. That is, just as Renaissance and early modern Europe, beholden to yet seeking to break away from the classical heritage, engendered "Rabelais and his World," to cite Bakhtin's classic text, so belated Jewish modernization set parodists against the beloved texts of the Jewish canon.[5]

Parody and satire are overlapping but distinct genres, and the relationship between them is complex. The chart below depicts the various sorts of parody that will be encountered throughout the course of this chapter:

TYPES OF PARODY

Serious:	Pietist	Humorous:	Benign	
	Subversive		Satiric:	
				Quiescent
				Subversive
				Mobilized

Parodies can be either serious or humorous. The former has no intent to amuse; it adopts the form of a universally known sacred text to drive home an ethical or political message. Serious parodies can revere the hypotext, employing its language in order to stimulate a return to the system of religious belief and practice the original text espoused. An example of this form of serious parody is the Yiddish Haggadah of 1885 composed by the Lithuanian *badhan* (wedding entertainer) Marechevsky. The Haggadah is replete with proverbs attacking the Haskalah and urging Jews towards piety and observance.[6] Equally serious, yet utterly secular, in intent were the kibbutz haggadot of the interwar period, which undermined the hypotext by transforming the story of divine liberation of the Jews into a celebration of natural rebirth and an epic of national and class struggle. Even more subversive were the early Soviet Union's "red haggadot," produced during the early years of the Bolshevik regime. These haggadot employ motifs from the Passover story in order to discourage celebration of the Passover holiday or any other aspects of Jewish religious life.[7]

Throughout history, Jewish parody has tended far more often to be humorous than serious; indeed, humorous parodies of biblical or rabbinic texts date back to the Middle Ages. During medieval and early modern times, such humor was usually benign, aiming not to ridicule individuals or institutions but simply to entertain through the inversion of sacred motifs for profane ends. Medieval Purim parodies, written in Talmudic or biblical style, indulge in boisterous praise for drinking alcohol, as in *Sefer Ha-vakbuk Ha-navi*, whose title punned the biblical prophet Habbakuk and the Hebrew word for bottle.[8] Similar parodies were produced in medieval Christendom, where drinkers' masses engaged in wordplay, such as changing the word "*oremus*" (let us pray) to "*potemus*" (let us drink).[9] Such works operated well within the margins of social propriety, indulging in harmless wordplay and paeans to the alcohol that lubricated social relations during the Jewish Carnival of Purim. Similarly safe, although more cerebral, is the venerable tradition of yeshiva students producing parodic sermons for Purim that employed talmudic casuistry in creative and humorous ways. This sort of parody, produced and consumed by a learned Jewish elite, was akin to medieval Latin Bible parodies, which jumbled biblical verses together for comic effect.[10]

Satire, as Hutcheon puts it, is "both moral and social in its focus and ameliorative in its intention."[11] Satire – and it is this which distinguishes it from parody alone – employs humor as a weapon, not merely as a source of good feeling. Nonetheless, even satiric parody can be essentially quiescent, lacking a sharp edge, if the objects of its attacks are abstract personalities, standard types found in any time or situation, such as the pompous doctor, the ignorant cleric, or the heartless miser, rather than identifiable individuals or institutions. In Jewish literature this kind of socially non-threatening parody persisted into modern times, as in the *Megilat Yuhasin* of 1834, attributed to R. Mendel Landsberg of Kremenitz. The parody consists of a variety of quotes from various portions of the Babylonian Talmud, presenting the reader with the pleasurable challenge of recalling their original context and witnessing how they are applied, via association or implicit meaning, to the satiric barbs in the text.[12]

Jewish satiric parody with a specific target first appeared in seventeenth- and eighteenth-century anti-Sabbatean literature, in which the Hebrew liturgy was altered to ridicule the false messiah Shabbatai Zvi's abrogation of Jewish law. But a full-blown subversive satiric parody, mimicking the style of revered texts in order to undermine traditional ways of thought and life, emerged only with the late eighteenth-century Haskalah, particularly in Eastern Europe. Maskilim (exponents of the Haskalah) employed satire to criticize what they considered to be the forces of backwardness and obscurantism in Jewish society. Hasidism was the most frequent target of ridicule, which was expressed in a variety of literary forms, including the observational essay and the fictional story, but the most famous of which was the parody of religious texts. The first Hebrew novel, Joseph Perl's *Megaleh Temirin* (The Revealer of Secrets, 1819), was a satiric parody of Hasidic epistles. Its power derived from the authenticity of its presentation, its liberal borrowing from Hasidic texts, and its accurate reproduction of their style and message.[13] A similar accuracy characterizes the Talmudic parodies composed by Eastern European maskilim throughout the nineteenth century, such as Moshe Leib Lilienblum's *Mishnat Elisha ben Abuya* (1877), which included a blend of authentic, inverted, and fabricated rabbinic dicta, intricate commentaries, and an authentic *Masoret Ha-shas*, providing biblical and rabbinic references for the texts cited. The elaborateness of the parodic apparatus gave such texts an air of authenticity.

By operating within the Talmudic tradition, they made an appearance of repairing the rabbinic system from within rather than attacking it from without.[14]

The chasm separating the authors of such parodies from traditional Jewish norms of behavior and belief, however, should not be obscured. As the nineteenth century progressed, Haskalah parodies moved beyond critiques of Hasidic obscurantism to the entire fabric of Eastern European Jewish life. Models of an enlightened Jewish piety gave way gradually to calls for total socio-economic transformation of the Jewish masses in Eastern Europe. Biting social criticism gave off a strong whiff of anti-clericalism, as in Isaac Meir Dick's *Masekhet 'Aniyut min Talmud Rash 'Alma* (Tractate Poverty From the Talmud of the Poor of the Earth) of 1844.[15]

Dick's text features crisp fabricated Hebrew *mishnayot* (apodictic statements) and rambling Aramaic gemara (talmudic exposition, commentary, and extension) that deal with classic issues of classification, limitation, extension, and illustration. It is accompanied by learned but fabricated commentaries that mainly serve to explain the text and only occasionally offer deadpan humor. Throughout, the rabbis are given humorous names recalling various Hebrew words for poverty and want. The text begins with the mishna "All are sure [*ne'emanim*] to be poor: even owners of courtyards and contractors, except for the stranger, the convert, the doctor, the rabbi, and the money lender." The gemara then asks, "All – including what? Rabbi *Yored* says to include the groom who dines at his father in law's home. . . . Rabbi *Ephes* says including the Gentile who has been circumcised but not immersed [in the mikvah] for although in every word he is an idol worshipper in this term he is fully a Jew and trustworthy."[16]

The text bemoans the apparently inalterable nature of Jewish poverty and compares the Jew's economic behavior unfavorably with that of gentiles:

> Rabbi *Doheka* said, "Everyone who is not poor is not of them [the Jews], and the fathers of any in whom there is no sign of poverty did not stand at Mt. Sinai." What is the sign of poverty? Rabbi *Batlan* said laziness, for it is argued that laziness brings about idleness and idleness bring about boredom and boredom leads to weakness and weakness leads to poverty and poverty leads to degradation and degradation leads to life in the world to come.[17]
>
> Every Jew is fit for marriage brokering, liturgical chanting (*hazanut*), and teaching even if he never read torah in his life or never went to school. . . . the Jew goes from pupil to groom to supported groom to marriage broker to wedding jester to beggar.[18]

Gentiles, on the other hand, are pillars of probity and economic stability:

> There is no Gentile without land and no Gentile without a craft that sustains him; he dies and his sons inherit his legacy and take his place,

> which is not the case for the Jew: He has no land, and he has no craft; he dies and his sons return to [begging in] doorways.[19]

Jews, the parody tells us, only enrich themselves through contact with Gentiles, as one may learn from the biblical stories of the patriarchs, who grew wealthy through their dealings with Pharaoh, Avimelekh, and Laban. And Jewish women are particularly wont to idleness:

> There is no difference between the daughters of Israel and the daughters of the idol worshipers except that the daughters of idol worshipers spin, weave, launder and hem while the daughters of Israel sit idly, make up their faces and eyes, and wait for deliverance in the form of a marriage.[20]

We see in this text many of the leitmotifs of Eastern European Haskalah literature: An exaggerated self-critique and admiration for the gentile, and a misogyny born of a projection of frustration over economic emasculation on to the Jewish female. We also encounter the Haskalah's tutelary agenda, for, although this text is indeed comic, its intended function was no less educational than a dry piece of Hebrew journalism. The parody was intended to shock Jews into changing their educational patterns, abandoning the *heder* for the government-sponsored Russian school and a life of talmudic study for one of labor in handicrafts. It communicated its message through an artfully designed parody that could not be appreciated without a good knowledge of Hebrew and a rudimentary education in rabbinic texts. Texts like Dick's appeared into the 1880s, but by the turn of the twentieth century Jewish satire in Europe had begun to break away from the Haskalah tradition of learned Hebrew parody. Hundreds of ephemeral humorous journals were founded throughout the Russian Empire, but most were in Yiddish (for example *Der Shaygetz* [The Gentile], *Der Bezim* [The Broom][21]) and the Haggadah replaced the talmudic tractate as the text of choice for parody. The Haggadah liturgy – brief, straightforward, and memorized in childhood by any Jewish child from an observant home – is extremely easy to manipulate, thanks to both its form and content. The seder's ritual objects can be replaced or given new meanings, as can the many items that are numbered or listed in the Haggadah's text. Moreover, the Haggadah's story of oppression and liberation can be reset in virtually any contemporary situation. In the early 1900s, politically radical Haggadah parodies, usually in Yiddish, flourished in the Pale of Settlement and among immigrant Jews in New York City. In twentieth-century Poland, Passover Haggadah parodies became increasingly fragmentary, appearing in newspapers with severe space limitations, and so referred to only the most celebrated parts of the seder, such as the four questions, four sons, and ten plagues.[22] Still, the tradition of learned Hebrew parody continued into the 1920s, in, for example, the columns of Aharon Tsafnet in the Warsaw daily *Ha-yom*.[23]

By contrast to Eastern European Jews (whether in the Russian Empire or in their new North American environment), Jewish satirists who had been culturally formed in the West did not possess strong links with the Jewish Book. Western European Jews produced only a handful of humorous periodicals, the most successful being *Schlemiel*, which appeared in Berlin from 1903 to 1905, and then irregularly from 1919 to 1924. True to its Zionist orientation, most of the satire in *Schlemiel* was directed against pretentious and assimilationist German Jews, and Eastern European Jewry tended to be viewed with a rather sentimentalized sympathy, admired for its alleged authenticity and cohesive collective identity. Some of the material assumed a familiarity with the customs and popular culture of Eastern European Jews but the material was always in German and did not assume Jewish textual literacy. One of *Schlemiel*'s chief contributors, the genial Zionist humorist Sammy Gronemann, was the son of the chief rabbi of Hannover and had a thorough yeshiva education, but he did not make use of his Judaic knowledge in his writing, which, despite its paeans to the Eastern European Jewish folk soul and its condemnation of assimilation, was destined for an audience of highly acculturated readers who were often unfamiliar with the textual basis of Eastern European Jewish civilization.[24]

A less obvious, but highly significant, difference between Jewish humorous periodicals in *fin-de-siècle* Eastern and Western Europe was the fact that the former were normally issued at the time of the major Jewish holidays, Passover in particular, whereas the latter appeared, funds and circulation permitting, on a regular monthly or bimonthly basis. The bond between sacred time and profane humor has a rich legacy in Jewish culture, from the annual revelry at Purim to the irreverent joking of the traditional wedding jester, the *badhan*, who operated within the sacred and ephemeral environment of the wedding canopy, the *huppa*. In Eastern Europe, this linkage persisted into the twentieth century, and with it the unspoken, perhaps unconscious, notion that satire was too frivolous, or too dangerous, for everyday use.

The same was the case in the Yishuv, where, from the start of Zionist settlement, humor, satire, and parody were integral components of Hebrew literature.[25] The Yishuv's first humorous newspaper, *La-Yehudim* (For the Jews), appeared at Purim 1909, but the real flourishing of Hebrew humor came in the 1920s, when the third and fourth waves of Zionist immigration gave the Yishuv a sizeable base of secularly oriented readers. The connection between humor and holiday was driven home by an article in the newspaper *Ha-Aretz* in 1931, which listed 118 humorous publications produced in Palestine between 1919 and 1931, almost three-quarters of which were published at the time of the Jewish holidays (Purim, 37; Passover, 19; Shavuot, 10; Hanukkah, 5; Rosh Hashanah, 5; Sukkot, 3; Tu Bishvat and other holidays, 7). Ten appeared at May Day or alongside of special events in the life of the Yishuv. Only 22, or less than one-fifth, had no connection with a holiday or special event.[26] Humorous columns were featured as well in the daily Hebrew press, but even these were at first tied to the holidays, becoming routine affairs only in the early 1930s, at which time satirical cabarets (*Hakumkum*, *Hametate*) became an integral part of Yishuv culture.

The most important figure in Yishuv satire before World War I, Kadish Yehuda Silman, inherited the Haskalah legacy of learned satiric parody. An educator and publicist who served on the editorial board of *Ha-Aretz*, in 1910 Silman authored *Megilat Shemitah*, a parody of the Book of Esther that lampooned ultra-Orthodox inflexibility during the *shemitah*, or sabbatical, year, during which, according to biblical law, the Land of Israel was to lay fallow. The work was extraordinarily popular; it sold over a thousand copies in Jerusalem in a single day.[27] Silman expended most of his satiric energy, however, on what became known as the "language struggle" in the Yishuv between proponents of Hebrew as opposed to German in higher education. Silman's chief opponent in the "language struggle" was the Hilfsverein der deutschen Juden, a German-Jewish philanthropy that maintained a network of primary schools within the Yishuv and laid the cornerstone in 1912 for a technical high school and university (Technikum) in Haifa. Paul Nathan, the secretary of the Hilfsverein, insisted that Hebrew be the main language of instruction in the Hilfsverein's primary schools, and no less a figure than the pioneering Hebrew linguist Eliezer Ben-Yehuda had the highest praise for the Hilfsverein's Jerusalem teachers' seminary, which he saw as a vital protector and nurturer of modern spoken Hebrew. But students at the seminary grumbled that the Hilfsverein was an agent of Germanization, because German was taught as a secondary language at the Hilfsverein's schools, and Zionists throughout the Yishuv and abroad were incensed by Hilfsverein plans to use German as a language of instruction for technical subjects at the institutions of higher education in Haifa.

Against this background, Silman produced the intricate parody *Bava Tekhnika* in 1913.[28] The text is a withering attack upon the directors and officers of the Hilfsverein, Paul Nathan, James Simon, Ephraim Cohen, and Bernard Kahn, as well as the Hilfsverein's defenders in the Yishuv, such as Ben-Yehuda and the ultra-Orthodox newspaper *Ha-Moriah*. The text contains fabricated commentaries (including *perush ras'i*, that is, Silman himself is in place of the customary Rashi, and *avot di-rav nathan*, a pun on Paul Nathan within a reference to a canonical midrashic text). The parody contains a blend of authentic, inverted, and altered mishnayot from several talmudic tractates, mainly *Bava Metsiya* and *Shabbat*. Silman chooses texts that would be familiar to anyone with a basic talmudic education; to wit, discussions in *Bava Metsiya* about property that is disputed or abandoned, and the rights and responsibilities of bailors and bailees. These mishnayot are accompanied by lengthy and at times complex gemara.

Beginning with the classic "Two are holding on to a garment," from the first chapter of *Bava Metsiya* (*shnayim ohazin be-talit*, rendered *shtayim ohazot*, thus finding humor in the cross-gendering of language, as the feminine form of the number is substituted for the masculine, the default form in Hebrew speech), the text reads, as per the original, that each claimant swears an oath of ownership and the garment (or its value) is divided, although in this case the division is unequal, and the authorities cited are the Zionist ideologue Ahad Ha-Am and the Liberal German rabbi Ludwig Phillipson, representing Eastern European and German Jewry, respectively. Then, in the fabricated gemara, Silman's tone turns hostile:

> What are we dealing with here? If you were to say a *talit* and *tefilin* [prayer shawl and phylacteries], [I would say that] he is of the West, where there is no *talit* and *tefilin*, as Mar said, "From the day that rights were given to the children of the West, Torah and commandments were forgotten by them." And if you say that we are dealing with the *talit* of Korach [who, according to the Midrash, challenged Moses by asking if an entirely blue garment required a ritual blue fringe], [I reply that] we are dealing with the Technikum, as Mar said, "What is the Technikum? A sort of cloak with which those sons of the West wrap themselves and make in it a bow to their master." You say that the *talit* of the Technikum is nothing but the *talit* of Korach as we have taught, "From the day that the Technikum came into the world betrayal and slander have multiplied and even, God forbid, chaos has entered the minds of the Jews," as it is written, "And did the children of Korach not die?"[29]

According to the parody, Jews in the West play God; invoking the language of the narrative in Genesis of the creation of Eve, they claim to make for man a helpmate (*'ezrah*, a pun on the Hebrew name for the Hilfsverein). Thus the Hilfsverein becomes a feminized force, just as disastrous as primal woman. *Ezrah* is a force of wanton destruction, and anyone who leaves a child in *Ezrah*'s care is guilty of a wrongdoing. *Ezrah* will bring gentile (meaning German) rule upon the Holy Land and tear youth away from it: "Rabbi Ephraim [Ephraim Cohen of the Hilfsverein] says, 'The Wise of Israel will look outwards,'" meaning that the schools in the Land of Israel must be multilingual and thus easy prey for those who would tear them asunder.[30] Much of the parody deals with *Ezrah*'s great wealth ("Rabbi [James] Simon says, 'Whoever has money in his hand has the upper hand.'"),[31] and even the cleverest of men succumb to *Ezrah*'s power. In a retelling of the classic Midrash about Rabbi Eliezer and the oven, here the protagonist is Eliezer Ben-Yehuda, who comes under a rabbinic ban for supporting the Hilfsverein.[32] Of all the groups in the Yishuv, the parody relates, only the socialist pioneers have the courage to resist *Ezrah*.

Silman's bitter polemic has much in common with its Haskalah predecessors, but the differences are striking. Maskilim wrote parodies in the style and language of their opponents, who would be infuriated by the parodies precisely because of their accuracy. Silman, on the other hand, composed a parody which most of its targets could not possibly understand. Haskalah parody was an offensive act by a self-confident elite with a sense of mission. Silman's text, on the other hand, is a defensive ploy designed to shore up the morale of a fragile Hebrew intelligentsia caught between the ultra-Orthodox majority and the western philanthropic agencies necessary for the Yishuv's survival. Haskalah parody was subversive of the religious status quo, yet in the raw and unformed Yishuv of the early twentieth century, there was no status quo, only entrenched interest groups that battled against one another on fairly equal terms. Finally, whereas learned parody was a major literary genre that flourished for over a century in Eastern Europe, its life span in Palestine was all too brief. So far as I know, Silman's parodies were the only ones of their type produced before World War I, and after the war there was little place for such intricate textual play in the secularized atmosphere of Tel Aviv, the cradle of literary culture in what was known at the time as the Jewish National Home.

Most of the humorous literature produced in the interwar Yishuv was of a piece with the sensibilities of the rising political establishment: hostile to the British, pro-Labor, and critical of Revisionism, the radical Left, and ultra-Orthodoxy. Like Silman's broadsides against the Hilfsverein, Hebrew satires directed against the British authorities were likely to go unnoticed by the intended targets, but they did serve the purpose of providing moral support and inspiring collective solidarity.

On the other hand, Hebrew satire in the interwar period featured scathing attacks against various forces within the Yishuv, recalling the internecine verbal warfare of nineteenth-century Eastern Europe. These attacks were couched in the language and genres of the Zionist sacred canon: the Hebrew Bible (in particular the narratives of the Exodus and the biblical kingdoms) and the story of the Maccabees. Only occasionally did satirists play with rabbinic sources, as in Menashe Polini's 1931 column in *Ha-Aretz* titled "Mili de-orayta le-furim" (Words of Torah for Purim): "What does the Arab Higher Committee say to [the dovish Zionist leader Judah] Leib Magnes? 'And you shall serve me for free [*ve-'avadetani hinam*, Gen. 29:15],' which in the Aramaic Targum is '*ve-tiflehinani magnes*' [a pun on the Targum's actual wording, *magan*]."[33] The Jewish liturgy was rarely a vehicle for satire, although before the autumn High Holidays in 1932 the humorous newspaper *Ve-'al kulam* (the title itself was taken from the Yom Kippur liturgy) produced a satiric *Kol Nidrei* (the proactive revocation of vows made to God recited on the evening of Yom Kippur). In this parody, the British ask God for permission to break all their vows to the Jewish people.[34]

Among biblical texts, Esther was the most commonly chosen text for parody. The Book of Esther had, of course, been the target of parody for centuries, and in Palestine, governed by the British and populated mostly by Arabs, the book's themes of collective danger, Jewish political dependence on gentiles, and the ambiguous quality of the gentile as both potential liberator (Ahashverush) and destroyer (Haman) all had particular relevance.

Examples of updating the Book of Esther may be found in a humorous newspaper, *Me-hodu Ve-'ad Kush* (From India even unto Ethiopia, a reference to Ahashverush's empire as described at the beginning of Esther). Six issues of this paper appeared between 1929 and 1935. The journal was edited, and one assumes largely written, by Avraham Lev, who used the pseudonym Yoshev Beseter (a reference to Psalm 91: "You who dwell in the shelter of the Most High"). An article of 1935 titled "Megilat Heskem" (The scroll of the agreement) was written at the time of the abortive Ben-Gurion–Jabotinsky accords, which sought to put an end to strife between the Labor and Revisionist movements. The piece features Jabotinsky as Ahashverush, Uri Zvi Greenburg as the king's disgraced wife Vashti, the Revisionist activist Von Weisel as the wicked counselor Haman, and both Chaim Weizmann and David Ben-Gurion playing different parts of the role of the wise Mordechai. The labor movement takes the place of the Persian Empire's Jewish masses (intriguingly, the story has no Esther). In this version of the classic tale, a heroic Ben-Gurion saves the "Jews" – to wit, his labor movement – through an "agreement game" and subsequent plebiscite.

More than any other text, the Passover Haggadah was the vehicle of Hebrew satirical parody during the interwar years. As noted, the Haggadah's simple structure lends itself to parody; its story of collective liberation by God might easily be transformed into a tale of national revival and the struggle for independence. Beginning in the 1920s, kibbutzim produced original haggadot, earnest and wholly secular tales of national liberation that conform to the literary genre of "serious parody." The satiric haggadot of the same time period also had serious intentions, such as celebrating the accomplishments of the Zionist project, criticizing Zionism's opponents, and expressing rage at apparent British mendacity.

Unlike Haskalah parody, which was one of the few weapons in the hands of the maskil minority against dominant Orthodoxy, the Yishuv's satiric haggadot reflected the sensibilities of what was, in that time and place, the Jews' leadership elite, namely the Zionist labor movement. Satire gradually shed its subversive qualities and became the expression of a mobilized, dynamic society seeking to discredit its enemies, internal and external alike. Whereas Haskalah satire worked indirectly, evoking a humorous response and an appreciation for the *maskilic* point of view from the clever juxtaposition of texts and imaginative commentaries, satiric parodies in the Yishuv were far less subtle; their humor lay in the shock of the politicization and secularization of the sacred text.

The earliest satiric haggadot I have encountered are relatively free of anti-British or anticlerical bile. A parody published in the humorous periodical *Ha-Darban* in 1926 poked fun at the corruption, inefficiency, and long-windedness of Zionist institutions, and it lampooned various Jewish types via the four sons, who take the form of a French professor, a free-thinking Russian artist, a wealthy and stupid American philanthropist, and a thick-headed *yekke* (German Jew) who can't learn Hebrew after twenty years in Palestine. This Haggadah also features stock references to Jewish poverty, a throwback to the socially conscious Haskalah parodies we discussed above.[35] The 1929 riots and spate in the following year of British investigatory commissions and government decrees, which appeared to threaten the very survival of the Jewish National Home, stimulated the writing of several satiric haggadot that featured a more bitter tone. Avraham Lev, the editor of *Me-hodu Ve-'ad Kush*, authored the 1931 parody *Mi-Mitsrayim Ve-'ad Henah* (From Egypt unto here).[36] The frontispiece displays the literal equation of the Exodus and Zionist narratives, with mirror-images of Chaim Weizmann and Lord Passfield (author of the 1930 British White Paper critical of the Zionist project), on the one hand, and Moses and Pharaoh, on the other, crowned by an inscription that in Hebrew numerology (*gematria*) Pharaoh and *Melekh Passfield* (King Passfield) are the same. The entire Haggadah that follows interprets the Zionist struggle against the British in terms of the ancient Passover story.

Each of the elements of the service, recited at the beginning (*kadesh urhatz*, *karpas*, *yahatz*, and so forth), is given a political meaning; for instance: "*Korekh* [the 'binding' of matzah and bitter herbs]: One binds together the Shaw [*shav*: worthless, in vain] and the [Hope–]Simpson Report and the Passfield White Paper." Similarly, the *matzot* in front of the leader are replaced by White Papers. The *mah nisthanah* (What makes this night different from all other nights?) asks, "What makes this time different from all other times? At all other times one promises and fulfills; this time only promises; at all other times one makes sweet and bitter promises; this time only bitter ones." In the narrative of the four sons, the wicked son is a Revisionist ("who says, 'we need blood, mud, and slave labor and nothing more. For what is free labor to you?' To you and not to him"). As in the traditional Haggadah, this son will not be redeemed because he has removed himself from the community: here, the Labor and Labor-affiliated sectors of society. The simple son is a member of the bi-national association Brit Shalom (Covenant of Peace), much reviled in the Yishuv for its advocacy of a Jewish–Arab agreement regarding the future of Palestine. The simple son asks, "What is this? Why do you have a land? And you will say to him, we left Egypt to be slaves." Finally, the son who does not know how to ask is presented as a Jewish communist.

This Haggadah reflects the anxiety of Zionists struggling against a welter of hostile forces – British, Arab, and Jewish alike – that appeared poised to strangle the Jewish National Home in its cradle. The prayer *Shfokh Hamatkhah* (Pour out thy wrath) is directed against the British, who are "the Gentiles who have deceived you and against the commissions which did not invoke your name." The invocation "*dam ve-'esh ve-timrot ashan*" (blood and fire and pillars of smoke) is rendered thus: '*Dam* (referring to the riots of 1929) *ve'e"sh* (an acronym based on *ve'idat Shav*, the Shaw Commission) *ve'-imrot resha*' (evil decrees, that is, The White Paper). The ten plagues include

"The White Paper, Husseinis, Dr. Shiels [Drummond Shiehls, Undersecretary of State at the time of the 1930 White Paper], Brit Shalom, Agudat Yisrael, factionalism, and Revisionist contempt."

Not surprisingly, the tone in *Mi-Mitsrayim Ve-'ad Henah* is often more cynical than celebratory. Water is drunk instead of wine. The *Ha-Lahma* (This is the bread of affliction) at the beginning of the service reads: "All who are hungry are hungry; all who are in need, let them come and be in need." An even more bitter flavor characterizes Binyamin Kaspi's parodic Haggadah of 1931, which appeared in the journal *Pitom ve-Ramses.*[37] Kaspi turns the recitation of the order of the service into a lamentation for Jews murdered in riots two years previously: *kadeshurhatz* refers to the British sanctioning the riots and washing their hands of the affair; *tsafun, barekh* refers to the conscience (*matspun*) of the enlightened public that has fled (*barah*). Kaspi is no less hostile to Jewish communists and radical socialist Zionists, whom he saw as being in thrall to the Soviet Union, whose programs for Jewish agricultural colonization in Crimea and Birobidzhan were thought to divert desperately needed human and financial resources away from the Yishuv. The *Ha-Lahma* reads: "This is the bread of affliction that our ancestors ate in the land of the Soviets. . . . All who are hungry, let them come to the Crimea; all who are in need, let them come to Stalin. This year in Birobidzhan, next year in the land of the *Komsomol* [the Communist Youth League]. This year, Trotsky; next year, Bukharin too." "We were slaves unto Pharaoh" is changed to read: "We were slaves unto the *Yevsektsiya* [the Jewish section of the Soviet Communist Party]". In the *mah nishtanah* we are told, "[o]n all other nights we work the land with the tractor and collectivization, tonight only collectivization; on all other nights we endure a variety of reprisals, but tonight just terror." And the narrative of Jacob and Laban is transmuted into the story of Reuven Brainin, a renegade Zionist who became an avid supporter of the Crimean project and so *persona non grata* within the Zionist movement.

The elements of self-criticism in Kaspi's Haggadah become full-blown self-hatred in a bizarre parody of 1930, *Shfokh Hamatkhah*, edited by Zvi Kashdai.[38] Here, the Haggadah's description of Jacob's uncle Laban as a greater threat to the Jews than Pharaoh is interpreted to mean that Jewish enemies of Zionism are more dangerous than antisemites. The *mah nisthanah* begins: "Jews are different from all other people because others hate, kill, respond to hatred in kind, [whereas] Jews turn the other cheek." The *shfokh hamatkhah*, after which this sclerotic work is named, calls upon God to "pour out thy wrath against the Gentiles who did not know you and on the Jews who have forgotten you . . . to forgive those who murder and plunder us." Harry Charles Luke, the acting High Commissioner at the time of the 1929 riots and himself of Jewish origin, is singled out for savage ridicule.

The parodic Haggadot of the early 1930s exude a secular, even anticlerical spirit, and they redirect the worship of God into veneration for and commitment to the Jewish National Home. In *Mi-Mitsrayim Ve-'ad Henah*, the refrain of the counting song "*Ehad mi-yode'a*," is not God who is one in Heaven and on earth, but, "Our people, in Exile and in the Land, are One." Similarly, in the song's last verse, in place of the thirteen attributes of God there are the thirteen years since the Balfour Declaration. The rest of the song gives secular and contemporary meanings to all of the numbers: three high commissioners, a five-day work week in the Haifa harbor, eleven stars of Mapai on the Yishuv's National Committee; but in these cases the intent is clearly humorous, whereas the Zionist sentiment in the refrain is utterly sincere. In this Haggadah, God is present only at the beginning, and even here He is quickly pushed aside. Following the examination for leaven (*hametz*) performed the evening before the commencement of Passover there is a blessing to God for releasing the individual from the commandment against engaging in the very act he or she has just performed. In the narrative of the four sons, the wise one is a religious Zionist who, we quickly learn, is an impediment to the Zionist project:

> "What? The testimonies and laws and judgments which God commanded belong to you? No! The Torah is mine, wisdom is mine, and I resign [from the various governing bodies of the Zionist movement and Yishuv]!" And you will say to him as according to the Law, one does not resign at any moment (*ayn mitpatrin* [a pun on *maftirin*] *bekhol rega*) *ve-al tifsachafnkoymen*.

In *Shfokh Hamatkhah*, the blessing *barukh hamakom, barukh hu* reads that Jews are obliged to thank the Lord for all the persecutions and evils that have befallen them throughout time. Rabbis are portrayed as indolent and useless, while praise is heaped upon their "sons," the pioneers, who come forth to redeem the land. True, *Shfokh Hamatkhah* claims Zionist ownership of the Western Wall of the ancient Temple compound, as shown in this Haggadah's version of the song *Had Gadya*, which comes at the end of the seder evening. In the song's parodied lyrics, "*Ha-kotel koteleinu ve-ha-aretz artzeinu*! [The Western Wall is our wall and the land is our land]." The underlying sensibility here, however, is not piety, rather Revisionist maximalism, a claim to ownership of a national treasure (Revisionist demonstrations at the Western Wall were one of the causes of the 1929 riots). In *Mi-Mitsrayim Ve-'ad Henah*, on the other hand, the Western Wall and other holy sites are overlooked altogether. The Haggadah's final words are "Next year in the rebuilt land!" as opposed to the standard "Next year in the rebuilt Jerusalem."

The forces of secularization that removed God from the Haggadah could make possible a trivialization of the revered text more shocking than the elevation of the Zionist project to the status of the abandoned godhead. In April of 1928, a multi-page advertisement in *Ha-Aretz* featured the "*Haggadah shel 'Yehuda'*," an insurance company, tied to the American

Zionist organization Bnei Zion, that claimed to keep all its profits and resources in Eretz Israel. This insurance company, like the night of the seder, is claimed to be separate from all others.[39]

A cleverer, but no less crass, application of modern consumerism to the Haggadah came in a parody prepared for the Levant Trade Fair of 1932 by Binyamin Kaspi, whom we encountered above, and Daniel Parski, who frequently wrote humorous retellings of Bible stories for *Ha-Aretz*.[40] The theme of the Haggadah is economic growth; patriotism is expressed through consumption of local products and by attendance at the fair ("What makes this night different from all other nights? For on all other nights we eat Australian butter and Egyptian cream, but tonight only products from [the labor movement's dairy co-operative] Tenuva"). The four sons are classified according to consumption patterns: the good son "buys everything" and is to be instructed "according to the laws of trade and industry." The wicked son is avaricious, but lazy; "*ulefi she-hotsi 'et 'atsmo min ha-hakla'ut kafar be-'ikar*" ("and because he has removed himself from the community he has sinned against the farmer," a series of puns on the original wording "and because he has removed himself from the community, he has committed a primal sin"). The text goes on to say, "*Methilah 'ovdei totseret hutz hayu 'avoteinu*" (in the beginning our fathers worshiped foreign merchandise – as opposed to foreign gods). The song *'avadim hayinu* (We were slaves) thanks God for removing the Jews from economically depressed Europe; the prayer *Be-khol dor ve-dor*, which in the traditional Haggadah refers to the series of enemies who have risen against the Jews over time, now describes the economic crises of every generation, and the *maggid*, the Haggadah's narrative of biblical history, here relates the Jews' economic woes, focusing on how in recent years they have been denied credit or even access to their own assets by large banks. In this Trade Fair Haggadah, capitalist entrepreneurs are the Jews' new saviors. Moshe Novomesky, founder of the Palestine Potash Company, later the Dead Sea Works, is likened to the biblical Moses; he was led to the other side of the Dead Sea, given a concession, and God multiplied his potash. The fair is itself a nearly miraculous event; the lyrics of the counting song "Who Knows One?" feature the likes of "Who knows three? Three weeks of the fair. ... Who knows four? Grain from four corners of the world."

Satiric Passover Haggadot and other forms of textual parody continued to appear throughout the 1930s, but they reached their peak early in the decade. The amount of religious-textual parody in *Me-hodu ve-'ad Kush* declined with each issue, from 1929 to 1935. Over this same period, the number and frequency of satiric columns in Hebrew notably increased. The textual parody gave way to a literary genre described by Dan Almagor as *tasa"m (tur satiri mehuraz)*, a newspaper column featuring rhymed satiric prose. Such columns made references to biblical and rabbinic texts and occasionally parodied them, but the main function of these columns was to comment humorously upon contemporary political affairs by means of a literary, yet highly accessible, Hebrew prose. Already in the mid-1920s, Yehuda Karni and Alexander Pen had begun to use this form in the newspapers *Ha-Aretz* and *Davar*, respectively, but the genre was made famous by Nathan Alterman, who began writing political verse for *Ha-Aretz* in 1934. Nine years later, he moved to *Davar*, and his column "Ha-tur ha-shevi'i" (The seventh column) became the Yishuv's most influential source of political commentary.[41]

The transition from the ephemeral periodical to the weekly column, and also, as mentioned earlier, to the nightly cabaret act, marked the freeing of humor from the confines of sacred space. These developments in the Yishuv can best be understood in terms of David Roskies's important observations about the transformation of the social function of the wedding jester, the *badhan*, in Eastern Europe in the second half of the nineteenth century. The *badhan*'s performance, notes Roskies, changed from an expression of folk to popular culture, and the circumstances in which it took place moved from sanctified to secular time, from the wedding feast or the *Purimspil* to every day. In the mid-1800s, certain *badhanim* became popular entertainers, authors of Yiddish popular songs that became "hits" well known throughout Eastern Europe. A tie to the past remained, however, in that many of these songs were anti-hasidic parodies, a vulgarized version of the learned Haskalah parodies with which we began this chapter. In the United States the *badhan* underwent a further transformation into the writers and performers in Second Avenue Yiddish theater. Yet even here there remained an element of parody, although now satire was blended with reverential and nostalgic imitation (hence the blending of western popular musical styles with the Phrygian mode of Jewish liturgical music). With the end of Second Avenue Yiddish theater and song, argues Roskies,

> American Jews lost the art of spoofing that which they held most sacred. Second Avenue preserved and protected the art of Jewish parody. ... What the *badkhan* was allowed at weddings and the folk was allowed at Purim became the sanctioned release mechanism for the largest mass of migratory Jews in history.

The loss of Jewish parody, Roskies concludes, is inextricably linked with the loss "of pragmatic Jewish politics and ... the immediate Jewish past."[42]

Jews newly arrived in Palestine did not suffer a deficiency of politics. Quite the opposite. Yet, otherwise, Roskies's comments about the transition from the *badkhan* to the Borsht Belt and the separation of satire from the realm of the sacred to that of the profane (from the "sabbath Jew" to the "weekday Jew," to parody Marx's famous distinction) are fruitfully applied to the early twentieth-century Yishuv. Roskies's remarks, and my own here, reflect a universal phenomenon connected with the modernization and secularization of society and the development of the mass media through which modern society expresses itself. Media scholars Elihu Katz and George Wedell have commented upon the difficulties in developing countries of performing traditional cultural practices on television. Among other things, there is an irresistible pull to broadcast occasional art forms associated with holidays, weddings, and the like on a regular basis: "the imported orthodoxy of broadcasting prescribes 'continuous performance.'"[43] I would argue that the modern Jewish press exerted a similar centrifugal force, but that for several decades it was balanced by the highly traditional nature of Jewish society, which cleaved to the rhythms of the sacred Jewish calendar, as well as the text-centered nature of Jewish high culture. The result was a flourishing of textual parody tied to Jewish holidays. As we have seen, however, those parodies' links with the Jewish heritage grew weaker over time. By the 1940s they had lost their Judaic roots in the thick overgrowth of political satire that characterized the modern Hebrew press.

This trend intensified after 1948, as Israeli satire became increasingly parochial. It certainly has made use of ethnic themes, lampooning the stereotypical characteristics of the various components – whether Polish, German, Moroccan, or other – of Israel's population, a kind of satire perfected by the comedy troupe Ha-gashash ha-hiver (The pale tracker). But this kind of humor does not demand *Jewish* literacy. Recent satiric television programs such as *Nikui rosh* (Head cleaning), *Ha-hartzufim* (The muppets), and today's sardonic *Zo 'artseinu* and *Ha-burgonim* (This is our land, The bourgeois) are intensely funny to the knowledgeable insider in Israeli society, but they are a far cry from the satiric parody of the Jewish Bookshelf. Contemporary satiric literature for children, some of it written by Israel's finest authors, does employ biblical language and refers to basic themes from the Genesis or Exodus narratives, but nothing more sophisticated than that is to be found.[44] This is not solely a question of lacking textual knowledge; rather, it is a sense of distance, even alienation, from the Jewish past and its creations.

How many secular Israelis today would identify themselves, as did Yishuv parodists during the 1920s and 1930s, with Israel in Egypt, and how many would conceive of the manifold crises confronting contemporary Israel in terms of the Passover narrative? Underneath the Yishuv parodists' wordplay and levity lay an utter seriousness of purpose, an identification with a national cause, which today has been thrown into uncertainty. Like Haskalah parody, the satiric haggadot of the interwar period were manifestos, products of a mobilized sub-group within Jewish society that was engaged in a revolutionary project. Parody of revered texts both lent legitimacy to the manifestos' message and highlighted distinctions between the old and desired orders. During the period before Israeli statehood, the parodic hypertext preserved the collective memory and awareness of the sacred hypotext. Over the past several decades, however, the chasm between secularism and Orthodoxy has magnified. The former lost its Judaic literacy

and the latter abandoned the irony that characterizes much of traditional Jewish exegesis. For all its apparently subversive qualities, textual parody was a manifestation of a healthy Jewish civilization struggling to establish equilibrium between tradition and modernity, and between memory and forgetting. It was a form of imitation without assimilation, and one whose loss is to be mourned for more than literary reasons.

10 Transmitting Jewish culture

Radio in Israel

The written sign is the linchpin of western civilization, the chief vehicle for the transmission of knowledge across time and space. Although rooted in an oral epic tradition, ancient societies from Babylonia to Rome assiduously transcribed and preserved foundational texts. The Hebrew Bible presented divine enunciation and human transcription of Torah as nearly simultaneous. The Jewish Oral Law of late antiquity metamorphosed into a massive corpus of written exegetical and legal texts, just as primitive Christianity's logocentrism ("In the beginning was the [spoken] Word," says the Gospel of John) engendered the medieval monastery, whose center was the scriptorium. In the early modern period, the development of print technology freed the word from its cloister and made possible the wide dissemination of abstract thought, which is most effectively expressed in concrete text.[1] The nineteenth-century newspaper further de-sacralized the written word – Hegel remarked that newspaper reading was the modern substitute for daily prayers – and democratized it. But from the epoch of the Bible to the era of the boulevard press, the written word remained the common vehicle for signification and communication.

Between the two world wars of the twentieth century, the cultural systems of the western world were challenged by radio, which, along with cinema, was a post-literary medium of mass communication. Radio restored the fallen pillars of pre-literary civilization, orality and aurality, by making the spoken word accessible to millions of listeners. But orality in the age of electronic communication – what Walter Ong refers to as "secondary orality" – and practices of listening were qualitatively different than in previous eras. In pre-literate society oral communication and comprehension occurred via direct, immediate interaction, while the body of transmitted cultural knowledge was fluid and subject to change with every act of narration. In the technologically sophisticated societies of the twentieth century, however, whatever potential for spontaneity lay in the broadcast of human speech was overwhelmed by the written, prepared text: the political manifesto, the news bulletin, the dramatic soliloquy, all corresponding to a fixed body of knowledge.[2] The spoken word, based on a written text, was broadcast from centers of power by disembodied yet widely recognized and trusted voices, to an unseen population of workers and citizens. Radio also presented the paradox of a non-verbal mass medium in that the most popular broadcast material was music, in which words were either absent or subordinated to melody. During the 1920s and 1930s throughout Europe and North America, intellectuals, policy-makers, and entrepreneurs debated whether broadcast speech or music should be seen as merely extensions of live performance or a new form of communication altogether, and whether the primary purpose of radio was entertainment or education.

All of these concerns came to play in the Zionist project, which, like other nationalist movements in the mid-twentieth century, saw in radio an important tool for the nationalization of the masses. The founders of Hebrew broadcasting in Palestine hoped that radio would be an equal partner, alongside journalism and formal education, in the creation of a Hebrew vernacular and a Zionist culture. Aspirations towards the development of a specifically Hebraic culture dwelled with a desire to instill into the Israeli populace an appreciation of cosmopolitan, mainly European, high culture, in the form of the international language of classical music or translations of classic dramatic and literary works. Radio was also meant to be a source of general social and scientific knowledge. Thus Hebrew broadcasting, first in Mandatory Palestine and then in the state of Israel, was accorded a mission similar to that of the Jewish press in nineteenth-century Europe – to serve as a *melits*, an intermediary, between a raw yet educable people and the high cultures, Judaic and European, that were at present just beyond its grasp.

The case of Israeli radio provides a unique opportunity to study the relationship between the electronic media and Jewish culture. During the previous century, outside of Palestine and Israel Jewish electronic media scarcely existed, at least not before the flourishing of Jewish cable television channels and internet sites at the century's end. Thus an important, and neglected, component of the rupture between diaspora and Israeli culture is the marginality of electronic media in the former versus their centrality in the latter. Moreover, the late introduction of television into Israel – regular broadcasts began only in 1968 – meant that during Israel's formative decades radio played a far greater cultural role than was the case in most western countries, where television established its dominance already during the 1950s, or in the developing world, where few people had access to radio receivers. For both of these reasons, the question of the impact of electronic media on mid-twentieth-century Jewish culture can be satisfactorily answered only via an intensive examination of Israeli radio. I shall attempt to do so here, beginning with the establishment of the Palestine Broadcast Service (PBS) by the British in 1936 and ending in the 1970s, with the diminution of Israeli radio's tutelary mission in the wake of the introduction of television and the social upheaval that followed the 1973 Arab–Israeli war.

This chapter is something of a counterpoint to the excellent study by Jeffrey Shandler and Elihu Katz on Jewish radio and television broadcasting in the postwar United States. Focusing on the program *The Eternal Light*, which was produced by the Jewish Theological Seminary for the National Broadcasting Company (NBC), Shandler and Katz demonstrate how the program's presentation of Jewish culture was framed by the "Sunday ghetto" of religious broadcasting into which it was placed and by its integrationist mission to present Jewish contributions to civilization and the universalist underpinnings of Jewish values.[3] Until the 1980s, when Jewish cultural material began to be broadcast on dedicated radio and cable television stations, a listener in North America desiring exposure to Jewish culture had access only to weekly doses of edification or slivers of light entertainment, such as Yiddish-inflected humor. The situation was entirely different in Israel, where a listener could be exposed to *yidishkayt* on any station, at any time. As a writer in Palestine's Hebrew radio magazine observed on the eve of Israel's declaration of statehood:

> There are indeed in the world several broadcasting stations that broadcast for Jews; and especially the famous program 'Ner Tamid' [Eternal Light] in America – in our struggle in this realm, too, redemption will come only with the establishment of the Jewish state with the Jewish broadcasting station special to it.[4]

The cultural agenda of Hebrew radio in Palestine and Israel was just as strong as that of its diaspora counterpart, but the two differed substantively in structure, practice, and effect.

Inventing Hebrew radio: the Palestine Broadcast Service

In the 1920s, radios were rare in Palestine. People longing to hear broadcast news and music from Europe flocked to public listening salons. There were only 5,000 receivers in Palestine in 1931, but 37,000 by the end of the decade, and 110,000 by 1943.[5] Ownership rates were six times higher among Jews than Arabs. This imbalance reflected not only greater Jewish affluence but also higher levels of cultural literacy. (According to Israeli surveys of the 1950s and 1960s, there was a direct correlation between education, reading, and attendance at cultural events, on the one hand, and listening to the radio, on the other.)[6] Most of Palestine's Jews were newcomers, eager to maintain connections with the outside world and, particularly after 1939, anxious to follow world events. Moreover, Zionist leaders in Palestine, inspired by Lenin's dictum that the radio would be the newspaper of tomorrow, and in general favoring the highest possible use of technological innovation in order to realize the gargantuan tasks of nation-building, decided early in the Mandate period that radio broadcasting would be an essential component of the Zionist project. Zionist efforts to establish a radio station in Palestine began in 1924. Two years later, David Ben-Gurion and Berl Katznelson established a Radio and Electrotechnical Institute, a

co-operative venture of the private sector and the General Trade Union's holding company, Hevrat Ovdim.[7]

Zionist attempts to establish a radio station were held up by the British authorities until 1932, when a permit was granted to Mendel Abramovitch, an engineer and employee of the Radio Institute, to construct a radio station to broadcast during that year's Levant Trade Fair. The experiment was short lived, as the Mandatory government decided that radio should be a governmental monopoly. Trying to draw lessons from the 1929 riots, the government believed radio should be mobilized to pacify the natives through the judicious interpretation and soothing exposition of news and to combat Arabic-language Soviet propaganda. (After 1939, the chief threat came from fascist propaganda emanating from Bari, Tirana, and Berlin.) The authorities also assumed that the technically sophisticated Zionists would set up unauthorized stations of their own at some point and so would best be co-opted into a governmentally supervised venture.[8] The result was the PBS, which featured, in addition to English and Arabic services, a Hebrew service known as Kol Yerushalayim (The voice of Jerusalem). This service continued until 1948, at which time it melded with the underground radio stations of the Haganah to form the state-controlled Kol Yisrael (The voice of Israel).

As was so often the case in the history of the British Mandate, actions taken by the British out of self-interest wound up primarily benefiting the Zionist project. For a variety of reasons – the presence of a large and capable pool of potential broadcasters and writers, a willingness to work on a volunteer basis when needed, and the pro-Zionist leanings of Edwin Samuel (son of Herbert Samuel, the first high commissioner), director of the PBS from 1945 to 1948 – the PBS was far more closely identified with the interests of the Zionist project than those of its Palestinian Arab rival. In 1946, for example, there were six hours of daily programming in Hebrew as opposed to only three in Arabic. In the dynamic and complex world of Zionist politics, Kol Yerushalayim was quickly added to the existing repertoire of political and cultural institutions. Hebrew radio programming was formulated in consultation with Palestinian Jewry's governing body, the National Committee, the cultural and educational departments of the Jewish Agency Executive, and a host of cultural bodies such as the Hebrew Language Committee, teachers' and journalists' organizations, the Hebrew University, and even the Ha-Bimah theatrical company.[9]

The directors of Kol Yerushalayim, Eliezer Lubrani (1936–42) and Mordechai Avida (1942–8) exalted Hebrew radio as not merely a symbol but also an instrument of Jewish cultural revival. Radio played its own role in the invention of modern Hebrew; Lubrani created the words "*shidur*" (broadcast or broadcasting), "*ulpan*" (studio), "*taskit*" (radio play), and the memorable phrase, pronounced at the beginning of each news bulletin, "*harei hahadashot ve-'ikaran tehilah*" (here follows the news, and first, the main points). More important, radio sought to standardize spoken Hebrew.

In a 1986 interview, an English veteran of the PBS administration recalled tensions between champions of Ashkenazic versus Sephardic pronunciation. (The interviewee called the latter "German," perhaps in reference to the veneration by adherents of the German Jewish Enlightenment of Sephardic culture and the adoption by modern German Jews of Sephardic pronunciation for Torah reading in the belief that it replicated the speech patterns of ancient biblical Hebrew.)[10] Kol Yisrael's official language handbook claims that during the Mandate period Sephardic pronunciation was chosen for broadcasting without an ideological agenda; Hebrew radio was merely following the precedent of other lands, where one particular dialect or form of pronunciation was chosen to be the standard for national broadcasting as a whole.[11]

This description is somewhat disingenuous. It masks the process of artful crafting of modern Hebrew speech through the political and educational institutions of the Zionist movement and the Jewish state in the making (the Yishuv). Already before World War I, and increasingly thereafter, the mixing together in Palestine of Jews of varied provenance yielded a vernacular that blended Sephardic and Ashkenazic elements, in general preserving the vowels and stresses of the former and the consonants of the latter. In 1913 the Hebrew Language Committee proclaimed that Sephardic pronunciation would henceforth be the pillar of Palestinian spoken Hebrew, but it accepted the penetration of certain Ashkenazic elements such as the pronunciation of the "*tsadi*" like a German "*zed*" rather than an Arabic "*zaay*."[12] Kol Yerushalayim made every effort, however, to render the language as purely Sephardic as possible. Radio's linguistic guidelines demanded that broadcasters not only employ the trilled "*resh*," glottal "*'ayin*," guttural "*khaf*," and aspirated "*het*" of Sephardic speech, but also punctiliously follow Masoretic guidelines for the pronunciation of the "*shva*," the glottal stop marked by the letter "*aleph*," and the doubling of consonants marked with a *dagesh hazak*.[13] (The artificiality of radio Hebrew, and its complex relationship with the evolving vernacular of the street, brings to mind the intricately wrought and aristocratic broadcast Hebrew and the upper-crust, but not quite Oxonian, English of the BBC.)

In addition to cultivating an idealized Hebrew, Kol Yerushalayim propagated a Eurocentric Zionist high culture. Ashkenazic belles-lettres and European fine arts held pride of place, with the culture of Middle Eastern Jewry relegated to the realm of folklore or used as the inspiration for a western cultural creation. Kol Yerushalayim's first broadcast on March 30, 1936, provides an excellent example of this approach and agenda. The program began with a reading of Haim Nahman Bialik's epic poem "The Scroll of Fire." It was followed by European classical music performed by pianist Vittorio Weinberg and singer Hanna Rovina, and then Yemenite songs performed by Bracha Zefira.[14] The Yemenite songs had a distinctively western sound, featuring an operatic singing style, an elegant piano arrangement, diatonic scales, and lush chords.[15] The overwhelming bulk of the music played on Kol Yerushalayim was western; in a playlist from 1945 "Oriental music" (*shirah mizrahit*) was presented in a special weekly half-hour program.[16] One could argue that this situation reflected the preponderance of Ashkenazim in the population at the time, yet the marginalization and bracketing of Middle Eastern Jewish culture continued on Israeli radio well into the 1960s, by which time nearly half the country's population was of North African or Middle Eastern origin.[17]

Kol Yerushalayim made no secret of its nationalizing agenda. Hemdah Feigenbaum Zinder, who was in charge of the children's programming, tried to inject as much Zionist and pedagogic content as possible into the programs without making them so heavy that children would simply turn the radio off.[18] (This was an important issue across the board, as a listener desiring pure entertainment could abandon Kol Yerushalayim in favor of the British army station in Jaffa or Radio Ramallah, which played light music.) The Haganah's underground radio stations featured educational programming as well.[19] The connection between radio and youth education was also present in the invention of Zionist traditions, adapted from ancient Jewish practices. Newly invented ceremonies were often recorded at kibbutzim and then disseminated, via radio, youth movements, and the schools, throughout the Yishuv. An excellent example is the broadcast of the tree planting at kibbutz Mishmar Ha-Emek on Tu Bishvat, 1944.

As is well known, Zionism refashioned Jewish holidays by emphasizing their agricultural roots, thereby demonstrating the antiquity of the Jews' presence in the Land of Israel and the association between them and lives of productive labor. In addition to modifying major festivals such as Passover and Shavuot, the Zionist movement elevated the importance of Tu Bishvat, which in antiquity had been merely a marker for determining the age of trees in order to determine the onset of *orlah*, the period when the fruit could not be picked. A kabbalistic Tu Bishvat liturgy developed from the sixteenth century onward, and Zionism transformed the mystical consumption of fruits and nuts into a celebration of Eretz Israel's late winter bounty. More important, Tu Bishvat became an occasion for the planting of trees, an ancient sanction for the Zionist greening of the land. In the broadcast from Mishmar Ha-Emek, Eliezer Lubrani, speaking a florid Hebrew, describes the ceremony in elaborate detail: the rows of muscular youth, their flags pointed heavenwards; the freshly dug holes in the black soil into which young saplings are planted. The youth utter a "planters' declaration" followed by trumpet blasts. They speak in unison, employing mock biblical language:

> And it shall come to pass, in the eleventh month, on the fifteenth day of the month, a day of planting shall be to you. Every tree, every plant, shall be counted upon that day. … And it shall come to pass when you come to the land, you shall plant every plant, and you shall bless and blow the shofar over the plants, and you shall rejoice over your land on this day … IT IS THE NEW YEAR FOR TREES.[20]

In the Tu Bishvat planting ceremony, a rabbinic commandment was cloaked in biblical raiment – not the divine authority of the Torah so much as the historical-esthetic power of the Hebrew Scriptures, the *Tanakh*, taken as a whole. The Bible was literally the foundation-stone for Hebrew broadcasting; in job interviews, aspiring announcers for Kol Yerushalayim were asked to read from the *Tanakh*. During the difficult days of the Arab Revolt or Israel's struggle for independence, stiff British censorship regulations could be circumvented through the recitation of or allusion to a particular biblical verse pregnant with contemporary relevance. In the late 1930s, following the Arab Revolt, British regulations limited readings from Jewish and Muslim Scriptures to a quarter-hour slot for each, on Friday evening (after sundown, and thus out of bounds for observant Jews who are enjoined against using electronic devices on the Sabbath).[21] The premier broadcast was of the first chapter of Isaiah, read by Shlomo Bertonov, who chanted the text in the traditional fashion, and without commentary.[22] After 1945, *Tanakh* readings took place every evening at 8 p.m., with two chapters read in a quarter-hour slot. Aside from *Tanakh* readings, there was little religious programming *per se*, largely due to conflicts between Zionist and anti-Zionist Orthodox Jews as to the appropriate subject matter and format for such broadcasts. Moreover, unlike Muslim and Christian prayer services, which were broadcast over the PBS every Friday and Sunday, Jewish prayer services could not be broadcast due to prohibitions against the use of electricity on the Jewish Sabbath. The problem was partially overcome in 1943 with the broadcasting on a Saturday evening of prayers for *Selihot*, which marks the onset of the High Holiday season but does not constitute a holiday in and of itself. Anti-Zionist Orthodox Jews opposed the broadcast nonetheless, though the chief Ashkenazic rabbi endorsed it, and the program attracted a wide listening audience, including Jewish soldiers in army camps and kibbutzniks; at one kibbutz in the Jezreel Valley the dining hall was packed full of listeners.[23]

All of the issues discussed so far – the cultivation of the Hebrew language, the nationalization of youth and immigrants of all ages, the invention of traditions and the centrality of the *Tanakh* therein, and an ambivalent, even strained, relationship with the Jewish religious tradition – carried over into the period of statehood. But the transfer of radio from British to sovereign Jewish control, a sharp increase in the amount of programming, and the demands of nation-building in an era of mass migration expanded both the mission and the audience of Israeli radio during the years following the state's establishment.

Creating culture in a mobilized state: Israeli radio, 1949–73

During Israel's first two decades, radio was under direct government control. Under the Provisional Government of 1948–9, radio was under the aegis of the Interior Ministry, but under the state it moved into the Prime

Minister's Office, where it remained, having assumed the name of the Haganah's station, Kol Yisrael, until the establishment of the semi-autonomous Israel Broadcasting Authority in 1965. Kol Yisrael featured a central radio station, Reshet Alef. There was also Reshet Bet, which was devoted solely to immigrant programming until 1960, when a so-called "light program" of entertainment and music was introduced, financed by commercials. Galei Tsahal, the army radio station, was set up in 1950, but its broadcast hours and influence were highly limited until the mid-1960s.[24] Ben-Gurion and members of his Mapai party called Kol Yisrael the "voice of the state" (*shofar ha-medinah*), although Ben-Gurion's critics dubbed the station the "voice of the government" (*shofar ha-memshalah*), noting its failure to broadcast the speeches of leaders of the opposition or include opposition parties' activities in public service announcements of upcoming political events.[25] Responsibility over radio was entrusted to activists in Mapai, or Mapai's sympathizers, or coalition partners. During the 1950s Ben-Gurion's personal secretary, Yitzhak Navon, and the director-general of the Prime Minister's Office, Teddy Kollek, intervened directly in broadcasting, particularly of news items.

Kol Yisrael's near-monopoly on Israeli radio broadcasting represented a continuation of the PBS tradition and also an adoption of the typical practice, in most post-colonial states, of securing radio within the state apparatus. But a number of factors made the Israeli case unusual, even unique. The one dominant radio station was juxtaposed against a proliferation of newspapers, themselves a product of the highly factionalized political culture and vibrant civil society of the pre-state period. The young state of Israel permitted the flourishing of newspapers in keeping with basic democratic principles of free speech; moreover, regardless of political affiliation all but the most radical newspapers submitted to governmental guidelines in the reporting of security matters, and, through a body known as the Editors' Committee, practiced a considerable degree of self-censorship in such affairs.

An intriguing sign of the distinction between the party press and government radio, and between the written and spoken word, lay in Israeli radio's shunning of Arabic-language programming for Jews, in contrast to the prevalence of Arabic-language newspapers in various forms of Judeo-Arabic for new immigrants. As Mustafa Kabha has observed, during the 1950s all the major political parties distributed Arabic-language newspapers in the immigrant transit camps and in immigrant neighborhoods (Mapai's *al-Watan*, Herut's *al-Hurriyah*, the General Zionists' *Nashrat al-Markaz*).[26] Clearly, the parties did so in order to reach out to the immigrants and secure their votes. Yet state-run radio, which had a mission to ease immigrants' entry into Israeli society, was extremely reluctant to broadcast to Jews in Arabic. Throughout the 1950s, immigrant broadcasts were offered in Yiddish, Ladino, and several other European languages. There was even some immigrant programming in Turkish and Persian. The Arabic Service, however, was intended for Christian and Muslim Arabs (though Mizrahi [Middle Eastern and North African] Jews did listen to it). Iraqi Jews ran Kol Yisrael's Arabic Service, but they were unsuccessful in their efforts to introduce immigrant broadcasts in Iraq's Judeo-Arabic dialect. There was a program in Arabic featuring Eliyahu Nawi, a future mayor of Beersheva, but he was a raconteur of tales about Palestinian Arab peasants, employing the name Daud al-Natur, David the Guard.[27] During the late 1950s, hundreds of thousands of immigrants from North Africa were offered scanty, short-term broadcasts in what was called "Mughrabi"; the word "Arabic" was never used in Kol Yisrael documentation. It was publicly, and inaccurately, stated that North African Jews were all conversant in French, a staple of immigrant and overseas broadcasting. And immigrants from Yemen had to make do with what was called the "special program for Yemenite immigrants," entirely in Hebrew.[28]

Kol Yisrael's distance from Arabic did not derive simply from a desire to nationalize immigrants quickly; immigrant programming in Yiddish continued on a daily basis into the 1960s. It reflects a general discomfort with the Arabness of the Mizrahi immigrants and the need for a sharp linguistic barrier between Jew and Arab. Whereas a politically partisan newspaper could employ populist means to reach voters, radio was intended to be above all interests; it was a disembodied vocalization of the general will, the voice of the state, which could not confuse its speech with that of the enemy. Thus radio, more than print, reflected the anxieties and linguistic politics of the young Israeli state as well as the authorities' view of the broadcast voice as the wellspring of a culture that would be uniquely Israeli yet rooted in the expressive core of Jewish civilization, the Hebrew language.

The anxieties expressed by the molders of Israeli broadcasting stemmed from the Herculean challenge of constructing a Jewish state in a hostile Middle Eastern environment and the need for constant vigilance and preparedness for battle while adhering to a democratic political order and civilian rule. The paradoxical quality of "mobilized voluntarism" (*hitnadvut meguyeset*) that characterized Israeli society manifested itself in Galei Tsahal. Not only does Galei Tsahal have no parallel within the framework of Jewish broadcasting, it has no parallel within global broadcasting as a whole. Many countries have army radio stations, which broadcast to soldiers on base at home and abroad, but Galei Tsahal broadcasts to the nation, or at least to its more youthful members. (There are states, like modern Thailand, where the army owns national radio stations, but in Thailand the army's stations are perceived by the press and the populace as agents of oppression, whereas Galei Tsahal is a national treasure which has shaped as much as it has mirrored Israeli culture.)[29]

A final, fascinating aspect of Israeli radio is the absence, until the end of the 1960s, of television, which in every land has been radio's fiercest natural predator. Discussion about introducing television went back as far as 1952, when David Sarnoff, president of the Radio Corporation of America (RCA), proposed a co-operative venture with the Israeli Defense Ministry, and Shimon Peres, at that time the ministry's director-general, eagerly endorsed the establishment of television with the military as a major partner in its creation.[30] But at this time Ben-Gurion and his finance ministers rejected television on both financial and moral grounds. The state could not afford to set up its infrastructure; nor did Israelis have the means to buy television sets. Moreover, television, they feared, would promote idleness and rampant consumerism. In the coming years, opposition to television came also from the extremes of the political spectrum: Mapam rejected it, especially during the mid-1960s recession, as a frivolous luxury; the ultra-Orthodox Agudat Yisrael warned that "television and Torah contradict each other" and that the former would promote juvenile delinquency and sexual libertinism.[31]

Only when the crisis between Israel and the Arab states worsened in the spring of 1967 did a meeting of minds develop between Israel Galilee, the minister of information, and Israeli academics regarding the need for Israeli television to combat televised propaganda from Arab lands. Except Jordan, all nearby Arab countries had introduced television by 1960, and their broadcasts, it was feared, would find easy prey in the 40 percent of the Israeli Jewish population who were of Middle Eastern or North African origin and for many of whom Arabic was a native tongue.[32] Immediately after the 1967 War, Galilee called for the introduction of television into the Territories as a propaganda source. Early plans for what was called "emergency television" proposed three hours of Arabic broadcasting per night, with only one hour for Hebrew.[33] Once regular broadcasts began in 1968, however, television was quickly "demilitarized." The 1968 Independence Day military parade was the occasion for Israeli television's first general broadcast, but it was not repeated. In general, television did not seek to play the explicitly mobilizing, nationalizing role previously undertaken by radio. The political and cultural climate of the country changed drastically after 1967; the 1969–71 War of Attrition with Egypt and, all the more so, the October War of 1973 left many Israelis feeling exhausted, betrayed by their government, and disillusioned with classic Zionist ideology. At the time when radio was becoming ancillary to television – the percentage of Israeli households owning televisions skyrocketed from 8 in 1968 to 75 by 1973 – Israel was itself maturing; evolving, as it were, from a society in khaki shorts to one in denim jeans. Conversely, the history of the mobilized young state of Israel is inseparable from that of its state-controlled radio.

The statist and tutelary agenda of Israeli radio was laid out as early as October of 1948, when the Interior Ministry of the Israeli provisional government convened a meeting of the Public Council for Radio Affairs (PCRA), a body of notables that was to guide the infant state's media policy. At the meeting, Menachem Soloveitchik (later Soleli), director of broadcasting, enunciated his vision of the relationship between broadcasting, the state, and the new Israeli society. "In other lands," he proclaimed, "radio serves the individual primarily. Among us radio needs to serve a) the state; b) the people; c) the individual." Guidance in the form of esthetic education, and not entertainment, was to be radio's chief function. "Above all else," Soloveitchik added, "radio is the only institution upon which is stamped the seal of the state."[34] Throughout the 1950s and early 1960s, radio was presented as an educational tool for new immigrants and as a source for instilling a psychological sense of belonging. At a PCRA meeting in 1952, Yehuda Yaari stated that the purpose of radio was "to make from the immigrant communities a single national unit." The following year, PCRA member Mordechai Breuer, a historian and Orthodox Jew, called upon radio to "draw the new immigrants nearer to the basic concepts of citizenship and life in the state, such as taxes, police, what is a queue, instruction about the laws of the land and guidance on the life of law and justice." Other members wanted rigorous literary programming "for the spiritual improvement of the immigrants" or proposed broadcasting stories about the lives of the pioneer settlers in order to encourage newcomers that they, too, could overcome great hardship.[35]

Galei Tsahal featured a similar pedagogic agenda. When the station began broadcasting in September of 1950, Chief of Staff Yigal Yadin claimed that the station's first function would be to assist the army in the defense of the country but that its second task was to educate and mold the nation, to fulfill the Israel Defense Force's task to "comprise a melting pot for all the exiles of Israel and their transformation into a single fighting nation."[36] David Ben-Gurion waxed far more eloquent:

> [T]he military broadcaster, as an additional link in the chain of tools and instruments of the army, for the mobilization and education of the youth and the nation in Zion, is designed to serve the public relations and educational system of an army in which all the tribes of Israel meet, mix together, and are united. The military broadcaster will serve as a tool of security and defense, a means for stimulating and activating all the forces of the regular and reserve army, an artistic and educational *ulpan* for Israeli youth in general and soldiers in uniform in particular, a cultural supplemental aid for new immigrants among the soldiers, for the acquisition of knowledge of the land, the history of the nation, for rooting the values of labor and defense, in forging the national will, in the development of the formation of the army and in forming a bridge between the soldier and the citizen in the state.[37]

According to the Israeli Defense Force newspaper, *Ba-mahaneh*, Galei Tsahal's goal was to present educational material, ranging from history and Hebrew lessons to radio plays based on Hebrew literature and programs of Jewish choral music, at a level suitable for an army private. One example of such programming would be a series of fictionalized interviews with biblical figures, who would speak in modern Hebrew, thus serving the dual goal of inculcating an appreciation for the Jewish national epic and a knowledge of the vernacular.[38]

There was universal agreement within the government and army about the centrality of radio as a means of disseminating a pure spoken Hebrew. In early 1954, members of the PCRA proclaimed that

> broadcasting is one of the determining factors behind the idiomatic vocabulary [*otsar halashon ha-shegurah ba-fi haberiyot*], both for good and for ill. . . . [T]he principal function of the Israeli broadcast service is to be an active force in the acquisition of the Hebrew language, in the improvement of the spoken language and in the production and strengthening of the connection between the community of listeners and the treasures of Hebrew literature and its values.

At the center of broadcasting was "the spoken word, the good word, which instructs and brings one near to the innermost recesses of the spirit, the word that influences and guides."[39]

Kol Yisrael's early years hardly lived up to these grandiose visions. In 1949, almost half of the 115 hours of broadcasting per week was devoted to classical and light music, news bulletins and immigrant programs in various languages, and short programs designated for particular segments within Israeli society – the armed forces, Arabs, women, and children, the latter two being the targets of the appositely named *Women's Corner* and *Children's Corner* – snug spaces into which political content was presented in a manner believed appropriate for the particular group in question. (A *Women's Corner* episode of 1954 featured a guide to the "presentation of tasty austerity menus.") There was not much cultural programming: the *Tanakh* reading every evening, a *kabbalat shabbat* program on Friday afternoons, and a *Farewell to the Sabbath Queen* on Saturday evening. In 1952 only thirty minutes per week were devoted to discussions of literature. As late as 1957, almost 80 percent of broadcasting hours were devoted to multilingual news and immigrant programming, the Arabic Service, and music, leaving relatively little time for public interest, cultural, or religious programming.[40] Similarly, almost two-thirds of Galei Tsahal's broadcast hours were devoted to music.[41]

The heavy emphasis on entertainment and information, as opposed to educational or cultural programming, reflected the tastes of the Israeli listenership. A stream of surveys carried out between 1949 and 1965 demonstrate as much; for example, in 1951 more than 80 percent of listeners listened to the daily news, 60 percent to light music, 35 percent to classical music, and only 20 percent to lectures, interviews, and talks. Despite Menachem Solieli's brave words in 1949 about the radio's educational mission, within a few years his successors had adopted a more pragmatic approach.

In 1952 serious cultural programming was moved to a second frequency; lovers of classical music would henceforth be considered a listening segment, one of many "*miutim*," as they were called. (Other segments included farmers and new immigrants.) Many members of the PCRA, led by the polymath scholar Yeshiyahu Leibowitz, thundered against the dumbing down of programming to cater to popular taste. Another member, calling on radio to wage war against "*shund* and *kitsch*," called for not only less dance music and jazz, but also a reduction in nineteenth-century Romantic music in favor of more contemporary, serious work. Letters from highbrow listeners complained about the cancellation of serious programs and the marginalization of classical music and spoken word in favor of popular music, which, it was said, promoted a hedonistic Tel Aviv lifestyle. As an article in *Maariv* put it, Kol Yisrael appeared to be veering between the deadly earnest and the frivolous – between Bing Crosby and *Kabbalah*.[42]

Regardless of content, Israeli radio played an educational role by its very essence, broadcasting mostly in Hebrew and striving to facilitate language acquisition through special news programs "at dictation speed" or with a simplified vocabulary. More important, a closer look at what was considered "western" or "light" programming testifies to the role of radio in promoting a broad-based cultural literacy, both Jewish and global. To be sure, Israelis loved to listen to Bing Crosby or to western-style music sung by Israeli crooners with names like Freddy Dorah or Bobby Pinchasi. Inane game shows received high ratings. Yet the facts that over one-third of the public listened to classical music and that the drama revue *The Curtain Rises* was one of the most popular programs in the mid-1950s were signs of a Jewish embrace of serious western culture that dated back almost two centuries and, when transplanted to Israel, not only continued but was now institutionalized by publicly subsidized or controlled bodies – schools, libraries, community centers, and theatrical companies as well as radio. Moreover, the single most popular program in the history of Israeli radio, the humorous *Three Men in a Boat*, centered around a well-tempered rivalry between the rough-hewn Dan Ben-Amotz, the embodiment of blunt native Israeli culture, and the urbane Shalom Rosenfeld, a master of dexterous and sophisticated Hebrew witticisms, based on a foundation of diaspora Jewish culture. Finally, the programs of Hebrew songs broadcast on Israeli radio were no less popular than western music. In 1965, the Friday afternoon *kabbalat shabbat* anthology of Hebrew ballads was the fifth most popular program on the air, with a 40 percent audience share.[43]

Israeli radio's cultural orientation remained overwhelmingly Ashkenazic despite mass migration from North Africa and the Middle East. In 1952, there were eight hours of western music broadcast daily and only fifteen minutes of *muzikah mizrahit*. At the end of the 1950s, Kol Yisrael began to broadcast performances by North African and Central Asian musical troupes, but these and other programs of Mizrahi music were still presented in special segments of short duration. Some of them were broadcast on

Saturday afternoon, when many Mizrahi Jews would, for religious reasons, not be able to listen to the radio. (In 1951, a survey limited almost entirely to Ashkenazic Jews showed that 13 percent refrained from turning on their radios on the Sabbath, but by 1965, in a survey reflecting the entire ethnic spectrum of the Jewish population, the figure had risen to 30 percent, testifying to the considerable number of traditional, though not rigidly Orthodox, Mizrahi Jews.) Moreover, a Eurocentric agenda could underlie even programs of or about Mizrahi music. For example, a program of 1961 on *Artists from the Oriental Communities* profiled the Yemenite opera singer Naomi Tsur, who was praised for her unique combination of Mizrahi folk music and the western classical repertoire. In 1965, the weekly *Mivhar Shirei Ha-'edot* (selection of songs of the Oriental communities) was the sixth most popular program on the air, with an almost 40 percent share of the listening audience, spread evenly across all age groups.[44] Yet, even then, much of the so-called "Mizrahi" music was, in fact, written by European Jews with a western musical sensibility. Oriental embellishments (and Oriental performers) were grafted on to western tonal and chord patterns.[45]

Kol Yisrael, like other agents of the young Israeli state, strove to cross ethnic lines, or obliterate them altogether, via the invention of Zionist traditions and the creation of a usable Jewish past. Important ceremonies at the time of the state's founding, such as the opening of the first session of the Israeli Knesset and the transfer of Theodor Herzl's remains from Vienna to Jerusalem, were broadcast live. Although the former broadcast was marred by technical difficulties and unruly behavior on the part of some members of Parliament, the latter went off smoothly and became an occasion for the inculcation of patriotic sentiment. On the day of the reinterment of the remains, Kol Yisrael featured a tour of Herzl's reconstructed library, housed in the Jewish National Fund building in downtown Jerusalem. The program presented Herzl in a hagiographic light, as a doting son, adoring father, and political visionary, whose ties to the Jewish heritage were demonstrated by one of the library's most striking features – a Torah scroll presented by the Vilna community.[46]

Starting in 1952, Kol Yisrael's semi-weekly news magazine covered events deemed to be of national importance. The docking of the first ship at the Gulf of Eilat following the Sinai campaign, the opening of Israel's first oil well, the building of roads, the draining of swamps, even the opening of the first petrol station at Kfar Yeruham in the Negev desert – all were grist for the magazine, whose creator, Nakdimon Rogel, said, "development is news." Radio closely covered the annual national parade, a vast pilgrimage of thousands of youth, soldiers, workers, and seniors to Jerusalem. In 1958, Kol Yisrael began its broadcasting of the five-day event with reports of soldiers throughout the country resting in groves, waiting for midnight, when trumpets would blare and the great march would begin. Broadcasts covered the entrance of paramilitary youth brigades and seniors' leagues into Jerusalem on the second day, of women soldiers and civilians on the third, and on the fifth, final, day the male soldiers, the cream of the nation. Despite the terrible heat, the radio reported, the entire population soldiered on, singing, "The road is long and steep. The road is long and perilous. They all go on the road to its end. They go on to its bitter end."[47]

Israeli radio featured a muscular, adventurous spirit, taking risks and engaging in constant technological innovation in order to bring the nation into the citizen's salon. The 1958 Independence Day celebrations pioneered the use of multiple live feeds. Kol Yisrael broadcast programs from Israeli air force jets and, in 1961, from the heart of the Judean desert, where letters from the ancient Jewish warrior and would-be messiah Simon Bar-Kokhba had been found. According to Kol Yisrael's weekly magazine, the many farmers, soldiers, and students at the archeological site

> did not feel ashamed to admit the wondrous feeling of attachment linking them – the generation of [the] Sinai [campaign] and border guarding – with another generation of Hebrew warriors who, with righteous anger and a hunger for independence, lay down their weapons of rebellion only when the last soldier fell.[48]

The "Voice of Israel" was, most of the time, that of an adult, but children's programming was an important educational tool, particularly for instilling Zionist values and historical interpretations. In a program of 1953 about the dedication of the youth village Yemin Orde, named after the British Christian Zionist Orde Wingate, an Israeli boy described Wingate's contributions to Jewish Palestine of the 1930s in an archetypally laconic and colloquial fashion: "At first, the Arabs would kill the Jews. Then he [Wingate] came and took the Jews and said, 'Comrades, let us go forth and be pioneers and build up our country and all that.'"[49] The confluence of pioneering and soldiering is also present in a 1963 children's radio play for Tel Hai day (11 Adar), the commemoration of the death in 1920 of the pioneer Yosef Trumpeldor at the hands of Arab raiders. Titled simply *The Man*, the program features music from Aaron Copeland's *Fanfare for the Common Man*, but the dramatization of Trumpeldor's life story that follows presents him as anything but ordinary. According to the narrator, Trumpeldor's family was distant from Judaism, but at the age of seven Yosef went to *heder* and came to a love of Torah and Judaism. Under Yosef's influence, his parents held a Passover seder, and he added to the Four Questions a new and extraordinary one: "Abba, once we were a people, and we had a state and land of our own. Why don't we have all this now?" The program goes on to feature melodramatic interactions between the adolescent Trumpeldor and gentiles, such as an antisemitic Russian military commander. When Trumpeldor defends his honor, the announcer intones, "Thus spoke Trumpeldor, the proud and courageous Jew." Despite losing an arm in the Russo-Japanese war, Trumpeldor implores his commander to allow him to return to the fight, claiming, "I have one hand remaining – but it is my right hand – and so I want to continue fighting alongside of my friends. I request from His Excellency to give me a sword and a pistol." The commander agrees, and says to his fellow Russian soldiers:

> This is a request from a true Russian officer, not by his name, but by his spirit. These words are to be inscribed in letters of gold in the history of our brigade. And the matter is especially important because the person saying them is a Jew. I have heard much about Trumpeldor. In battle he has displayed great courage.

The officer wishes to promote Trumpeldor into the officer corps, but Trumpeldor demurs, claiming that he is not a professional soldier and will only take weapons in hand in an emergency, when he has no other choice.[50]

The remainder of the program traces Trumpeldor's Zionist activity as a Japanese prisoner of war, his Zionist vision and immigration to Palestine, collaborative efforts with Vladimir Jabotinsky during World War I to establish a Jewish fighting force under British auspices, and his heroic death. Much of this program conforms to Trumpeldor's actual biography, although the crucial interactions between Trumpeldor, his parents, and his gentile peers are fictionalized. The anachronistic projection of Trumpeldor's Zionism back into childhood, the emphasis on winning gentile respect, and the conflation of Zionism and the Jewish religious tradition testify to the values that the program's writers wished to instill in young listeners. As Michael Stanislawski has noted in his recent study of Theodor Herzl, Max Nordau, and Vladimir Jabotinsky, Zionist historiography has traditionally been uncomfortable with the notion of an individual's undergoing a complete about-face from assimilation to Zionism. Such actions imply emotional capriciousness and intellectual promiscuity. Thus, in classic biographies of Zionist leaders the embers of Jewish nationalism are presented as being ever-present, awaiting the circumstances that will fan them into full-blown Zionist fervor.[51] I would add that a similar desire for continuity and harmony informs popular conceptions of the relationship between secular Zionism and Judaism. The Trumpeldor program presented this idealized relationship in a crude fashion, but it was the source of considerable attention and tension within Kol Yisrael, one of whose listening "segments" consisted of Orthodox Jews.

In the early 1950s, Kol Yisrael aired weekly programs of cantorial music and talmudic study in addition to its Friday afternoon *kabbalat shabbat* and daily Bible readings. Mordechai Breuer of the PCRA complained that the religious programs were too simplistic for the religious and too dry and flat to attract secular listeners. Worse still, he observed, religious life and experience were ghettoized, limited to specifically religious programming. Radio dramas did not touch religious themes, and any sort of religious music was corralled into the programs of *hazanut* (cantorial music). Breuer felt that traditional Jewish culture was being reduced by Kol Yisrael to a variety of folklore, something distant and unchanging, and noted that, on occasion, radio programs explicitly presented religious culture within a folkloric framework. As another sign that traditional Jewish culture was being divorced from the rhythm of life in the Jewish state, Breuer noted that religious programming was sometimes scheduled on the Sabbath or holidays, when observant Jews could not listen. Finally, radio programming intended for the secular majority undermined the religious underpinnings of Jewish culture; for example, a program on a new humor book was aired on *Shabbat hazon*, a day of somber reflection in anticipation of the mournful holiday of Tisha Be-av.[52]

Based on Breuer's litany alone, one might think that Israeli radio was fundamentally no different from its North American Jewish counterpart and that Jewish religious programming in Jerusalem was just as ghettoized as *The Eternal Light*, which we discussed at the beginning of this chapter. But such a view would neglect the substantial amount of mainstream programming that wove religious themes into a new national narrative. For example, holiday programming was central to Kol Yisrael. In 1954 an Orthodox member of the PCRA noted, quite correctly, that the holiday celebrations introduced by the Zionist movement and Israeli state were attempts to invent traditions and should not be identified with tradition as such. Thus his and others' discontent that programs for the festival of Shavuot that year described it entirely in agricultural terms and neglected its religious meaning as the commemoration of the giving of the Torah.[53] Similar complaints about the desacralization of Jewish holy days could be, and no doubt were, made about the entire Zionist/Israeli calendar, but the fact that that calendar was a shared inheritance made debate about its meaning possible in the first place. Similarly, there was universal agreement regarding the need for daily *Tanakh* readings, which, as we saw earlier, date back to the Mandate period. There were differences of opinion about the length of the readings, whether they should be accompanied by commentary, and what sort of commentary should be employed – traditional or modern, pious or secular. In the early 1950s, the daily readings were done without commentary, much to the liking of Breuer, who claimed that listening to the *Tanakh* was an emotional, not intellectual experience, a direct contact with the divine word.[54] By the mid-1960s, however, commentary had been added, and the result was highly successful; according to the massive 1965 listeners' survey, the daily bible readings enjoyed a share of more than 30 percent, appealing to listeners of all ages.[55]

As listeners' response to the *Tanakh* readings indicates, the new Israeli national culture was more responsive to certain manifestations of the Jewish tradition than others. Zionist Bible-centrism made significant inroads among Israel's Jewish population. Other aspects of Jewish culture fared more poorly; in 1965, programs on the Talmud were near the bottom of the ratings, at 10 percent, drawing mostly on listeners over forty-five. This much might be expected, given Zionism's deprecation of rabbinic culture, but another aspect of diaspora Jewish culture marginalized by Zionist ideology, liturgical music, remained highly popular. Kol Yisrael's weekly program of cantorial music attracted a healthy 25 percent share despite being broadcast on the Sabbath and hence being out of bounds to observant Jews. Although listeners under thirty were not wont to tune in, the program attracted considerably more listeners in the thirty to forty-five bracket than the program on Talmud. (Interestingly, this program narrowly beat out sports programming in the overall ratings.) *Hazanut* appealed to even secular listeners because of melody's well-known ability to overpower lyrics and to exert powerful effects on memory and the senses. Cantorial music transmitted the pre-Holocaust past in a sensual, not cerebral, fashion.

Radio clearly reflected broader currents in Israeli society, in terms of not only the government's cultural policies but also the levels of acceptance, adaptation, or rejection of those policies by the Israeli Jewish populace. In the wake of the 1967 War, as the collectivist Zionist ethos began to fade and Israelis became enamored of western youth culture, Kol Yisrael found itself challenged by competing stations with a more lively spirit. In 1971, Abie Nathan began offshore broadcasts of the Voice of Peace, which played mostly western pop music. Galei Tsahal, whose popularity had grown steadily through the 1960s, exploded into prominence after 1967. Under directors Yitzhak Livni (1967–74) and Mordechai Naor (1974–8), Galei Tsahal developed a youthful and informal style and an appealing mixed format of popular music and talk. Livni set out to change the way Hebrew was spoken on the air. He claimed that, unlike in European countries, where people could learn to speak the vernacular by imitating what they heard on the radio, in Israel the language of broadcasting was too stilted and alien, and it was Galei Tsahal's responsibility to adopt a "more flexible style of presenting and announcing."[56] Faced with the mounting popularity of the Voice of Peace and Galei Tsahal, Kol Yisrael founded a pop music station, Reshet Gimmel, in 1976, and it gradually loosened its own regulations for spoken Hebrew, with the hourly news remaining one of the few bastions of Masoretic pronunciation.

The conversation on Galei Tsahal was warm and casual but not frivolous, occasionally irreverent but never subversive. As Livni said, the Hebrew spoken on the air may have been relaxed, but it "took pains to follow the rules of grammar." Israeli radio in the 1970s hardly lost its educational mission. Israel's most prominent Jewish studies scholars lectured over the air regularly. Israeli radio remained "Jewish" not simply in that its programming was written, presented, and consumed mainly by Jews, or because the contents of programming reflected the day-to-day concerns of individuals living in a Jewish state. At times, the programming had an explicitly Jewish cultural content; more important, at all times it was delivered in the vernacular, a spoken Hebrew whose increasing informality should not be associated, as it sometimes is, with de-Judaization in general and Americanization in particular. As Ron Kuzar has observed, Palestinian, then Israeli, spoken Hebrew has undergone continuous evolution for over a century. It is a creole, influenced by many linguistic sources in the past and destined to continue to be so in the future.[57] The Americanization of contemporary Hebrew is akin to the Hellenization of Second Temple Hebrew, which produced a vast vocabulary of loanwords and considerably enriched the language.

Was Israeli radio a motor, rather than merely a mirror, of cultural change? The question is difficult to answer precisely because the key agents of Israeli culture were interdependent, and one cannot estimate the significance of radio alone. Yet it is clear that certain newly invented Israeli cultural traditions like the National Bible Quiz (begun in 1958) would have been unthinkable without radio, which broadcast the proceedings live and whose weekly magazine provided charts of the participants so that listeners at home could keep score. Israeli popular music, which through the 1970s featured an unashamedly romantic-nationalistic tone, was disseminated primarily over the radio and only secondarily via individually owned phonograph recordings. No less than popular culture, Israeli historical consciousness was molded by radio, as exemplified by the broadcasting of the 1961 trial of the Nazi war criminal Adolf Eichmann. (Sixty percent of all listeners over the age of fourteen listened to one of the two first sessions of the trial, and one-third listened to both. Teenagers were just as likely to have listened to a session as those over eighteen.)[58] In a society where radios were ubiquitous and the population lived in a state of perpetual mobilization, the hunger for news and information was ever present. Like a narcotic, radio stoked this craving by the very act of satisfying it. The five daily news bulletins of the 1950s changed to hourly broadcasts after 1967, and then, a decade later, were broadcast on the half-hour.[59] Until the 1990s, it was common for drivers of public buses to turn the volume up for hourly news bulletins, during which the passengers would listen in rapt attention. In the silence of those moments, a sense of common fate would fill the air. Radio did not create such sentiments, but it did augment them, just as in contemporary Israel the fracturing of society is both reflected and hastened by the proliferation of private radio and cable television stations.[60]

From the 1920s through the 1960s, the politicians and bureaucrats who shaped Israeli radio attributed tremendous importance to broadcasting: not merely as an accoutrement of sovereignty or an educational tool, but rather as a means of direct contact with the spoken Hebrew word, which was accorded a redemptive, quasi-mystical power. The veneration of the voice can be seen as an inherent component of Zionist ideology, an aspect of the social and psychological normalization for which the Zionist project strove. The awakening of Jews from political dormancy, the inculcation of a fighting spirit and a commitment to productive labor were intended to remedy the defects of Jewish diaspora culture. Similarly, the broadcast voice, offering direct, concrete, and unmediated contact between leader and led, was seen as an electrifying alternative to the abstract and distant written word, the pillar of rabbinic Jewish culture.

The restoration of the Hebrew voice reflected not only a desire for Jewish political or social normalization but also a yearning to align Jewish civilization with the privileging of voice over writing that has characterized most of the history of human civilization. This chapter began with a description of the centrality of the written word in the transmission of culture, but for millennia this social reality has co-existed with a deeply rooted idealization of the spoken word as primal and authentic. As Jacques Derrida demonstrated in his classic book *Of Grammatology*, since antiquity "the voice, producer of *the first symbols*, has [had] a relationship of essential and immediate proximity with the mind."[61] Western civilization's logocentrism "is also a phonocentrism: absolute proximity of voice and being, of voice and the meaning of being, of voice and the ideality of being." From Aristotle's claim that "spoken words are the symbols of mental experience and written words are the symbols of spoken words" to Jean-Jacques Rousseau's accusation that writing "enervates" speech, western civilization has valorized forms of writing and texts that are tightly bound with the spoken word.[62]

The development of modern literary Hebrew began in Europe, but the revival, as it was called, of spoken Hebrew occurred in the Yishuv, at first spontaneously by immigrants in the late 1800s and then, self-consciously, by educators and publicists. Hebrew radio was part and parcel of this process of attempted restoration of the Hebrew voice, and the importance attributed to broadcasts of Bible reading nicely demonstrates the Zionist search for the sort of linguistic totality described by Derrida: the oral transmission of a written text, which itself is imbedded in speech acts, human and divine. Hebrew radio transmitted some aspects of traditional Jewish culture or preserved aspects of others in a transmuted form, but the choice of the medium of transmission was itself an ideological as well as a pragmatic act: an internalization of romantic phonocentrism, a search for totality within the particularism of a nationalist movement.

The grandiose visions of Israel's broadcasting policies were only partially fulfilled in reality. In its heyday, Israeli radio was indeed the primary source for exposure to spoken Hebrew outside of the environments of home, work, and school. For new immigrants, radio was undoubtedly an important means for learning how to speak and read the language. Its usefulness was limited, however, as only about one-third of new immigrants listened regularly. This was the case partly because of limited access to receivers and partly because immigrants tended to have low levels of formal education, which is strongly correlated with radio listening. For the native born, whose listening rates were more than twice as high, radio no doubt had educational value, but as an auxiliary to literacy rather than a framework for attaining it.

Unlike television, which threatens literacy by replacing printed signs with images, in a highly literate society such as Israel radio complements the written word. Hebrew radio surrounded but did not engulf the Jewish text. Jewish culture, graphocentric to its core, was never displaced by radio, just as today it is not endangered by the internet (which, although a visual medium, is primarily used for the presentation of text). To be sure, print and radio are processed in radically different ways. The text is reflected upon by the voiceless speech of the mind; it can be analyzed repeatedly as the reader jumps back and forth in the text at will. Broadcast words, however, wash over the listener in a ceaseless flow. There is no possibility for reflection, and only small amounts of knowledge can be retained, but sentiments evoked by the broadcast voice hold fast. Reading is a solitary activity, whereas listening, even when alone, is social, an engagement with a fellow human. In Israel, where Hebrew radio has been a staple of everyday life, broadcasting has helped forge a sense of national community, abstract in that the broadcast voice is disembodied and most likely not known to the listener, yet concrete in the voice's warmth and texture (its "grain," as Roland Barthes calls it),[63] in the informality that pervades Israeli discourse, and in the very fact of communication in a language spoken almost solely by Jews. Israelis have retained the Jewish self-ascription as a people of the book, but Israeli popular consciousness has been shaped by the broadcast voice as well as the written sign.

Notes

Introduction

1 *Zionism and Technocracy: The Engineering of Jewish Settlement in Palestine, 1870–1918*, Bloomington and Indianapolis: Indiana University Press, 1991. Hebrew version: *Tikhnun ha-utopiyah ha-tsiyonit: itsuv ha-hityashvut ha-yehudit be-eretz yisra'el, 1870–1918*, Sede Boker and Jerusalem: Midreshet Ben-Gurion/ Yad Ben-Zvi, 2000.

2 The first serious histories of Zionism written in North America were Arthur Hertzberg, *The Zionist Idea*, Philadelphia: Athanaeum, 1958; and Ben Halpern, *The Idea of the Jewish State*, Cambridge, Mass.: Harvard University Press, 1961. Work in the 1970s era on Zionism in the diaspora includes Jehuda Reinharz, *Fatherland or Promised Land? The Dilemma of the German Jew, 1893–1914*, Ann Arbor, Mich.: University of Michigan Press, 1975, Stephen Poppel, *Zionism in Germany, 1897–1933: The Shaping of a Jewish Identity*, Philadelphia: Jewish Publication Society, 1976; Paula Hyman, *From Dreyfus to Vichy: The Remaking of French Jewry, 1906–1939*, New York: Columbia University Press, 1979; and Ezra Mendelsohn, *Zionism in Poland: The Formative Years, 1915–1926*, New Haven, Conn.: Yale University Press, 1981.

3 Marc Bloch, "A Contribution towards a Comparative History of European Societies," *Land and Work in Medieval Society*, Berkeley and Los Angeles: University of California Press, 1967, 58.

4 Michael N. Barnett, "Israel in the World Economy: Israel as an East Asian State?," in Michael N. Barnett, ed., *Israel in Comparative Perspective: Challenging the Conventional Wisdom*, Albany, N.Y.: State University of New York Press, 1996, 107–40.

5 Sammy Smooha, "The Viability of Ethnic Democracy as a Mode of Conflict Management: Comparing Israel and Northern Ireland," in ed. Todd Endelman, *Comparing Jewish Societies*, Ann Arbor, Mich.: University of Michigan Press, 1997, 267–312; *idem*, "Ethnic Democracy: Israel as an Archetype," *Israel Studies* II, 2 (1997), 198–241; Ian Lustick, *Unsettled States, Disputed Lands: Britain and Ireland, France and Algeria, Israel and the West Bank-Gaza*, Ithaca, New York: Cornell University Press, 1993; Gershon Shafir, "Zionism and Colonialism: A Comparative Approach," in Barnett, *Israel in Comparative Perspective*, 227–42.

6 This crucial subject is not covered in the otherwise outstanding collection of essays *Comparing Jewish Societies* (see note 5). Although five of the volume's eleven essays deal with Israel, three of the five are informed by presentist, social-scientifc analysis, and the only one that offers a detailed historical analysis of Zionist state-building approaches the subject from the point of view of Palestinian Arab labor history.

7 Comparative history constitutes a field within itself, and the theoretical literature on comparative historical methods is vast. For an introduction, see Theda

Skocpol and Margaret Somers, "The Uses of Comparative History in Macrosocial Inquiry," *Comparative Studies in Society and History* 22, 2 (1980), 174–97; Stefan Berger, "Comparative History," in eds. Stefan Berger, Heiko Feldner, and Kevin Passmore, *Writing History: Theory and Practice*, London: Hodder Arnold, 2003, 61–79; and Chris Lorenz, "Comparative Historiography: Problems and Perspectives," *History and Theory* 38 (1999), 25–39. For an up-to-date critique of the state or nation as the basis for comparative analysis, see Phillip Ther's thoughtful article "Beyond the Nation: The Relational Basis of a Comparative History of Germany and Europe," *Central European History* 36, 1 (2003), 45–73.

8 Lorenz, "Comparative Historiography," 37.

9 For an astute analysis of the dynamic intellectual field in which national consciousness takes form, see Rogers Brubaker, *Nationalism Reframed: Nationhood and the National Question in the New Europe*, New York: Cambridge University Press, 1996; and Ther, "Beyond the Nation."

10 Walter Laqueur's classic *A History of Zionism* was written in 1972. Howard Morley Sachar's *A History of Israel from the Rise of Zionism to Our Time*, which first appeared in 1979, has been updated to cover recent developments, but its fundamental presentation remains locked in a Mapai-centered universe. Despite its title, Ahron Bregman's *A History of Israel* (Palgrave Macmillan, 2003) is yet another conflict-centered work. Michael Brenner's *Zionism: A Brief History* (Markus Wiener, 2003) offers a useful but intentionally brief overview of developments up to 1948. Two excellent recent synthetic works are written by social scientists with a presentist agenda: Baruch Kimmerling, *The Invention and Decline of Israeliness*, Berkeley and Los Angeles: University of California Press, 2001; and Gershon Shafir and Yoav Peled, *Being Israeli: The Dynamics of Multiple Citizenship*, Cambridge, UK, and New York: Cambridge University Press, 2002. More historically oriented, but still driven by social-scientific approaches and themes, is Alan Dowty's *The Jewish State: A Century Later*, Berkeley and Los Angeles: University of California Press, 1998.

11 For a few praiseworthy winners, see Ilan Pappé, *Britain and the Arab–Israeli Conflict, 1948–1951*, London: Palgrave Macmillan, 1988; Rashid Khalidi, *Palestinian Identity*, New York: Columbia University Press, 1998; and Benny Morris, *The Road to Jerusalem: Glubb Pasha, Palestine and the Jews*, London: Tauris, 2002.

1 Israel's "new history"

1 Benny Morris, "The New Historiography: Israel and Its Past," in *idem*, *1948 and After: Israel and the Palestinians*, Oxford, UK: Oxford University Press, 1990, 6. Cf. the citation from John Lukacs, *The Great Powers and Eastern Europe*, New York: American Book Company, 1953, viii, in the Oxford English Dictionary's definition of revisionism: "The somewhat vague concept of historical revisionism is applicable only when there is an abundance of well-documented historical writing which, because of its unilateral emphasis on perspective, needs to be counter-balanced."

2 Morris, "The New Historiography," 7.

3 Israel Kolatt, "'Al mehkar ve-ha-hoker shel toledot ha-yishuv ve-ha-tsiyonut," *Cathedra*, no.1, 1976, 3–35.

4 Israel Kolatt, "Ideologiah u-metsiut bi-tenuat ha-'avodah be-eretz yisra'el, 1905–19," Ph.D. diss., Hebrew University of Jerusalem, 1964; Elkana Margalit, *Ha-Shomer ha-Tza'ir-Me-'adat ne'urim le-marksizm mahapakhant, 1913–1936*, Tel Aviv: Ha-kibbbutz Ha-me'uhad, 1971; Yosef Gorny, *Ahdut ha-Avodah: ha-yesodot ha-ra'yoniyim ve-ha-shitah ha-medinit*, Tel Aviv: Ha-kibbbutz Ha-me'uhad, 1973; Dan Giladi, *Ha-yishuv bi-tekufat ha-aliyah ha-revi'it (1924–1929)*, Tel

Aviv: 'Am 'Oved, 1973; Anita Shapira, *Ha-ma'avak ha-nikhzav: 'avodah 'ivrit, 1929–1939*, Tel Aviv: The Institute for the Study of the History of Zionism, 1977.

5 Yonathan Shapiro, *The Formative Years of the Israeli Labour Party: The Organization of Power, 1919–1930*, London: Sage, 1976; Dan Horowitz and Moshe Lissak, *Origins of the Israeli Polity: Palestine under the Mandate*, Chicago: University of Chicago Press, 1978,

6 *Cathedra*'s purview, according to its masthead, is "the history of *Eretz Israel* and its *Yishuv*." Most of the items published in it, particularly those dealing with the modern period, have dealt with the Yishuv or matters directly affecting it, as opposed to Palestinian history as a whole.

7 Giladi is an important exception. See the discussion of Yishuv economic historiography below.

8 Daniel Capri, *Ha-Tsiyonut* 1, 1970, 2.

9 Israel Bartal, "Post-Mapai," *Ha-Aretz*, October 5, 1994.

10 Josef Heller, "The End of Myth: Historians and the Yishuv (1918–48)," *Studies in Contemporary Jewry* 10, 1994, 112–38.

11 Dina Porat, *The Blue and Yellow Stars of David: The Zionist Leadership in Palestine and the Holocaust, 1939–1945*, Cambridge, Mass.: Harvard University Press, 1990; Yechiam Weitz, *Muda'ut ve-hoser onim: Mapai nokhah ha-shoah, 1943–1945*, Jerusalem: Yad Ben-Zvi, 1994. In the Introduction, Weitz claims that he has no polemical intent and rejects the view, held by some hostile critics of Mapai's wartime behavior, that a conspiracy of silence has long existed between the Israeli political and academic establishments. Rather, he argues, scholarly research on this subject could not have begun before the mid-1980s due to the need for distance from the subject matter and the growing availability of archival documentation, which make possible the writing of academic history about many controversial and traumatic issues, of which his story is one. In other words, Weitz, like Morris, claims to be a mere innovator, not a "revisionist." See the discussion of revisionism below.

12 On the Orthodox Yishuv, see Yehoshua Kaniel, *Hemshekh u-temurah: Ha-yishuv ha-yashan ve-ha-yishuv he-hadash bi-tekufat ha-'aliyah ha-rishonah ve-ha-sheniyah*, Jerusalem: Yad Ben-Zvi, 1981; Israel Bartal's important collection of essays *Galut ba-aretz: yishuv eretz yisra'el terem ha-tsiyonut*, Jerusalem: Ha-sifriyah Ha-tsiyonit, 1995; and Menachem Friedman, *Hevrah ve-dat: Ha-ortodoksiah ha-lo tsionit be-eretz yisra'el 1918–1936*, Jerusalem: Yad Ben-Zvi, 1977.

13 Interestingly, one of the first archivally based monographs on Yishuv history was Eliezer Livneh's biography of the hero of the Zionist Right, *Aharon Aaronsohn, the Man and His Time*, Jerusalem: Yad Ben-Zvi, 1969. As of the mid-1990s, major scholarly work on the Zionist Right remained slim; see Yaakov Shavit, *Jabotinsky and the Revisionist Movement, 1925–1948*, London: Frank Cass, 1988, and Joseph Heller, *The Stern Gang: Ideology, Politics and Terror, 1940–1949*, London: Frank Cass, 1995.

14 The most important economic-historical writing on the Yishuv has been done by Nachum Gross and Jacob Metzer, who at times work collaboratively. Other significant work has been done by Dan Giladi and Hagit Lavsky. Much of the literature takes the form of articles published in *Cathedra* and *Ha-Tsiyonut* and little is available in English. I have synthesized much of the Hebrew literature for the period up to 1920 in my *Zionism and Technocracy: The Engineering of Jewish Settlement in Palestine, 1870–1918*, Bloomington, Ind.: Indiana University Press, 1991.

15 Among the major Israeli historical geographers are Ran Aaronsohn, Yossi Ben-Artzi, Yehoshua Ben-Arieh, Gideon Biger, Ruth Kark, Yosef Katz, Shalom Reichman, and Zvi Shiloni. Many of these authors' publications are, or soon will be, available in English translation.

16 As of the mid-1990s, the few monographs on Yishuv women's history were by sociologists; e.g. Deborah S. Bernstein, *The Struggle for Equality: Urban Women Workers in Prestate Israeli Society*, New York: Praeger, 1987. See also *idem*, ed., *Pioneers and Homemakers: Jewish Women in Pre-State Israel*, Albany, New York: State University of New York Press, 1992. The 11 contributors to the volume include 5 sociologists, 2 historians, 2 literary critics, one geographer and an archivist.

17 See the critique of writing on Jewish nationalism and nation-building in Mitchell Cohen, "A Preface to the Study of Jewish Nationalism," *Jewish Social Studies* 1, n.s., no.1, 1994, 73–93.

18 David Vital, *The Origins of Zionism*, Oxford, UK: Oxford University Press, 1975. Vital is quite the opposite of a scion of the Labor movement; he is the son of the Revisionist Zionist statesman Meir Grossman.

19 See Jií Koalka, "Czechoslovakia," in the October 1992 issue of *American Historical Review*, which contains a series of articles on the historiography of the countries of Eastern Europe.

20 Maria Todorova, "Bulgaria," ibid., 1117. See also the articles by Keith Hitchins and Ivo Banac on Romania and Yugoslavia, respectively.

21 Communication from Professor Toivo Raun, Indiana University, 20 January 1995.

22 Segev's books include *1949: The First Israelis*, New York: Free Press, 1986; and *The Seventh Million: The Israelis and the Holocaust*, New York: Hill and Wang, 1993. Morris's major early works were *1948 and After: Israel and the Palestinians*, Oxford, UK: Oxford University Press, 1990; *The Birth of the Palestinian Refugee Problem, 1947–1949*, Cambridge, UK: Cambridge University Press, 1987; and *Israel's Border Wars, 1949–1956*, Oxford, UK: Oxford University Pres, 1993. (See Chapter 2 for a discussion of Morris's more recent writings.)

23 Shlaim is the author of several books. Germane to our discussion here is *Collusion across the Jordan: King Abdullah, the Zionist Movement, and the Partition of Palestine*, Oxford, UK: Oxford University Press, 1988. A significantly revised and abridged edition was published as *The Politics of Partition: King Abdullah, the Zionists, and Palestine, 1921–1951*, New York: Oxford University Press, 1990.

24 Pappé's first books were *Britain and the Arab–Israeli Conflict, 1948–1951*, New York: Macmillan, 1988; and *The Making of the Arab Israeli Conflict, 1947–1951*, London and New York: I.B. Tauris, 1992.

25 Uri Milstein, *Toledot milhemet ha-atsma'ut*, 4 vols., Tel Aviv: Zimora Bitan, 1989–91. Three volumes of this work have been published in English translation by the University Press of America.

26 The "strong state–weak state" dichotomy is put to good use in Pierre Birnbaum's *Anti-Semitism in France*, London: Blackwell, 1992.

27 Robert O. Paxton, *Vichy France: Old Guard and New Order, 1940–1944* New York: Columbia University Press, 1972; Michael R. Marrus and Robert O. Paxton, *Vichy France and the Jews*, New York: Basic Books, 1981; Henry Rousso, *The Vichy Syndrome: History and Memory in France since 1944*, Cambridge, Mass.: Harvard University Press, 1991.

28 The documentation of the *Historikerstreit* may be found in *Forever in the Shadow of Hitler? Original Documents of the Historikerstreit*, trans. James Knowlton and Truett Cates, Atlantic Highlands, N.J.: Humanities Press, 1993. For analysis of the controversy, see Peter Baldwin, ed., *Reworking the Past: Hitler, the Holocaust, and the Historians' Debate*, Boston: Beacon Press, 1990.

29 On imperialism, see R.K. Webb, *Modern England*, New York: Harper & Row, 1968, 349; on Canaanism, see James Diamond, *Homeland or Holy Land?*, Bloomington,

Ind.: Indiana University Press, 1986; and Shmuel Dothan, *A Land in the Balance*, Tel Aviv: Ministry of Defense, 1993, 419–29.

30 For overviews of this literature, see Peter Novick, *That Noble Dream: The "Objectivity Question" and the American Historical* Profession, New York: Cambridge University Press, 1988, 417–57; and Jacob Heilbrun, "The Revision Thing," *New Republic*, 15 August 1994, 31–9.

31 Novick, *That Noble Dream*, 453

32 For several years, most of the polemical literature attacking the new historians was available only in Hebrew. For examples of these polemics in English, see Shabtai Teveth, "Charging Israel with Original Sin," *Commentary* 88, no. 3 (September 1989), 24–33; and the translation in *The Jerusalem Post*, 17 June 1994, of Aharon Megged's piece on "Israel's Suicidal Impulse," which had appeared in *Ha-Aretz*, June 10, 1994.

33 Novick makes this point in *That Noble Dream*, 467–8.

34 Segev, *The Seventh Million*, 35–64.

35 For a useful corrective to Shlaim, see Avraham Sela, "Ha-melekh 'Abdallah u-memshelet yisrael bi-milhemet ha-ha'atsmau't – ha'arakhah me-hadash," *Cathedra*, no. 57, 1990, 120–62, and no.58, 1990, 172–93; *idem*, "Transjordan, Israel and the 1948 War: Myth, Historiography and Reality," *Middle Eastern Studies* 28, no. 4, 1992, 623–58.

36 Take, for example, the Arab siege of Jewish sectors of Jerusalem. Shlaim, in *Collusion across the Jordan*, 251, writes: "The operation in Jerusalem was relatively small and limited"; Pappé, in *The Making of the Arab–Israeli Conflict*, 79, describes the siege of Jerusalem as more threatening in appearance than in reality and, in any case, of only a few months' duration.

37 Shlaim acknowledges the non-viability of the partition proposal and the impossibility of a Zionist–Mufti rapprochement in *Collusion across the Jordan*, 107 and 117, and he makes this point more explicitly in *The Politics of Partition*, 104–5. The term "Jewish aggressiveness" shows up on p. 177 of *Collusion across the Jordan*. For Pappé, cf. *Britain and the Arab–Israeli Conflict*, 49, and *The Making of the Arab–Israeli Conflict*, 153.

38 Pappé, *The Making of the Arab–Israeli Conflict*, 122–34.

39 Ibid., 108–13; Shlaim, *Collusion across the Jordan*, 139, 153–4.

40 Morris, *Israel's Border Wars*, 20n. See Itamar Rabinovich, *The Road Not Taken: Early Arab–Israeli Negotiations*, New York: Oxford University Press, 1991; Michael Oren, *Origins of the Second Arab–Israeli War: Egypt, Israel, and the Great Powers, 1952–1956*, London: Frank Cass, 1992. Morris has claimed that scholars such as Rabinovich, Oren, and Sela have, despite their defensive posture, internalized the new historians' essential arguments into their own narratives. Similar observations were made in the 1970s by Cold War revisionists about "postrevisionism" which "incorporated many of the revisionist findings . . . within a context which emphasized Soviet depravity and American virtue." Novick, *That Noble Dream*, 454.

41 The quotations are taken from Morris, "Response to Finkelstein and Masalha," *Journal of Palestine Studies* 21, 1, autumn 1991, 103–4; "The Eel and History," *Tikkun*, January–February 1990, 20; and "The New Historiography," 27.

42 Shlaim, *Collusion across the Jordan*, viii.

43 Novick, *That Noble Dream*, 422–3.

44 Fritz Fischer, *Germany's War Aims in the First World War*, New York: Chatto & Windus, 1967 (German original edn. 1961). Fischer's case also provides a nice demonstration of the importance of the outsider as a source of historical revisionism. Although Fischer was a veteran university professor, a true German mandarin, when he began the research for this book, his main field until then had been medieval and early modern church history.

45 Baruch Kimmerling, "Ha-vikuah 'al ha-historiographiah ha-tsiyonit," typed ms., November 1994. I would like to than Nachum Gross for bringing this ms. to my

attention. See *idem*, *Zionism and Territory: The Socio-Territorial Dimensions of Zionist Politics*, Berkeley: Institute of International Studies of the University of California, 1983.

46 Gershon Shafir, *Land, Labor, and the Origins of the Israeli–Palestinian Conflict, 1882–1914*, Cambridge, UK: Cambridge University Press, 1989. Shafir is eager to prove that from its very beginning in Ottoman Palestine the Yishuv economy was molded, more than anything else, by the threat posed by cheap Arab labor. To be sure, the issue of Arab labor was central to the Zionist Labor movement and influenced many of its policies. Twenty years before Shafir, Anita Shapira analyzed the ramifications of this problem during the 1930s in her monograph *The Futile Struggle* (Anita Shapira, *Ha-maavak ha-nikhzav: 'avodah 'ivrit 1929–1939*, Tel Aviv: Tel Aviv University, 1977). But Shafir mistakenly projects the mentalities of the Mandatory period back to Ottoman times. At the *fin de siècle* the founders of Zionist nation-building instruments such as the Jewish National Fund were largely ignorant of conditions in Palestine. Contrary to his claims, the pioneers of the Second Aliyah did not uniformly esteem farm managers who employed only Hebrew labor; nor did they despise all managers who employed Arab labor. And although the formation of the celebrated collective settlement Deganyah was inspired in part by the perceived need for a separate Jewish economy, these motives did not apply to other pioneer collectives established in Palestine at approximately the same time.

47 See the works by Baruch Kimmerling, Ilan Pappé, Gershon Shafir, and Yoav Peled discussed in Chapter 2.

2 Beyond Revisionism

1 Tom Segev, *1949: The First Israelis*, New York: Free Press, 1986; Benny Morris, *The Birth of the Palestinian Refugee Problem, 1947–1949*, Cambridge, UK: Cambridge University Press, 1987; rev. and expanded edn., 2004; *idem*, *1948 and After: Israel and the Palestinians*, New York: Oxford University Press, 1990; *idem*, *Israel's Border Wars, 1949–1956*, Oxford, UK: Oxford University Press, 1993; Avi Shlaim, *Collusion Across the Jordan: King Abdullah, the Zionist Movement, and the Partition of Palestine*, Oxford, UK: Oxford University Press, 1988; Ilan Pappé, *Britain and the Arab–Israeli Conflict, 1948–51*, London: Palgrave Macmillan, 1988; *idem*, *The Making of the Arab–Israeli Conflict, 1947–1951*, London: I.B. Tauris, 1992.

2 There is now a sizeable literature on the Israeli historiographical debates and their significance for contemporary Israeli society and culture: *History & Memory* VII, 1995 (Special Issue: Israeli Historiography Revisited); *Iyunim bitekumat Yisra'el*, 1996 (Thematic Series: *Tsiyonot: Polmus bein zemaneinu*, Yechiam Weitz, ed., *Bein hazon le-reviziyah: me'ah shenot hitoriographiyah tsiyonit*, Jerusalem: Shazar Centre, 1997); Laurence Silberstein, *The Postzionism Debates: Knowledge and Power in Israeli Culture*, New York: Routledge, 1999; *The Journal of Israeli History* XX, 2–3, 2001, published in book form as *Israeli Historical Revisionism From Left to Right*, Anita Shapira and Derek J. Penslar, eds., London: Frank Cass, 2002.

3 Benny Morris, "The New Historiography: Israel and Its Pasts," in *1948 and After*, 1–34. An earlier version of this article was published in *Tikkun*, November–December 1988.

4 Aharon Megged, "Israels' Suicidal Impulse," *Jerusalem Post*, June 17, 1994 (originally published in *Ha-Aretz* on June 10).

5 Motti Golani, personal communication, May 18, 2003; *idem*, "The Limits of Interpretation and the Permissible in Historical Research Dealing with Israel's Security: A Reply to Bar-On and Morris," eds. Laura Zittrain Eisenberg, Neil

Caplan, Naomi B. Sokoloff, and Mohammed Abu-Nimer, *Traditions and Transitions in Israel Studies: Books on Israel, Volume VI*, Albany, N.Y.: State University of New York Press, 2003, 33–34.

6 Benny Morris, "The Crystallization of Israeli Policy against a Return of the Arab Refugees: April-December 1948," *Studies in Zionism* VI, 1, 1985, 85–118.

7 These themes are explored in greater depth in Chapter 1.

8 For an overview of the most recent trends in historiography on the German *Kaiserreich*, see Volker Berghahn, "The German Empire, 1871–1914: Reflections on the Direction of Recent Research," and Margaret Lavinia Anderson, "Reply to Volker Berghahn," in *Central European History* 31, 1, 2002, 75–90. See also Geoff Eley and James Retallack, eds., *Wilhelminism and Its Legacies: German Modernities, Imperialism, and the Meanings of Reform, 1890–1930: Essays for Hartmut Pogge Von Strandmann*, New York: Berghahn, 2003, 1–9. For a trenchant critique of master narratives in German history, see Konrad Jarausch and Michael Geyer, *Shattered Past: Reconstructing German Histories*, Princeton, N.J.: Princeton University Press, 2003.

9 See the useful Introduction to George Boyce and Alan O'Day, eds., *The Making of Modern Irish History: Revisionism and the Revisionist Controversy*, London and New York: Routledge, 1996.

10 See the pioneering essay by Nachum Gross, "Ha-mediniyut ha-kalkalit shel ha-mimshal ha-briti ha-mandatory be-eretz yisra'el," *Cathedra*, 24, 1982, 153–80; and 25, 1983, 135–68.

11 Tom Segev, *Yemei ha-kalaniyot: Eretz yisra'el bi-tekufat ha-mandat*, Jerusalem: Keter, 2000 (English version: New York: Metropolitan, 2000); Amos Oz, *Sipur ahavah ve-hoshekh*, Jerusalem: Keter, 2002.

12 The major synthetic works include Arthur Hertzberg, *The Zionist Idea*, New York: Atheneum, 1959; Ben Halpern, *The Idea of the Jewish State*, Cambridge, Mass: Harvard University Press, 1961; Walter Laqueur, *A History of Zionism*, New York: Schocken, 1972; Noah Lucas, *The Modern History of Israel*, London: Weidenfeld and Nicolson, 1974; Howard M. Sachar, *A History of Israel from the Rise of Zionism to Our Time*, New York: Knopf, 1976, 2nd rev. edn. 1996; Ben Halpern and Jehuda Reinharz, *Zionism and the Creation of a New Society*, New York: Oxford University Press, 1998; Gideon Shimoni, *The Zionist Ideology*, Hanover, N.H.: University Press of New England, 1995; Leslie Stein, *The Hope Fulfilled: The Rise of Modern Israel*, Westport, Conn.: Praeger, 2003; and Michael Brenner, *Zionism: A Brief History*, Princeton, N.J.: Markus Wiener, 2003.

13 The few historically situated works on Israel by North American social scientists are Mitchell Cohen, *Zion and State: Nation, Class and the Shaping of Modern Israel*, New York: Columbia University Press, 1987; Gershon Shafir, *Land, Labour and the Origins of the Israeli–Palestinian Conflict, 1882–1914*, Cambridge, UK: Cambridge University Press, 1982; Yael Zerubavel, *Recovered Roots: Collective Memory and the Making of Israeli National Tradition*, Chicago: University of Chicago Press, 1995; and Alan Dowty, *The Jewish State: A Century Later*, Berkeley and Los Angeles: University of California Press, 1998.

14 For example, Stanford's Joel Beinin publishes mainly on Egypt, though he has written some interesting articles on Israel. New York University's Zackary Lockman has written an important book on Jewish–Arab relations in Mandate Palestine, which I analyze below. Both Beinin and Lockman have trained several doctoral students who have recently taken positions in American universities.

15 Alon Tal, *Pollution in a Promised Land: An Environmental History of Israel*, Berkeley and Los Angeles: University of California Press, 2002.

16 Boyce and O'Day, *The Making of Modern Irish History*, 10.

17 Joseph Heller, *The Birth of Israel, 1945–1949: Ben-Gurion and his Critics*, Gainesville, Fl.: University of Florida Press, 2000.

18 On the fear of civil war between the Labour government and the Right, see the survey published on March 2, 1948, by the Haganah's Department of Public Opinion Research, Haifa. Haganah Archive, 80/54/2.

19 Ehud Luz, *Makbilim nifgashim: dat u-le'umiyut ba-tenu'ah ha-Tsiyonit be-Mizrah-Eropah be-reshitah (1882–1904)*, Tel Aviv: 'Am 'Oved, 1985 (English version: *Parallels Meet: Religion and Nationalism in the Early Zionist Movement, 1882–1904*, Philadelphia: Jewish Publication Society, 1988); Yosef Salmon, *Dat ve-tsiyonut: 'imutim rishonim*, Jerusalem: Ha-sifriyah ha-tsiyonit, 1990 (English version: *Religion and Zionism: First Encounters*, Jerusalem: Magnes, 2002).

20 Aviezer Ravitzky, *Ha-kets ha-meguleh u-medinat ha-Yehudim: meshihiyut, tsiyonut ve-radikalizm dati be-yisra'el*, Tel Aviv: 'Am 'Oved, 1994 (English version: *Messianism, Zionism, and Jewish Religious Radicalism*, Chicago: University of Chicago Press, 1996).

21 Arye Naor, *Eretz Yisra'el ha-sheleimah: emunah u-mediniyut*, Jerusalem: Zimora Bitan, 1999, 71–2, 84.

22 E.g. Anita Shapira, "The Religious Motifs of the Labor Movement," in eds. Shmuel Almog, Jehuda Reinharz, and Anita Shapira, *Zionism and Religion*, , Hanover, N.H.: University of New England Press, 1998, 251–72.

23 Zeev Sternhell, *Binyan umah o-tikun hevrah? Le'umiyut ve-sotsializm bi-tenua't ha-'avodah ha-yisre'elit 1904–1940*, Tel Aviv: 'Am 'Oved, 1995 (English version: *The Founding Myths of Israel*, Princeton, N.J.: Princeton University Press, 1998).

24 See my review essay on Sternhell, "Ben-Gurion's Willing Executioners," *Dissent*, winter 1999, 114–18.

25 Tel Aviv: Dvir; Bloomington, Ind.: Indiana University Press.

26 Anita Shapira, "The Debate in Mapai on the Use of Violence, 1932–35" *Studies in Zionism* III, 1981, 99–124; *idem, Land and Power: The Zionist Resort to Force*, Stanford, Calif.: Stanford University Press, 1992.

27 Martin Van Creveld, *The Sword and the Olive Branch: A Critical History of the Israel Defense Force*, New York: Public Affairs, 1998; Motti Golani, *Milhemot lo korot me-'atsman: 'al zikaron, koah u-vehirah*, Moshav Ben Shemen: Modan, 2002.

28 Yona Hadari-Ramage, *Mashiah rakhuv 'al tank. Ha-mahshavah ha-tsiburit be-yisra'el bein mivtsa Sinai le-milhemet yom ha-kippurim 1955–75*, Jerusalem: Hartman Institute; Ramat Gan: Bar-Ilan University Press; Tel Aviv: Ha-kibbutz ha-me'uhad, 2002.

29 Margalit Shilo, "Tovat ha-aretz o-tovat ha-'am? Yahsah shel ha-tenua'h ha-tsiyonit le-'aliyah bitekufat ha-'aliyah ha-sheniyah," *Cathedra* 46, 1987, 109–22; Yehiam Weitz, *Muda'ut ve-hoser onim – Mapai le-nokhah ha-shoah 1943–45*, Jerusalem: Yad Ben-Zvi, 1994, ch. 5; Tom Segev, *The Seventh Million: The Israelis and the Holocaust*, New York: Hill and Wang, 1993, 113–22; Avi Picard, "Reshitah shel ha-hageirah ha-selektivit bi-shenot ha-50," *Iyunnim bi-tekumat Yisra'el* IX, 1999, 338–93; Eli Tzur, "Hehelah yetsiat mitzrayim – u mah asu halutseinu ba-kibbutz be-mivhan ha-'aliyah ha-hamonit," ibid., 316–38; Hagit Lavsky, "Le'umiyut, hageirah ve-hityashvut: ha'im haytah mediniyut kelitah tsiyonit?," eds. Avi Bareli and Nahum Karlinsky, Sede Boker: Midreshet Ben-Gurion, *Kalkalah ve-hevrah bimei ha-mandat. Iyunnim bi-tekumat Yisra'el: Sidrat le-noseh*, 2003, 153–78; Aviva Halamish, "'Aliyah lefi yikholet ha-kelitah ha-kalkalit: Ha-'ikaronot ha-manhim, darkhei ha-bitsua' ve-ha-hashlakhot ha-demografiyot shel mediniyut ha-'aliyah bein milhemot ha-'olam," ibid., 179–216.

30 Tom Segev, *1949: ha-yisre'elim ha-rishonim*, Jerusalem: Domino, 1984 (English edition: *1949: The First Israelis*, New York: Free Press, 1986); Idith Zertal, *Zehavam shel ha-yehdim: Ha-hagerah ha-yehudit ha-mahtertit le-erets yisra'el 1945–48*, Tel Aviv: 'Am 'Oved, 1996 (English edition: *From Catastrophe to Power: Holocaust Survivors and the Emergence of Israel*, Berkeley and Los Angeles: University of California Press, 1998).

31 Zertal, *From Catastrophe to Power*, 131–2.
32 Dina Porat, "Attitudes of the Young State of Israel toward the Holocaust and Its Survivors," ed. Laurence Silberstein, *New Perspectives on Israeli History*, New York: New York University Press, 1991, 157–74.
33 Esther Meir-Glitzenstein, *Ha-Tenu'ah ha-tsiyonit vi-yehude 'irak*: *1941–1950*, Tel Aviv: 'Am 'Oved 1994 (*Zionism in an Arab Country: The Jews in Iraq in the 1940s*, London: Routledge 2004).
34 E.g. Devorah HaCohen, *'Olim be-se'arah: ha-'aliyah ha-gedolah u-kelitatah be-yisra'el 1948–1953*, Jerusalem: Yad Ben-Zvi, 1994 (English version: *Immigrants in Turmoil: Mass Immigration to Israel and its Repercussions in the 1950s and After*, Syracuse, N.Y.: Syracuse University Press, 2003).
35 Shlomo Swirski, *Israel: The Oriental Majority*, London: Zed Publishers, 1989 (Hebrew original 1981).
36 For overviews of changing trends in Mizrahi studies over the past twenty years, see the essays by Ella Shohat, Aziza Khazzoom, Sami Shalom Chetrit, and Uri Ram in *Israel Studies Forum* 17, 2002, 86–130.
37 See the analysis of Shas voters' hawkish political views in Ephraim Yuchtman-Yaar and Tamar Hermann, "Shass: The Haredi-Dovish Image in a Changing Reality," *Israel Studies* V, 2, 2000, 32–77.
38 Lavsky, "Le'umiyut, hageirah ve-hityashvut"; Gur Alroey, "Journey to Twentieth-Century Palestine as an Immigrant Experience," *Jewish Social Studies* IX, 2003, 28–64; *idem*, *Ha-hagirah ha-yehudit be-reshit ha-me'ah ha-esrim*: *ha-mikreh shel Erets-Yisra'el ("ha-'Aliyah ha-sheniyah")*, Jerusalem: Yad Ben-Zvi, 2004.
39 Anat Helman, "East or West? Tel Aviv in the 1920s and 1930s," *People of the City: Jews and the Urban Challenge. Studies in Contemporary Jewry*, XV, New York: Oxford University Press, 1999, 68–79; "European Jews in the Levant Heat: Climate and Culture in 1920s and 1930s Tel-Aviv," *Journal of Israeli History*, 22,1, 2003, 71–90; "Hues of Adjustment: *Landsmanshaftn* in Inter-War New York and Tel Aviv," *Jewish History* 20,1 2006, 41–67.
40 Jacob Metzer, *Hon le'umi le-bayit le'umi*, Jerusalem: Yad Ben-Zvi, 1979; Nachum Gross, *Lo 'al ruah levadah: 'iyunim ba-historyah ha-kalkalitshel eretz-yisra'el ba-'et ha-hadashah*, Jerusalem, Magnes, 1999; Nahum Karlinsky, *Perihat he-hadar: yazemut peratit ba-yishuv, 1890–1939*, Jerusalem: Magnes, 2000, (*California Dreaming: Ideology, Society and Technology in the Citrus Industry of Palestine, 1890–1939*, State University of New York Press, 2005).
41 Deborah Bernstein, ed., *Pioneers and Homemakers: Jewish Women in Pre-State Israel*, Albany, N.Y.: State University of New York Press, 1992.
42 Mikhal Ben Ya'akov, "'Olot le-eretz yisra'el: defusei hageirah shel nashim mi-tsafon afrikah le-eretz yisra'el ba-me'ah ha-19," eds. Margalit Shilo, Ruth Kark, and Galit Hazan-Rokem, *Ha-'ivryot ha-hadashot: nashim ba-yishuv u-va-tsiyonut bi-re'i ha-migdar*, Jerusalem: Yad Ben-Zvi, 2001, 63–83.
43 Margalit Shilo, *Nesikhah o-shevuyah?*, Haifa: Zimorah Bitan, 2001 (English version: *Princess or Prisoner?* Hanover, New Hampshire: University Press of New England 2005).
44 Yossi Ben-Artsi, "Ha'im shinu heker nashim u-migdar et yahaseinu le-havanat ha-historyah shel ha-aliyah ve-ha-hityashvut?," in *Ha-'ivriyot ha-hadashot*, 26–44.
45 Zachary Lockman, *Comrades and Enemies: Arab and Jewish Workers in Palestine, 1906*–1948, Berkeley and Los Angeles: University of California Press, 1996.
46 Deborah Bernstein has produced a book similar to Lockman's in argument, but with a more limited chronological and geographical scope – Haifa during the interwar period. The tightening of parameters allows for a more focused examination of the Arab side of the equation. See *Constructing Boundaries: Jewish and Arab Workers in Mandatory Palestine*, Albany, N.Y.: State University of New York Press, 2000.

47 Ilan Pappé, *A History of Modern Palestine: One Land, Two Peoples*, Cambridge, UK: Cambridge University Press, 2004.
48 Mahmoud Yazbek, "Mi-falahim le-mordim: gormim kalkaliyim le-hitpartsut ha-mered ha-'aravi be-1936," *Ha-tsiyonut 22*, 2000, 185–206; Mustafa Kabha, "Tafkidah shel ha-'itonut ha-'aravit-ha-falastinit be-irgun ha-shevitah ha-falastinit ha-kelalit, april–oktober 1936," *Iyunim bi-tekumat yisra'el* 11, 2001, 212–29.
49 Baruch Kimmerling and Joel Migdal, *Palestinian People: A History*, Cambridge, Mass.: Harvard University Press, 2003.
50 Baruch Kimmerling, *The Invention and Decline of Israeliness*, Berkeley and Los Angeles: University of California Press, 2001; Gershon Shafir and Yoav Peled, *Being Israeli: The Dynamics of Multiple Citizenship*, Cambridge, UK, and New York: Cambridge University Press, 2002.
51 Shafir and Peled, *Being Israeli*, 56–7, 231–59.
52 Ibid., 261–70.
53 It can be argued that Morris, whose earlier work highlighted Israeli acts of aggression against the Palestinians in order to pillory the state leadership for unjustified cruelty, now does so in order to justify a harsh military response to the current Palestinian uprising. Morris has, in fact, justified Israeli expulsions of Palestinians in 1948 in terms of military and demographic necessities of the era and has suggested it would perhaps have been best to expel all the Palestinians dwelling within what would become Israel's post-1949 borders (*Ha-Aretz*, January 9 and 23, 2004). Yet Morris's latest monograph on 1948, analyzed below, offers no apology or warrant for Israeli aggression in 1948.
54 Benny Morris, *The Road to Jerusalem: Glubb Pasha, Palestine and the Jews*, London: Tauris, 2002, 240.
55 Ibid., 241.
56 Motti Golani, *Tihyeh milhamah ba-kayits: ha-derekh le-milhemet sinai, 1955–1966*, Tel Aviv: Ministry of Defense, 1997 (English Version: *Israel in Search of a War: The Sinai Campaign, 1955–1956*, Brighton, UK: Sussex Academic Press, 1998).
57 Mordechai Bar-On, *The Gates of Gaza. Israel's Road to Suez and Back, 1955–1957*, New York: St. Martin's Press, 1994.
58 See also the exchange between Bar-On, Golani, and Morris cited in note 5.
59 Michael Oren, *Six Days of War: June 1967 and the Making of the Modern Middle East*, New York: Oxford University Press, 2002.
60 Ibid., 55, 59, 83, 95.
61 Ibid., 23, 39, 231, 261, 278–80.
62 Avi Shlaim, *The Iron Wall: Israel and the Arab World*, New York: Norton, 2000, 235.
63 Ibid., 249–50.
64 Compare Shlaim, *The Iron Wall*, 258, with Oren, *Six Days of War*, 317–23.
65 See Shlaim's review of Oren's book in the *Manchester Guardian*, June 8, 2002.
66 Efraim Karsh, *Fabricating Israeli History: The 'New Historians'*, London: Frank Cass, 1997, 18.
67 Anita Shapira, *Berl*, 2 vols., Tel Aviv: 'Am 'Oved, 1980. The book sold 26,000 cloth copies in its first two years – this in a country with a Hebrew-reading population of 3.5 million.
68 E.g. Oz, *A Tale of Love & Darkness*; A.B. Yehoshua, *Mr. Mani*, New York: Doubleday, 1992.
69 Amos Funkenstein, *Perceptions of Jewish History*, Berkeley and Los Angeles: University of California Press, 1993, 50–3.

3 Historians, Herzl, and the Palestinian Arabs

1 Eliezer Be'eri, *Reshit ha-sikhsukh Yisra'el-'Arav 1882–1911*, Tel Aviv: Sifriyat Po'alim, 1985, 34.

2 See the brief discussions in such standard works as Amos Elon, *Herzl*, New York: Holt, Rinehart and Winston, 1975, 261; Anita Shapira, *Land and Power: The Zionist Resort to Force, 1881–1948*, New York: Oxford University Press, 1992, 51; Israel Kolatt, "The Zionist Movement and the Arabs" (orig. 1982), in Jehuda Reinharz and Anita Shapira, eds., *Essential Papers on Zionism*, New York: New York University Press, 1995, 624; as well as the more extended analysis in Be'eri, *Reshit*.

3 Elon, *Herzl*, 310–11; Yosef Gorny, *Zionism and the Arabs, 1882–1948: A Study of Ideology*, Oxford, UK: Oxford University Press, 1987, 30–3; Be'eri, *Reshit*, 89–91. Herzl's reply to al-Khalidi has been translated and published in Walid Khalidi, *From Haven to Conquest: Readings in Zionism and the Palestine Problem until 1948*, Beirut: The Institute for Palestine Studies, 1971, 92. Quotations that support Gorny's argument may be found on pp. 68, 120, and 123 of the English translation (New York: Herzl Press, 1960).

4 Theodor Herzl, ed. Raphael Patai, *Complete Diaries*, trans. Harry Zohn, New York: Herzl Press, 1960, 88–9.

5 E.g. Alex Bein, *Theodore Herzl: A Biography of the Founder of Modern Zionism*, New York: Atheneum, 1970 (1941); Elon, *Herzl*; Ernst Pawel, *The Labyrinth of Exile: A Life of Theodor Herzl*, New York: Farrar, Straus, Giroux, 1989.

6 Shabtai Teveth, *The Evolution of "Transfer" in Zionist Thinking*, Tel Aviv: Dayan Center, 1989, 2–4.

7 Shapira, *Land and Power*, 16.

8 Chaim Simons, *A Historical Survey of Proposals to Transfer Arabs from Palestine, 1895–1947*, Hoboken, N.J.: Ktav, 1988; Teveth (*The Evolution of "Transfer"*) notes a similar study by Dr. Moshe Yegar of the Israeli Foreign Ministry, an old time Revisionist, who published a study of Dr. Avraham Sharon, an early proponent of transfer, and of his alleged impact on a host of his contemporaries, including the dovish Arthur Ruppin.

9 Joseph Nedava, "Herzl and the Arab Problem," *Forum on the Jewish People, Zionism and Israel* 27, 2, 1977, 64–72.

10 Benny Morris, *The Origins of the Palestinian Refugee Problem Revisited*, Cambridge, UK: Cambridge University Press, 2004, 41. Morris first raised the issue of Herzl's June 12, 1895, diary entry in 1998, at which time he was critical of the concept of transfer. As of now Morris does not explicitly endorse transfer but claims it to be a historical desideratum, which, if carried out in full in 1948, would have strengthened the young state of Israel and mitigated the future Arab–Israeli conflict (Benny Morris, "Looking Back: A Personal Assessment of the Zionist Experience," *Tikkun*, March 1998).

11 Walid Khalidi, "The Jewish–Ottoman Land Company: Herzl's Blueprint for the Colonization of Palestine," *Journal of Palestine Studies* XXII, 2, 1993, 40.

12 Zachary Lockman, *Comrades and Enemies: Arab and Jewish Workers in Palestine, 1906–1948*, Berkeley and Los Angeles: University of California Press, 1996, 32–3. The original quote runs:

> What interested me most [about the lecture] was the striking number of intelligent-looking young Egyptians who packed the hall. They are the coming masters. It is a wonder that the English don't see this. They think they are going to deal with *fellahin* forever. . . . What the English are doing today is splendid. They are cleaning up the Orient, letting light and air into the filthy corners, breaking old tyrannies, and destroying abuses. But along with freedom and progress they are also teaching the *fellahin* how to revolt.
>
> (Entry of March 26, 1902, *Complete Diaries*, 1449)

13 Muhammad Ali Khalidi, "Utopian Zionism or Zionist Proselytism? A Reading of Herzl's *Altneuland*," *Journal of Palestine Studies* 30, 4, 2001, 58.
14 Edward Said, "Zionism from the Standpoint of Its Victims" (orig. 1979), reproduced in Anne McClintock, Aamar Mufti, and Ella Shohat, eds., *Dangerous Liaisons: Gender, Nation and Postcolonial Difference*, Minneapolis, Minn.: University of Minnesota Press, 1997, 15–38, esp. 25.
15 Lockman, *Comrades and Enemies*, 32–3, 380–1. The quote is from 381.
16 Desmond Stewart, *Theodor Herzl: Artist and Politician. A Biography of the Father of Modern Israel*, Garden City, N.Y.: Doubleday, 1974, 190.
17 Cited in Stewart, *Theodor Herzl*, 185.
18 Herzl, *Complete Diaries*, 89.
19 Daniel Boyarin, *Unheroic Conduct: The Rise of Heterosexuality and the Invention of the Jewish Man*, Berkeley and Los Angeles: University of California Press, 1997, 302.
20 Adolf Friedmann, *Das Leben Theodor Herzls*, Berlin: Jüdischer Verlag, 1914, 20.
21 Entry for March 29, 1903, *Complete Diaries*, 1454.
22 W. Khalidi, "The Jewish–Ottoman Land Company," 44–5. The original *Übereinkommen über die Privilegien, Rechte, Schuldigkeiten u. Pflichten der Jüdische-Ottomanischen Land-Compagnie (J.O.L.C.) zur Besiedelung von Palästina und Syrien* is in the Central Zionist Archive, Jerusalem (CZA), H VI A 2.
23 Wolffsohn's draft charter, in CZA W10, remains unpublished.
24 Adolf Boehm, *Die zionistische Bewegung*, Berlin, Jüdischer Verlag, 1935, I, 705–7; Paul Alsberg, "Mediniyut ha-hanhalah ha-tsiyonit mi-moto shel Hertsl ve-ad milhemet ha-olam ha-rishonah," Ph.D. diss., Hebrew University of Jerusalem, 1958, 24; Be'eri, *Reshit*, 100; Ben Halpern, *The Idea of the Jewish State*, Cambridge, Mass.: Harvard University Press, 1961, 263.
25 W. Khalidi, "The Jewish–Ottoman Land Company."
26 M. Khalidi, "Utopian Zionism or Zionist Proselytism?," 59, 64–5.

4 Is Israel a Jewish state?

1 E.g. Shmuel Eisenstadt, *The Transformation of Israeli Society: An Essay in Interpretation*, London: Weidenfeld and Nicolson, 1985; Daniel J. Elazar, *The Jewish Polity*, Bloomington, Ind.: Indiana University Press, 1985.
2 For the second generation, see Dan Horowitz and Moshe Lissak, *Origins of the Israeli Polity: Palestine under the Mandate*, Chicago: University of Chicago Press, 1978; Yonathan Shapiro, *The Formative Years of the Israeli Labour Party: The Organisation of Power, 1919–1930*, London: Sage, 1976. For the third, see Gershon Shafir, *Land, Labor, and the Origins of the Israeli–Palestinian Conflict, 1882–1914*, rev. edn., Berkeley and Los Angeles: University of California Press, 1996; Uri Ben-Eliezer, *The Origins of Israeli Militarism*, Bloomington, Ind.: Indiana University Press, 1998.
3 Gershon Shafir and Yoav Peled, *Being Israeli: The Dynamics of Multiple Citizenship*, New York: Cambridge University Press, 2002; Baruch Kimmerling, *The Invention and Decline of Israeliness*, Berkeley and Los Angeles: University of California Press, 2001.
4 There is the important exception of *Divergent Jewish Centers: Israel and America*, eds. Deborah Dash Moore and S. Ilan Troen, New Haven, Conn.: Yale University Press, 2001. But, as the title indicates, most of the essays in this volume stress areas of discontinuity rather than linkage between Jewish life in Israel and in the United States.
5 Yosef Salmon, *Dat ve-tsiyonut: imutim rishonim: kovets maamarim*, Jerusalem: Ha-sifriyah ha-tsiyonit, 1990; Michael Silber, "The Emergence of Ultra-Orthodoxy: The Invention of a Tradition," in ed. Jack Wertheimer, *The Uses of Tradition: Jewish Continuity in the Modern Era*, Cambridge, Mass.: Harvard

University Press, 1992, 23–84; Israel Bartal, *Galut ba-aretz. Yishuv eretz-yisra'el be-terem tsiyonut*, Jerusalem: Ha-sifriyah ha-tsiyonit, 1994.

6 Jonathan Frankel, *Prophecy and Politics: Socialism, Nationalism, and the Russian Jews, 1862–1917*, New York: Cambridge University Press, 1981; Ezra Mendelsohn, *On Modern Jewish Politics*, New York: Oxford University Press, 1993; Derek J. Penslar, *Shylock's Children: Economics and Jewish Identity in Modern Europe*, Berkeley and Los Angeles: University of California Press, 2001, chs. 5 and 6.

7 Benedict Anderson, *The Spectre of Comparisons: Nationalism, Southeast Asia, and the World*, London: Verso, 1998, 30–45.

8 Ron Kuzar, *Hebrew and Zionism: A Discourse Analytic Cultural Study*, Berlin and New York: Mouton de Gruyter, 2001, 120–36.

9 Ernst Feder, *Politik und Humanität: Paul Nathan, Ein Lebensbild*, Berlin: Deutsche Verlagsgesellschaft für Politik und Geschichte, 1929, 85–90, 97–9.

10 *Toldot ha-yishuv ha-yehudi be-eretz yisra'el me'az ha-'aliyah ha-rishonah. Beniyatah shel tarbut 'ivrit: helek rishon*, gen. ed. Moshe Lissak, vol. ed. Zohar Shavit, sec. author Rafael Nir, Jerusalem: Mosad Bialik, 1998, 119–22.

11 Benjamin Harshav, *Language in Time of Revolution*, Berkeley and Los Angeles: University of California Press, 1993.

12 Derek Penslar, "Broadcast Orientalism: Representations of Mizrahi Jewry in Israeli Radio, 1948–67," eds. Ivan Kalmar and Derek Penslar, *Orientalism and the Jews*, Hanover, N.H.: University Press of New England, 2004, 182–200.

13 Compare *The Jewishness of Israelis: Responses to the Guttman Report*, Charles S. Liebman and Elihu Katz, eds., Albany, N.Y.: State University of New York Press, 1997; with *A Portrait of Israeli Jewry: Beliefs, Observances and Values Among Israeli Jews*, Jerusalem: Avi Chai Foundation/Israeli Democracy Institute, 2002. The results of the 2000 survey are interpreted by its authors, Shlomit Levy, Hanna Levinsohn, and Elihu Katz, in "The Many Faces of Jewishness in Israel," in Uzi Rebhun and Chaim I. Waxman, eds., *Jews in Israel: Contemporary Social and Cultural Factors*, Hanover, N.H.: University Press of New England, 2004, 265–84.

14 These figures are extrapolated from tables provided in Sergio DellaPergola, "Jewish Women in Transition: A Comparative Sociodemographic Perspective," *Studies in Contemporary Jewry* XVI, 2000, 209–42.

15 Anita Shapira, "The Religious Motifs of the Labor Movement," in eds. Shmuel Almog, Jehuda Reinharz, and Anita Shapira, *Zionism and Religion*, Hanover, N.H., and London: University Press of New England, 1999, 251–72.

16 1965 Kol Yisrael listeners' survey, Israel State Archive 45g 6858/023/g, p. 3.

17 Mizrahi Jewish flexbility may be on the wane, however, as increasing numbers of Mizrahi youth receive a rigid yeshiva education, often inspired by Ashkenazic models.

18 Israel Bartal, "The Closeness which Alienates or the Alienation which Brings Closer? Jewish Religion and Israeli Culture," in Liebman and Katz, *The Jewishness of Israelis*, 121–4.

19 Elan Ezrahi, "The Quest for Spirituality among Secular Israelis," in Uzi Rebhun and Chaim Waxman, eds., *Jews in Israel: Contemporary Social and Cultural Patterns*, Hanover, N.H.: University Press of New England, 2004, 315–28.

20 Michael Brenner, *The Jewish Renaissance in Weimar Germany*, New Haven, Conn.: Yale University Press, 1994.

21 Reproduced in Michael Walzer, Menachem Lorberbaum, and Noam J. Zohar, eds., *The Jewish Political Tradition: Volume One: Authority*, New Haven, Conn., and London: Yale University Press, 2000, 476–9.

22 The separation of temporal and religious authority in *dar al-Islam* was the work of the medieval jurist Ibn Taymiyyah; he intended thereby for the state to create favorable conditions for adherence to Islamic law, but in practice religion and politics drifted into separate spheres.

23 Daniel Elazar, ed., *Kinship and Consent: The Jewish Political Tradition and Its Contemporary Uses*, Philadelphia: Turtledove, 1981.
24 Alan Dowty, *The Jewish State: A Century Later*, Berkeley and Los Angeles: University of California Press, 1998, 7–12, 30–3, 83–4.
25 Kimmerling, *The Invention and Decline of Israeliness.*
26 Walzer, Lorberbaum, and Zohar, eds., *The Jewish Political Tradition*, 490–7. The quotation is from p. 494.
27 Ibid., 468.
28 United Nations Population Division and World Bank, http://www.wri.org/wr-00-01/pdf/ei1n_2000.pdf, Table EI.
29 David Bartram, "Foreign Workers in Israel: History and Theory," *International Migration Review* 32, 2, 1998, 303–25.
30 Penslar, *Shylock's Children*, esp. ch. 4.
31 *The Jerusalem Report*, 28 January 2002, 36–7.
32 National Insurance Institute Report of December 1999, http://www.shemayisrael.com/chareidi/VCapoverty.htm.
33 Yakir Plessner, *The Political Economy of Israel: From Ideology to Stagnation*, Albany, N.Y.: State University of New York Press, 1994; Michael N. Barnett, "Israel in the World Economy: Israel as an East Asian State?," in ed. Michael N. Barnett, *Israel in Comparative Perspective: Challenging the Conventional Wisdom*, Albany, N.Y.: State University of New York Press, 1996, 107–40.
34 Nahum Karlinsky, *Perihat he-hadar*: *yazemut peratit ba-yishuv, 1890–1939*, Jerusalem: Magnes, 2000.
35 Eli Shaltiel, *Pinhas Rutenberg*: *aliyato u-nefilato shel ish hazak be-Erets-Yisrael, 1879–1942*, Tel Aviv: 'Am 'Oved, 1990.
36 There is a large literature on the relationship between Israeli society and the Holocaust: Tom Segev, *The Seventh Million: The Israelis and the Holocaust*, New York: Hill and Wang, 1993; Anita Shapira, "The Holocaust: Private Memories, Public Memory," *Jewish Social Studies* IV, 2, 1998, 40–58; Yosef Gorny, *Ben Aushvitz li-Yerushalayim*, Tel Aviv: 'Am 'Oved, 1998; Dalia Ofer, "The Strength of Remembrance: Commemorating the Holocaust During the First Decade of Israel," *Jewish Social Studies* VI, 2, 2000, 24–55; Roni Stauber, *Ha-lekah la-dor*: *sho'ah u-gevurah ba-mahashavah ha-tsiburit ba-arets bi-shenot ha-hamishim*, Jerusalem and Beersheva: Yad Ben-Tsevi and Ha-merkaz le-moreshet Ben-Gurion, 2000; Gulie Ne'eman Arad, "Shoah as Israel's Political Trope," in *Divergent Jewish Cultures: Israel & America*, 192–216; and Sidra DeKoven Ezrahi, "The Future of the Holocaust: Storytelling, Oppression and Identity. See under: 'Apocalypse'," *Judaism* 51, 1, 2002, 61–70; Idith Zertal, *Israel's Holocaust and the Politics of Nationhood*, New York: Cambridge University Press, 2005. On changes in Israeli history curricula and text books, see Dan Porat's highly useful doctoral thesis "One Text at a Time. Reconstructing the Past, Building the Future in Israeli History Text books," Stanford University, 1999; and *idem*, "From the Scandal to the Holocaust in Israeli Education," *Journal of Contemporary History* 39, 2004, 619–36.
37 Porat, "From the Scandal to the Holocaust in Israeli Education."
38 Benny Morris, *Righteous Victims: A History of the Zionist–Arab Conflict, 1881–1999*, New York: Knopf, 1999, 514–15. Yoram Bilu has noted the significance of Menachem Begin's choice to be buried in the Jewish sacred terrain of the Mount of Olives, Mount Herzl, the memory-site for the fallen heroes of the Israeli state and the resting place for many of its political leaders.
39 Moshe Zuckermann, "Ha-yehudi ha-klassi," *Shoah be-heder atum: Ha-"shoah" ba-itonut ha-yisre'elit be-milhemet ha-mifrats*, Tel Aviv: 'Am 'Oved, 1993, 220–35 (the quotation is from 235); *idem*, "Fluch des Vergessens" and "Geschichte, Angst und Ideologie: Aspekte der politischen Kultur in Israel," in *Zweierlei*

Holocaust: Der Holocaust in den politischen Kulturen Israels und Deutschland, Göttingen: Wallstein, 1998, 13–37 and 60–77.

40 Motti Golani, "We've Been to the Carmel, Now Let's Take a Trip to Auschwitz: The Founding of Israel, the Holocaust, and the Youth's Journeys to Poland," *Israel Studies Forum*, 17, 2, 2002, 54.

41 Cited in Arad, "Shoah as Israel's Political Trope," 209.

42 "Intermarriage, Low Birth Rates Threaten Diaspora Jewry," *Ha-Aretz*, 13 February 2002.

43 On the curricular changes, see Porath, "One Text at a Time." On Israeli historiographical controversies, see Eyal Naveh and Esther Yogev: *Historiyot: Likrat dialog 'im ha-'etmol*, Tel Aviv: Bavel, 2002. On the representation of Mizrahi Jews in Israeli textbooks, see Amnon Raz-Krakozkin, "History Textbooks and the Limits of Israeli Consciousness," *The Journal of Israeli History* 20, 2/3, 2001, 155–72.

44 This positive potential of the new curriculum was, unfortunately, not appreciated by the previous education minister, Limor Livnat, who banned one controversial (and little used) textbook and demanded that schools offer separate instructional units in Zionist values.

45 See Chapters 1 and 2; see also Derek J. Penslar, "Narratives of Nation-Building: Major Themes in Zionist Historiography," eds. David Myers and David Ruderman, *The Jewish Past Revisited*, New Haven, Conn.: Yale University Press, 1998, 104–27.

46 For example, the historian Benny Morris, whose work has established Israel's partial responsibility for the creation of the Palestinian refugee problem in 1948 and the Israeli–Egyptian border wars of the early 1950s, considers himself ideologically a Zionist, and in the wake of the Al-Aqsa Intifada became politically hawkish. See the exchange between Morris and Avi Shlaim in the *Manchester Guardian*, 21 and 22 February 2002; see also Morris, "'Asiti ma'aseh tsiyoni," *Ha-Aretz*, 16 June 1997. For an overview of the post-Zionist terrain in Israel, see Laurence Silberstein, ed., *The Postzionism Debates: Knowledge and Power in Israeli Culture*, New York: Routledge, 1999.

47 Menachem Brinker, "The End of Zionism? Thoughts on the Wages of Success," in ed. Carol Diament, *Zionism: The Sequel*, New York: Hadassah, 1998, 293–9; Silberstein, *The Postzionism Debates*, 123, 222 n.4; Tom Segev, *Ha-tsiyonim ha-hadashim*, Jerusalem: Keter, 2001, 39–40. There are intriguing parallels between the evolution of the terms "post-Zionism" and "post-colonialism:" during the 1950s post-colonialism referred to the state-system in the post-colonial era, but during the 1980s it came to mean a new way of thinking about history and culture that challenged the hegemony of western forms of knowledge and discourse. Robert Young, *Postcolonialism: An Introduction*, Oxford, UK: Blackwell, 2001, 58–61.

48 Gadi Taub, "The Shift in Israeli Ideas Concerning the Individual and the Collective," in ed. Hazim Saghie, *The Predicament of the Individual in the Middle East*, London: Saqi, 2001, 187–99; Daniel Gutwein, "The Imagined Critique: Left and Right Post-Zionism and the Privatization of Israeli Collective Memory," *Journal of Israeli History* 20, 2/3, 2001, 9–42.

49 The post-Zionist sociologist Uri Ram thinks highly of the message of this story, which, in his view, relates a narrative of liberation. Uri Ram, "Bizekhut ha-shikhehah," in ed. Adi Ophir, *50 le-48: Hamishim le-arbai'm u-shemonah: momentim bikortiyim be-toldot medinat yisra'el: te'ud eruim: masot u-ma'amarim*, Jerusalem: Van Leer Institute and Ha-kibbutz ha-me'uhad, 1999, 349–57.

50 Gutwein, "The Imagined Critique."

51 Yosi Yonah and Yehuda Shenhav, "Ha-matsav ha-rav-tarbuti," *Teoryah u-Vikoret* 17, 2000, 163–88.

52 Amnon Raz-Krakotzkin, "A Peace Without Arabs: The Discourse of Peace and the Limits of Israeli Consciousness," in eds. George Giacaman and Dag Jorund

Lonning, *After Oslo: New Realities, Old Problems*, London: Pluto Press, 1998, 59–76; *idem*, "Moreshet Rabin: hiloniyut, le'umiyut ve-oriyentalizm," unpublished ms.; also personal communications, April 29 and 30, 2002.

53 Adi Ophir, "'The Poor in Deed Facing the Lord of All Deeds': A Postmodern Reading of the Yom Kippur *Mahzor*," *Interpreting Judaism in a Postmodern Age*, ed. Steven Kepnes, New York: New York University Press, 1996, 181–217.

54 Bethamie Horowitz, "Blinded by the Light unto the Nations," *Forward*, April 23, 2004.

55 Oz Almog, *The Sabra: The Creation of the New Jew*, Berkeley and Los Angeles: University of California Press, 2000.

5 Is Zionism a colonial movement?

1 Ronen Shamir, *The Colonies of Law: Colonialism, Zionism, and Law in Early Mandate Palestine*, Cambridge, UK: Cambridge University Press, 2000, 17. See also the works of Baruch Kimmerling, Zachary Lockman, and Gershon Shafir cited in Chapter 2.

2 Compare Partha Chatterjee, *Nationalist Thought and the Colonial World: A Derivative Discourse?*, London: Zed Books, 1986; with *idem*, *The Nation and its Fragments: Colonial and Postcolonial Histories*, Princeton, N.J.: Princeton University Press, 1993. Both books stress Third World nationalisms' ongoing struggle to free themselves from the western epistemological categories that make nationalist sensibility possible in the first place. Particularly in the second book, Indian nationalism is presented as the product of a ceaseless *agon* with western thought as opposed to an adaptation of it.

3 Robert J.C. Young, *Postcolonialism: An Historical Introduction*, Oxford, UK: Blackwell, 2001, 57–69. The quotation is from p. 61.

4 E.g. Edward Said, *The Question of Palestine*, New York: Vintage, 1979.

5 Maxine Rodinson, *Israel: A Colonial Settler-State?*, New York: Monad, 1973, 39. The same is true for stateless European peoples who throughout the nineteenth century presented themselves as serving the interests of the dominant Powers. In the Hapsburg Empire, Poles and Czechs won autonomy and bilingualism respectively as rewards for their loyalty, and during World War I leaders of both national movements constantly lobbied the Great Powers just as the Zionists did.

6 Ibid., 92.

7 See the essays in Part II of economic historian Nachum Gross's collected works, *Lo 'al ha-ruah levadah: 'iyunim ba-historiyah ha-kalkalit shel heretz-yisra'el ba-'et ha-hadashah*, Jerusalem: Magnes and Yad Ben-Zvi, 1999. Many of Gross's arguments have been popularized by Tom Segev in *One Palestine, Complete: Jews and Arabs under the British Mandate*, New York: Metropolitan, 2000.

8 Daniel Boyarin, "Zionism, Gender and Mimicry," in eds. Fawzia Afzal-Khan and Kalpana Seshadri-Crooks, *The Pre-Occupation of Postcolonial Studies*, Durham, N.C., and London: Duke University Press, 2000, 256; Gershon Shafir, "Zionism and Colonialism: A Comparative Approach," in Michael N. Barnett, ed., *Israel in Comparative Perspective: Challenging the Conventional Wisdom*, Albany, N.Y.: State University of New York Press, 1996, 227–42.

9 Jacob Mester, *The Divided Economy of Mandatory Palestine*, Cambridge, UK: Cambridge University Press, 1998, 174–5.

10 Kenneth Stein, *The Land Question in Palestine: 1917–1939*, Chapel Hill, N.C.: University of North Carolina Press, 1984; Arieh L. Avneri, *The Claim of Dispossession: Jewish Land-Settlement and the Arabs, 1878–1948*, New Brunswick, N.J.: Transaction, 1984.

11 A bizarre scholarly alliance has developed between critics of Israel, who believe that Zionism sought from the outset to expel the native population in the fashion

of European settlement colonialisms, and right-wing Israeli scholars who wish to claim a historical pedigree for their own support for "transfer," that is, the expulsion, of Arabs from the Territoriies conquered in 1967. In fact, although there were occasional statements by Zionist activists, dating back to the turn of the twentieth century, supporting expelling the native population, the discourse of transfer only became serious and systematic in the wake of the 1937 Peel Commission partition proposal, whose territorial division would have left almost as many Arabs as Jews in the area allotted for the Jewish state. See Chapter 3.

12 Derek J. Penslar, *Zionism and Technocracy: The Engineering of Jewish Settlement in Palestine, 1870–1918*, Bloomington and Indianapolis, Ind.: Indiana University Press, 1991, 94–6.

13 Yael Simpson Fletcher, "'Irresistible Seductions': Gendered Representations of Colonial Algeria around 1930," in Julia Clancy-Smith and Frances Gouda, eds., *Domesticating the Empire: Race, Gender and Family Life in French and Dutch Colonialism*, Carlottesville, Va., and London: University of Virginia Press, 1998, 193–210.

14 Mary Louise Pratt, *Imperial Eyes: Travel Writing and Transculturation*, London and New York: Routledge, 1992, 7.

15 Yaron Peleg, "Moshe Smilansky and the Making of a Noble Jewish Savage," *Prooftexts*, forthcoming.

16 Ibid. Smilansky's stories do present an eroticized image of the Bedouin male, but his relationship with Jews is a friendship among equals, not the domination by the older European man of the young native boy found in Gide.

17 Lora Wildenthal, *German Women for Empire, 1884–1945*, Durham, N.C., and London: Duke University Press, 2001. On women in the Yishuv, see Deborah Bernstein, *Pioneers and Homemakers: Jewish Women in Pre-State Israel*, Albany, N.Y.: State University of New York Press, 1992.

18 Aron Rodrigue, *Images of Sephardi and Eastern Jewries in Transition, 1860–1939: The Teachers of the Alliance Israelite Universelle*, Seattle, Wa.: University of Washington Press, 1993.

19 The term "human material" (*homer enushi*) was most likely derived from the German *Menschenmaterial*, a word popularized during the interwar period and associated with the brutal materialism of both fascism and communism.

20 Shafir, *Land, Labour, and the Origins of the Palestinian–Israeli Conflict*, Cambridge, UK: Cambridge University Press, 1989, 91–122; Yehuda Nini, *He-hayit o-halamti halom? Temanei Kineret: parashat hityashvutam ve-'akiratam, 1912–1930*, Tel Aviv: 'Am 'Oved, 1996.; Gabi Peterberg, "Domestic Orientalism: The Representation of 'Oriental' Jews in Zionist/Israeli Historiography," *British Journal of Middle Eastern Studies* 23, 2 (1996), 140–44.

21 Yehouda Shenhav, *Ha-yehudim ha-'aravim: le'umuit, dat ve-etniut*, Tel Aviv: 'Am 'Oved, 2003, chs. 1 and 2.

22 Ibid.; Peterberg, "Domestic Orientalism;" Ella Shohat, "Rupture and Return: Zionist Discourse and the Study of Arab Jews," *Social Text* 75, 21, 2003, 49–74.

23 Ann Stoler, "Sexual Affronts and Racial Frontiers: European Identities and the Cultural Politics of Exclusion in Colonial Southeast Asia," 1992, reproduced in Geoff Eley and Ronald Grigor Suny, eds., *Becoming National*, New York and Oxford, UK: Oxford University Press, 1996, 295.

24 I discuss this subject in detail in my book *Shylock's Children: Economics and Jewish Identity in Modern Europe*, Berkeley and Los Angeles: University of California Press, 2001, ch. 1.

25 Peter van der Veer, "The Moral State: Religion, Nation, and Empire in Victorian Britain and British India," in Peter van der Veer and Hartmut Lehmann, eds., *Nation and Religion: Perspectives on Europe and Asia*, Princeton, N.J.: Princeton University Press, 1999, 32–4.

26 Compare Thongchai Winichakul, *Siam Mapped: A History of the Geo-Body of a Nation*, Honolulu: University of Hawaii Press, 1994, 39–40; with Chatterjee's essay "Histories and Nations," in *The Nation and Its Fragments: Colonial and Postcolonial Histories*, Princeton, N.J.: Princeton University Press, 1993. For a comparison of Zionist and colonial African intellectuals, see Dan Segre, "Colonization and Decolonization: The Case of Zionist and African Elites," in ed. Todd Endelman, *Comparing Jewish Societies*, Ann Arbor, Mich.: University of Michigan Press, 1994, 217–34.
27 Susannah Heschel, *Abraham Geiger and the Jewish Jesus*, Chicago: University of Chicago Press, 1998, 20–1. See also Christian Wiese, "Struggling for Normality: The Apologetics of Wissenschaft des Judentums in Wilhelmine Germany as an Anti-colonial Intellectual Revolt against the Protestant Construction of Judaism," in eds. Rainer Liedtke and David Rechter, *Towards Normality? Acculturation and Modern German Jewry*, Tübingen: Mohr Siebeck, 2003, 77–101.
28 Van der Veer, "The Moral State," 30–1.
29 Ibid.
30 Compare Chatterjee, "The Nation and Its Women," in *The Nation and Its Fragments*; with Paula Hyman, *Gender and Assimilation in Modern Jewish History*, Seattle, Wa., and London: University of Washington Press, 1995; and Marion Kaplan, *The Making of the Jewish Middle Class: Women, Family, and Identity in Imperial Germany*, New York and Oxford, UK: Oxford University Press, 1991.
31 Benedict Anderson, *The Spectre of Comparisons: Nationalism, Southeast Asia, and the World*, London: Verso, 1998, 30–45.
32 See Chatterjee's essays "The Nation and Its Pasts" and "Histories and Nations," in *The Nation and Its Fragments.*
33 On this point Bhabha was adumbrated by Albert Memmi, whose 1957 book *The Colonizer and the Colonized* described Jews as a colonized minority engaging in "self-colonization" by aping the dominator. See Rachel Feldhay Brenner, *Inextricably Bonded: Israeli Arab and Jewish Writers Re-visioning Culture*, Madison, Wisc.: University of Wisconsin Press, 2003, 54.
34 Discussed in Chatterjee's essay "The Nationlist Elite," in *The Nation and Its Fragments*, 45–51.
35 Amos Funkenstein, "Zionism, Science, and History," *Perceptions of Jewish History*, Berkeley and Los Angeles: University of California Press, 1993, 347–50.
36 Compare Sylvia Walby, "Woman and Nation," reproduced in Gopal Balakrishnan and Benedict Anderson, eds., *Mapping the Nation*, London: Verso, 1996, 235–54; with Chatterjee's essay "The Nation and Its Women," in *The Nation and Its Fragments.*
37 Chatterjee, "The National State," in *The Nation and Its Fragments.*
38 These themes are further developed in Penslar, *Shylock's Children*, ch. 6.
39 Chatterjee, "Whose Imagined Community?," in *The Nation and Its Fragments.*
40 Penslar, *Shylock's Children*, 29–32.
41 Cited in Mauro Moretti, "The Search for a 'National' History: Italian Historiographical Trends Following Unification," in Stefan Berger, Mark Donovan, and Kevin Passmore, eds., *Writing National Histories*, London and New York: Routledge, 1999, 114.
42 Ibid., 118.
43 Despite its many problems, Liah Greenfeld's *Nationalism: Five Roads to Modernity* (Cambridge, Mass.: Harvard University Press, 1992) argues this point convincingly.
44 Chatterjee, *Nationalist Thought and the Colonial World*, 10.
45 Ibid., 30; see also p. 169.
46 Dipesh Chakrabarty, *Provincializing Europe: Postcolonial Thought and Historical Difference*, Princeton, N.J.: Princeton University Press, 2000, 45–6.

47 Ella Shohat, "Sephardim in Israel: Zionism from the Standpoint of Its Jewish Victims," orig. 1988, reproduced in eds. Anne McClintock, Aamir Mufti, and Ella Shohat, *Dangerous Liaisons: Gender, Nation & Postcolonial Perspectives*, Minneapolis, Minn., and London: University of Minnesota Press, 1997, 39–68; *idem*, *Israeli Cinema: East/West and Political Representation*, Austin, Tex.: University of Texas Press, 1989; Shlomo Swirski, *Israel: The Oriental Majority*, London: Zed Publishers, 1989 (Hebrew original 1981). For overviews of changing trends in Mizrahi studies over the past twenty years, see the essays by Ella Shohat, Aziza Khazzoom, Sami Shalom Chetrit, and Uri Ram in the *Israel Studies Forum* 17, 2002, 86–130.

48 Mahmood Mamdani, *When Victims Become Killers: Colonialism, Nativism and the Genocide in Rwanda*, Princeton, N.J.: Princeton University Press, 2001, 23, cited in Gil Anidjar, *The Jew, the Arab. A History of the Enemy*, Stanford, Calif.: Stanford University Press, 2003, xv. See also Terence Ranger, "The Invention of Tradition in Colonial Africa," in Eric Hobsbawm and Terence Ranger, eds., *The Invention of Tradition*, Cambridge, UK: Cambridge University Press, 1992, 211–62.

49 By the 1980s, as much as 40 percent of the Occupied Territories' labor force was employed in Israel, and their collective income comprised at least one-quarter of the Territories' total product. Metzer, *The Divided Economy of Mandatory Palestine*, 174–5.

50 On this point, see Young, *Postcolonialism*, chs. 2 and 3.

51 Joseph Massad, "The 'Post-Colonial' Colony: Time, Space, and Bodies in Palestine/Israel," in eds. Afzal-Khan and Seshadri-Crooks, *The Pre-Occupation of Postcolonial Studies*, 311–46.

6 Antisemites on Zionism

1 Theodor Herzl, *Der Judenstaat*, 8th edn., Berlin: Jüdischer Verlag, 1920, 9–10.

2 Andrew Handler, *An Early Blueprint for Zionism: Győző Istóczy's Political Antisemitism*, Boulder, Col.: Greenwood, 1989, 42–51.

3 Ibid., 152.

4 "Un Congrès israélite," *La Libre Parole*, August 17, 1897.

5 "Le Sionisme et la haute banque," *La Libre Parole*, September 4, 1897.

6 "Le Congrès sioniste," *La Libre Parole*, August 20, 1907.

7 "L'Agonie du sionisme," *La Libre Parole*, September 11, 1913.

8 Ibid.

9 "Le Congrès sioniste: nouvelle orientation," *La Libre Parole*, August 31, 1913; Frederick Busi, "Anti-Semites on Zionism," *Midstream*, Februrary 1979, 18–27.

10 Georges Bernanos, *La Grande Peur des bien-pensants, Edouard Drumont*, Paris: B. Grasset, 1931.

11 André Lavagne, quoted in Michael Marrus and Robert O. Paxton, *Vichy France and the Jews*, New York: Basic Books, 1981, 315. Compare the treatment of Vichy's flirtation with Zionism on pp. 310–15 with Francis Nicosia's discussion of changes in Nazi policy towards Zionism over the years 1937–40 in his *The Third Reich and the Palestine Question*, Austin, Tex.: University of Texas Press, 1985, chs. 7–9.

12 "Intorno alla Questione del Sionismo," *La Civiltà cattolica*, April 2, 1938, a. 89, vol. II, quad. 2107, 76.

13 Furio Biagini, *Mussolini e il sionismo*, Milan: M&B, 1998, 14, 23–4, 49–52, 63, 72, 78, 122, 128, 137.

14 Mosche Zimmermann, *Wilhelm Marr: The Patriarch of Antisemitism*, New York: Oxford University Press, 1986, 88.

15 Eugen Dühring, *Die Judenfrage als Frage der Rassenschädlichkeit für Existenz, Sitte und Cultur der Völker*, 4th edn., Berlin: H. Reuther, 1892, 122–3.

16 Eugen Dühring, *Die Judenfrage als Frage des Rassencharakters und seiner Schädlichkeiten für Existenz der Völker*, 6th edn., Leipzig: O.R. Reisland, 1930, 127–8.
17 I have compared the 1886, 1892, 1907, and 1910 editions of the work, which was published at first by the author in Leipzig, but which as of 1907, if not earlier, was published by the Hanseatischer Druck- und Verlagsanstalt in Hamburg.
18 Theodor Fritsch, *Handbuch der Judenfrage*, 36th edn., Leipzig: Hammer-Verlag, 1934, 146–55, 170. Similarly, Fritsch's book *The Riddle of the Jew's Success*, published in many editions during the 1920s, does not even raise the issue of Zionism in its final chapter about World War I and Jewish control over wartime finance.
19 Houston Stewart Chamberlain, *The Foundations of the Nineteenth Century*, New York: H. Fertig, 1968, 477n.
20 For Rosenberg's and Hitler's views on Zionism, see Nicosia, *The Third Reich and the Palestine Question*, 20–8; and Robert Wistrich, *Hitler's Apocalypse: Jews and the Nazi Legacy*, London: Weidenfeld and Nicolson, 1985, 154–63. Quotation from *Mein Kampf* on p. 155.
21 Quoted by Marvin Kurz, "Ernst Zundel Is More Dangerous than You Realize," *Globe and Mail*, February 26, 2003, A15.
22 On the history of the *Protocols*, see Norman Cohn, *Warrant for Genocide: The Myth of the Jewish World Conspiracy and the Protocols of the Elders of Zion*, New York: Harper & Row, 1967; Binjamin Segel, *A Lie and a Libel: The History of the Protocols of the Elders of Zion*, Lincoln, Neb.: University of Nebraska Press, 1995; and Stephen Erich Bronner, *A Rumor about the Jews: Reflections on Antisemitism and the Protocols of the Learned Elders of Zion*, New York: St. Martin's Press, 2000.
23 Bronner, *A Rumor about the Jews*, 92.
24 Thanks to Steven Zipperstein for this observation.
25 Cohn, *Warrant for Genocide*, 108. See also Segel, *A Lie and a Libel*, 71–9.
26 See the excerpts in Richard S. Levy, ed., *Antisemitism in the Modern World: An Anthology of Texts*, Lexington, Mass.: D.C. Heath 1991, 169–77.
27 Yehoshafat Harkabi, "On Arab Antisemitism Once More," in Shmuel Almog, ed., *Antisemitism through the Ages*, Oxford, UK: Pergamon, 1988, 227–40. The Hebrew edition of the book in which this article appeared, based on a 1978 conference, was published in 1980.
28 The book *Arab Attitudes to Israel*, published in English in 1972 (Jerusalem: Israel Universities Press), first appeared in Hebrew in 1967.
29 Mark Cohen, *Under Crescent and Cross: The Jews in the Middle Ages*, Princeton, N.J.: Princeton University Press, 1994, 3–14.
30 Ron Nettler, "Islamic Archetypes of the Jews: Then and Now," in Robert Wistrich, ed., *Anti-Zionism and Antisemitism in the Modern World*, London: Macmillan, 1990, 63–73.
31 Cohen, *Under Crescent and Cross*, 167.
32 Yehoshua Porath, "Anti-Zionist and Anti-Jewish Ideology in the Arab Nationalist Movement in Palestine," in Almog, ed., *Antisemitism through the Ages*, 217–26.
33 Eliezer Be'eri, "The Jewish–Arab Conflict during the Herzl Years," *Jerusalem Quarterly* 41, 1987, 13.
34 Muhammad Muslih, *The Origins of Palestinian Nationalism*, New York: Columbia University Press, 1988, 75, 77–8. Quotation on p. 78.
35 Elyakim Rubinstein, "'Ha-protokolim shel ziknei tziyon' ba-sikhsukh ha-aravi-yehudi," *Ha-Mizrah he-Hadash* 25, 1985, 37–42.
36 Reeva Spector Simon, *Iraq between the Two World Wars: The Militarist Origins of Tyranny*, 2nd edn., New York: Columbia University Press, 2004.
37 Porath, "Anti-Zionist and Anti-Jewish Ideology," 223.
38 Muslih, *Origins of Palestinian Nationalism*, 169.

39 Constantine Zurayk, *The Meaning of the Disaster*, Beirut: Khayat's College Book Co-operative, 1956, 2.
40 Paul Berman, *Terror and Liberalism*, New York: Norton, 2003, 85–6.
41 Emmanuel Sivan, "Islamic Fundamentalism, Antisemitism, and Anti-Zionism," in Wistrich, ed., *Anti-Zionism and Antisemitism in the Modern World*, 82.
42 Yehoshafat Harkabi, "On Arab Antisemitism Once More," in Almog ed., *Antisemitism through the Ages*, 238.

7 Zionism and Jewish social policy

1 Jürgen Habermas, *The Structural Transformation of the Public Sphere*, Cambridge, Mass.: MIT Press, 1991.
2 In this chapter I prefer the terms "social policy" and "social welfare" over "philanthropy" when describing the international relief and colonization projects of various Jewish organizations. In doing so I respond to the spirit of the *fin de siècle*, when the word "philanthropy" (*Wohltätigkeit*) took on the negative connotation of unplanned giving motivated by sentiment alone. "Social policy" (*Sozialpolitik*) and "social welfare" (*soziale Fürsorge, Wohlfahrtspflege*) gained currency and respectability as signifiers of rationalized forms of income redistribution, usually involving some level of state intervention. Christoph Sachsse and Florian Tennstedt, *Geschichte der Armenfürsorge in Deutschland*, Stuttgart: Kohlhammer, 1980, 220–1; Rolfe Landwehr and Rüdiger Baron, *Geschichte der Sozialarbeit. Hauptlinien ihrer Entwicklung im 19. und 20. Jahrhundert*, Weinheim-Basel: Beltz, 1983, 40, 67, 147; Rüdiger vom Bruch, ed., *Weder Kommunismus noch Kapitalismus: bürgerlicher Sozialreform in Deutschland vom Vormärz bis zur Ära Adenauer*, Munich: C.H. Beck, 1985, 65–6.
3 Jacob Toury, "'The Jewish Question:' A Semantic Approach," *Leo Baeck Institute Year Book XI*, 1966, 85–106; Peter Pulzer, *Jews and the German State: The Political History of a Minority, 1848–1933*, London: Blackwell, 1992, 28–43.
4 It is difficult to date the precise origins of terms such as the "Negro question" or the "social question." A perusal of various bibliographic databases for English, French, and German texts suggests that the former term began to appear in writings as early as 1800, and the latter seems to have gained currency around mid-century. In 1838, Thomas Caryle's book *Chartism* posed the famous "Condition-of-England Question," which had a strong social component.
5 Ezra Mendelsohn, *On Modern Jewish Politics*, New York: Oxford University Press, 1993.
6 Moshe Rinott, *Hevrat ha-'ezrah liyehudei Germaniyah bi-yetsirah u-ve-ma'avak*, Jerusalem: Bet sefer le-hinukh shel ha-universitah ha-ivrit, 1971, 26.
7 For an excellent analysis of the relationship between the Alliance's political strategies, educational policies, and underlying ideologies, see Aron Rodrigue, *French Jews, Turkish Jews: The Alliance Israelite and the Politics of Jewish Schooling in Turkey, 1860–1925*, Bloomington, Ind.: Indiana University Press, 1990.
8 Georg Herlitz, *Das Jahr der Zionisten*, Jerusalem and Luzern: Ullmann, 1949, 139.
9 Rodrigue, *French Jews, Turkish Jews*, 23; Zosa Szajkowski, "Conflicts in the Alliance Israélite Universelle and the Founding of the Anglo-Jewish Association, the Vienna Allianz, and the Hilfsverein," *Jewish Social Studies* 1–2, 1957, 44, 49.
10 Membership figures and listings of the provenance of members and branches may be found in the *Jahresberichte der Israelitischen Allianz zu Wien*. See, in particular, XIV, 1887, xix.
11 Szajkowski, "Conflicts," 39–42.
12 Compare Yehuda Bauer, *My Brother's Keeper. A History of the American Jewish Joint Distribution Committee*, Philadephia: Jewish Publication Society, 1974, 17–22;

with *30 Years. The Story of the J.D.C.*, New York: Joint Distribution Committee, 1945. In the 1940s, the Joint's National Council numbered some 5,200 activists drawn from the communal leadership. But this was only the base of a pyramid, at the top of which stood an elite group of at most a half-dozen men who ran the day-to-day operations of the Joint and set its course. The quotation is from Bauer, p. 26.

13 Leonard Robinson and Frank Rosenblatt to Herbert Lehman, July 26, 1922, Archive of the American Jewish Joint Distribution Committee, New York, AR21/32/104.

14 Bernard Kahn to Herbert Lehman, November 21, 1923, AAJDC AR21/32/105.

15 Louis Oungre to Herbert Lehman, October 23 and November 10, 1923, AAJDC AR21/32/105.

16 Compare Ehud Luz, *Parallels Meet: Religion and Nationalsm in the Early Zionist Movement, 1882–1904*, Philadelphia: Jewish Publication Society, 1988; with Jacob Kellner, *Le-ma'an Tsiyon. Ha-hit'arvut ha-klal yehudit bi-metsukat ha-yishuv 1869–1882*, Jerusalem: Yad Ben-Zvi, 1977, ch. 3; and Rinott, *Hevratha-'ezrah*, 22–3.

17 Theodore Norman, *An Outstretched Arm: A History of the Jewish Colonization Association*, London: Routledge and Kegan Paul, 1985, 161.

18 Haim Avni, "Hevrat IKA ve-ha-tsiyonut," in Haim Avni and Gideon Shimoni, eds., *Ha-tsiyonut u-mitnagdeihah ba-'am ha-yehudi*, Jerusalem: Ha-sifriyah Ha-tsiyonit, 1990, 125–46; Ya'akov Goldstein and Batsheva Stern, "PIKA – Irgunah u-mataroteihah," *Cathedra* 59, 1991, 102–26.

19 Compare Derek J. Penslar, *Zionism and Technocracy: The Engineering of Jewish Settlement in Palestine 1870–1918*, Bloomington, Ind.: Indiana University Press, 1991, 27–33; with Yoram Mayorek, "Emil Meyerson ve-reshit ha-me'uravut shel hevrat IKA be-Eretz Yisra'el," *Cathedra* 62, 1991, 67–79.

20 JCA Paris to James Rosenberg, 21 September 1923, AJDC AR21/32/104.

21 "Not the need, not the poverty of the Jewish people, are the impulsive force of Zionism, but the riches of the Jewish people accumulated in thousands of years. Instead of fleeing to the Jewish state out of need and misery, we want to go down to the pits of our inner life, to unearth the treasures which are concealed there in sufficient quantities to make us strong and powerful." The striving for a Jewish state is important, said Kahn, but if "it gets the upper hand in the Zionist movement . . . then it kills the soul of Zionism, or let me rather say, the soul of Judaism because Zionism in its pure form is the soul of Judaism." Archives of the Leo Baeck Institute (ALBI), New York, Bernard Kahn archive, Box No. 1.

22 For biographical information on Kahn, see the "Biographische Notizen" (typed ms., dated 1936) and Shalom Adler-Rudel's long obituary, in the June 10, 17, and 24, 1955, issues of *Allgemeine*, ALBI, Bernard Kahn Archive, Box No. 1; and the biographical sketch by Joseph van Gelder in AJDC AR21/32/50b.

23 That is, $8 million out of $74 million. Joseph Hyman to W.K. Wasserman, March 18, 1928, YIVO Archives, New York, RG 358/26.

24 David De Sola Pool to JDC Reconstruction Committee, March 22, 1922, AJDC AR21/32/297.

25 De Sola Pool to JDC Reconstruction Committee, September 19, 1921, AJDC AR21/32/297.

26 I document the links between the proletarian radicalism of the Second Aliyah *halutzim* and the bourgeois social-reformism of the WZO's settlement officers in *Zionism and Technocracy*, esp. ch. 4.

27 Derek J. Penslar, "The Origins of Modern Jewish Philanthropy," *Philanthropy in the World's Traditions*, Warren Ilchman, Stanley Katz, and Edward Queen II, eds., Bloomington, Ind.: Indiana University Press 1998, 197–214; *idem*, "Philanthropy, the 'Social Question,' and Jewish Identity in Imperial Germany," *Leo Baeck Institute Yearbook XXXVIII*, 1993, 51–73.

28 Cf. Kellner, *Le-ma'an Tsiyon*, ch. 3, esp. 88; Penslar, *Zionism and Technocracy*, 13–18.

29 The quote is from the *Israelitische Wochenschrift*, 1873, 278; cited in Jacob Toury, *Die politischen Orientierungen der Juden in Deutschland*, Tübingen: Mohr, 1966. For scholarly confirmation of this observation, see anke Richter, "Das jüdische Armenwesen in Hamburg in der 1. Hälfte des 19. Jahrhunderts," in eds. Peter Freimark and Arno *Die Hamburger Juden in der Emanzipationsphase (1780–1870)*, Herzig, Hamburg: H. Christian, 1990, 244; and the sources cited in Marie-Elisabeth Hilger, "Probleme jüdischer Industriearbeiter in Deutschland," in eds. Peter Freimark, Alice Jankowksi, and Ina Lorenz, *Juden in Deutschland. Emanzipation, Integration, Verfolgung und Vernichtung. 25 Jahre Institut für die Geschichte der deutschen Juden, Hamburg*, Hamburg: H. Cristians Verlag, 1991, 305.

30 There were some important exceptions. The situation at Brody in 1881 was so flammable that the Vienna Allianz's man on the scene suffered from nightmares that refugees burst into his bedroom and threatened him with bodily harm. In the United States, the Ward's Island revolt of October 1882 profoundly affected Emma Lazarus, whose subsequent writings on the Jewish refugees breathed a frigid Social Darwinism. Jacob Kellner, *Immigration and Social Policy: The Jewish Experience in the USA, 1881–82*, Jerusalem: Hebrew University, 1979, 2–3, 66–7.

31 This is a major theme in Rainer Liedtke, *Jewish Welfare in Hamburg and Manchester, c. 1850–1914*, Oxford, UK: Oxford University Press, 1995. See also Penslar, "Philanthropy, the 'Social Question,' and Jewish Identity in Imperial Germany."

32 Compare the *IAzW Jahresberichte* 1893; 1906, 17; 1910, 7; with Liedtke, *Jewish Welfare in Hamburg and Manchester*, ch. 6.

33 *IAzW Jahresbericht*, 1882, 98.

34 The phrase "selected human material" was used by Meyerson in a speech of 1898. Mayorek, "Emil Meyerson," 84.

35 Ruppin, so far as I know, never received a reply to his petition to the antisemitic politician Otto Böckel; Ford was not impressed by Rosenberg's gesture. Compare Allan Laine Kagedan's discussion of Rosenberg in *Soviet Zion: The Quest for a Russian Jewish Homeland*, New York: St. Martin's Press, 1994, 49–56; with my treatment of Ruppin in *Zionism and Technocracy*, 83–4.

36 According to George Mosse, before World War I the term "human material" had negative connotations because it appeared to "den[y] the human spirit." The term gained currency during the interwar period as a result of the "mechanization of all aspects of life." See George Mosse, *Fallen Soldiers*, New York: Oxford University Press, 1985, 179. The late Amos Funkenstein claimed that Zionist concepts of "human material" were offset by a romantic streak asserting human ineffability. Amos Funkenstein, "Zionism, Science, and History," *Perceptions of Jewish History*, Berkeley and Los Angeles: University of California Press, 1993, 347–50.

37 On Zionist concepts of the need for selective immigration, because of both the limited absorptive capacity of the region and the need to filter out asocial elements that could endanger the Jewish national project, see Margalit Shilo, "Tovat ha-aretz o-tovat ha-'am? Yahsah shel ha-tenua'h ha-tsiyonit le-'aliyah bitekufat ha-'aliyah ha-sheniyah," *Cathedra* 46, 1987, 109–22; Moshe Mossek, *Palestine Immigration Policy under Sir Herbert Samuel*, London: Frank Cass, 1978; Yehiam Weitz, *Muda'ut ve-hoser onim – Mapai le-nokhah ha-shoah 1943–45*, Jerusalem: Yad Ben-Zvi, 1994, ch. 5; Tom Segev, *The Seventh Million: The Israelis and the Holocaust*, New York: Hill and Wang, 1993, 113–22.

38 The history of the conferences held between 1869 and 1882 is narrated in detail in Jacob Kellner, "Philanthropy and Social Planning in Jewish Society (1842–

82)," Ph.D. dissertation, Hebrew University of Jerusalem, 1973. Details of post-1903 relief work may be found in the *IAzW Jahresberichte*, 1904, 7; 1906, 9–12.

39 *Le Baron Maurice de Hirsch et la Jewish Colonisation Association*, Paris: Jewish Colonization Association, 1936, 44–6.

40 Kurt Grunwald, *Türkenhirsch*, Jerusalem: Israel Program for Scientific Translations, 1969, 123, also 76–85. See also Shalom Adler-Rudel, "Moritz Baron Hirsch: Profile of a Great Philanthropist," *Leo Baeck Institute Year Book* VIII, 1963, 42–8.

41 See Chapter 8.

42 The issue of the commission of experts takes up most of the famous three-page memorandum to the Russian Choveve Tsiyon which Hirsch penned in August of 1891. The document is reproduced in Grunwald, *Türkenhirsch*, 123ff.

43 Born in Moscow, Rosen was exiled to Siberia at age seventeen for revolutionary activities. He escaped and reached Germany, where he attended the University of Heidelberg. In 1903 he immigrated to the United States, where he obtained a doctorate in agronomy, won fame as the discoverer of a new variety of winter rye, and established a career introducing American grains and fodder crops into Russia. In 1921 he joined the staff of the American Relief Administration in the USSR as the JDC's representative. See Rosen to a Miss Adlerstein, AJDC AR21/32/52a and the obituary press release in AJDC AR21/32/3188.

For examples of Rosen's effect on the leadership of the Joint and similar bodies, see American Relief Administration to James Rosenberg, 5 September 1922, AJDC AR21/32 52a; Felix Warburg's remarks at a June 17, 1924 JDC Executive Committee meeting, YIVO Archives, New York, RG 358/17; paeans to Rosen by Warburg, Bernard Lehman, and Rosenberg, dated between December 31, 1924 and March 25, 1925, in AJDC AR21/32 508; Felix Warburg's diary of his travels through the USSR, May 1927, typescript ms., AJDC AR21/32 534; and Hyman's account of his Russian journey, dated December 27, 1928, in the same file.

44 Yigal Elam, *Ha-sokhnut ha-yehudit: shanim rishonot*, Jerusalem: Ha-sifriya Ha-tsiyonit, 1990, 81–82, 91–92.

45 On the London Board of Jewish Guardians' inability to respond to the crush of petitions for assistance, see David Cesarani, *The Jewish Chronicle and Anglo-Jewry, 1841–1991*, Cambridge, UK: Cambridge University Press, 1994, 72; and Geoffrey Alderman, "English Jews or Jews of the English Persuasion? Reflections on the Emancipation of Anglo-Jewry," eds. Pierre Birnbaum and Ira Katznelson, *Paths of Emancipation: Jews, States, and Citizenship*, Princeton, N.J.: Princeton University Press, 1995, 141–3. For examples from German communities, compare the discussion of Memel in Jacob Kellner, *Reshito shel tikhnun hevrati klal-yehudi*, Jerusalem, 1974, 8–9, with the memorandum from the Darmstadt Verein zur Beschränkung des jüdischen Wanderbettlerei to the Deutsche Zentralstelle für jüdische Wanderarmenfürsorge, March 19, 1913, in the Hamburg Staatsarchiv, JG 483.

46 Kellner, *Reshito shel tikhnun hevrati klal-yehudi*, 16, 25.

47 Kellner, *Immigration and Social Policy*, 8–9.

48 *IAzW Jahresbericht*, 1880, 73–82; 1904, *passim.*; 1910, 5. Note also the changes in the style and content of the *Jahresberichte* of the Hilfsverein der deutschen Juden over the years 1902–6.

49 Hilfsverein der deutschen Juden, *Viertes Geschäftsbericht (1905)*, 1906, 13–49; *Zeitschrift für Demographie und Statistik der Juden III*, 4, April 1907, 60. A figure of 600,000 Jewish immigrants would account only for those who arrived in the United States over this period; smaller numbers went to Canada, South America, and Palestine. Most of the Jewish immigrants who crossed the Atlantic departed from German ports.

50 Between 1918 and 1933 the WZO expended $9,521,000 on agricultural settlement; this sum amounted to two-thirds of the budget for immigration, agricultural, and

urban settlement and almost one-third of the total WZO budget (excluding land purchase) over this period. Nachum Gross and Jacob Metzer, *Public Finance in the Jewish Economy in Interwar Palestine*, Jerusalem: Falk Institute for Economic Research, 1977, 52–3, 57. (Gross and Metzer's figures are given on an annual basis in Palestine pounds; I converted them to dollars using the exchange rates in R.L. Bildwell, *Currency Conversion Tables*, London: Rex Collings, 1970.)

51 The figure for Argentina, from the 1913 JCA annual report, is reproduced in Haim Avni, *Argentina and the Jews: A History of Jewish Immigration*, Tuscaloosa, Ala.: University of Alabama Press, 1991, 61.
52 Joseph Hyman to Felix Warburg *et al.*, May 13, 1925, AJDC AR21/32/508.
53 Bauer, *My Brother's Keeper*, 61–5.
54 Hyman to Warburg *et al.*, May 13, 1925, AJDC AR21/32/508; and Bernard Kahn, "My Trip to Russia," typewritten ms. in YIVO Archive, RG358/21, 6–7. When Felix Warburg visited the Agro-Joint colonies, he was very impressed by Tel Chai, mainly because it had nicely irrigated fields and its settlers spoke Hebrew rather than Yiddish, which, he wrote, is "not to my liking." Warburg's diary of his journey to the Soviet Union, entry dated May 15, 1927, AJDC AR21/32/534.
55 For the number of Agro-Joint employees, see Rosen to James Rosenberg, July 28, 1936, AJDCA AR21/32 510.
56 Elam, *Ha-sokhnut ha-yehudit*, 74.
57 Bauer, *My Brother's Keeper*, 61–5, 88.
58 Kahn to JDC New York, July 1, 1925, AJDC AR21/32/508.
59 Kagedan, *Soviet Zion*, 77–8, 80–3.
60 Bauer, *My Brother's Keeper*, 66–7, 81–6, 90–8.
61 Rosen to Hyman, February 7, 1939, AR21/32/52a.
62 Zecharias Frankel, "Die gegenwärtige Lage der Juden in Palästina," *Monatsschrift fur die Geschichte und Wissenschaft des Judenthums*, 3, 1854, 291.
63 The quotation is reproduced in Kellner, *Reshito shel tikhnun hevrati klal-yehudi*, 14; see also ibid., 1–2; and *idem*, *Le-ma'an Tsiyon*, 12–15; as well as Michael Graetz, *Les Juifs en France au XIXe siècle: De La Révolution française à l'Alliance Israélite Universelle*, Paris: Editions du Seuil, 1989, ch. 10.
64 Ludger Heid, "Melocho welo Zedoko: 'Arbeit, nicht Wohltätigkeit' für ostjüdische Proletarier im Ruhrgebiet," *Zedaka: Jüdische Sozialarbeit im Wandel der Zeit. 75 Jahre Zentralwohlfahrtsstelle in Deutschland 1917–92*, eds. Frank Kind and Esther Alexander-Ihme, Frankfurt am Main: Jüdisches Museum, 1992, 80. The importance of social welfare as a source of collective Jewish identity is a major theme in several of the essays in *In Search of Jewish Community: Collective Jewish Identities in Germany and Austria, 1918–1933*, Michael Brenner and Derek J. Penslar, eds., Bloomington, Ind.: Indiana University Press, 1998.

8 Technical expertise and the rural Yishuv

1 This definition follows the description of the term in Yehuda Slutsky, *Mavo le-toldot tnua't ha-'avodah ha-yisre'elit*, Tel Aviv: 'Am 'Oved, 1973, 231.
2 Such inclusive descriptions of technical expertise abound in the social-scientific literature on technocracy. See, for example, Langdon Winner, *Autonomous Technology*, Cambridge, Mass.: MIT Press, 1977; and Frank Fischer, *Technocracy and the Politics of Expertise*, Newbury Park, Calif.: Sage, 1990. A nice historical confirmation of this point comes from early twentieth-century German census data on civil service employees, in which "technically trained supervisory officials" were combined with "economists" in a single category. Verein zur Abwehr

des Antisemitismus, *Die wirtschaftliche Lage, soziale Gliederung, und die Kriminalstatistik der Juden*, Berlin, 1912, 25.

3 *Die wirtschaftliche Lage ... der Juden*, 6, 11, 19.

4 In 1925, 15.5 percent of Prussia's medical doctors were Jewish, but only 1.7 percent of its engineers, architects, and chemists. The sociologist Jacob Lestschinsky attributed this disparity directly to antisemitism in the civil service and in big business. Jacob Lestschinsky, *Das jüdische Volk im neuen Europa*, Prague: Jüdische Akademie Technischer Verbesserung "Barissia," 1934, 93–4.

5 Konrad Jarausch, *The Unfree Professions: German Lawyers, Teachers, and Engineers, 1900–1950*, New York: Oxford University Press, 1990, 218.

6 As with so many other aspects of European Jewish history, the German case has been studied more extensively than those of other countries. See, e.g., Ernest Hamburger, *Juden im öffentlichen Leben Deutschlands*, Tübingen: Mohr, 1968, 63–5; David Lawrence Preston, "Science, Society, and the German Jews, 1870–1933," Ph.D. diss., University of Illinois at Champagne-Urbana, 1971, 139; Shulamit Volkov, "Soziale Ursachen des jüdischen Erfolgs in der Wissenschaft," *Jüdisches Leben und Antisemitismus im 19. und 20. Jahrhundert*, Munich: Beck, 1991, 146–65; and Harold Pollins, "German Jews in British Industry," in Werner Mosse and Julius Carlebach, eds., *Second Chance: Two Centuries of German-Speaking Jews in the United Kingdom*, Tübingen: Mohr, 1991, 362–77.

7 Derek J. Penslar, "Philanthropy, the 'Social Question,' and Jewish Identity in Imperial Germany," *Leo Baeck Institute Yearbook XXXVIII*, 1993, 51–74; Jürgen Sielemann, "Eastern Jewish Migration via the Port of Hamburg, 1880–1914;" and "Records Regarding Emigrants in the Hamburg State Archives," typed mss., n.d., Hamburg Staatsarchiv.

8 *Thirty Years. The Story of the J.D.C.*, New York: American Jewish Joint Distribution Committee, 1945, 14. There is a similar description in Joseph Hyman, *Twenty Five Years of American Aid to Jews Overseas*, New York: American Jewish Joint Distribution Committee, 1939, 16. The JDC commanded impressive resources; between 1914 and 1925 its expenditures amounted to $46 million, whereas the WZO's expenditures for immigration, urban settlement, and rural colonization during the entire interwar period were only $25 million.

9 On the JCA's agricultural activities in interwar Europe, see Chapter 7.

10 This was particularly true during the Ottoman period. See D. Jonathan Penslar, "Hashpa'ot tsorfatiyot 'al hityashvut yehudit hakla'it be-erets yisra'el, 1870–1914," *Cathedra* 62, December 1991, 54–66.

11 On the tension within all forms of modern thought, including Zionism, between the materialistic conception of the individual as a meliorable *tabula rasa* and the romantic view of man as spontaneous essence, see Amos Funkenstein, "Zionism, Science and History," in *Perceptions of Jewish History*, Berkeley and Los Angeles: University of California Press, 1993, 347–50.

12 Yosef Gorny, "Utopian Elements in Zionist Thought," *Studies in Zionism* V, 1, 1984, 19–27.

13 Cf. Heinz Gollwitzer, *Europe in the Age of Imperialism, 1880–1914*, New York: Thames & Hudson, 1969; Daniel Headrick, *The Tools of Empire: Technology and European Imperialism in the Nineteenth Century*, New York: Oxford University Press, 1981; Fritz Stern, "Fritz Haber: The Scientist in Power and in Exile," *Dreams and Delusions: The Drama of German History*, New York: Knopf, 1987, 51–76.

14 Derek J. Penslar, *Zionism and Technocracy: The Engineering of Jewish Settlement in Palestine, 1870–1918*, Bloomington, Ind.: Indiana University Press, 1991, 60–8, 70.

15 Ibid., 101–2, 139, 142.

16 The Zionist Executive was divided between London and Jerusalem.

17 *Report of the Executive to the 13th Zionist Congress*, London, 1923, 34–6; Arthur Ruppin, "A Period of Crisis" (1927), *Building Israel: Selected Essays, 1907–1935*, New York: Schocken, 1949, 176–7; and *idem*, *Tagebücher, Briefe, Erinnerungen*, Königstein/Ts.: Jüdischer Verlag/Atheneum, 1985, entry for April 26, 1920, 314.

18 The members were Akiva Ettinger and Abraham Harzfeld of Ahdut ha-'Avodah, Yitzhak Wilkansky and Eliezer Joffe of Ha-Po'el Ha-Tsa'ir, Eliyahu Krause, the director of Mikveh Yisra'el and a longtime friend of the pioneer community, and Judah Raab and Aharon Eisenberg, who represented the capitalist moshavot.

19 I. Wilkansky (Elazar-Volcani), *The Communistic Settlements in the Jewish Colonization of Palestine*, Tel Aviv, 1927; reprint, Westport, Conn.: Hyperion, 1976, 11–12, 15.

20 Jacob Metzer, *Hon le'umi le-bayit le'umi, 1919–1921*, Jerusalem: Yad Ben-Zvi, 1979, 40–53; *idem*, "Economic Structures and National Goals: The Jewish National Home in Inter-war Palestine," *Journal of Economic History* XXXVIII, 1, December 1978, 101–19; Alon Gal, "Brandeis' Views on the Upbuilding of Palestine, 1914–23," *Studies in Zionism* 6, 1982, 211–40.

21 Alex Bein, *The Return to the Soil*, Jerusalem: World Zionist Organization, 1952, 273; Henry Near, *The Kibbutz Movement: A History, Volume I: Origins and Growth, 1909–1939*, London: Littman Library, 1992, 183, 389.

22 Ruppin, *Tagebücher*, entries for April 13, 1923, 348; December 31, 1928, 411; and December 31, 1931, 434–5.

23 Akiva Ettinger, *'Im hakla'im 'ivriyim be-artseinu*, Tel Aviv: 'Am 'Oved, 1945, 128–33. The quotation is from p. 133.

24 Nachum Gross, "Klitat 'olim akademayim bi-shenot ha-'esrim ve-ha-mehkar ha-hidrologi," *Ha-Tsionut* XII, 1987, 127–31; *idem*, "The Development of Agricultural Techniques in the Jewish Economy in Mandatory Palestine," in Harald Winkel and Klaus Herrmann, eds., *The Development of Agricultural Technology in the 19th and 20th Centuries/Die Entwicklung der Agrartechnik im 19. und 20. Jahrhundert*, Ostfildern: Scripta Mercaturae Verlag, 1984, 164.

25 See Shlomo Kaplansky's speech at the 14th Zionist Congress, *Stenographisches Protokoll der Verhandlungen des XIV. Zionisten Kongresses*, London, 1925, 100; and Kaplansky's letter to the Jewish National Fund of November 20, 1925, reproduced in Mendel Singer, *Shlomo Kaplansky: Hayyav u-fo'olo*, Jerusalem: Ha-sifriyah Ha-tsiyonit, 1971, II, 24. On Zemach's activities, see his memoirs, *Sipur Hayai*, Jerusalem: Devir, 1983, 135–6.

26 Gross, "The Development of Agricultural Techniques," 166. Indeed, even in the 1930s, when irrigation became technically and financially feasible, kibbutzim were slow to respond to the blandishments of citriculture; as one official of the Histadrut's Merkaz Hakla'i (Agricultural Center) explained, "No explanation or demand for agricultural planning can hush the clink of the shillings in the pocket of the orange-grower." Quoted in Near, *The Kibbutz Movement*, 180.

27 Gross, "The Development of Agricultural Techniques," 165–6.

28 Zemach, *Sipur Hayai*, 134.

29 Shaul Katz and Joseph Ben David, "Scientific Research and Agricultural Innovation in Israel," *Minerva* XIII, 2, 1975, 158.

30 For example, in 1923 the Experiment Station reported that it had experimented with what it called a "Chinese" method of growing wheat, wherein the grain is grown, like rice, in flooded fields. Although the report did not acknowledge as much, this technique had been first employed before World War I by agricultural laborers at Kinneret. Compare the *Report of the Executive to the 13th Zionist Congress*, 171, with Shaul Katz, *Aspektim sotsiologiyim shel tsemihat ha-yeda' (ve-tahalufato) be-hakla'ut be-Yisra'el: hofa'atan shel ma'arekhot huts-mada'iyot*

le-hafakat yeda' hakla'i, 1880–1940, Ph.D. dissertation, Jerusalem: Hebrew University, 1986, 163–7.

31 Shlomo Zemach, "Ha-hakla'ut u-tmuroteihah," in his essay collection *'Avoda ve-'adamah*, Jerusalem: World Zionist Organization/Reuven Mass, 1950, 107.

32 The formulation is from Magali Sarfatti Larson, "The Production of Expertise and the Constitution of Expert Power," in Thomas Haskell, ed., *The Authority of Experts: Studies in History and Theory*, Bloomington, Ind.: Indiana University Press, 1984, 67. Thus the Yishuv was quite different from the depoliticized public sphere envisioned throughout modern history by champions and opponents of technocracy alike. For historical and philosophical surveys of the anti-democratic element in technocratic speculation, see Winner, *Autonomous Technology*, 141–72; and Willem H. Vanderberg, "Political Imagination in a Technical Age," and Marie Fleming, "Technology and the Problem of Democratic Control: The Contribution of Jürgen Habermas," in Richard B. Day, Ronald Beiner, and Joseph Masciulli, eds., *Democratic Theory and Technological Society*, Armonk, N.Y.: M.E. Sharpe, 1988, 3–35, 90–109. Policy-oriented analyses include Larson, "The Production of Expertise"; and Jack DeSario and Stuart Langton, "Citizen Participation and Technocracy," in Jack DeSario and Stuart Langton, eds., *Citizen Participation in Public Decision Making*, New York: Greenwood, 1987, 3–17.

33 Wilkansky, *The Communistic Settlements in the Jewish Colonization of Palestine*, 59–93; *idem*, *The Transition from Primitive to Modern Agriculture in Palestine*, Tel Aviv: Hapoel Hazair, 1925, 25.

34 Wilkansky, *The Communistic Settlements in the Jewish Colonization of Palestine*, 102–8.

35 Katz and Ben David, "Scientific Research," 160–1.

36 Ruppin, *Tagebücher*, entry for March 27, 1926, 379.

37 Ettinger, *'Im hakla'im 'ivriyim be-artseinu*, 135–6, 141; Bein, *Return to the Soil*, 208, 251, 294–9, 317–25.

38 Bein, *Return to the Soil*, 352.

39 Cf. Kaplansky's speech at the 14th Zionist Congress, *Stenographisches Protokoll*, 95–112; his detailed report within the *Bericht des Landwirtschaftlichen Kolonisations-Department an den XV. Zionisten-Kongress*, 1927, 81–100; and Bein, *Return to the Soil*, 354. In the Hebrew version of Bein's work, Kaplansky is described as "an engineer, not an agronomist; his manner of thinking was cautious, systematic, and thorough, like a German professor." (*Toldot ha-hityashvut ha-tsionit*, Jerusalem: World Zionist Association, 1942, 310).

40 See, for example, Kaplansky's account of his visit of April 14, 1927, to the kvutzah at Yagur, reproduced in Singer, *Shlomo Kaplansky*, II, 25–6.

41 Bein, *Return to the Soil*, 303–6, 329.

42 See "Bericht der Landwirtschaftlichen Versuchsstationen der Zionistischen Organization," in *Bericht der Executive der Zionistischen Organization an den XVI. Zionisten-Kongress*, 1929; Zemach, "Ha-hakla'ut u-temuroteihah," in *'Aovdah ve-'adamah*, 107–9.

43 Singer, *Shlomo Kaplansky*, II, 20, 28; Bein, *Return to the Soil*, 355–61.

44 *Report of the Executive of the Zionist Organization Submitted to the XVIth Zionist Congress at Zurich, July 28 – August 7, 1929*, 231; *Bericht der Executive der Jewish Agency für Palästina an den Council der Agency zur II. Tagung, Basel, der 14. Juli 1931*, 113–16; *Bericht der Executive der Zionistischen Organization an den XVIII. Zionisten-Kongress*, 1933, 321.

45 Ettinger, *'Im hakla'im 'ivriyim be-artseinu*, 118–19; Bein, *Return to the Soil*, 389–91; 405–6.

46 Penslar, *Zionism and Technocracy*, 133–5, 153.

47 See Gal, "Brandeis' Views on the Upbuilding of Palestine," especially 229–30 and 234–5; and Ben Halpern, *A Clash of Heroes: Brandeis, Weizmann, and American*

Zionism, New York: Oxford University Press, 1987, 210–36. On American Progressive-era concepts of efficiency and scientific management, see William Akin, *Technocracy and the American Dream: The Technocratic Movement, 1900–1941*, Berkeley and Los Angeles: University of California Press, 1977.

48 Halpern, *A Clash of Heroes*, 260.

49 Weizmann to Max Warburg, December 2, 1929, and Weizmann to Felix Warburg, December 6, 1929, ed. Camillo Dresner, *The Letters and Papers of Chaim Weizmann*, Oxford, UK: Oxford University Press, 1978, XIV, 126–7, 148–55.

50 *Report of the Executive of the Zionist Organization to the Council of the Jewish Agency*, 1929, 58, 63–8; Henry Near, *Ha-Kibbutz ve-ha-hevrah: Ha-Kibbutz ha-Me'uhad, 1923–1933*, Jerusalem: Yad Ben-Zvi, 1984, 193–4; Abraham Rozenman, *Ha-Shamashim: Ruppin ve-Eshkol*, Jerusalem: World Zionist Organization, 1992, 122.

51 See Camillo Dressner's editorial comment in *The Letters and Papers of Chaim Weizmann*, XIV, 125n.

52 *Report of the Executive of the Zionist Organization to the Council of the Jewish Agency*, 85; Bein, *Return to the Soil*, 287.

53 Soskin had been a Zionist functionary between 1903 and 1906, when he collaborated with Otto Warburg on investigative and publicistic projects. Soskin left the WZO to work as an adviser in Germany's African colonies, but, upon his return to Europe after the war, Nehemia de Lieme, the director of the JNF's office in the Hague and a fiscal conservative, dismissed Kaplansky from his position as head of the JNF's Palestine Department, and put Soskin in his place. See De Lieme to Ussishkin, January 16, 1920, CZA A24/145/1(I); and the undated JNF notice about Soskin in CZA A121/103.

54 14th Zionist Congress, *Stenographisches Protokoll*, 113–36. The quotation is from pp. 131–2. See also Soskin's presentation at the 12th Zionist Congress, *Stenographisches Protokoll*, 1921, 342–51 and 420–1. Soskin's views are more fully developed in his book *Small Holding and Irrigation*, London: Allen and Unwin, 1920. Soskin went on to join the Revisionist movement, which he served as an agricultural theorist. Ya'akov Shavit, *Me-rov li-medinah*, Tel Aviv: Yariv, 1978, 145–7, 181–3.

55 Before World War I Dyk had been the manager of Merhavia, an experimental co-operative run according to the teachings of the utopian socialist economist Franz Oppenheimer. Despite its co-operative elements, Oppenheimer's system was a tutelary one featuring an expert administrator and a wage system tied to productivity. Dyk, an ardent disciple of Oppenheimer, got along badly with the workers at Merhavia, was dismissed from his position in 1914, and left Palestine for Germany. See the letters from Dyk to Oppenheimer from 1915 through 1919 in CZA, uncatalogued material; and Penslar, *Zionism and Technocracy*, 120–2.

56 See the *Report of the Experts Submitted to the Joint Palestine Survey Commission*, Boston, 1928.

57 See, e.g., Wilkansky's remarks at the 14th Zionist Congress, *Stenographisches Protokoll*, 413; Kaplansky's letter to Chaim Weizmann of September 30, 1928, excerpted in Singer, *Shlomo Kaplansky*, II, 21; Ruppin's comments at the nineteenth Zionist Congress, 1935, reprinted as "The Record of Twenty-Five Years," in *Building Israel*, 293–4; Bein, *Return to the Soil*, 261–3, 286–7, 370–1.

58 Wilkansky at the 14th Zionist Congress, *Stenographisches Protokoll*, 1925, 407–8.

59 *Bericht des Landwirtschaftlichen Kolonisations-Departments an den XV. Zionisten-Kongress*, 83–5.

60 See the series of entries in Ruppin's diary from March through July of 1928, *Tagebücher*, 398–405.

61 The same cannot be said of the agronomist Aaron Aaronsohn, a child of Zikhron Ya'akov and a luminary in the Zionist Yishuv. Aaronsohn was associated with the capitalist moshavot and was harshly critical of the workers' movement and

collective settlement. His untimely death in 1919 deprived the opponents of *hityashvut ovedet* of a powerful champion. See Eliezer Livneh, *Aaron Aaronsohn: Ha-ish u-zmano*, Tel Aviv: Mosad Bialik, 1969.

62 Weizmann to Salman Shocken, February 25, 1928, and Weizmann to Harry Sacher, March 1, 1928, in *The Letters and Papers of Chaim Weizmann*, XIII, 385–7, 391–4.

63 Weizmann to Oskar Wasserman, February 13, 1928, ibid., 366.

64 Compare Wilkansky, *The Communistic Settlements in the Jewish Colonization of Palestine*, 94–101, 134; with Eliezer Joffe, *Yesud Moshvei 'Ovdim*, Jaffa: Ha-Po'el Ha-Tsa'ir, 1919, 12–13, 31–2.

65 Anita Shapira, *Berl*, Tel Aviv: 'Am 'Oved, 1980, I, 281.

66 Although Ben-Gurion did not succeed, he did force Kaplansky out of the Ahdut ha-'Avodah leadership in 1929. Yonatan Shapiro, *The Formative Years of the Israeli Labour Party: The Organization of Power, 1919–1930*, London: Sage, 1976, 168–84; Shabtai Teveth, *Ben-Gurion: The Burning Ground 1886–1948*, Boston: Houghton Mifflin, 1987, 308–23, 361. Soon thereafter Kaplansky became the president of the Haifa Technion, and he supervised the JA Technical Department's work with agricultural machinery. *Bericht der Executive der Zionistischen Organization an den XIX. Kongress*, 1935, 359.

67 Shapira, *Berl*, I, 21; Shapiro, *Formative Years*, 138, 218–25.

68 Shimon Kushnir, *The Village Builder: A Biography of Abraham Harzfeld*, New York: Herzl Press, 1967, 299–303, 316–17.

69 Rozenman, *Ha-Shamashim*, 164–6.

70 Near, *The Kibbutz Movement*, 316.

71 This summary is based on Elhannan Orren, *Hityashvut bi-shenot ma'avak*, Jerusalem: Yad Ben-Zvi, 1978. See also Rozenman, *Ha-Shamashim*, 116, 168, 175–9.

72 Orren, *Hityashvut bi-shenot ma'avak*, 17–32, 65–75. On the cultural significance of Hanita, see Anita Shapira, *Land and Power: The Zionist Resort to Force, 1881–1948*, New York: Oxford University Press, 1992, 253–4.

73 On the plan, see Orren, *Hityashvut bi-shenot ma'avak*, 122–30. For evidence of Avidar's military bent from youth on, see his memoirs, *Ba-derekh le-Tsahal*, Tel Aviv: Ma'arakhot, 1970, 9.

74 Orren, *Hityashvut bi-shenot ma'avak*, 25, 27–8; Rozenmann, *Ha-Shamashim*, 135, 168–71.

75 Benny Morris, in "Yosef Weitz and the Transfer Committees, 1948–49," *Middle Eastern Studies* XXII, 4, October 1986, 522–61; and in *The Birth of the Palestinian Refugee Problem, 1947–49*, Cambridge, UK: Cambridge University Press, 1987, presents Weitz as a key figure behind the expulsion of Palestinians during the War of Independence. A similar claim is made by Nur Masalha in a work of questionable scholarship, *Expulsion of the Palestinians: The Concept of "Transfer" in Zionist Political Thought, 1882–1948*, Washington, D.C.: Institute for Palestine Studies, 1992. Morris's claims were challenged by Shabtai Teveth, "The Palestinian Arab Refugee Problem and Its Origins," *Middle Eastern Studies* XXVI, 2, April 1990, 214–49. In a rebuttal to Teveth's many criticisms of his work, Morris offered no substantive defense of his views on Weitz. Benny Morris, *1948 and After*, Oxford, UK: Oxford University Press, 1990, 27–34.

76 E.g. the words of Lenin: "Communist society, as you know, cannot be built unless we restore industry and agriculture, and that, not in the old way. They must be re-established on a modern basis, in accordance with the last word in science. You know that electricity is that basis, and that only after the electrification of the entire country, of all branches of industry and agriculture, only when you have achieved that aim, will you be able to build for yourselves the communist society which the older generation will not be able to build." "The

Tasks of the Youth Leagues," 1920, *Lenin: Selected Works*, Moscow: Progress Publishers, 1971, 607.

9 The continuity of subversion

1 Mary Douglas, "Jokes," 1975, reproduced in Chandra Mukerji and Michael Schudson, eds., *Rethinking Popular Culture: Contemporary Perspectives in Cultural Studies*, Berkeley and Los Angeles: University of California Press, 1991, 296–7.
2 Ibid., 295.
3 Ibid., 302.
4 For a concise analysis of Bakthin's approach to parody see Margaret A. Rose, *Parody: Ancient, Modern and Post-Modern*, Cambridge, UK: Cambridge University Press, 1993, 145–53. A good overview of the state of scholarly debate over parody may be found in Simon Dentith, *Parody*, London and New York: Routledge, 2000. Hutcheon's views, which are applied to the visual, plastic, and musical arts as well as literature, are expressed concisely in her *A Theory of Parody: The Teachings of Twentieth-Century Art Forms*, London: Methuen, 1985. The quotation is from p. 6.
5 David Roskies employs a similar distinction between what he calls "sanctioned" and "militant" parody in his article "Major Trends in Yiddish Parody," in the *Jewish Quarterly Review* 94, 1, 2004, 109–22.
6 Edward Portnoy discussed this Haggadah in his paper on satirical Yiddish haggadot in interwar Eastern Europe, delivered at the December, 2000, meeting of the Association for Jewish Studies. On serious parody as a genre, see Ziva Ben Porat, "Ideology, Genre, and Serious Parody," *Proceedings of the Ninth International Congress of the ICLA*, New York: Garland, 1982, 380–7.
7 Anita Shapira, "The Religious Motifs of the Labor Movement," in Shmuel Almog, Jehuda Reinharz, and Anita Shapira, eds., *Zionism and Religion*, Hanover, N.H.: Brandeis University Press, 1998, 265–9; Anna Shternshis, "Passover in the Soviet Union, 1917–41," *East European Jewish Affairs* 31, 1, 2001, 61–4.
8 "Parody, Hebrew," *Encyclopedia Judaica*, XIII, 129.
9 Dentith, *Parody*, 50.
10 Ibid., 52–3.
11 Hutcheon, *A Theory of Parody*, 16.
12 Yehuda Friedlander, *Be-misterei ha-satirah: Perakim ba-satirah ha-ivrit ha-hadashah ba-me'ot ha-yod-het ve-ha-yod-tet*, Jerusalem: Bar Ilan University, 1989, II, 113–39, esp. 122.
13 The classic works on Hebrew satire are Joseph Chotzner, *Hebrew Humour and Other Essays*, London: Luzac, 1905; *idem*, *Hebrew Satire*, London: K. Paul, Trench, Trübner, 1911; and Israel Davidson, *Parody in Jewish Literature*, New York: AMS Press, 1907, 58–77. For more recent insights on Perl, see Yehuda Friedlander, "The Struggle of the Mitnagedim and Maskilim against Hasidism: Rabbi Jacob Emden and Judah Leib Mises," and Immanuel Etkes, "Magic and Miracle Workers in the Literature of the *Haskalah*," in eds. Shmuel Feiner and David Sorkin, *New Perspectives on the Haskalah*, London and Portland, Ore.: Littman Library, 2001, 103–12 and 113–27.
14 Friedlander, *Be-misterei ha-satirah*, III, 1994, 160–1.
15 The edition I have used was printed in Vilna in 1878.
16 Isaac Meir Dick, *Masekhet 'Aniyut*, 10.
17 Ibid., 14.
18 Ibid., 18.
19 Ibid., 20.

20 Ibid., 22–4.
21 Sarah Abrevaya Stein, *Making Jews Modern: The Yiddish and Ladino Press in the Russian and Ottoman Empires*, Bloomington, Ind.: Indiana University Press, 2004, 90.
22 See note 6.
23 Dan Almagor, "Ha-turim she-kadmu la-'tur ha-shevi'i'," *Kesher* 17,1995, 98.
24 Yehuda Eloni, "The Immortal 'Schlemiel,'" *Kesher* 8, 1990, 94–102. See also the obituary for Gronemann in the Central Zionist Archives, Jerusalem (CZA), A135/69.
25 For the early history of Hebrew humor and satire in the Yishuv, see Almagor, "Ha-turim she-kadmu la-'tur ha-shevi'i'," 87–107; and Getzl Kressel, "Toldot sifrut ha-hitul be-eretz yisra'el," in ed. Getzl Kressel, *Otsar sifrut ha-humor ha-satirah ve-ha-karikaturah be-eretz yisra'el*, Tel Aviv: Mazkret, 1984, 113–17.
26 "Ha-Itonut ha-humoristit ha-ivrit," *Ha-Aretz*, March 6, 1931.
27 Kressel, *Otsar sifrut ha-humor*, 80.
28 *Masekhet Bava Tekhnika: 'im perush Rasi ve-tosafot be-yahad 'im Mahari Shif u-ferush avot (he-horim) de-R. Nathan ve-'im masoret ha-shas ve-hilufei girsa'ot ha-kol kemo she-nidpas bi-defus. vilna, amsterdam, frankfurt a.M.* (not the real cities of publication), n.d., dated by Kressel to 1913.
29 Ibid., 3–4.
30 Ibid., 12.
31 Ibid., 15.
32 Ibid., 19.
33 *Ha-Aretz*, March 3, 1931.
34 *Ve-'al kulam. Hoveret sifrutit humoristit u-metsuyeret le-rosh hashanah*, 1932, in CZA J/97.
35 *Ha-Darban*, Purim 1926, 8–10, CZA J/97.
36 *Haggadah Passfield Simpson Husseini. Mi-Mitsrayim Ve-'ad Henah*, Tel Aviv, 1931. Fisher Rare Book Library, University of Toronto.
37 From pp. 19–22 of the journal. In CZA J/97.
38 *Shfokh Hamatkhah: Hoveret le-fesah u-le-khol yemot ha-shanah*, Haifa, 1930, CZA J/97. For bibliographic information, see Kressel, *Otsar sifrut ha-humor*, 110.
39 *Ha-Aretz*, April 4, 1928.
40 *Ha-Gamal Ha-Me'ofef: Hagadah shel Pesah*, Tel Aviv: Satirikon, 1932, CZA J/97.
41 Dan Almagor, "Tura'im, tura'im rishonim ve-rabei tura'im ba-'itonut ha-ivrit," *Kesher* 19, 1996, 106–13; *idem*, "Ha-turim she-kadmu la-'tur ha-shevi'i'," 103, 105; *idem*, "Bibliyographiyah shel ha-tasa'm," *Kesher* 19, 1996, 114–30; Hanan Hever, "Shivhei 'amal u-folmus politi: reshit tsemihato shel ha-shir ha-politi be-eretz yisra'el: shmoneh pirkei mavo," in ed. Pinhas Ginosar, *Ha-sifrut ha-'ivrit u-tnua't ha-'avodah*, Beersheva: Ben-Gurion University Press, 1989.
42 David Roskies, "The Golden Peacock: The Art of Song," in *The Jewish Search for a Usable Past*, Bloomington and Indianapolis, Ind.: Indiana University Press, 1999, 89–119. The quotations are from pp. 118 and 119.
43 Elihu Katz and George Wedell, *Broadcasting in the Third World: Promise and Performance*, Cambridge, Mass.: Harvard University Press, 1977, 191–203.
44 Yaakova Sacerdoti, "Prophecy of Wrath: Israeli Society as Reflected in Satires for Children," in eds. Laura Zittrain Eisenberg and Neil Caplan, *Review Essays in Israel Studies: Books on Israel, Volume V*, Albany, N.Y.: State University of New York Press, 2000, 119–36.

10 Transmitting Jewish culture

1 Most effectively, but not solely, for example the sophisticated oral literature, including epics, romances, legal and ethical treatises, and chronicles, among non-literate peoples in contemporary Africa and the South Pacific. See Ruth

Finnegan, *Literacy and Orality: Studies in the Technology of Communication*, Oxford, UK: Blackwell, 1988.

2 Walter J. Ong, *Orality and Literacy: The Technologizing of the Word*, London and New York: Methuen, 1982, 136–7; Finnegan, *Literacy and Orality*, 69.

3 Jeffrey Shandler and Elihu Katz, "Broadcasting American Judaism," in ed. Jack Wertheimer, *Tradition Renewed: A History of the Jewish Theological Seminary of America*, New York: Jewish Theological Seminary, 1997, II, 363–402.

4 *Ha-galgal*, February 26, 1948.

5 These figures are cited in the first of a three-part radio program, aired in 1986, on the history of Hebrew radio broadcasting in Palestine over the period 1936–48. The program, *Otot u-Moftim*, was written and narrated by Eytan Almog, currently director of Kol Yisrael's Reshet Aleph and the author of a doctoral thesis in progress on the program's subject. I would like to thank Mr. Almog for his conversations with me and his assistance on a variety of points related to this section of the chapter.

6 Derek J. Penslar, "Radio and the Shaping of Modern Israel, 1936–73," in ed. Michael Berkowitz, *Zionism, Ethnicity, and National Mobilisation*, Leiden: Brill, 2004, 60–82.

7 *Otot u-Moftim*, first episode.

8 High Commissioner for Palestine to Sir Philip Cunliffe-Lister, Secretary of State for the Colonies, December 23, 1933; and the "Report of the Broadcasting Committee" attached to this letter, in Kew Public Record Office (PRO) CO733/266/7; see also Zevi Gil, "Mi-'Kol Yerushalayim' le-'Kol Yisrael'," *Emtsa'ei tikshoret hamoniyim be-Yisrael*, eds. Dan Caspi and Yehiel Limor, Tel Aviv: Open University, 1998, 237. This article was written in 1950.

9 Mordechai Avida, "Sheloshet ha-kolot," in ed. Yitzhak Tishler, *'Al 'itona'im ve-'itona'ut. 'Arbayim shanah le-agudat ha-'itona'im bi-Yerushalayim*, Jerusalem, 1976, 92.

10 Ismar Schorsch, "The Myth of Sephardi Supremacy," reproduced in *From Text to Context: The Turn to History in Modern Judaism*, Hanover, N.H.: University Press of New England, 1994, 71–92.

11 *Madrikh lashon la-radiyo u-la-televiziyah*, eds. Abba Bendavid and Hadassah Shai, Jerusalem: Reshut Hashidur, 1974, 9–11. The guidelines discussed in this section were promulgated in 1966 and were probably based on earlier practices.

12 *Toledot ha-yishuv ha-'ivri be-erets yisra'el me-az ha-'aliyah ha-rishonah. Beniyatah shel tarbut 'ivrit*, gen. ed. Moshe Lissak, vol. ed. Zohar Shavit, sec. author Rafael Nir, Jerusalem: Mosad Bialik, 1998, 119–22.

13 Ibid., 12–16.

14 "The Opening of the Palestine Broadcast Service," http://www.israelradio.org/history/pbs1.html.

15 Fragments of the program have survived and were included into *Otot u-Moftim*, first episode.

16 *Ha-galgal*, May 30, 1945.

17 Derek J. Penslar, "Broadcast Orientalism: Representations of Mizrahi Jewry in Israeli Radio, 1948–67," *Orientalism and the Jews*, eds. Ivan Kalmar and Derek Penslar, Hanover, N.H.: University Press of New England, 2004, 182–200.

18 Interview in *Otot u-Moftim*, first episode.

19 Douglas Boyd, "Hebrew-language Clandestine Radio Broadcasting during the British Palestine Mandate," article posted on http://www.israelradio.org/history/pal-clan.html.

20 *Otot u-Moftim*, second episode.

21 Arthur Wauchope, High Commissioner for Palestine, to W.G.A. Ormsby-Gore, Secretary of State for the Colonies, February 8, 1938, PRO CO/323/1588/2:

> it would probably be desirable ... to increase the time devoted to religious talks and readings from the Quran; but in Palestine there are reasons which I do not think it is necessary to explain in detail in this despatch, why this is not feasible. The whole question of broadcasting in this country is fraught, as you are aware, with special and peculiar difficulties which, it is to be supposed, would be less likely to be encountered in a broadcasting service organized solely or mainly for Moslem populations in racially homogeneous territories.

22 Interview with Yossi Rosen in *Otot u-Moftim*, second episode; see also the 1946 PBS broadcast schedule at http://www.israelradio.org/history/pbs1946.html.
23 Interview with Mordechai Avida in *Otot u-Moftim*, second episode.
24 There are a number of overviews of the history of Israeli radio broadcasting, though none employ archival sources. See Dan Caspi and Yehiel Limor, *The In/ Outsiders: Mass Media in Israel*, Creskill, N.J.: Hampton Press, 1999; Amit Schejter, "Media Policy as Social Regulatory Policy: The Role of Broadcasting in Shaping National Culture in Israel," Ph.D. diss., Rutgers University, 1995; and Tamar Liebes, "Performing a Dream and Its Dissolution: A Social History of Broadcasting in Israel," in *De-Westernizing Media Studies*, eds. James Curran and Myung-Jin Park, London: Routledge, 2000, 305–23. On the beginnings of Galei Tsahal, see Eliezer Shmueli, "Galei Tsahal ba-derekh le-ma'alah," in Tishler, *'Al 'itona'im ve-'itona'ut*, 133–4. For Galei Tsahal's history, see Raphael Mann and Tzippy Gon-Gross, *Galei Tsahal kol ha-zeman*, Tel Aviv: Ministry of Defense, 1991. An excellent overview history is provided by Yossi Beilin, "Ha-tadmit ha-tse'irah shel Galei Tsahal," *Davar*, September 22, 1975.
25 Israeli Knesset protocols (Hebrew): 1st Knesset, 220th sitting, VIII, January 30, 1951, 912–13; 2nd Knesset, 43rd sitting, X, January 16, 1952, 1006–10; 3rd Knesset, 621st sitting, XXVI, March 30, 1959, 1690–3.
26 Mustafa Kabha, "The Role of Middle Eastern Jews in Reconstructing Arabic Journalistic Discourse in Israel, 1948–67," paper presented at the annual meeting of the Association for Israel Studies, Vale, Colorado, May 27, 2002.
27 Personal communications from Esther Meir-Glitzenstein, June 11 and 30, 2002.
28 Penslar, "Broadcast Orientalism." The programs for Moroccan *olim* were cut altogether in 1961, just as another wave of immigrants began to arrive, and it took the intervention of a Moroccan-born member of the Knesset and Jewish Agency funding to reinstate the broadcasts.
29 Ubonrat Sirihuvasak, "Regulation Reform and the Question of Democratising the Broadcast Media in Thailand," paper presented at the International Conference on Democratization and the Media: Comparative Perspectives from Europe and Asia, Bellagio, Italy, April 8–12, 2001.
30 Undated set of guidelines for Ministry of Defense delegation to the United States to explore the introduction of television, arrival date stamped as December 15, 1952; H. Ben-David to Israeli Defense Force attaché in Washington, D.C., December 28, 1952; Shimon Peres to B. Shamir, December 30, 1952; Archive of the Israel Defense Force (AIDF), 540/55/42.
31 H.L. Gotliffe, "Israeli General Television," Ph.D. dissertation, Wayne State University, 1981, 68; Zvi Gil, *Beit ha-yahalomim. Sipur ha-televiziyah ha-yisre'e-lit*, Tel Aviv: Sifriat Ha-Po'alim, 1986, 22–30.
32 Tasha Oren, "Living Room Levantine: Immigration, Ethnicity and the Border in Early Israeli Television," *Velvet Light Trap* 44, 1999, 20–30.
33 Gil, *Beit ha-yahalomim*, 34–55; Elihu Katz, "Television Comes to the People of the Book," in David Horowitz, ed., *The Use and Abuse of Social Science*, New Brunswick, N.J.: Transaction, 1971, 249–71.

34 Protocol dated October 31, 1948, in Israel State Archive, Jerusalem (ISA), Archive of the Israel Broadcast Authority (Group 45g), 19/499/12.
35 Protocols dated July 28, 1952, ISA 2387/11g, 3; and June 15, 1953, ISA 2387/10g, 2–3.
36 Transcript in IDFA 540/55/8.
37 "Galei Tsahal: Shidurei tsva haganah le-Yisra'el," in IDFA 68/55/47.
38 *Ba-mahaneh*, September 28, 1950, 3; August 16, 1951, 4; October 1, 1951, 28–9. These dialogues may be placed within the framework of Yael Zerubavel's study of encounters between Jewish and Zionist heroes from times past and contemporary youth in Israeli children's literature. See Yael Zerubavel, "Masa' be-merhavei ha-zeman ve-ha-makom: sifrut agadit ke-makhshir le-'itsuv zikaron kibutsi," *Teyoriyah u-vikoret* 10, 1997, 69–80.
39 "Digest of Suggestions and Recommendations of the Council," dated January 1954, ISA 2387/10/g, 1–2.
40 "Roshei perakim le-diyun al ba'ayot ya-yesod shel sherut ha-shidur," 1949(?), ISA 6862/1; PCRA meeting of July 28, 1952, ISA 2387/11/g; Moshe Pearlman, director of Kol Yisrael, to L. Wallenborn, January 11, 1954, ISA 2387/9/g; "Halukat ha-shidurim lefi ha-matsav be-yom 1.12.57," ISA 6862/48; http://www.israelradio.org/history/1949.html.
41 *Ba-mahaneh*, October 1, 1951, 28–9; "Galatz be-mabat le-ahor," *Ha-Aretz*, October 3, 1980.
42 "Survey of Listening in Israel Carried out by the Institute for Applied Social Research at the Beginning of 1951," ISA 2387/11/g; PCRA meeting of February 11, 1952, ISA 2387/11/g; "Mah nishtanah be-Kol Yisrael," *Ma ariv*, April 18, 1952; PCRA meeting of December 22, 1953, ISA 2387/10/g; 1956 listeners' survey by the Institute for Practical Social Research, Jerusalem, manuscript dated April 1957, in ISA 6858/042/g; 1965 listeners' survey carried out by the Central Statistical Office of the Office of the Prime Minister, ISA 6858/0423/g.
43 See the 1956 and 1965 listeners' surveys cited in note 42. On *Three Men in a Boat*, see A. Dankner, *Dan Ben-Amotz: Biografiyah*, Jerusalem, 1992, 161–2, cited in Oz Almog, *The Sabra: The Creation of the New Jew*, Berkeley and Los Angeles: University of California Press, 2000, 12; and "A Brief History of Radio in the Country," http://www.israelradio.org/history.html. An anthology of material from the program was assembled by Yehuda Haezrahi and Yitzhak Shimoni, *Sheloshah be-sirah ahat*, Tel Aviv: Tsabar, 1956–7.
44 Listeners' survey of 1951, cited in note 35 (this survey intentionally reflected the ethnic distribution of the country as of May 1948); "Halukat ha-shidurim lefi ha-matsav be-yom 1.12.57" (see note 34); Knesset Protocol of July 27, 1959, XXVII, 2702–3; *Radiyo*, December 8, 1960, 10; February 2, 1961, 18, 20, 23; 1965 listeners' survey (see note 42).
45 Gila Flam, "Hishtakfut ha-mizrah ba-zemer ha-ivri," in ed. Mordechai Bar-On, *Etgar ha-ribonut: Yetsirah ve-hagut ba-asor ha-rishon la-medinah*, Jerusalem: Yad Ben-Zvi, 1999, 248–61. Contemporary *muzikah mizrahit* is also in many ways a western phenomenon, featuring western-style twelve- or sixteen-bar melodies, fixed rhythms, and chord patterns, though employing Middle Eastern instruments and nasalized, melismatic vocals. See Jeff Harper, Edwin Seroussi, and Pamela Squires-Kidron, "Musica Mizrahit: Ethnicity and Class Culture in Israel," *Popular Music* 8, 1989, 131–42; Amy Horowitz, "Musikah yam tikhonit yisre'elit (Israeli Mediterranean Music): Cultural Boundaries and Disputed Territories," Ph.D. diss., University of Pennsylvania, 1994.
46 On the Knesset opening fiasco, see the letter from Rita Prasitz, dated February 17, 1949, in ISA 500/4. On the Herzl ceremony, see the script for the program *Bein kirot hadero shel Herzl*, dated August 17, 1949, in ISA 500/1/g.

47 "Mi-alef ve-'ad elef: tokhnit le-siyum elef ha-geliyonot ha-rishonim shel yoman ha-hadashot, 1952–60," 1960, ed. Nakdimon Rogel, Harvard University, Widener Library, JCKY 613.
48 *Radiyo*, March 23, 1961, 13.
49 "Mi-alef ve-ad elef," ed. Rogel.
50 "Ha-adam," Harvard University, Widener Library, JCKY 819. On Trumpeldor's function as a Zionist cultural icon, see Yael Zerubavel, *Recovered Roots: Collective Memory and the Making of Israeli National Tradition*, Chicago: University of Chicago Press, 1995.
51 Michael Stanislawski, *Zionism and the Fin-de-Siecle*, Berkeley and Los Angeles: University of California Press, 2001.
52 PCRA meetings of March 17, 1952, and September 14, 1954, ISA 2387/10/g.
53 PCRA meetings of May 26, 1954, and June 22, 1954, in ISA 2387/11/g and 2387/10/g, respectively.
54 PCRA meetings of February 11, 1952, and March 17, 1952, ISA 2387/10/g and 2387/11/g.
55 1965 listeners' survey (see note 42), 21, 28, 31.
56 "100 elef lirot le-shiputz be-galei tsahal" (interview with Yitzhak Livni), *Ha-Aretz*, July 1, 1971. On the general development of Galei Tsahal, see Beilin, "Ha-tadmit ha-tse'irah shel galei tsahal."
57 Ron Kuzar, *Hebrew and Zionism: A Discourse Analytic Cultural Study*, Berlin: Mouton de Gruyter, 2001.
58 *Seker haazanah le-shidur shetei ha-yeshivot ha-rishonot shel mishpat Eichmann*, April 25, 1961, ISA 6863/405.
59 "Yurhavu shidurei ha-hadashot be-radio u-ve-galei tsahal," *Davar*, May 17, 1977.
60 On the segmentation of Israeli broadcasting, see Liebes, "Performing a Dream and Its Dissolution."
61 Jacques Derrida, *Of Grammatology*, corrected ed., trans. Gayatri Chakravorty Spivak, Baltimore, Md.: Johns Hopkins University Press, 1998, 10–11; emphasis in original.
62 Ibid., 17.
63 Roland Barthes, "The Grain of the Voice," in S. Firth and A. Goodwin, eds., *On Record: Rock, Pop and the Written Word*, New York: Routledge, 1990, 293–300.

Select Bibliography

This bibliography is limited to books, journal articles, book chapters, and unpublished doctoral theses. When a Hebrew book is available in English translation, the English version is listed.

Akin, William, *Technocracy and the American Dream: The Technocratic Movement, 1900–1941*, Berkeley and Los Angeles: University of California Press, 1977.

Almagor, Dan, "Ha-turim she-kadmu la-'tur ha-shevi'i',", *Kesher* 17, 1995, 87–107; 19, 1996, 114–30.

——"Tura'im, tura'im rishonim ve-rabei tura'im ba-'itonut ha-'ivrit," *Kesher* 19, 1996, 106–13.

——"Bibliyographiyah shel ha-tasa'm," *Kesher* 19, 1996, 114–30.

Almog, Oz, *The Sabra: The Creation of the New Jew*, Berkeley and Los Angeles: University of California Press, 2000.

Almog, Shmuel, Reinharz, Jehuda, and Shapira, Anita, eds., *Zionism and Religion*, Hanover, N.H.: Brandeis University Press, 1998.

Alroey, Gur, "Journey to Twentieth-Century Palestine as an Immigrant Experience," *Jewish Social Studies* IX, 2003, 28–64.

——*Imigrantim: ha-hagirah ha-yehudit le-Eretz Yisrael be-reshit ha-me'ah ha-esrim*, Jerusalem: Yad Ben-Zvi, 2004.

Alsberg, Paul, *Mediniyut ha-hanhalah ha-tsiyonit mi-moto shel Hertsl ve-ad milhemet ha-olam ha-rishonah*, Ph.D. diss., Jerusalem: Hebrew University of Jerusalem, 1958.

Anderson, Benedict, *The Spectre of Comparisons: Nationalism, Southeast Asia, and the World*, London: Verso, 1998.

Anidjar, Gil, *The Jew, the Arab. A History of the Enemy*, Stanford, Calif.: Stanford University Press, 2003.

Arad, Gulie Neeman, ed., *Israeli Historiography Revisited*. Special issue of *History & Memory* 7, 1995.

——"The Shoah as Israel's Political Trope," in Deborah Dash Moore and S. Ilan Troen, eds., *Divergent Jewish Cultures: Israel & America*, New Haven, Conn.: Yale University Press, 2001, 192–216.

Avi Chai Foundation/Israeli Democracy Institute, *A Portrait of Israeli Jewry: Beliefs, Observances and Values Among Israeli Jews*, Jerusalem: Avi Chai Foundation/ Israeli Democracy Institute, 2002.

Avneri, Arieh L., *The Claim of Dispossession: Jewish Land-Settlement and the Arabs, 1878–1948*, New Brunswick, N.J.: Transaction, 1984.

Avni, Haim, "Hevrat IKA ve-ha-tsiyonut," in Haim Avni and Gideon Shimoni, eds., *Ha-tsiyonut u-mitnagdeihah ba-'am ha-yehudi*, Jerusalem: Ha-sifriyah Ha-tsiyonit, 1990, 125–46.

——*Argentina and the Jews: A History of Jewish Immigration*, Tuscaloosa, Ala.: University of Alabama Press, 1991.

Baldwin, Peter, ed., *Reworking the Past: Hitler, the Holocaust, and the Historians' Debate*, Boston: Beacon Press, 1988.

Barnett, Michael N., "Israel in the World Economy: Israel as an East Asian State?," in Michael N. Barnett, ed., *Israel in Comparative Perspective: Challenging the Conventional Wisdom*, Albany, N.Y.: State University of New York Press, 1996, 107–40.

Bar-On, Mordechai, *The Gates of Gaza. Israel's Road to Suez and Back, 1955–1957*, New York: St. Martin's Press, 1994.

Bartal, Israel, *Galut ba-aretz. Yishuv eretz-yisra'el be-terem tsiyonut*, Jerusalem: Ha-sifriyah ha-tsiyonit, 1994.

Barthes, Roland, "The Grain of the Voice," in S. Firth and A. Goodwin, eds., *On Record: Rock, Pop and the Written Word*, New York: Routledge, 1990, 293–300.

Bartram, David, "Foreign Workers in Israel: History and Theory," *International Migration Review* 32, 2, 1998, 303–25.

Bauer, Yehuda, *My Brother's Keeper. A History of the American Jewish Joint Distribution Committee*, Philadephia: Jewish Publication Society, 1974.

Be'eri, Eliezer, *Reshit ha-sikhsukh Yisra'el-'Arav 1882–1911*, Tel Aviv: Sifriyat Po'alim, 1985.

——"The Jewish–Arab Conflict during the Herzl Years," *Jerusalem Quarterly* 41, 1987, 3–18.

Bein, Alex, *The Return to the Soil*, Jerusalem: World Zionist Organization, 1952.

——*Theodore Herzl: A Biography of the Founder of Modern Zionism*, New York: Atheneum, 1970.

Bendavid, Abba and Shai, Hadassah, eds., *Madrikh lashon la-radiyo u-la-televiziyah*, Jerusalem: Reshut Hashidur, 1974.

Ben-Eliezer, Uri, *The Origins of Israeli Militarism*, Bloomington, and Indianapolis: Indiana University Press, 1998.

Ben Porat, Ziva, "Ideology, Genre, and Serious Parody," *Proceedings of the Ninth International Congress of the ICLA*, New York: Garland, 1982, 380–7.

Berger, Stefan, "Comparative History," in Stefan Berger, Heiko Feldner, and Kevin Passmore, eds., *Writing History: Theory and Practice*, London: Hodder Arnold, 2003, 61–79.

Berkowitz, Michael, *Zionist Culture and West European Jewry before the First World War*, Cambridge, UK: Cambridge University Press, 1993.

——*Western Jewry and the Zionist Project, 1914–1933*, Cambridge, UK: Cambridge University Press, 1997.

Berman, Paul, *Terror and Liberalism*, New York: Norton, 2003.

Bernanos, Georges, *La Grande Peur des bien-pensants, Edouard Drumont*, Paris: B. Grasset, 1931.

Bernstein, Deborah, *The Struggle for Equality: Urban Women Workers in Prestate Israeli Society*, New York: Praeger, 1987.

——*Pioneers and Homemakers: Jewish Women in Pre-State Israel*, Albany, N.Y.: State University of New York Press, 1992.

——*Constructing Boundaries: Jewish and Arab Workers in Mandatory Palestine*, Albany, N.Y.: State University of New York Press, 2000.

Biagini, Furio, *Mussolini e il sionismo*, Milan: M&B, 1998.

Birnbaum, Pierre, *Anti-Semitism in France*, London: Blackwell, 1992.

Birnbaum, Pierre and Katznelson, Ira, eds., *Paths of Emancipation: Jews, States, and Citizenship*, Princeton, N.J.: Princeton University Press, 1995.

Böhm, Adolf, *Die Zionistische Bewegung*, Berlin: Jüdischer Verlag, 1935.

Boyarin, Daniel, *Unheroic Conduct: The Rise of Heterosexuality and the Invention of the Jewish Man*, Berkeley and Los Angeles: University of California Press, 1997.

——"Zionism, Gender and Mimicry," in Fawzia Afzal-Khan and Kalpana Seshadri-Crooks, eds., *The Pre-Occupation of Postcolonial Studies*, Durham, N.C., and London: Duke University Press, 2000, 234–65.

Boyce, George and O'Day, Alan, eds., *The Making of Modern Irish History: Revisionism and the Revisionist Controversy*, London and New York: Routledge, 1996.

Brenner, Michael, *The Jewish Renaissance in Weimar Germany*, New Haven, Conn.: Yale University Press, 1994.

——*Zionism: A Brief History*, Princeton, N.J.: Markus Wiener, 2003.

Brenner, Michael and Penslar, Derek J., eds., *In Search of Jewish Community: Collective Jewish Identities in Germany and Austria, 1918–1933*, Bloomington and Indianapolis; Indiana University Press, 1998.

Brenner, Rachel Feldhay, *Inextricably Bonded: Israeli Arab and Jewish Writers Revisioning Culture*, Madison, Wisc.: University of Wisconsin Press, 2003.

Brinker, Menachem, "The End of Zionism? Thoughts on the Wages of Success," in Carol Diament, ed., *Zionism: The Sequel*, New York: Hadassah, 1998, 293–9.

Bronner, Stephen Erich, *A Rumor about the Jews: Reflections on Antisemitism and the Protocols of the Learned Elders of Zion*, New York: St. Martin's Press, 2000.

Brubaker, Rogers, *Nationalism Reframed: Nationhood and the National Question in the New Europe*, New York: Cambridge University Press, 1996.

Caspi, Dan and Limor, Yehiel, *The In/Outsiders: Mass Media in Israel*, Creskill, N.J.: Hampton Press, 1999.

Cesarani, David, *The Jewish Chronicle and Anglo-Jewry, 1841–1991*, Cambridge, UK: Cambridge University Press, 1994.

Chakrabarty, Dipesh, *Provincializing Europe: Postcolonial Thought and Historical Difference*, Princeton, N.J.: Princeton University Press, 2000.

Chamberlain, Houston Stewart, *Foundations of the Nineteenth Century*, New York: H. Fertig, 1968.

Chatterjee, Partha, *The Nation and its Fragments: Colonial and Postcolonial Histories*, Princeton, N.J.: Princeton University Press, 1993.

Chotzner, Joseph, *Hebrew Humour and Other Essays*, London: Luzac, 1905.

——*Hebrew Satire*, London: K. Paul, Trench, Trübner, 1911.

Cohen, Mark, *Under Crescent and Cross: The Jews in the Middle Ages*, Princeton, N.J.: Princeton University Press, 1994.

Cohen, Mitchell, *Zion and State: Nation, Class and the Shaping of Modern Israel*, New York: Columbia University Press, 1987.

——"A Preface to the Study of Jewish Nationalism," *Jewish Social Studies* 1 (n.s.), 1, 1994, 73–93.

Cohn, Norman, *Warrant for Genocide: The Myth of the Jewish World Conspiracy and the Protocols of the Elders of Zion*, New York: Harper & Row, 1967.

Davidson, Israel, *Parody in Jewish Literature*, New York: AMS Press, 1907.

DellaPergola, Sergio, "Jewish Women in Transition: A Comparative Socio-demographic Perspective," *Studies in Contemporary Jewry* XVI, 2000, 209–42.

Dentith, Simon, *Parody*, London and New York: Routledge, 2000.
Derrida, Jacques, *Of Grammatology*, corrected edn., trans. Gayatri Chakravorty Spivak, Baltimore, Md.: Johns Hopkins University Press, 1998.
DeSario, Jack and Langton, Stuart, eds., *Citizen Participation in Public Decision Making*, New York: Greenwood, 1987.
Diamond, James, *Homeland or Holy Land?*, Bloomington, Ind.: Indiana University Press, 1986.
Dick, Isaac Meir, *Masekhet 'Aniyut min Talmud Rash 'Alma*, Vilna, 1878.
Dothan, Shmuel, *A Land in the Balance*, Tel Aviv: Ministry of Defense, 1993.
Dowty, Alan, *The Jewish State: A Century Later*, Berkeley and Los Angeles: University of California Press, 1998.
Dresner, Camillo, ed., *The Letters and Papers of Chaim Weizmann*, Oxford, UK: Oxford University Press, 1978.
Dühring, Eugen, *Die Judenfrage als Frage der Rassenschädlichkeit für Existenz, Sitte und Cultur der Völker*, 4th edn., Berlin: H. Reuther, 1892.
Eisenstadt, Shmuel, *The Transformation of Israeli Society: An Essay in Interpretation*, London: Weidenfeld and Nicolson, 1985.
Elam, Yigal, *Ha-sokhnut ha-yehudit: shanim rishonot*, Jerusalem: Ha-sifriya Hatsiyonit, 1990.
Elazar, Daniel, ed., *Kinship and Consent: The Jewish Political Tradition and Its Contemporary Uses*, Philadelphia: Turtledove, 1981.
——*The Jewish Polity*, Bloomington, Ind.: Indiana University Press, 1985.
Eley, Geoff and Retallack, James, eds., *Wilhelminism and Its Legacies: German Modernities, Imperialism, and the Meanings of Reform, 1890–1930: Essays for Hartmut Pogge Von Strandmann*, New York: Berghahn, 2003.
Elon, Amos, *Herzl*, New York: Holt, Rinehart and Winston, 1975.
Eloni, Yehuda, "The Immortal 'Schlemiel,'" *Kesher*, 8, 1990, 94–102.
Etkes, Immanuel, "Magic and Miracle Workers in the Literature of the *Haskalah*," in Shmuel Feiner and David Sorkin, eds., *New Perspectives on the Haskalah*, London and Portland, Oreg.: Litman Library, 2001, 113–27.
Ettinger, Akiva, *'Im hakla'im 'ivriyim be-artseinu*, Tel Aviv: 'Am 'Oved, 1945.
Ezrahi, Elan, "The Quest for Spirituality among Secular Israelis," in Uzi Rebhun and Chaim I. Waxman, eds., *Jews in Israel: Contemporary Social and Cultural Factors*, Hanover, N.H.: University Press of New England, 2004, 315–28.
Ezrahi, Sidra DeKoven, "The Future of the Holocaust: Storytelling, Oppression and Identity. See under: 'Apocalypse,'" *Judaism* 51, 1, 2002, 61–70.
Feder, Ernst, *Politik und Humanität: Paul Nathan, Ein Lebensbild*, Berlin: Deutsche Verlagsgesellschaft für Politik und Geschichte, 1929.
Finnegan, Ruth, *Literacy and Orality: Studies in the Technology of Communication*, Oxford, UK: Blackwell, 1988.
Fischer, Frank, *Technocracy and the Politics of Expertise*, Newbury Park, Calif.: Sage, 1990.
Fischer, Fritz, *Germany's War Aims in the First World War*, New York: Chatto & Windus, 1967.
Flam, Gila, "Hishtakfut ha-mizrah ba-zemer ha-ivri," in Mordechai Bar-On, ed., *Etgar ha-ribonut: Yetsirah ve-hagut ba-asor ha-rishon la-medinah*, Jerusalem: Yad Ben-Zvi, 1999, 248–61.
Fleming, Marie, "Technology and the Problem of Democratic Control: The Contribution of Jürgen Habermas," in Richard B. Day, Ronald Beiner, and Joseph

Masciulli, eds., *Democratic Theory and Technological Society*, Armonk, N.Y.: M.E. Sharpe, Inc., 1988, 90–109.

Fletcher, Yael Simpson, "'Irresistible Seductions': Gendered Representations of Colonial Algeria around 1930," in Julia Clancy-Smith and Frances Gouda, eds., *Domesticating the Empire: Race, Gender and Family Life in French and Dutch Colonialism*, Charlottesville, Va., and London: University of Virginia Press, 1998, 193–210.

Frankel, Jonathan, *Prophecy and Politics: Socialism, Nationalism, and the Russian Jews, 1862–1917*, New York: Cambridge University Press, 1981.

Freimark, Peter, Jankowksi, Alice, and Lorenz, Ina, eds., *Juden in Deutschland. Emanzipation, Integration, Verfolgung und Vernichtung. 25 Jahre Institut für die Geschichte der deutschen Juden, Hamburg*, Hamburg: H. Christians, 1991.

Friedlander, Yehuda, *Be-misterei ha-satirah: Perakim ba-satirah ha-ivrit ha-hadashah ba-me'ot ha-yod-het ve-ha-yod-tet*, Jerusalem: Bar Ilan University, 1989.

——"The Struggle of the Mitnagedim and Maskilim against Hasidism: Rabbi Jacob Emden and Judah Leib Mises," in Shmuel Feiner and David Sorkin, eds., *New Perspectives on the Haskalah*, London and Portland, Oreg.: Litman Library, 2001, 103–12.

Friedman, Menachem, *Hevrah ve-dat:Ha-ortodoksiah ha-lo tsionit be-eretz yisra'el 1918–1936*, Jerusalem: Yad Ben-Zvi, 1977.

Friedmann, Adolf, *Das Leben Theodor Herzls*, Berlin: Jüdischer Verlag, 1914.

Fritsch, Theodor, *Handbuch der Judenfrage*, 36th edn., Leipzig: Hammer-Verlag, 1934.

Funkenstein, Amos, *Perceptions of Jewish History*, Berkeley and Los Angeles: University of California Press, 1993.

Gal, Alon, "Brandeis' Views on the Upbuilding of Palestine, 1914–23," *Studies in Zionism*, 6, 1982, 211–40.

Gil, Zvi, *Beit ha-yahalomim. Sipur ha-televiziyah ha-yisre'elit*, Tel Aviv: Sifriat Ha-Po'alim, 1986.

——"Mi-'kol yerushalayim' le-'kol yisra'el'," in Dan Caspi and Yehiel Limor, eds., *Emtsa'ei tikshoret hamoniyim be-Yisrael*, Tel Aviv: Open University, 1998, 235–50.

Giladi, Dan, *Ha-yishuv bi-tekufat ha-aliyah ha-revi'it (1924–1929)*, Tel Aviv: 'Am 'Oved, 1973.

Golani, Motti, *Israel in Search of a War: the Sinai Campaign, 1955–1956*, Brighton, UK: Sussex Academic Press, 1998.

——*Milhemot lo korot me-'atsman: 'al zikaron, koah u-vehirah*, Moshav Ben Shemen: Modan, 2002.

Goldstein, Ya'akov and Stern, Batsheva, "PIKA – Irgunah u-mataroteihah," *Cathedra* 59, 1991, 102–26.

Gollwitzer, Heinz, *Europe in the Age of Imperialism, 1880–1914*, New York: Thames & Hudson, 1969.

Gorny, Yosef, *Ahdut ha-Avodah: ha-yesodot ha-ra'yoniyim ve-ha-shita ha-medinit*, Tel Aviv: Ha-kibbbutz Ha-me'uhad, 1973.

——"Utopian Elements in Zionist Thought," *Studies in Zionism* V, 1, 1984, 19–27.

——*Zionism and the Arabs, 1882–1948: A Study of Ideology*, Oxford, UK: Oxford University Press, 1987.

——*Bein aushvitz liyerushalayim*, Tel Aviv: 'Am 'Oved, 1998.

Gotliffe, H. L., "Israeli General Television," Ph.D. diss., Wayne State University, 1981.

Graetz, Michael, *Les Juifs en France au XIXe siècle: De la révolution française à l'Alliance Israélite Universelle*, Paris: Editions du Seuil, 1989.
Greenfeld, Liah, *Nationalism: Five Roads to Modernity*, Cambridge, Mass.: Harvard University Press, 1992.
Gross, Nachum, "The Development of Agricultural Techniques in the Jewish Economy in Mandatory Palestine," in Harald Winkel and Klaus Hermann, eds., *The Development of Agricultural Technology in the 19th and 20th Centuries*, St. Katarinen: Scripta Mercaturae, 1984, 157–68.
——"Entrepreneurship of Religious and Ethnic Minorities," in Werner E. Mosse and Hans Pohl, eds., *Jüdische Unternehmer in Deutschland im 19. u. 20. Jahrhundert*, Stuttgart: F. Steiner, 1992, 11–23.
——*Lo 'al ha-ruah levadah:'iyunim ba-historiyah ha-kalkalit shel eretz-yisra'el ba-'et ha-hadashah*, Jerusalem: Magnes and Yad Ben-Zvi, 1999.
Gross, Nachum and Metzer, Jacob, *Public Finance in the Jewish Economy in Interwar Palestine*, Jerusalem: Falk Institute for Economic Research, 1977.
Grunwald, Kurt, *Türkenhirsch*, Jerusalem: Israel Program for Scientific Translations, 1969.
Gutwein, Daniel, "The Imagined Critique: Left and Right Post-Zionism and the Privatization of Israeli Collective Memory," *Journal of Israeli History* 20, 2/3, 2001, 9–42.
Habermas, Jürgen, *The Structural Transformation of the Public Sphere*, Cambridge, Mass.: MIT Press, 1991.
Hacohen, Devorah, *Immigrants in Turmoil: Mass Immigration to Israel and Its Repercussions in the 1950s and After*, Syracuse, N.Y.: Syracuse University Press, 2003.
Hadari-Ramage, Yonah, *Mashiah rakhuv 'al tank. Ha-mahshavah ha-tsiburit be-yisra'el bein mivtsa Sinai le-milhemet yom ha-kippurim 1955–75*, Jerusalem: Hartman Institute; Ramat Gan: Bar-Ilan University Press; Tel Aviv: Ha-kibbutz ha-me'uhad, 2002.
Haezrahi, Yehuda and Shimoni, Yitzhak, *Sheloshah be-sirah ahat*, Tel Aviv: Tsabar, 1956.
Halamish, Aviva, "'Aliyah lefi yikholet ha-kelitah ha-kalkalit: Ha-'ikaronot ha-manhim, darkhei ha-bitsua' ve-ha-hashlakhot ha-demografiyot shel mediniyut ha-'aliyah bein milhemot ha-'olam," in Avi Bareli and Nahum Karlinsky, eds., *Kalkalah ve-hevrah biyemei ha-mandat, 1918–1948*, Sede Boker: Midreshet Ben-Gurion, 2003, 179–216.
Halpern, Ben, *The Idea of the Jewish State*, Cambridge, Mass.: Harvard University Press, 1961.
——*A Clash of Heroes: Brandeis, Weizmann, and American Zionism*, New York: Oxford University Press, 1987.
Halpern, Ben and Reinharz, Jehuda, *Zionism and the Creation of a New Society*, New York: Oxford University Press, 1998.
Hamburger, Ernest, *Juden im öffentlichen Leben Deutschlands*, Tübingen: Mohr, 1968.
Handler, Andrew, *An Early Blueprint for Zionism: Gyöznö Istóczy's Political Antisemitism*, Boulder, Col.: Greenwood, 1989.
Harkabi, Yehoshafat, *Arab Attitudes to Israel*, Jerusalem: Israel Universities Press, 1972.
——"On Arab Antisemitism Once More," in Shmuel Almog, ed., *Antisemitism through the Ages*, Oxford, UK: Pergamon, 1988, 227–40.

Harper, Jeff, Seroussi, Edwin, and Squires-Kidron, Pamela, "Musica Mizrahit: Ethnicity and Class Culture in Israel," *Popular Music* 8, 1989, 131–42.

Harshav, Benjamin, *Language in Time of Revolution*, Berkeley and Los Angeles: University of California Press, 1993.

Headrick, Daniel, *The Tools of Empire: Technology and European Imperialism in the Nineteenth Century*, New York: Oxford University Press, 1981.

Heller, Joseph, "The End of Myth: Historians and the Yishuv (1918–48)," *Studies in Contemporary Jewry* 10, 1994, 112–38.

——*The Stern Gang: Ideology, Politics and Terror, 1940–1949*, London: Frank Cass, 1995.

——*The Birth of Israel, 1945–1949: Ben-Gurion and His Critics*, Gainesville, Fl.: University of Florida Press, 2000.

Helman, Anat, "East or West? Tel Aviv in the 1920s and 1930s," *People of the City: Jews and the Urban Challenge*," *Studies in Contemporary Jewry XV*, 1999, 68–79.

——"European Jews in the Levant Heat: Climate and Culture in 1920s and 1930s Tel-Aviv," *Journal of Israeli History* 22, 1, 2003, 71–90.

——"Hues of Adjustment: *Landsmanshaftn* in Inter-War New York and Tel Aviv," *Jewish History* XX, 1, 2006, 41–67.

Herlitz, Georg, *Das Jahr der Zionisten*, Jerusalem and Luzern: Ullmann, 1949.

Hertzberg, Arthur, *The Zionist Idea*, New York: Atheneum, 1959.

Herzl, Theodor, *Der Judenstaat*, 8th edn., Berlin: Jüdischer Verlag, 1920.

——*Complete Diaries*, ed. Raphael Patai, trans. Harry Zohn, New York: Herzl Press, 1960.

Heschel, Susannah, *Abraham Geiger and the Jewish Jesus*, Chicago: University of Chicago Press, 1998.

Hever, Hanan, "Shivhei 'amal u-folmus politi: reshit tsemihato shel ha-shir ha-politi be-eretz yisra'el: shmoneh pirkei mavo," in Pinhas Ginosar, ed., *Ha-sifrut ha-'ivrit u-tnua't ha-'avodah*, Beersheva: Ben-Gurion University Press, 1989, 116–57.

Horowitz, Amy, "Musikah yam tikhonit yisre'elit (Israeli Mediterranean Music): Cultural Boundaries and Disputed Territories," Ph.D. diss., University of Pennsylvania, 1994.

Horowitz, Dan and Lissak, Moshe, *Origins of the Israeli Polity: Palestine under the Mandate*, Chicago: University of Chicago Press, 1978.

Hutcheon, Linda, *A Theory of Parody: The Teachings of Twentieth-Century Art Forms*, London: Methuen, 1985.

Hyman, Joseph, *Twenty Five Years of American Aid to Jews Overseas*, New York: Joint Distribution Committee, 1939.

Hyman, Paula, *From Dreyfus to Vichy:The Remaking of French Jewry, 1906–1939*, New York: Columbia University Press, 1979

——*Gender and Assimilation in Modern Jewish History*, Seattle, Wa., and London: University of Washington Press, 1995.

Jarausch, Konrad, *The Unfree Professions: German Lawyers, Teachers, and Engineers, 1900–1950*, New York: Oxford University Press, 1990.

Jarausch, Konrad and Geyer, Michael, *Shattered Past: Reconstructing German Histories*, Princeton, N.J.: Princeton University Press, 2003.

Jewish Colonization Association, *Le Baron Maurice de Hirsch et la Jewish Colonisation Association*, Paris: Jewish Colonization Association, 1936.

Joffe, Eliezer, *Yesud moshvei 'ovdim*, Jaffa: Ha-Po'el Ha-Tsa'ir, 1919.

Joint Distribution Committee, *Thirty Years. The Story of the J.D.C.*, New York: Joint Distribution Committee, 1945.

Kabha, Mustafa, "Tafkidah shel ha-'itonut ha-'aravit-ha-falastinit be-irgun ha-shevitah ha-falastinit ha-kelalit, april-oktober 1936," *Iyunim bi-tekumat yisra'el* 11, 2001, 212–29.

Kagedan, Allan Laine, *Soviet Zion: The Quest for a Russian Jewish Homeland*, New York: St. Martin's Press, 1994.

Kaniel, Yehoshua, *Hemshekh u-temurah: ha-yishuv ha-yashan ve-ha-yishuv he-hadash bi-tekufat ha-'aliyah ha-rishonah ve-ha-sheniyah*, Jerusalem: Yad Ben-Zvi, 1981.

Kaplan, Eran, *The Jewish Radical Right: Revisionist Zionism and Its Ideological Legacy*, Madison, Wisc.: University of Wisconsin Press, 2004.

Kaplan, Marion, *The Making of the Jewish Middle Class: Women, Family, and Identity in Imperial Germany*, New York and Oxford, UK: Oxford University Press, 1991.

Karlinsky, Nahum, *California Dreaming: Ideology, Society and Technology in the Citrus Industry of Palestine, 1890–1939*, Albany, N.Y.: State University of New York Press, 2005.

Karsh, Efraim, *Fabricating Israeli History: The 'New Historians,'* London: Frank Cass, 1997.

Katz, Elihu, "Television Comes to the People of the Book," in David Horowitz, ed., *The Use and Abuse of Social Science*, New Brunswick, N.J.: Transaction, 1971, 249–71.

Katz, Elihu and Wedell, George, *Broadcasting in the Third World: Promise and Performance*, Cambridge, Mass.: Harvard University Press, 1977.

Katz, Shaul, *Aspektim sotsiologiyim shel tsemihat ha-yeda' (ve-tahalufato) be-hakla'ut be-Yisra'el: hofa'atan shel ma'arekhot huts-mada'iyot le-hafakat yeda' hakla'i, 1880–1940*, Ph.D. diss., Hebrew University of Jerusalem, 1986.

Katz, Shaul and Ben David, Joseph, "Scientific Research and Agricultural Innovation in Israel," *Minerva* XIII, 2, 1975, 152–82.

Kellner, Jacob, "Philanthropy and Social Planning in Jewish Society (1842–82)," Ph.D. diss., Hebrew University of Jerusalem, 1973.

——*Le-ma'an Tsiyon. Ha-hit'arvut ha-klal yehudit bi-metsukat ha-yishuv 1869–1882*, Jerusalem: Yad Ben-Zvi, 1977.

——*Immigration and Social Policy: The Jewish Experience in the USA, 1881–82*, Jerusalem: Hebrew University, 1979.

Khalidi, Muhammad Ali, "Utopian Zionism or Zionist Proselytism? A Reading of Herzl's *Altneuland*," *Journal of Palestine Studies* 30, 4, 2001, 55–67.

Khalidi, Rashid, *Palestinian Identity*, New York: Columbia University Press, 1998.

Khalidi, Walid, *From Haven to Conquest: Readings in Zionism and the Palestine Problem until 1948*, Beirut: Institute for Palestine Studies, 1971.

——"The Jewish–Ottoman Land Company: Herzl's Blueprint for the Colonization of Palestine," *Journal of Palestine Studies* XXII, 2, 1993, 30–47.

Kimmerling, Baruch, *Zionism and Territory: The Socio-Territorial Dimensions of Zionist Politics*, Berkeley: Institute of International Studies of the University of California, 1983.

——*The Invention and Decline of Israeliness*, Berkeley and Los Angeles: University of California Press, 2001.

Kimmerling, Baruch and Migdal, Joel, *Palestinian People: A History*, Cambridge, Mass.: Harvard University Press, 2003.

Kind, Frank and Alexander-Ihme, Esther, eds., *Zedaka: Jüdische Sozialarbeit im Wandel der Zeit. 75 Jahre Zentralwohlfahrtsstelle in Deutschland 1917–92*, Frankfurt am Main: Jüdisches Museum, 1992.

Kolatt, Israel, "Ideologiah u-metsiut bi-tenuat ha-'avodah be-eretz yisra'el, 1905–19," Ph.D. diss., Hebrew University of Jerusalem, 1964.

——"'Al mehkar ve-ha-hoker shel toledot ha-yishuv ve-ha-tsiyonut," *Cathedra* 1, 1976, 3–35.

——"The Zionist Movement and the Arabs," 1982, in Jehuda Reinharz and Anita Shapira, eds., *Essential Papers on Zionism*, New York: New York University Press, 1995, 617–47.

Kressel, Getzl, ed., *Otsar sifrut ha-humor ha-satirah ve-ha-karikaturah be-eretz yisra'el*, Tel Aviv: Mazkret, 1984.

Kushnir, Shimon, *The Village Builder: A Biography of Abraham Harzfeld*, New York: Herzl Press, 1967.

Kuzar, Ron, *Hebrew and Zionism: A Discourse Analytic Cultural Study*, Berlin and New York: Mouton de Gruyter, 2001.

Landwehr, Rolfe and Baron, Rüdiger, *Geschichte der Sozialarbeit. Hauptlinien ihrer Entwicklung im 19. und 20. Jahrhundert*, Weinheim-Basel: Beltz, 1983.

Laqueur, Walter, *A History of Zionism*, New York: Schocken, 1972.

Larson, Magali Sarfatti, "The Production of Expertise and the Constitution of Expert Power," in Thomas Haskell, ed., *The Authority of Experts: Studies in History and Theory*, Bloomington, Ind.: Indiana University Press, 1984, 28–80.

Lavsky, Hagit, "Le'umiyut, hageirah ve-hityashvut: ha'im haytah mediniyut kelitah tsiyonit?," in Avi Bareli and Nahum Karlinsky, eds., *Kalkalah ve-hevrah bimei ha-mandat*, Sede Boker: Midreshet Ben-Gurion, 2003, 153–78.

Lestschinsky, Jacob, *Das jüdische Volk im neuen Europa*, Prague: Jüdische Akademie Technischer Verbesserung "Barissia," 1934.

Levy, Shlomit, Levinsohn, Hanna, and Katz, Elihu, "The Many Faces of Jewishness in Israel," in Uzi Rebhun and Chaim I. Waxman, eds., *Jews in Israel: Contemporary Social and Cultural Factors*, Hanover, N.H.: University Press of New England, 2004, 265–84.

Liebes, Tamar, "Performing a Dream and Its Dissolution: A Social History of Broadcasting in Israel," in James Curran and Myung-Jin Park, eds., *De-Westernizing Media Studies*, London: Routledge, 2000, 305–23.

Liebman, Charles S. and Katz, Elihu, eds., *The Jewishness of Israelis: Responses to the Guttman Report*, Albany, N.Y.: State University of New York Press, 1997.

Liedtke, Rainer, *Jewish Welfare in Hamburg and Manchester, c. 1850–1914*, Oxford, UK: Oxford University Press, 1995.

Livneh Eliezer, *Aharon Aaronsohn: ha-ish u-zemano*, Jerusalem: Mosad Bialik, 1969.

Lissak, Moshe, *Toldot ha-yishuv ha-yehudi be-eretz yisra'el me-az ha-'aliyah ha-rishonah: beniyatah shel tarbut 'ivrit be-eretz yisra'el*, Jerusalem: Mosad Bialik, 1998.

Lockman, Zachary, *Comrades and Enemies: Arab and Jewish Workers in Palestine, 1906–1948*, Berkeley and Los Angeles: University of California Press, 1996.

Lorenz, Chris, "Comparative Historiography: Problems and Perspectives," *History and Theory* 38, 1999, 25–39.

Lucas, Noah, *The Modern History of Israel*, London: Weidenfeld and Nicolson, 1974.

Lustick, Ian, *Unsettled States, Disputed Lands: Britain and Ireland, France and Algeria, Israel and the West Bank–Gaza*, Ithaca, N.Y.: Cornell University Press, 1993.

Luz, Ehud, *Parallels Meet: Religion and Nationalism in the Early Zionist Movement, 1882–1904*, Philadelphia: Jewish Publication Society, 1988.

Mamdani, Mahmood, *When Victims Become Killers: Colonialism, Nativism and the Genocide in Rwanda*, Princeton, N.J.: Princeton University Press, 2001.

Mann, Raphael and Gon-Gross, Tzippy, *Galei Tsahal kol ha-zeman*, Tel Aviv: Ministry of Defense, 1991.

Margalit, Elkana, *Ha-Shomer ha-Tza'ir: Me-'adat ne'urimle-marksizm mahapakhani, 1913–1936*, Tel Aviv: Ha-kibbbutz Ha-me'uhad, 1971.

Marrus, Michael R. and Paxton, Robert O., *Vichy France and the Jews*, New York: Basic Books, 1981.

Masalha, Nur, *Expulsion of the Palestinians: The Concept of "Transfer" in Zionist Political Thought, 1882–1948*, Washington, D.C.: Institute for Palestine Studies, 1992.

Massad, Joseph, "The 'Post-Colonial' Colony: Time, Space, and Bodies in Palestine/Israel," in Fawzia Afzal-Khan and Kalpana Seshadri-Crooks, eds., *The Pre-Occupation of Postcolonial Studies*, Durham, N.C., and London: Duke University Press, 2000, 311–46.

Mayorek, Yoram, "Emil Meyerson ve-reshit ha-me'uravut shel hevrat IKA be-Eretz Yisra'el," *Cathedra* 62, 1991, 67–79.

Meir-Glitzenstein, Esther, *Zionism in an Arab Country: The Zionist Establishment and the Jews in Iraq in the 1940s*, New York: Routledge, 2004.

Memmi, Albert, *The Colonizer and the Colonized*, Boston: Beacon, 1969.

Mendelsohn, Ezra, *On Modern Jewish Politics*, New York: Oxford University Press, 1993.

Metzer, Jacob, "Economic Structures and National Goals: The Jewish National Home in Inter-war Palestine," *Journal of Economic History* XXXVIII, 1, December 1978, 101–19.

——*Hon le'umi le-bayit le'umi*, Jerusalem: Yad Ben-Zvi, 1979.

——*The Divided Economy of Mandatory Palestine*, Cambridge, UK: Cambridge University Press, 1998.

Milstein, Uri, *Toledot milhemet ha-atsma'ut*, 4 vols, Tel Aviv: Zimora Bitan, 1989–91.

Moore, Deborah Dash and Troen, S. Ilan, eds., *Divergent Jewish Centers: Israel and America*, New Haven, Conn.: Yale University Press, 2001.

Morris, Benny, "The Crystallization of Israeli Policy against a Return of the Arab Refugees: April–December 1948," *Studies in Zionism* VI, 1, 1985, 85–118.

——"Yosef Weitz and the Transfer Committees, 1948–49," *Middle Eastern Studies* XXII, 4, October 1986, 522–61.

——*The Birth of the Palestinian Refugee Problem, 1947–1949*, Cambridge, UK: Cambridge University Press, 1987.

——*1948 and After: Israel and the Palestinians*, Oxford, UK: Oxford University Press, 1990.

——*Israel's Border Wars, 1949–1956*, Oxford, UK: Oxford University Press, 1993.

——*Righteous Victims: A History of the Zionist–Arab Conflict, 1881–1999*, New York: Knopf, 1999.

——*The Road to Jerusalem: Glubb Pasha, Palestine and the Jews*, London: Tauris, 2002.

——*The Origins of the Palestinian Refugee Problem Revisited*, Cambridge, UK: Cambridge University Press, 2004.

Mosse, George, *Fallen Soldiers*, New York: Oxford University Press, 1985.

Mossek, Moshe, *Palestine Immigration Policy under Sir Herbert Samuel*, London: Frank Cass, 1978.

Muslih, Muhammad, *The Origins of Palestinian Nationalism*, New York: Columbia University Press, 1988.

Naor, Arye, *Eretz Yisra'el ha-sheleimah: emunah u-mediniyut*, Jerusalem: Zimora Bitan, 1999.

Naveh, Eyal and Yogev, Esther, *Historiyot: Likrat dialog 'im ha-'etmol*, Tel Aviv: Bavel, 2002.

Near, Henry, *Ha-Kibbutz ve-ha-hevrah: Ha-Kibbutz ha-Me'uhad, 1923–1933*, Jerusalem: Yad Ben-Zvi, 1984.

——*The Kibbutz Movement: A History. Volume I: Origins and Growth, 1909–1939*, London: Littman Library, 1992.

Nedava, Joseph, "Herzl and the Arab Problem," *Forum on the Jewish People, Zionism and Israel* 27, 2, 1977, 64–72.

Nettler, Ron, "Islamic Archetypes of the Jews: Then and Now," in Robert Wistrich, ed., *Anti-Zionism and Antisemitism in the Modern World*, London: Macmillan, 1990, 63–73.

Nicosia, Francis, *The Third Reich and the Palestine Question*, Austin, Tex.: University of Texas Press, 1985.

Nini, Yehuda, *He-hayit o-halamti halom? Temanei Kineret: parashat hityashvutam ve-'akiratam, 1912–1930*, Tel Aviv: 'Am 'Oved, 1996.

Norman, Theodore, *An Outstretched Arm: A History of the Jewish Colonization Association*, London: Routledge and Kegan Paul, 1985.

Novick, Peter, *That Noble Dream: The "Objectivity Question" and the American Historical Profession*, New York: Cambridge University Press, 1988.

Ofer, Dalia, "The Strength of Remembrance: Commemorating the Holocaust during the First Decade of Israel," *Jewish Social Studies* VI, 2, 2000, 24–55.

Ong, Walter J., *Orality and Literacy: The Technologizing of the Word*, London and New York: Methuen, 1982.

Ophir, Adi, "The Poor in Deed Facing the Lord of All Deeds: A Postmodern Reading of the Yom Kippur *Mahzor*," in Steven Kepnes, ed., *Interpreting Judaism in a Postmodern Age*, New York: New York University Press, 1996, 181–217.

Oren, Michael, *Origins of the Second Arab–Israeli War: Egypt, Israel, and the Great Powers, 1952–1956*, London: Frank Cass, 1992.

——*Six Days of War: June 1967 and the Making of the Modern Middle East*, New York: Oxford University Press, 2002.

Oren, Tasha, "Living Room Levantine: Immigration, Ethnicity and the Border in Early Israeli Television," *The Velvet Light Trap* 44, 1999.

——*Demon in the Box: Jews, Arabs, Politics, and Culture in the Making of Israeli Television*, New Brunswick, N.J.: Rutgers University Press, 2004.

Orren, Elhannan, *Ba-derekh le-Tsahal*, Tel Aviv: Ma'arakhot, 1970.

——*Hityashvut bi-shenot ma'avak*, Jerusalem: Yad Ben-Zvi, 1978.

Pappé, Ilan, *Britain and the Arab–Israeli Conflict*, 1948–51, Basingstoke: Macmillan, 1988.

——*The Making of the Arab-Israeli Conflict, 1947–1951*, London and New York: I.B. Tauris, 1992.

——*A History of Modern Palestine: One Land, Two Peoples*, Cambridge, UK: Cambridge University Press, 2004.

Pawel, Ernst, *The Labyrinth of Exile: A Life of Theodor Herzl*, New York: Farrar, Straus, Giroux, 1989.
Paxton, Robert O., *Vichy France: Old Guard and New Order, 1940–1944*, New York: Columbia University Press, 1972.
Peleg, Yaron, "Moshe Smilansky and the Making of a Noble Jewish Savage," *Prooftexts*, forthcoming.
Penslar, Derek J., *Zionism and Technocracy: The Engineering of Jewish Settlement in Palestine, 1870–1918*, Bloomington and Indianapolis, Ind.: Indiana University Press, 1991.
——"Hashpa'ot tsorfatiyot 'al hityashvut yehudit hakla'it be-erets yisra'el, 1870–1914," *Cathedra* 62, December 1991, 54–66.
——"Philanthropy, the 'Social Question,' and Jewish Identity in Imperial Germany," *Leo Baeck Institute Yearbook XXXVIII*, 1993, 51–73.
——"Narratives of Nation-Building: Major Themes in Zionist Historiography," in David Myers and David Ruderman, eds., *The Jewish Past Revisited*, New Haven, Conn.: Yale University Press, 1998, 104–27.
——"The Origins of Modern Jewish Philanthropy," in Warren Ilchman, Stanley Katz, and Edward Queen II, eds., *Philanthropy in the World's Traditions*, Bloomington and Indianapolis: Indiana University Press, 1998, 197–214.
——"Ben-Gurion's Willing Executioners," *Dissent*, winter 1999, 114–18.
——*Shylock's Children: Economics and Jewish Identity in Modern Europe*, Berkeley and Los Angeles: University of California Press, 2001.
——"Broadcast Orientalism: Representations of Mizrahi Jews in Israeli Radio, 1948–67," in Ivan Kalmar and Derek Penslar, eds., *Orientalism and the Jews*, Hanover, N.H.: University Press of New England, 2004, 182–200.
——"Radio and the Shaping of Modern Israel, 1936–73," in Michael Berkowitz, ed., *Zionism, Ethnicity, and National Mobilisation*, Leiden: Brill, 2004, 60–82.
Peterberg, Gabi, "Domestic Orientalism: The Representation of 'Oriental' Jews in Zionist/Israeli Historiography," *British Journal of Middle Eastern Studies* 23, 2, 1996, 140–4.
Picard, Avi, "Reshitah shel ha-hageirah ha-selektivit bi-shenot ha-50," *Iyunnim bi-tekumat Yisra'el* IX, 1999, 338–93.
Plessner, Yakir, *The Political Economy of Israel: From Ideology to Stagnation*, Albany, N.Y.: State University of New York Press, 1994.
Pollins, Harold, "German Jews in British Industry," in Werner Mosse and Julius Carlebach, eds., *Second Chance: Two Centuries of German-Speaking Jews in the United Kingdom*, Tübingen: Mohr, 1991, 362–77.
Poppel, Stephen, *Zionism in Germany, 1897–1933: The Shaping of a Jewish Identity*, Philadelphia: Jewish Publication Society, 1976.
Porat, Dan, "One Text at a Time: Reconstructing the Past, Building the Future in Israeli History Texbooks," Ph.D. diss., Stanford University, 1999.
——"From the Scandal to the Holocaust in Israeli Education," *Journal of Contemporary History* 39, 2004, 619–36.
Porat, Dina, *The Blue and Yellow Stars of David: The Zionist Leadership in Palestine and the Holocaust, 1939–1945*, Cambridge, Mass.: Harvard University Press, 1990.
——"Attitudes of the Young State of Israel toward the Holocaust and Its Survivors," in Laurence Silberstein, ed., *New Perspectives on Israeli History*, New York: New York University Press, 1991, 157–74.

Porath, Yehoshua, "Anti-Zionist and Anti-Jewish Ideology in the Arab Nationalist Movement in Palestine," in Shmuel Almog, ed., *Antisemitism through the Ages*, Oxford, UK: Pergamon, 1988, 217–26.

Pratt, Mary Louise, *Imperial Eyes: Travel Writing and Transculturation*, London and New York: Routledge, 1992.

Preston, David Lawrence, *Science, Society, and the German Jews, 1870–1933*, Ph.D. diss., Urbana, Ill.: University of Illinois at Champagne-Urbana, 1971.

Pulzer, Peter, *Jews and the German State: The Political History of a Minority, 1848–1933*, London: Blackwell, 1992.

Rabinovich, Itamar, *The Road Not Taken: Early Arab–Israeli Negotiations*, New York: Oxford University Press, 1991.

Ram, Uri, "Bizekhut ha-shikhehah," in Adi Ophir, ed., *50 le-48:Hamishim le-arbai'm u-shemonah: momentim bikortiyim be-toldot medinat yisra'el: te'ud eruim: masot u-ma'amarim*, Jerusalem: Van Leer Institute and Ha-kibbutz ha-me'uhad, 1999, 349–57.

Ranger, Terence, "The Invention of Tradition in Colonial Africa," in Eric Hobsbawm and Terence Ranger, eds., *The Invention of Tradition*, Cambridge, UK: Cambridge University Press, 1992, 211–62.

Ravitzky, Aviezer, *Messianism, Zionism, and Jewish Religious Radicalism*, Chicago: University of Chicago Press, 1996.

Raz-Krakotzkin, Amnon, "A Peace without Arabs: The Discourse of Peace and the Limits of Israeli Consciousness," in George Giacaman and Dag Jorund Lonning, eds., *After Oslo: New Realities, Old Problems*, London: Pluto Press, 1998, 59–76.

——"History Textbooks and the Limits of Israeli Consciousness," *Journal of Israeli History* 20, 2/3, 2001, 155–72.

Reinharz, Jehuda, *Fatherland or Promised Land? The Dilemma of the German Jew, 1893–1914*, Ann Arbor, Mich.: University of Michigan Press, 1975.

Richter, Anke, "Das jüdische Armenwesen in Hamburg in der 1. Hälfte des 19. Jahrhunderts," in Peter Freimark and Arno Herzig, eds., *Die Hamburger Juden in der Emanzipationsphase (1780–1870)*, Hamburg: H. Christian, 1990, 234–54.

Rinott, Moshe, *Hevrat ha-'ezrah li-yehudei Germaniyah bi-yetsirah u-ve-ma'avak*, Jerusalem: Bet sefer le-hinukh shel ha-universitah ha-ivrit, 1971.

Rodinson, Maxine, *Israel: A Colonial Settler-State?*, New York: Monad, 1973.

Rodrigue, Aron, *French Jews, Turkish Jews: The Alliance Israelite and the Politics of Jewish Schooling in Turkey, 1860–1925*, Bloomington Ind.: Indiana University Press, 1990.

——*Images of Sephardi and Eastern Jewries in Transition, 1860–1939: The Teachers of the Alliance Israelite Universelle*. Seattle, Wa.: University of Washington Press, 1993.

Rose, Margaret A., *Parody: Ancient, Modern and Post-Modern*, Cambridge, UK: Cambridge University Press, 1993.

Roskies, David, "The Golden Peacock: The Art of Song," *The Jewish Search for a Usable Past*, Bloomington and Indianapolis: Indiana University Press, 1999, 89–119.

——"Major Trends in Yiddish Parody," *Jewish Quarterly Review* 94, 1, 2004, 109–22.

Rousso, Henry, *The Vichy Syndrome: History and Memory in France since 1944*, Cambridge, Mass.: Harvard University Press, 1991.

Rozenman, Abraham, *Ha-Shamashim: Ruppin ve-Eshkol*, Jerusalem: World Zionist Organization, 1992.
Rubinstein, Elyakim, "'Ha-protokolim shel ziknei tziyon' ba-sikhsukh ha-aravi-yehudi," *Ha-Mizrah he-Hadash* 25, 1985, 37–42.
Ruppin, Arthur, *Building Israel: Selected Essays, 1907–1935*, New York: Schocken, 1949.
——*Tagebücher, Briefe, Erinnerungen*, Königstein/Ts.: Jüdischer Verlag/Atheneum, 1985.
Sacerdoti, Yaakova, "Prophecy of Wrath: Israeli Society as Reflected in Satires for Children," in Laura Zittrain Eisenberg and Neil Caplan, eds., *Review Essays in Israel Studies: Books on Israel, Volume V*, Albany, N.Y.: State University of New York Press, 2000, 119–36.
Sachar, Howard M., *A History of Israel from the Rise of Zionism to Our Time*, New York: Knopf, 2nd rev. edn. 1996.
Sachsse, Christoph and Tennstedt, Florian, *Geschichte der Armenfürsorge in Deutschland*, Stuttgart: Kohlhammer, 1980.
Said, Edward, *The Question of Palestine*, New York: Vintage, 1979.
——"Zionism from the Standpoint of its Victims," in Anne McClintock, Aamar Mufti, and Ella Shohat, eds., *Dangerous Liaisons: Gender, Nation and Postcolonial Perspectives,* Minneapolis, Minn.: University of Minnesota Press, 1997, 15–38.
Salmon, Yosef, *Religion and Zionism: First Encounters*, Jerusalem: Magnes, 2002.
Schejter, Amit, "Media Policy as Social Regulatory Policy: The Role of Broadcasting in Shaping National Culture in Israel," Ph.D. diss., Rutgers University, 1995.
Schorsch, Ismar, *From Text to Context: The Turn to History in Modern Judaism*, Hanover, N.H.: University Press of New England, 1994.
Segel, Binjamin, *A Lie and a Libel: The History of the Protocols of the Elders of Zion*, Lincoln, Neb.: University of Nebraska Press, 1995.
Segev, Tom, *1949: The First Israelis*, New York: Free Press, 1986.
——*The Seventh Million: The Israelis and the Holocaust*, New York: Hill and Wang, 1993.
——*One Palestine, Complete: Jews and Arabs under the British Mandate*, New York: Metropolitan, 2000.
——*Elvis in Jerusalem*, New York: Metropolitan, 2002.
Segre, Dan, "Colonization and Decolonization: The Case of Zionist and African Elites," in Todd Endelman, ed., *Comparing Jewish Societies*, Ann Arbor, Mich.: University of Michigan Press, 1994, 217–34.
Sela, Avraham, "Ha-melekh 'Abdallah u-memshelet yisrael bi-milhemet ha-ha'atsmau't – ha'arakhah me-hadash," *Cathedra* 57, 1990, 120–62, 58; 1990, 172–93.
——"Transjordan, Israel and the 1948 War: Myth, Historiography and Reality," *Middle Eastern Studies* 28, 4, 1992, 623–58.
Shafir, Gershon, *Land, Labor, and the Origins of the Israeli–Palestinian Conflict, 1882–1914*, rev. edn., Berkeley and Los Angeles: University of California Press, 1996.
——"Zionism and Colonialism: A Comparative Approach," in Michael N. Barnett, ed., *Israel in Comparative Perspective: Challenging the Conventional Wisdom*, Albany, N.Y.: State University of New York Press, 1996, 227–42.
Shafir, Gershon and Peled, Yoav, *Being Israeli: The Dynamics of Multiple Citizenship*, Cambridge, UK, and New York: Cambridge University Press, 2002.

Shaltiel, Eli, *Pinhas Rutenberg: aliyato u-nefilato shel ish hazak be-Erets-Yisrael, 1879–1942*, Tel Aviv: 'Am 'Oved, 1990.

Shamir, Ronen, *The Colonies of Law: Colonialism, Zionism, and Law in Early Mandate Palestine*, Cambridge, UK: Cambridge University Press, 2000.

Shandler, Jeffrey and Katz, Elihu, "Broadcasting American Judaism," in Jack Wertheimer, ed., *Tradition Renewed: A History of the Jewish Theological Seminary of America*, New York: Jewish Theological Seminary, 1997, II, 363–402.

Shapira, Anita, *Ha-ma'avak ha-nikhzav:'avodah 'ivrit, 1929–1939*, Tel Aviv: Institute for the Study of the History of Zionism, 1977.

——*Berl*, 2 vols., Tel Aviv: 'Am 'Oved, 1980.

——"The Debate in Mapai on the Use of Violence, 1932–35," *Studies in Zionism* III 1981, 99–124.

——*Land and Power: The Zionist Resort to Force, 1881–1948*, New York: Oxford University Press, 1992.

——"The Holocaust: Private Memories, Public Memory," *Jewish Social Studies* IV, 2, 1998, 40–58.

——"The Religious Motifs of the Labor Movement," in Shmuel Almog, Jehuda Reinharz, and Anita Shapira, eds., *Zionism and Religion*, Hanover, N.H., and London: University Press of New England, 1999, 251–72.

Shapira, Anita and Penslar, Derek J., *Israeli Historical Revisionism: From Left to Right*, London: Frank Cass, 2002.

Shapiro, Yonathan, *The Formative Years of the Israeli Labour Party: The Organisation of Power, 1919–1930*, London: Sage, 1976.

Shavit, Ya'akov, *Me-rov li-medinah*, Tel Aviv: Yariv, 1978.

——*Jabotinsky and the Revisionist Movement, 1925–1948*, London: Frank Cass, 1988.

Shenhav, Yehouda, *Ha-yehudim ha-'aravim: le'umuit, dat ve-etniut*, Tel Aviv: 'Am 'Oved, 2003.

Shilo, Margalit, "Tovat ha-aretz o-tovat ha-'am? Yahsah shel ha-tenua'h ha-tsiyonit le-'aliyah bitekufat ha-'aliyah ha-sheniyah," *Cathedra* 46, 1987, 109–22.

——*Princess or Prisoner? Jewish Women in Jerusalem, 1840–1914*, Hanover, N.H.: University Press of New England, 2005.

Shilo, Margalit, Kark, Ruth, and Hazan-Rokem, Galit, eds., *Ha-'ivriyot ha-hadashot:nashim ba-Yishuv u-ve-tsiyonut ba-re'l ha-migdar*, Jerusalem: Yad Ben-Zvi, 2001.

Shimoni, Gideon, *The Zionist Ideology*, Hanover, N.H.: University Press of New England, 1995.

Shlaim, Avi, *Collusion across the Jordan: King Abdullah, the Zionist Movement, and the Partition of Palestine*, Oxford, UK: Oxford University Press, 1988.

——*The Politics of Partition: King Abdullah, the Zionists, and Palestine, 1921–1951*, New York: Oxford University Press, 1990.

——*The Iron Wall: Israel and the Arab World*, New York: Norton, 2000.

Shohat, Ella, *Israeli Cinema: East/West and Political Representation*, Austin, Tex.: University of Texas Press, 1989.

——"Sephardim in Israel: Zionism from the Standpoint of Its Jewish Victims," in Anne McClintock, Aamir Mufti, and Ella Shohat, eds., *Dangerous Liaisons: Gender, Nation & Postcolonial Perspectives*, Minneapolis, Minn., and London: University of Minnesota Press, 1997, 39–68.

——"Rupture and Return: Zionist Discourse and the Study of Arab Jews," *Social Text* 75:21, 2003, 49–74.

Silber, Michael, "The Emergence of Ultra-Orthodoxy: The Invention of a Tradition," in Jack Wertheimer, ed., *The Uses of Tradition: Jewish Continuity in the Modern Era*, Cambridge, Mass.: Harvard University Press, 1992, 23–84.

Silberstein, Laurence, *The Postzionism Debates: Knowledge and Power in Israeli Culture*, New York: Routledge, 1999.

Simon, Reeva Spector, *Iraq between the Two World Wars: The Militarist Origins of Tyranny*, 2nd edn., New York: Columbia University Press, 2004.

Simons, Chaim, *A Historical Survey of Proposals to Transfer Arabs from Palestine, 1895–1947*, Hoboken, N.J.: Ktav, 1988.

Singer, Mendel, *Shlomo Kaplansky: Hayyav u-fo'olo*, Jerusalem: Ha-Sifriyah Ha-Tsiyonit, 1971.

Sivan, Emmanuel, "Islamic Fundamentalism, Antisemitism, and Anti-Zionism," in Robert Wistrich, ed., *Anti Zionism and Antisemitism in the Modern World*, London: Macmillan, 1990, 74–84.

Skocpol, Theda and Somers, Margaret, "The Uses of Comparative History in Macrosocial Inquiry," *Comparative Studies in Society and History* 22, 2, 1980, 174–97.

Slutsky, Yehuda, *Mavo le-toldot tnua't ha-'avodah ha-yisre'elit*, Tel Aviv: 'Am 'Oved, 1973.

Smooha, Sammy, "The Viability of Ethnic Democracy as a Mode of Conflict Management: Comparing Israel and Northern Ireland," in Todd Endelman, ed., *Comparing Jewish Societies*, Ann Arbor, Mich.: University of Michigan Press, 1997, 267–312.

——"Ethnic Democracy: Israel as an Archetype," *Israel Studies* II, 2, 1997, 198–241.

Soskin, Selig, *Small Holding and Irrigation*, London: Allen and Unwin, 1920.

Stanislawski, Michael, *Zionism and the Fin-de-Siecle: Cosmopolitanism & Nationalism from Nordau to Jabotinsky*, Berkeley and Los Angeles: University of California Press, 2001.

Stauber, Roni, *Ha-lekah la-dor: sho'ah u-gevurah ba-mahashavah ha-tsiburit ba-arets bi-shenot ha-hamishim*, Jerusalem and Beersheva: Yad Ben-Tsevi and Ha-merkaz le-moreshet Ben-Gurion, 2000.

Stein, Kenneth, *The Land Question in Palestine: 1917–1939*, Chapel Hill, N.C.: University of North Carolina Press, 1984.

Stein, Leslie, *The Hope Fulfilled: The Rise of Modern Israel*, Westport, Conn.: Praeger, 2003.

Stein, Sarah Abrevaya, *Making Jews Modern: The Yiddish and Ladino Press in the Russian and Ottoman Empires*, Bloomington, Ind.: Indiana University Press, 2004.

Stern, Fritz, *Dreams and Delusions: The Drama of German History*, New York: Knopf, 1987.

Sternhell, Zeev, *The Founding Myths of Israel*, Princeton, N.J.: Princeton University Press, 1998.

Stewart, Desmond, *Theodor Herzl: Artist and Politician. A Biography of the Father of Modern Israel*, Garden City, N.Y.: Doubleday, 1974.

Stoler, Ann, "Sexual Affronts and Racial Frontiers: European Identities and the Cultural Politics of Exclusion in Colonial Southeast Asia," in Geoff Eley and Ronald Grigor Suny, eds., *Becoming National*, New York and Oxford, UK: Oxford University Press, 1996, 286–324.

Swirski, Shlomo, *Israel: The Oriental Majority*, London: Zed Publishers, 1989.

Szajkowski, Zosa, "Conflicts in the Alliance Israélite Universelle and the Founding of the Anglo-Jewish Association, the Vienna Allianz, and the Hilfsverein," *Jewish Social Studies* 19, 1–2, 1957, 29–50,

Tal, Alon, *Pollution in a Promised Land: An Environmental History of Israel*, Berkeley and Los Angeles: University of California Press, 2002.

Taub, Gadi, "The Shift in Israeli Ideas Concerning the Individual and the Collective," in Hazim Saghie, ed., *The Predicament of the Individual in the Middle East*, London: Saqi, 2001, 187–99.

Teveth, Shabtai, *Ben-Gurion: The Burning Ground 1886–1948*, Boston, Mass.: Houghton Mifflin, 1987.

——*The Evolution of "Transfer" in Zionist Thinking*, Tel Aviv: Dayan Center, 1989.

——"Charging Israel with Original Sin," *Commentary* 88, 3, September 1989, 24–33.

——"The Palestinian Arab Refugee Problem and Its Origins," *Middle Eastern Studies* XXVI, 2, April 1990, 214–49.

Ther, Phillip, "Beyond the Nation: The Relational Basis of a Comparative History of Germany and Europe," *Central European History* 36, 1, 2003, 45–73.

Toury, Jacob, *Die politischen Orientierungen der Juden in Deutschland*, Tübingen: Mohr, 1966.

——"'The Jewish Question:' A Semantic Approach," *Leo Baeck Institute Year Book XI*, 1966, 85–106.

Tzur, Eli, "Hehelah yetsiat mitzrayim – u mah asu halutseinu ba-kibbutz be-mivhan ha-'aliyah ha-hamonit," *Iyunnim bi-tekumat Yisra'el* IX, 1999, 316–38.

Van Creveld, Martin, *The Sword and the Olive Branch: A Critical History of the Israel Defense Force*, New York: Public Affairs, 1998.

Vanderberg, Willem H., "Political Imagination in a Technical Age," in Richard B. Day, Ronald Beiner and Joseph Masciulli, eds., *Democratic Theory and Technological Society*, Armonk, N.Y.: M.E. Sharpe, Inc., 1990, 3–35.

van der Veer, Peter and Lehmann, Hartmut, eds., *Nation and Religion: Perspectives on Europe and Asia*, Princeton, N.J.: Princeton University Press, 1999.

Vital, David, *The Origins of Zionism*, Oxford, UK: Oxford University Press, 1975.

——*Zionism: The Formative Years*, Oxford, UK: Oxford University Press, 1982.

——*Zionism: The Crucial Phase*, Oxford, UK: Oxford University Press, 1987.

Volkov, Shulamit, "Soziale Ursachen des jüdischen Erfolgs in der Wissenschaft," *Jüdisches Leben und Antisemitismus im 19. und 20. Jahrhundert*, Munich: Beck, 1991, 146–65.

vom Bruch, Rüdiger, ed., *Weder Kommunismus noch Kapitalismus: bürgerlicher Sozialreform in Deutschland vom Vormärz bis zur Ära Adenauer*, Munich: C.H. Beck, 1985.

Walby, Sylvia, "Woman and Nation," in Gopal Balakrishnan and Benedict Anderson, eds., *Mapping the Nation*, London: Verso, 1996, 235–54.

Walzer, Michael, Lorberbaum, Menachem, and Zohar, Noam J., eds., *The Jewish Political Tradition: Volume One: Authority*, New Haven, Conn., and London: Yale University Press, 2000.

Webb, R.K., *Modern England*, New York: Harper & Row, 1968.

Weitz, Yechiam, *Muda'ut ve-hoser onim: Mapai nokhah ha-shoah, 1943–1945*, Jerusalem: Yad Ben-Zvi, 1994.

——, ed., *Bein hazon le-reviziyah: me'ah shenot hitoriographiyah tsiyonit*, Jerusalem: Shazar Centre, 1997.

Wiese, Christian, "Struggling for Normality: The Apologetics of Wissenschaft des Judentums in Wilhelmine Germany as an Anti-colonial Intellectual Revolt against the Protestant Construction of Judaism," in Rainer Liedtke and David Rechter, eds., *Towards Normality? Acculturation and Modern German Jewry*, Tübingen: Mohr Siebeck, 2003, 77–101.

Wildenthal, Lora, *German Women for Empire, 1884–1945*, Durham, N.C., and London: Duke University Press, 2001.

Wilkansky, Yitzhak, *The Transition from Primitive to Modern Agriculture in Palestine*, Tel Aviv: Hapoel Hazair, 1925.

——*The Communistic Settlements in the Jewish Colonization of Palestine*, Tel Aviv: Palestine Economic Society, 1927; reprint, Westport, Conn.: Hyperion, 1976.

Winichakul, Thongchai, *Siam Mapped: A History of the Geo-Body of a Nation*, Honolulu: University of Hawaii Press, 1994.

Winner, Langdon, *Autonomous Technology*, Cambridge, Mass.: MIT Press, 1977.

Wistrich, Robert, *Hitler's Apocalypse: Jews and the Nazi Legacy*, London: Weidenfeld and Nicolson, 1985.

Yazbek, Mahmoud, "Mi-falahim le-mordim: gormim kalkaliyim le-hitpartsut ha-mered ha-'aravi be-1936," *Ha-tsiyonut 22*, 2000, 185–206.

Yonah, Yosi and Shenhav, Yehuda, "Ha-matsav ha-rav-tarbuti," *Teoryah u-Vikoret* 17, 2000, 163–88.

Young, Robert J.C., *Postcolonialism: An Historical Introduction*, Oxford, UK: Blackwell, 2001.

Yuchtman-Yaar, Ephraim and Hermann, Tamar, "Shass: The Haredi-Dovish Image in a Changing Reality," *Israel Studies* V, 2, 2000, 32–77.

Zemach, Shlomo, *'Avoda ve-adamah*, Jerusalem: World Zionist Organization/Reuven Mass, 1950.

——*Sipur Hayai*, Jerusalem: Devir, 1983.

Zertal, Idith, *From Catastrophe to Power: Holocaust Survivors and the Emergence of Israel*, Berkeley and Los Angeles: University of California Press, 1998.

——*Israel's Holocaust and the Politics of Nationhood*, New York: Cambridge University Press, 2005.

Zerubavel, Yael, *Recovered Roots: Collective Memory and the Making of Israeli National Tradition*, Chicago: University of Chicago Press, 1995.

——"Masa' be-merhavei ha-zeman ve-ha-makom: sifrut agadit ke-makhshir le-'itsuv zikaron kibutsi," *Teyoriyah u-vikoret* 10, 1997, 69–80.

Zimmermann, Mosche, *Wilhelm Marr: The Patriarch of Antisemitism*, New York: Oxford University Press, 1986.

Zuckermann, Moshe, *Shoah be-heder atum: Ha-"shoah" ba-itonut ha-yisre'elit be-milhemet ha-mifrats*, Tel Aviv: 'Am 'Oved, 1993.

——*Zweierlei Holocaust: Der Holocaust in den politischen Kulturen Israels und Deutschlands*, Göttingen: Wallstein, 1998.

Zurayk, Constantine, *The Meaning of the Disaster*, Beirut: Khayat's College Book Co-operative, 1956.

Index

Aaronsohn, Aaron 53
Abdul Hamid, Sultan 55, 125
Abdullah, Emir of Transjordan and King of Jordan 22, 45, 46
Abramovich, Mendel 190
Africa 58, 91, 92, 95, 98
Agadut Yisrael 74, 136, 138
Agro-Joint 140, 141, 143, 145–8, 152
Ahad Ha-Am 177
Ahdut ha-'Avodah (United Labor) 15, 154–5, 159, 162
Algeria 95, 110
Aliyah, waves of Zionist immigration to Palestine: First 139; Fourth 155; Second 157, 163; Third 15, 155, 157, 158
Alliance Israélite Universelle 97, 120, 135, 136–7, 138, 144, 148
Almog, Oz 36
Alroey, Gur 39
Alterman, Nathan 184
Altneuland (Herzl, T.) 53, 55, 57, 58, 60–61, 153
American Jewish Joint Distribution Committee (JDC) 104, 137–8, 143, 151–2
American Society for Farm Settlements in Russia 146
Amir, Gafi 84–5
'Amr, Abd al-Hakim 47
Anderson, Benedict 67, 68, 101, 103, 105
Anglo-Jewish Association 120, 135, 137
antisemitism 6, 17, 19, 57, 61, 80, 121, 123, 144, 151, 201; anti-Zionism and 112–29; Christian 54, 117; European 40, 54, 83, 112–13, 121–2, 123, 125, 149; Freemasonry and 120; Internet 56; irrationality of 83; Italian 117; 'Jewish Question' in Europe and 134–5; Middle Eastern 123–9; modern revival in Europe of 149; political 118, 134, 141–2; state-sanctioning of 108–9; and support for Zionism 115–16; in Vichy France 117
Antisemitism Catechism (Fritsch, T.) 119–20
Arab Higher Committee 178
Arab-Israeli conflict 7, 8–9, 16–17, 20, 81; new consensus on 44–50
Arab-Israeli War (1973) 14
Arab Legion of Jordan 45
Arab Revolt (1936-9) 43, 109, 163, 193
Arabic language 31
Arabs of Palestine *see* Palestinian Arabs
Arafat, Yasser 81
Argentina 7, 104, 144, 145
Armenia 124
Arya Samaj 100
Ashkenazim 27, 37–9, 43–4, 69, 72, 73, 82, 83, 97–8, 110, 192, 199–200
Asia 91, 92; Indo-Europeans in colonial 98
Auschwitz 82
Australia 3, 92
Austria 98; antisemitism in 122

Averni, Uri 84
Avida, Mordechai 190
Avidar (Rokhel), Yosef 164
Azuri, Najib 125

Bamahaneh 197–8
Biarritz (Goedsche, H.) 122
Bakhtin, Mikhail 170
Balfour Declaration 30, 51, 113, 133, 139, 182
Bank ha-Po'alim (Workers' Bank) 154
Barak, Chief Justice Aharon 77
Barak, Ehud 82
Bar-Kokhba, Shimon 49, 201
Bar-On, Mordechai 46–7
Bartal, Israel 15, 73
Barthes, Roland 207
Baruch, Adam 73
Bava Tekhnika (Silman, K.Y.) 169, 176
Bavli, Eliezer 160
Beardsley, Aubrey 1
Bebel, August 114
Bedouin of Palestine 95, 96
Be'er, Chaim 73
Be'eri, Eliezer 52
Begin, Menachem 34, 76, 81
Bein, Alex 56
Being Israeli: The Dynamics of Multiple Citizenship (Shafir, G. and Peled, Y.) 43, 66
Beit Shean Valley 164
Ben Shemen, Experiment Station at 157, 158, 159
Ben Ya'akov, Mikhal 40
Ben-Amotz, Dan 199
Ben-Arieh, Yehoshua
Ben-Artsi, Yossi 41
Ben-Eliezer, Uri 36
Bengal 91–2, 99, 100, 102
Ben-Gurion, David 25–7, 33–4, 46, 76–7, 162, 163, 179, 189–90, 194, 196, 197
Ben-Gurion-Jabotinsky Accords 179
Ben-Yehuda, Eliezer 69, 176
Berdichevsky, Micha 102
Berlin 175; Congress of 144
Bernstein, Eduard 19
Bertonov, Shlomo 193
Bevin, Ernest 22
Bhabha, Homi 101
Bialik, Haim Nahman 191
Birnbaum, Nathan 74
Birnbaum, Pierre 19
Birobidzhan 181
Bloch, Marc 3
Bnei Zion 183
Boehm, Adolf 60
Bohemia 108
Bolshevism 15, 126, 143, 146, 171
Boyarin, Daniel 58, 94
Boyce, George 33
Brafman, Iakov 120
Brandeis, Louis 150, 155, 160
Breuer, Mordechai 197, 202–3
Brit Shalom (Covenant of Peace) 180, 181
British Guiana 147
British Mandate *see* Mandatory Palestine
Buddhism 99
Bulgaria 17
Bund 135–6
Bush, George 81

Cahen, Emile 116
Camp David 128, 129; Peace Accords 124
Canaanism 20, 84
Carpi, Daniel 15
From Catastrophe to Power – Holocaust Survivors and the Emergence of Israel (Zertal, I.) 37
Cathedra (Ben Zvi Institute) 14, 15
Caucasian Muslims 96
Central Europe 122, 133, 144, 152; Jewish political organizations in 135
Centralverein deutscher Staatsbürger jüdischen Glaubens 125
Cervantes, Miguel de 170
Chakrabarty, Dipesh 107
Chamberlain, Houston S. 121

Chatterjee, Partha 91–2, 100, 102, 103, 104–5, 106, 107
Chattopadhyay, Tarnicharan 101
Chetrit, Sami Shalom
Choveve Tsiyon 139, 143
Christian Socialism 122
Christianity 54, 55, 75, 91, 108, 117, 124–7, 193, 195; antisemitism and 124–7; Assyrian Christians 126; influences of, colonialism and 99–102; Italian Catholocism and antisemitism 117
La Civiltà Cattolica 117
Cohen, Ephraim 176, 177
Cohen, Mark 124
Cohn, Norman 123
Cold War 20, 21–2, 29
colonialism: anti-colonialism and Zionism 91; Christianity and 99–102; colonized intelligentsia 98–102; Dutch East Indies 98; European 92, 93–4, 95; French Indochina 98; Herzl's colonialist aspirations 56–7, 60–61; of Mandatory Palestine 93–4; nationalism, Zionism and 91–2, 101–2; nationalism and 91, 104, 107; Zionism and 90–111; *see also* post-colonialism
Colonization Department of Palestine Zionist Executive 154, 155
Commission Palestinienne (CP) 139
comparative history 3–4
Comrades and Enemies: Arab and Jewish Workers in Palestine (Lockman, Z.) 42
Conrad, Joseph 96
Crémieux, Adolphe 148
Crimea 143, 146–7, 181; *see also* Agro-Joint
Croce, Benedetto 106
Crosby, Bing 199
Czechoslovakia 17

Davar 184
Dayan, Moshe 46, 47
De Sola Pool, David 140
Dearborn Independent 123
Deganiah Bet 1–2
Deir Yasin 22
DellaPergola, Sergio 71
Dentith, Simon 170
Deri, Arieh 74
Derrida, Jacques 107, 206
Deutsche Conferenz Gemeinschaft 137
A Dialogue in Hell (Joly, M.) 122
Dick, Isaak Meir 169, 173–4
Dinur, Ben-Zion 106
Dohm, Friedrich Wilhelm von 105
Dominican Republic 147
Douglas, Mary 169–70
Dowty, Alan 76
Dreyfus, Alfred 120
Droysen, Johann Gustav 106
Drumont, Edouard 114–17, 118
Druze of Palestine 96
Dühring, Eugen 118–19
Dutch East Indies 98
Dyk, Solomon 161

An Early Blueprint of Zionism (Handler, A.) 114
East India Company 92
Eastern Europe 7–8, 68, 69, 76, 105, 144, 150, 169; ethnic cleansing in 109; Jewish political organizations in 135
Eastern European Jewry 7–8, 66, 74, 80, 97, 105, 150, 175; Ahad Ha-Am as representative of 177; badkhan (wedding jester) of 171, 184; crisis of 141–2, 143–6; culture of 172–4, 178; economic life of 80; Haskalah in (Jewish Enlightenment) 69, 169, 172–4; international activity on behalf of 148; politics of 76, 135; poverty, persecution and migration of 133, 135, 137, 152; Yiddish speech of 68
Egypt 32, 46–8, 55, 99, 124–6, 128, 180, 185, 196
Eichmann, Adolf 81, 205
Elazar, Daniel J. 75
Elon, Amos 56, 84

England 106; 'Irish Question' in 134
Eretz aharet: ketav et al yisre'eliyut ve-yahadut 73
Eretz Yisrael Ha-sheleimah:emunah u-mediniyut (Naor, A.) 34
Eshkol (Shkolnik), Levi 8, 48, 163, 164
Esther, Book of 176, 178–9
The Eternal Light (NBC) 189, 203
The Eternity of Israel (Ben-Gurion, D.) 76–7
Ettinger, Akiva 154, 155, 156, 158–9, 162
Etzel 34
Exodus 178, 180, 185
Eyal, Gil 39

Felsenthal, Rabbi Bernhardt 120
Fichte, Johann Gottlieb 114
Fischer, Fritz 23
Folkists 136
Ford, Henry 123, 142
The Foundations of the Nineteenth Century (Chamberlain, H.S.) 121
France 18–19, 102, 106, 114–17; 'civil improvement' in 105; Dreyfus Affair 118, 124–5; 'Jewish Question' in 134; Napoleonic era in 107; Vichy 19, 29, 117
Frankel, Zecharias 148
Freemasonry 120
French Indochina 98
French Jewry 105–6
Friedmann, Adolf 58–9
Fritsch, Theodor 119–21
Funkenstein, Amos 49, 102
The Futile Struggle (Shapira, A.) 15

Galei Tsahal 195, 197–8, 204
Galilee 47, 109, 139, 164, 196
Gandhi, Mohandas 107
Gaza Strip 46, 110, 127
Geiger, Abraham 99–100
Gelber, Yoav 46
Genette, Gerard 170–71
Germany 18–19, 101, 106, 114; anti-semitism in 118–22; Bielefeld School of historiography 29; 'civil improvement' in 105; Colonial Service of 153; Magdeburg Law 76; Nazi Germany 19, 29, 113, 126, 128, 149; Nazi ideology 121; occupational diversity of Jewish population 151–2; philanthropic activism in 152; programs for Jewish civil improvement 135; Transfer Agreement (Ha'avarah) 113; Weimar Republic 73, 74, 148; Wilhelmine Empire 29; Wissenschaft des Judentums 86, 99, 100, 101–2, 108; Zentralwohlfahrtsstelle 148
Gide, André 96
Glinert, Eliezer 69
Goedsche, Hermann 122
Golan Heights 47, 110
Golani, Motti 27, 36, 46–7, 82
Goren, Shmuel 37
Gorny, Yosef 14, 15
Graetz, Heinrich 101
Of Grammatology (Derrida, J.) 206
Greenburg, Uri Zvi 179
Gronemann, Sammy 175
Gross, Nachum 40
Guizot, Francois 106
Guttman Center, Israel Democracy Institute 70
Guttman Reports 71, 73, 87

Ha-Aretz 33, 73, 175, 178, 182–3, 184
Ha-Bimah theatrical company 190
Ha-Moriah 176
Ha-Po'el Ha-Tsa'ir (The Young Worker) 154, 162
Ha-Shomer 2
Ha-yom 174
Habbakuk 172
Habermas, Jürgen 7, 133
Hadari-Ramage, Yonah 36–7
Hadassah 97
Haddayah, Rabbi Ovadyah 74–5
Haganah 46, 190; Technical Department 164; underground radio stations 192, 194

Haggadah 8, 169–71, 174, 179–83
Halpern, Ben 60
Hammer, Zevulun 81
Handler, Andrew 114
Hanukkah 175
Hapsburg Empire 101, 136
Harkabi, Yehoshafat 123–4, 129
Harshav, Benjamin 69
Harzfeld, Abraham 163
Haskalah (Jewish Enlightenment) 8, 69, 72–3, 86, 91, 99–101, 108, 138, 169, 171–4, 176–80, 184–5
HaTsiyonut (Weizmann Institute) 15
Hazanut (Kol Yisrael) 204
Hebrew language 6, 30–31, 65, 67–70, 121, 190, 193, 195, 198
Hebrew Language Committee 69, 190, 191
Hebrew satire in Mandate Palestine 169–86; Eastern European Haskalah literature 174, 175; Jewish parody 171–2, 176–7; Jewish satiric parody 172–3, 175, 176, 178–9; literary analyses of parody 170–71; parody and satire, overlapping genres 171, 172; religious-textual parody 183–5; satiric haggadot 179–84; Western European satire 175
Hegel, Georg Wilhelm Friedrich 49, 187
He-Halutz 136, 146
Heller, Joseph 15, 33, 34
Helman, Anat 39
Herder, Johann Gottfried von 114
Herzl, Theodor 5, 91, 94, 112, 114–16, 120, 122, 125, 136–7, 142–3, 153, 200, 202; colonialist aspirations of 56–7, 60–61; controversy of June 12, 1895 diary entry 53–5, 57, 58, 60; disregard for Palestinian Arabs 52–3, 55–6; expropriation ideas concerning Palestinian Arabs 53, 57–8, 59; Jewish-Ottoman Land Company 59–60; opposition to 'infiltration' 58–9; significance as political leader 51; Stewart's critical biography of 56–7
Heschel, Susannah 99
Hess, Moses 114
Hevrat Ovdim (Society of Workers) 163, 190
Hildesheimer, Rabbi Esriel 138
Hilfsverein der deutschen Juden 69, 135, 136, 137, 138, 139, 144–5, 152, 176–8
Hinduism 99, 100, 101, 102
Hirsch, Maurice de 116, 137, 142–3
Hirsch, Sampson Raphael 138
Histadrut (General Federation of Labor) 2, 15, 40, 97, 162–3
historiography: Bielefeld School of 29; critics of new history 25–6; current directions in Israeli 25–50; gender relations and women 40–41; immigration policy and experiences of immigrants 37–40; of Israel 3–6, 9–10, 13–24; militarism, political culture and 35–7; military historiography of Israel 22–3; Palestinisn Arabs 41–3; sociology, influence of 28; *see also* new history; revisionism
History & Memory (Tel Aviv University) 28
History of India (Chattopadhyay, T.) 101
A History of Modern Palestine (Pappé, I.) 42
History of the Jews (Graetz, H.) 101
Hitler, Adolf 81, 121
hityashvut ovedet 150, 155, 156, 162–3, 164, 165
The Holocaust 7, 15, 74, 78–9, 149; French complicity in 19, 29; German scholarship on 19; impact on early years in Israel 27, 80–81; Israeli political discourse and 76, 81; re-experience of 81–2; 'revisionism' and 19–20, 121; survivors 37–8
Holy Land 40, 66, 93, 95, 111, 127, 141, 177
Hope-Simpson Report 180
Horowitz, Dan 14
Horseman without a Horse (Egyptian television) 128
al-Husayni, Haj Amin 125

Al-Hurriyah 194
Hussein, King of Jordan 47, 48
Hussein, Saddam 81
Hutcheon, Linda 170, 172
Hyman, Paula 100–101

The Idea of the Jewish State (Halpern, B.) 60
The Immoralist (Gide, A.) 96
Imperialism 20, 61, 90; European 95, 111; French 236; Zionism as product of age of 108, 153
India 91–2, 98–9, 100–103, 106, 107; partition of 109
Internet 56
The Invention and Decline of Israeliness (Kimmerling, B.) 43, 66
Iran 109; Iranian Revolution 128
Iraq 126; Farhoud of 1941 in 126
Iraq War 149
Iraqi Jews 97
Ireland 108; Act of Union 106
The Iron Wall: Israel and the Arab World (Shlaim, A.) 47–8
Islam 31, 99, 124, 126–7
Israel: Ashkenazic cultural orientation of radio in 199–200; austerity of young state 79; capital transfers, reliance on 79–80; capitalist entrepreneurship in 80; classic Israeli social science 90; contemporary Israeli economy 79–80; contemporary political activity 76; contemporary religious life 73; Israeli radio 1949-73 193–207; declaration of statehood 189; diaspora links with 65–7, 87–9; economics 77–80, 87; educational role of radio in 199, 206–7; ethnic democracy 3; Hebrew language 6, 30–31, 65, 67–70, 121, 190, 193, 195, 198; Hebrew radio, invention of 189–93; historical consciousness 80–83; historiography of 3–6, 9–10; Independence Day in 196, 201; Jewish identity and 87–8; Jewish Renewal movement 74; Land of (Eretz Yisrael) 3, 34, 65, 85, 93, 95–6, 108, 165, 183, 192; language 67–70, 87; Law of Return 93; militarization in society 76–7; 'mobilized voluntarism' in 195; multiculturalism 85–6; non-religious Jews in 70–71; politics 74–7, 87; post-Zionism 83–6; Provisional Government (1948-9) 193–4, 196; Public Council for Radio Affairs (PCRA) 196–7, 198, 199, 202–3; radio in 187–207; radio listenership in 198–9; religion 70–74, 87; religious radio broadcasting in 202–4; ritual observance in 71–2; secularization in 72, 73–4; social-scientific work on 66; sovereignty in, conditions of 76; structural similarity with France and Germany 19; Supreme Court of 44; television, late arrival in 195–6; transplantation of diaspora economic life to 78–9; War of Independence 45, 48, 165; Yiddish language 67–70
Israel: A Colonial Settler State (Rodinson, M.) 93
Israel Broadcasting Authority 194
Israel Defense Force 37, 46, 197
Israel Democracy Institute 70
Israel-Egyptian War of Attrition (1969-71) 196
Israel in Exile (Dinur, B-Z.) 106
Israel Studies (Ben-Gurion University) 33
Israeli Defense Ministry 46, 196
Der Israelit 138
Israelitische Allianz zu Wien 135, 136–7, 141, 144–5
Istóczy, Győző 114
Italy 106, 117–18; antisemitism in 117; Fascism in 29

Jabotinsky, Vladimir 34–5, 179, 202
Japan: atomic attack on 21; Meiji Japan 99

Jerusalem 45–6, 48, 55, 79, 110, 125, 176, 182, 200, 203
Jewish Agency for Palestine 82, 104, 140, 143, 146, 148, 160, 163, 190; Political Department 164
Jewish Bookshelf 73–4, 85, 185
Jewish Colonization Association (JCA) 104, 137–40, 152
Jewish diaspora 3, 6, 30, 65, 67, 79–80, 82, 84, 87–8, 103, 119, 129, 205; links with Israel 65–7, 87–9
Jewish Enlightenment *see* Haskalah
Jewish National Fund (JNF) 159, 163, 164, 200
Jewish National Home 113, 120, 121, 123, 142, 178, 180
Jewish-Ottoman Land Company 59–60
'Jewish Problem/Question' 134–5, 140, 143–4, 147–8, 149
The Jewish Question as a Question of Racial Noxiousness for the Existence, Morals and Culture of Nations (Dühring, E.) 118–19
The Jewish State: A Century Later (Dowty, A.) 76
The Jewish State (Herzl, T.) 57, 112, 137, 142, 153
Jewish Theological Seminary 189
Jezreel Valley 58, 159, 163, 193
Joffe, Eliezer 158, 162
Joly, Maurice 122
Jordan, Hashemite Kingdom of 45–6
Journal of Israeli History (Tel Aviv University) 33
Judaism 2, 73, 83, 84–5, 102, 125, 201; Arab sensibilities about 113; Hebrew language and 121; Jewishness and 67, 74, 86; Liberal Judaism 99; 'muscular' 40; New Age Judaism 74; Rabbinic 75, 100, 101; Reform Judaism 99, 100; Zionism and 34, 123, 202
Judeophobia 101, 117; traditional Muslim 126–7
Kabha, Mustafa 43, 194
Kahn, Bernard 137, 139, 140, 143, 146, 176
Kahn, Zadoc 138, 139
Kaplan, Marion 100–101
Kaplansky, Shlomo 155, 159, 161
Karlinsky, Nahum 40, 80
Karni, Yehuda 184
Karsh, Efraim 48
Kashdai, Zvi 181
Kaspi, Binyamin 181, 183
Katz, Elihu 185, 188–9
Katz, Jacob 15
Katznelson, Berl 48–9, 189–90
Kedourie, Elie 107
Keren Heyesod 139
Kfar Yeruham 200
Khalidi, Muhammad Ali 55, 58, 60
Khalidi, Walid 54–5, 60
al-Khalidi, Youssuf Zia 52
Khartoum Arab Summit (1967) 48
Khazzoom, Aziza 39
Kimmerling, Baruch 24, 43, 66
Kinneret 97
Kiryat Anavim 156
Kiryat Arba 53
Kishinev Pogrom (1903) 142, 144
Kohn, Rabbi Leopold 120
Kol Yerushalayim 190–192
Kol Yisrael 72, 137, 190, 191, 194, 195, 198–204
Kolatt, Israel 14–15
Kollek, Teddy 194
Komsomol (Communist Youth League) 181
Kook, Isaac Abraham 34
Kook, Zvi Yehuda 34
Koran 124, 128
Kosman, Amiel 73
Kremenetzky, Johann 152
Kuzar, Ron 68, 205

Labor Zionism 15, 35, 44, 49, 72, 77–8, 85, 104, 165; technical ethos of 154–63

Land, Labor and the Origins of the Israeli-Palestinian Conflict (Shafir, G.) 41–2
Land and Power: The Zionist Resort to Force (Shapira, A.) 36, 53
language: Arabic language 31; Hebrew language 6, 30–31, 65, 67–70, 121, 190, 193, 195, 198; in Israel 67–70, 87; secularism and 70; Yiddish language 67–70
Latin America 92, 106
Latrun 45
Lavi, Shlomo 158
Lavsky, Hagit 39
Lazarus, Morritz 148
Lebanon 35, 47; Israeli invasion of 128
Lebanon War (1982) 28, 36, 81, 128
Lechi militia 34
Leibowitz, Yeshiyahu 199
Letter to the Jews of Yemen (Maimonides, M.) 124
Lev, Avraham 179, 180
Lev, Raphael 164
Levant Trade Fair (1932) 183, 190
Leven, Narcisse 139, 144
Liberal Judaism 99
La Libre Parole 115
Likud party 35, 49, 70, 76
Lilienblum, Moshe Leib 172
Lissak, Moshe 14,
Lithuania 171
Livni, Yitzhak 204
Lockman, Zachary 55
Lorenz, Chris 4
Lubavitcher Hasidism 74, 81–2
Lubrani, Eliezer 190, 192
Lueger, Karl 57, 122
Luke, Harry Charles 181
Luz, Ehud 34, 138

Ma'agan Michael 1, 2
Maariv 73, 199
Maccabees 178
Machiavelli, Niccolò 122
Maghreb 97, 110
Maimonides, Moses 124
The Making of the Arab-Israeli Conflict (Pappé, I.) 22
Mamdani, Mahmood 109–10
Mandatory Palestine 16, 34, 46, 72, 109–10, 118, 145, 180–81, 203; colonialism of 93–4; economic cooperation in 42–3; establishment of 122–3; gender relations in 40–41; Hebrew broadcasting in 188, 189–91; Hebrew satire in 169–86; hydroelectric power in 80; image of British rule in 30; immigration to 37, 39–40, 142, 145; Jewish-Arab relations in 55, 94; social stratification in 43; social-welfare in 97; technocracy in 143, 152–3, 154
Mapai Labor-Zionist party 15, 16, 34, 182, 194
Margalit, Elkana 14
Marr, Wilhelm 118
Marrus, Michael 19
Marshall, Louis 137, 143
Masalha, Nur 54
Masekhet 'Aniyut (Dick, I.M.) 169, 173–4
Mashrek 97, 110
Maskilim 172, 177
Masoretic pronunciation 191, 204
Massad, Joseph 111
Maunier, René 93
Me-hodu Ve-'ad Kush (From India unto Ethiopia) 179, 180, 183–4
Mead, Dr. Elwood 161–2
Megaleh Temirin (Perl, J.) 172
Megged, Aharon 21, 25
Megilat Shemitah (Silman, K.Y.) 176
Megilat Yuhasin (attributed to Landsberg, R.M.) 172
Mein Kampf (Hitler, A.) 121
Meir-Glitzenstein, Esther 38
Mekong River Valley 109
Mendelsohn, Ezra 135–6
Meretz party 70
Meridor, Sallai 82
Merkaz Ha-Rav Yeshiva 34

Merkaz Hakla'i 163
Messiah rides a tank (Hadari-Ramage, Y.) 36–7
Metzer, Jacob 40
Meyerson, Emil 137, 139, 141
Mi-Mitsrayim Ve-'ad Henah (Lev, A.) 180–81, 182
Middle East 31, 39, 76, 97, 108; Jews from the 37–9, 44, 66–7, 69, 72–3, 79, 83, 86, 97, 109, 126, 148, 191–2, 195–6
Migdal, Joel 43
Mikveh Israel 138–9
Milstein, Uri 18
Mishmar 146
Mishmar Ha-Emek 192
Mishnat Elisha ben Abuya (Lilienblum, M.L.) 172
Mitla Pass 27
Mizrahim 27, 38–9, 42–3, 43–4, 48, 69, 79, 85–6, 97, 109, 110, 195, 199–200
Mohammad 124
Montesquieu, Charles Louis, Baron de la Brède et de 122
Morocco 109
Morris, Benny 13, 18, 20–23, 25–6, 28, 45–7, 54
Motzkin, Leo 52, 53, 54
Mussolini, Benito 118

Naor, Mordechai 204
Napoleon III 122
Nashrat al-Markaz 194
Nasser, Gamal Abdel 47, 81, 128
Nathan, Abie 204
Nathan, Paul 136, 176
National Bible Quiz 205
national consciousness 7, 26, 49, 74, 76, 109, 205; *see also* historical consciousness
National Religious Party 81
nationalism 3, 32, 42, 92, 135; Afro-Asian 111; Arab 52, 126, 127; colonialism and 91, 104, 107; European 92, 105, 106, 107, 108; French 106; German 106–7; hyper-nationalism 70; Indian 103; Jewish 101, 115–16, 202; modernization and 43, 108; Palestinian 42, 110; Social Democracy 35; socialism and 165; territorial 76; Thai 109; Zionism and other forms of, comparison between 3
Nationalist Thought and the Colonial World: A Derivative Discourse? (Chatterjee, P.) 107
Navon, Yitzhak 194
Nazi Germany 19, 29, 113, 126, 128, 149
Near, Henry 163
Nedava, Joseph 53–4
Negev 164
Netter, Charles 144
new history 5, 25–7, 28, 30, 35–6, 41, 84; Arab-Israeli conflict, new consensus 44–50; Benny Morris on 'new history' and revisionism 13, 20; Israeli historians, two generations of 14–24; methodology of 23–4
New Zealand 103
Nicholas II, Tsar of Russia 122
Niégo, Joseph 139
Nikui rosh (Head cleaning) 185
1949: The First Israelis (Segev, T.) 37, 38
Nordau, Max 40, 52, 115–16, 120, 202
North African Jews 37, 39, 40, 69, 72–3, 79, 192, 195, 196, 199
Northern Ireland 3
Novick, Peter 20
Novomesky, Moshe 183

Occupied Territories 34, 42, 77, 85, 88, 110, 111
O'Day, Alan 33
One Palestine, Complete (Segev, T.) 30
Ong, Walter J. 187
oral literature 8, 187, 206
Oren, Michael 23, 47, 48
Oriental Jews 21, 27, 38–9, 97, 109
Orientalism 1, 59, 90–91, 95, 96, 111, 127
The Origins of Israeli Militarism (Ben-Eliezer, U.) 36
The Origins of Zionism (Vital, D.) 16

Orthodox Jews 15, 27, 34, 40, 70–73, 79, 86–8, 179, 200; American Jewish Joint Distribution Committee and 104, 137–8, 143, 151–2; economic life of 79; institutions of 71, 79; Jewish Colonization Association (JCA) and 137–40; Kol Yisrael and 202–3; Neo-Orthodox Jews 138; political parties of 71; secularism and 185–6; ultra-Orthodox Jews 27, 68, 74, 77, 79, 81, 85, 103, 135, 140, 176, 178, 196, 197; Zionists and anti-Zionists, conflict between 193
Oslo Peace Accords (and process) 26–7, 45, 85, 128
Ottoman Empire 52, 54–5, 58–9, 75–6, 93, 99, 124–5, 135–6
Ottoman Palestine 16, 24, 40, 51–2, 54–5, 142, 145, 152
Oungré, Louis 139
Oz, Amos 30

Pale of Settlement 76, 144, 174
Palestine 18; Arab loss of 127; desertification under Arab and Turkish rule 95–6; German Templer colonies in 156; Jewish restoration to, discourse on 114; Mandatory Palestine 16, 34, 46, 72, 109–10, 118, 145, 203; gender relations in 40–41; Hebrew broadcasting in 188, 189–91; Hebrew satire in 169–86; hydroelectric power in 80; image of British rule in 30; immigration to 37, 39–40, 142, 145; Jewish-Arab economic cooperation in 42–3; Jewish-Arab relations in 55, 94; Sephardic pronunciation for broadcasting in 191; social stratification in 43; social-welfare in 97; technocracy in 143, 152–3, 154; Ottoman Palestine 16, 24, 40, 51–2, 54–5, 142, 145, 152
Palestine Broadcast Service (PBS) 8, 188, 189–93
Palestine Economic Corporation 104, 139
Palestine Jewish Colonization Association (PICA) 139, 152–3
Palestine Joint Survey Commission 161, 162
Palestine Zionist Executive (PZE) 154, 155, 162, 163
Palestinian Arabs 5–6, 41; disregard of Herzl for 55–6; expulsion of, discussion concerning 53–4, 55–6; expropriation ideas of Herzl for 53, 57–8, 59; reflections of Herzl concerning 51–61; refugee problem, origins of 54, 56; relevance to international Zionism of 52–4
Palestinian Intifadas 28, 45, 81, 149
Palestinian Territories 39; *see also* Occupied Territories
Pappé, Ilan 18, 21, 22, 28, 42, 45
Parallels Meet (Luz, E.) 34
Parski, Daniel 183
Passfield (Sidney James Webb), Lord 180
Passfield White Paper 180–81
Passover 55, 70, 72, 85, 171, 175, 180, 182, 185, 192, 201
Passover Haggadah 8, 169, 170, 174, 179, 183
Peel Commission (1937) 51, 164, 165
Peled, Yoav 43–4, 66
Pen, Alexander 184
Peres, Shimon 46, 196
Perl, Joseph 172
Pétain, Marshall Philippe 117
Philippson, Rabbi Ludwig 148, 177
Pinsker, Leo 26, 144
Pioneers and Homemakers: Jewish Women in Pre-State Israel (Bernstein, D., Ed.) 40
Pitom ve-Ramses 181
Poalei Tsion (Workers of Zion) 136, 155, 159
Poland 82, 108; Prussian Poland 94, 98
Porat, Dina 15, 38
postcolonialism: as conceptual framework 92; postcolonial state building

and Zionism 91, 94, 103–8; and women's suffrage 102–3
Pratt, Mary Louise 96, 109
propaganda 38, 196; Arab 56, 125; fascist 190; Soviet 190; Zionist 53
The Protocols of the Elders of Zion 121–3, 125, 128
Proudhon, Pierre-Joseph 114
Prussia 98
Pulzer, Peter 134
Purim 171, 172, 175, 178, 184
Puritanism 108

Qutb, Sayyid 127–8

Rabbinic Judaism 75–6, 100
Rabinovich, Itamar 23
radio broadcasting in Israel 187–207
Radio Corporation of America (RCA) 196
Radio Ramallah 192
Rama IV, King of Siam 99
Ramakrishna, Vivekananda 98–9
Rathenau, Emil 151–2
Ravitzky, Aviezer 34
Raz-Krakotzkin, Amnon 85–6
Reform Judaism 99, 100
Reinach, Joseph 116
relativism 8, 9, 23
Reshet Gimmel 204
Le Reveil de la nation arabe (Azuri, N.) 125
revisionism 19–21, 23–4, 25–6, 53, 104, 143, 179–82; American 20, 21, 23; Benny Morris on 'new history' and 13; counter-narratives to 29; historical 5, 14, 27, 28–30, 35–6, 41, 46–9, 84; Holocaust and 19–20, 121; in Ireland 30; in Israeli historiography 30; on war and Arab-Jewish conflict 33–4; Zionism, colonialism and 90; *see also* historiography
Revisionist Zionism 36
Rhodes, Cecil 56
Ridha, Rashid 124–5
The Road to Jerusalem: Glubb Pasha, Palestine and the Jews (Morris, B.) 45
Rodinson, Maxine 93
Rogel, Nakdimon 200
Romania 76, 144
Rosen, Joseph 143, 146
Rosenberg, Alfred 121
Rosenberg, James 141–2
Rosenfeld, Shalom 199
Rosenwald, Julius 146
Rosh Hashanah 175
Roskies, David 184
Rothschild, Baron Edmond de 138–9, 152–3
Rothschild, James de 139
Rothschild, family 56, 57, 120, 121, 139
Rousseau, Jean-Jacques 206
Rovina, Hanna 191
Roy, Rammohan 100
The Ruin of Palestine (Palestinian play) 126
Ruppin, Arthur 141–2, 153–5, 158, 161, 162, 164–5
Russia 76, 96, 98, 101, 142, 144, 174; antisemitism in 122; Russian Empire, State Rabbinate of 73; Russian-Jewish communities 120
Rutenberg, Pinchas 80
Rwanda, genocide in 110

Sabbath 71, 72, 193, 200, 203, 204
The Sabra (Almog, O.) 36
Sacher, Harry 160, 162
Sadat peace initiative 128
Said, Edward 56, 99
Salmon, Yosef 34
Samuel, Edwin 190
Saravati, Dayananda 100
Sarnoff, David 196
Schlemiel 175
Schoenerer, Georg von 57
Scholem, Gershom 102
The Scroll of Fire (Bialik, H.N.) 191
secularism 8, 26–7, 44, 77, 79, 82–3, 86–7, 89, 97, 138, 148, 169–71; anti-

clericalism and 70–71; Christianity and 102; of haggadot 179, 181–3; Labor Zionism and 72–3; language and 70; Orthodox community and 185–6; radio programming for secular majority 203–4; and religious forms of Israeli identity 73–5; secular Arab nationalism 127–8; secular Judaic scholarship 100–101; secular post-Zionism 85; secular Zionism 2, 43, 44, 74, 80, 82, 202; secularization of society 184–5; and socialism 126; of Tel Aviv 178
Segev, Tom 17–18, 30, 37
Senesh, Hannah 80
Sephardic pronunciation 69, 191
September 11, 2001 149
settlements 7, 145, 147, 156, 159, 161, 164; agricultural 41, 138; Galilean 157; Jezreel Valley 159, 163; management of 158–9; religious settlement movement 49; settlement-colonialism 2, 6, 90–91, 92–6, 104; settlement policies in 156–7; technocrats in 159–63; Tower and Stockade settlements 164; West Bank and Gaza 127; WZO settlement activities 150, 153–4, 159; *see also* Aliyah; Pale of Settlement; WZO Settlement Department
Shafir, Gershon 24, 41–2, 43–4, 66, 94
Shalem Institute, Jerusalem 47, 85
Shaltiel, Eli 80
Shamir, Ronen 90–91
Shamir, Yithzak 82
Shandler, Jeffrey 188–9
Shapira, Anita 14, 15, 36, 48–9, 53, 72
Shapira, Yair 85
Shapiro, Yonathan 14, 15
Sharett (Shertok), Moshe 164
Sharon, Ariel 82
Shas political party 38, 43, 74, 79
Shavuot 175, 192, 203
Shaw Commission 180
Sheleg, Bambi 73
Shenhav, Yehouda 39, 85
Shiels, Drummond 181
Shilo, Margalit 40
Shinui party 70
Shlaim, Avi 18, 21, 22, 23, 28, 45, 46, 47–8
Shlonsky, Abraham 20
Silman, Kadish Yehuda 169, 176–8
Simon, James 176
Sinai campaign (1956) 27
Sinai Peninsula 27, 37, 46, 110, 200–201
Sivan, Emmanuel 128
Six Day War (1967) 128
Six Days of War: June 1967 and the Making of the Modern Middle East (Oren, M.) 47
slavery 134
Selihot 193
Slovakia 3
Smilansky, Moshe 96
Smithsonian Institute 21
Social Darwinism 138, 141, 152
Social Democracy 35
social policy: essential component of contemporary Jewish life 148–9; origins of 133; social engineering and 142–3; ‘social question’ for bourgeois society 134; welfare, philanthropy and 246n2; Yishuv, Zionism and 138–40; Zionism as form of Jewish 133–49; *see also* Agro-Joint; Jewish Problem/Question
Soloveitchik (Solieli), Menachem 196–7, 198–9
Soskin, Selig 161
South Africa 3, 6, 56, 93
South America 58
South Korea 3, 79
Soviet Union 7, 20, 27, 70–71, 87, 143, 146–7, 147, 171, 181; ethnic Germans expelled from 109; gulags of the 29
Spielberg, Steven 74
Stalin, Josef 147
Stanislawski, Michael 202
Stern, David 160
Sternhell, Zeev 35–6

Stewart, Desmond 56–7
Stöcker, Adolf 114
Stoler, Ann 98
A Story of Love and Darkness (Oz, A.) 30
Studies in Zionism (Tel Aviv University) 27
Suez Canal 47, 136
Suez Crisis 46, 47
Sukkot 175
Swirski, Shlomo 38
Switzerland 102
Syria 47–8, 59, 124
Syrkin, Nachman 53

Taiwan 79
Talmon, Jacob 15
Talmud 8, 173, 203–4; Babylonian 172
Tanakh 193, 198, 203
Tel Amal 164
Tel Chai 146
Teoryah u-Vikoret 85, 86
Territorialism 116
Teveth, Shabtai 21, 53, 54
Thailand (Siam) 99, 109, 195
Thierry, Augustin 106
Timmendorfer, Berthold 137
Tisha Be-av 203
Todorova, Maria 17
Torah 37, 77, 177, 178, 182, 191, 193, 200, 201; divine origins of 71; foundational text 187; in Herzl's library 200; Jewish law and 75; promotion of study of 34; television and 196
Toury, Jacob 134
Treblinka 81
Treitschke, Heinrich von 106, 114
Truman administration 20
Trumpeldor, Yosef 201–2
Tsafnet, Aharon 174
Tsur, Naomi 200
Tu Bishvat 175, 192–3

Ukraine 104, 143, 146–7; *see also* Agro-Joint
United Jewish Appeal 148
United Jewish Communities – United Jewish Appeal 79–80
United Nations 45; Partition Resolution 45–6, 51, 117, 164
United States 3, 19, 20, 21, 71, 73, 74, 87–8, 104, 108, 144, 189; Interior Department 161; Israel's relationship with 127
Upanishads 100
Ussishkin, Menachim 34

Vambery, Arminius 59
Van Creveld, Martin 36
Vatican 117, 118
Vendata 100
Vichy France and the Jews (Marrus, M. and Paxton, R.O.) 19
Vichy France 19, 29
Villari, Pasquale 106
Vital, David 16
Voice of Peace 204
Volpe, Gioacchino 106

Walby, Sylvia 102–3
Warburg, Felix 143, 146, 160
Warburg, Otto 95, 153
Al-Watan 194
Weber, Eugene 105–6
Weinberg, Vittorio 191
Weitz, Yechiam 15
Weitz, Yosef 159, 164, 165
Weizmann, Chaim 136, 140, 143, 160, 162, 179, 180
Weizmann Institute 15
Wertheimer, Joseph Ritter von 141
West Bank 45, 47, 48, 82, 110, 127
Western Wall 37, 182
Wilkansky, Yitzhak 154, 156–8, 160, 162
Wingate, Orde 201
Wolffsohn, David 59–60
World War I 19, 28, 29, 51, 154, 202
World War II 19, 20, 21, 28, 29, 80, 95, 116, 126

World Zionist Organization (WZO) 58, 59, 94, 95, 97, 103, 118, 146, 148, 153–4, 155–6, 158–9, 160–1, 163, 165; Financial Council 159; immigration, budget for 145–6; international politics of the 136–40; long-term, national goals 162; settlement activities 150, 153–4, 159; Settlement Department 156, 159, 162, 164; technocratic elite 143; Va'ad Hakla'i (Agricultural Committee) 155, 160, 163; Yishuv labor movement, relationship with 142, 150, 154; Zionist labor, antipathy towards 150–51

Yaari, Yehuda 197
Yadin, Yigal 197
Yahuda, Abraham Shalom Ezekiel 54
Yamin, Antoine 125
Yazbek, Mahmoud 43
Yediot Aharonot 81
Yemenite Jews 97
Yishuv (Jewish community in Palestine, pre-1948) 2–3, 7, 90, 95, 123–4, 180, 181, 182, 184; academic study of 13–18, 21–2, 24, 27–8, 32, 33, 38–40, 66, 72, 80; Agency for Clandestine Immigration 38; agricultural sector 150; Arab labor in, dependence on 147; Arab Revolt (1936-9) 163, 164; co-operative sector 155–6; development of 33–4, 104, 150, 163, 164, 191; expansion of 164; female suffrage 103; financial crisis 160; hityashvut ovedet and 162–3; humorous literature in 175, 178, 179; labor movement 143, 150, 154, 158–9; National Committee 182; national economy of 160, 162; New Yishuv 41, 169; Old Yishuv 40, 41, 68, 69; plantation colonies (moshavot) 156; relations between native population and 54; rural Yishuv, technical expertise and development of 145, 150–65; satirical parody in 170, 175–7, 178, 179, 185; socio-economic change of 138–40; speech of 68–9; spoken Hebrew in 206; womens' role 96; Zionism in 7–8, 93
Yom Kippur 70, 71, 86, 178
Yonah, Yossi 85
Young Turks 114

Zaid, Alexander 2
Zangwill, Israel 52, 53, 54
Zefira, Bracha 191
Zemach, Shlomo 156–7, 160
Zertal, Idith 37–8
Zinder, Hemdah Feigenbaum 192
Zionism: American Zionism 155; anti-colonialism and 91; anti-Zionism and antisemitism 113, 114; antisemites on 112–29; Ashkenazic leadership of 97–8; broadcast radio and 188–9, 190; collective identity in 2; colonialism and 90–111, 151; comparative history and study of 4–5; Histadrut leadership 162–3; hityashvut ovedet 150, 155, 156, 162–3, 164, 165; ideology of 2–3; immigration of Jews from Middle East and North Africa, effect on 109–11; intelligentsia and 98–102; post-Zionism 83–6; Jewish holidays refashioned by 192; Jewish politics and, structural comparisons 135–8; Judaism and 34, 123, 202; *mission civilisatrice* of 95–6, 105–6; Orientalist elements within 96; Palestinian Arabs and 95–7; political economics of 150; as product of age of Imperialism 108, 111, 153; Revisionist Zionism 36; science, Jewish social policy and 151–4; secular Zionism 2, 43, 44, 74, 80, 82, 202; as settlement-colonialism 92–5; settlement management 158–9; settlement technocrats 159–63; as social policy 133–49; state building and postcolonialism 91, 94, 103–8; technical ethos of Labor Zionism 154–63;

technology and ideology of 153; technophilia of 151–4, 154–63; victimization and 91; in the Yishuv 7–8, 93; Yishuv, social policy and 138–40
Zionism and Territory (Kimmerling, B.) 24
Zionist Congresses 59, 123, 139, 161; Eleventh (1913) 116; First (1897) 60, 115, 118, 122; Second (1898) 52, 103
Die zionistische Bewegung (Boehm, A.) 60
Zuckermann, Moshe 81–2
Zundel, Ernst 121
Zurayk, Constantine 127